THEOLOGICAL INVESTIGATIONS

Volume II

Also in this series

THEOLOGICAL INVESTIGATIONS

Vol. I

God, Christ, Mary and Grace

THEOLOGICAL INVESTIGATIONS

VOLUME II

MAN IN THE CHURCH

by

KARL RAHNER

Translated by

KARL-H. KRUGER

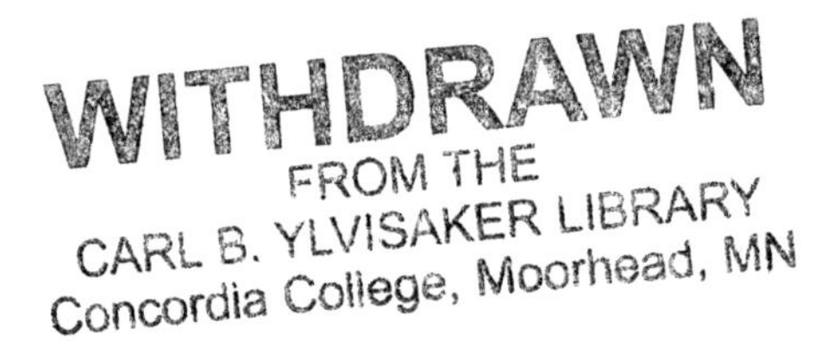

BALTIMORE
HELICON PRESS

HELICON PRESS
1120 North Calvert Street, Baltimore, Md. 21202.

A Translation of
SCHRIFTEN ZUR THEOLOGIE, II
published by Verlagsanstalt Benziger & Co. AG., Einsiedeln

First published 1963
Second printing: June 1964
Third printing: April 1966

Library of Congress Catalog Card No. 61–8189

Nihil obstat Joannes M. T. Barton, S.T.D., L.S.S. Censor deputatus. Imprimatur ✠ Georgius L. Craven. Epus Sebastopolis Vic. Cap, Westmonasterii, die 9a, Julii 1963. The Nihil obstat and Imprimatur are a declaration that a book or pamphlet is considered to be free from doctrinal or moral error. It is not implied that those who have granted the Nihil obstat and Imprimatur agree with the contents, opinion or statements expressed.

Printed in the United States of America

CONTENTS

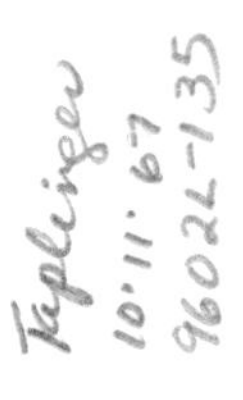

ACKNOWLEDGEMENTS

I wish to express my profound gratitude and appreciation to Rev A. Monaghan for his great care in reading the manuscript and his many valuable suggestions.

My sincere gratitude is also due to many other friends, and in particular to Revs V. Moffat, S.T.L., D. McGuinness, M.A., J. McNamara, B.Ed., J. Symon, M.A., S.T.L., D. Henry, H. White and Mr A. Lamont for their helpful suggestions on individual Chapters, as well as to Rev M. Macnamara for his help in reading the proofs.

Finally, I wish also to thank the B. Herder Book Co. (London) for kind permission to quote from *The Church Teaches*, and the Mercier Press, Ltd. (Cork) for kind permission to quote from L. Ott, *Fundamentals of Catholic Dogma*.

St Andrew's College
Drygrange
Melrose
Scotland

Karl-H. Kruger

ABBREVIATIONS

AAS	*Acta Apostolicae Sedis*
CIC	*Codex Iuris Canonici*
Denz	Denzinger-Rahner, *Enchiridion Symbolorum* (1953)
DAFC	*Dictionnaire Apologétique de la Foi Catholique*
DTC	*Dictionnaire de Théologie Catholique*
NRT	*Nouvelle Revue Théologique*
PG	*Patrologia, series graeca*, ed. Migne (Paris 1844 *sqq.*)
PL	*Patrologia, series latina*, ed. Migne (Paris 1857 *sqq.*)
RSPT	*Revue des Sciences Philosophiques et Théologiques*
RSR	*Recherches de Science Religieuse*
RT	*Revue Thomiste*
TQ	*Theologische Quartalschrift*
TS	*Theological Studies* (U.S.A.)
TWNT	*Theologisches Wörterbuch zum Neuen Testament*
ZKT	*Zeitschrift für Katholische Theologie*

Note.—The author very rarely quotes Scripture directly in German, and when he does so appears to make his own translations. In the present translation, accordingly, the author's renderings are retained, though of course the standard English versions have been consulted.

I

MEMBERSHIP OF THE CHURCH ACCORDING TO THE TEACHING OF PIUS XII's ENCYCLICAL 'MYSTICI CORPORIS CHRISTI'

THE repercussions which Pius XII's Encyclical '*Mystici Corporis Christi*' (29th June 1943) has had in certain quarters, induces us to pose the following questions: Who, according to the teaching laid down in this Encyclical, belong to the Church as members in the fullest sense and who do not belong to it in this sense? What follows, or what does not necessarily follow with regard to justification, state of grace and union with Christ, from *this* kind of non-membership of the Church? Finally, what insights into the nature of the Church itself result from this teaching about membership and non-membership of the Church?

This is a relatively restricted subject compared with the burning questions of present-day Ecclesiology. Indeed it becomes even more confined by basing our investigations exclusively (in as far as this is practicable) on the aforesaid Encyclical.[1]

[1] The following should serve as a select bibliography of the most recent literature on this question: J. Beumer, 'Die kirchliche Gliedschaft in der Lehre des hl. Robert Bellarmin', *Theologie und Glaube* XXXVIII (1948), pp. 243–257; J. Gribimont, 'Du sacrement de l'Eglise et de ses réalisations imparfaites', *Irénikon* XXII (1949), pp. 345–367; C. Lialine, 'Une étape en ecclésiologie', *Irénikon* XIX (1946), pp. 129–152; pp. 283–317; XX (1947), pp. 34–54; L. Malevez, 'Quelques enseignements de l'encyclique "Mystici Corporis"', NRT LXXVII (1945), pp. 385–407; A. Chavasse, 'Ordonnés au corps mystique', NRT LXXX (1948), pp. 690–702; V. Morel, 'Le corps mystique du Christ et l'Eglise catholique romaine', NRT LXXX (1948), pp. 703–726; A. Liégé, 'L'appartenance à l'Eglise et l'encyclique "Mystici corporis"', RSPT XXXII (1948), pp. 351–357; J. Brinktrine, 'Was lehrt die Enzyklika "Mystici Corporis" über die Zugehörigkeit zur Kirche?', *Theologie und Glaube* XXXVIII (1947–48), pp. 290–300; L. Valpertz, 'Kirchliche Mitgliedschaft und Nichtkatholiken nach der Enzyklika Mystici Corporis', *Theologie und Glaube* (= *Th. und Seelsorge*) (1944), pp. 43–46; E. Brunet, 'Les dissidents de bonne foi sont-ils membres de l'église?', *Analecta Gregoriana* LVIII (Rome 1954), pp. 199–218.

Yet it is an important, as well as difficult, question. Important and difficult, first of all because the particular doctrine of this Encyclical which is the subject of our present considerations, has given rise to the opinion that the teaching authority has come to positively new decisions on this matter, and that these are of such a nature as to be offensive to non-Catholics and detrimental to the efforts towards Union. If this were true, and if the gulf between Catholics and non-Catholics had indeed widened as a result of these particular authoritative pronouncements, then this would of course be very sad and most regrettable (humanly speaking) in an age of a new awakening of love for the *Una Sancta*. Hence this question of the membership of the Church is not simply a matter for subtle treatment by the Canonists, but a vital question for all those who love the Church of Christ and who own themselves in duty bound by our Lord's will that all be one. This is precisely why we must know dispassionately and objectively to what extent all Christians are in reality already one in Christ and in the Church (in spite of outward appearances which would point rather to a separation between Christians), and to what extent these same Christians are actually separated from one another (although their yearning for unity and their mutual love might make them believe that they are more or less united already).

The subject under discussion is important, furthermore, as an instance of the work of the theologian. For it must be stressed most emphatically from the outset that a great deal in our problem is still unclarified and obscure. If we wish to proceed as true theologians in this matter, then we will have to take the doctrinal pronouncements of the Church as our starting-point (for these are the beginning and end of all theology),[2] instead of starting with some impressive and lucid,

[2] But not the 'end' in the sense that theology has, in spite of this, no other task in the last analysis than to defend and comment on the present (and earlier) clear and explicit doctrinal pronouncements of the *magisterium* of the Church. In other words, we do not mean that the theologian can engage only in a 'Denzinger-theology'—which is unfortunately often precisely all he does. But the 'end' must be understood here in the sense that the doctrinal pronouncements of the Church are not only the starting-point, but also the abiding norm of all dogmatic theology. Whenever theology, sustained by faith and the desire for salvation, does moreover not forget its existential source and aim, then it will also continually serve the teaching authority itself, and it will then ultimately be possible to include it, with its newly gained insights, in the very teaching of that authority.

but ultimately uncompelling and subjective speculation. But the employment of this theological method will immediately bring to light a fact which is fairly familiar to the theologian, but which never ceases to puzzle the layman (and how many 'theologians' are really 'laymen'). We refer to the fact that the magisterium of the Church, supported by Tradition, simply lays down this or that particular point about a certain question, without it being at once apparent how all these individual pronouncements are to be logically combined into one systematic framework. Indeed the very attempt at logical systematization not only encounters grave difficulties, but perhaps has still to achieve any real success in theology. Thus it is a fact that there still remain important tasks for the theologian, which are of consequence even beyond the special province of the theologian as such.

Finally, our subject is important too for Ecclesiology in general. It is true, as will be seen in the course of our considerations, that any question about the membership of the Church necessarily and rightly presupposes a certain knowledge of the nature of the Church. For only in that way can it be logically determined who belongs to the Church and who does not. Yet, on the other hand, the ecclesiastical teaching authority has made pronouncements on the question of membership of the Church. Hence it is in turn possible to collect certain evidence about the nature of the Church from the positive elements of these pronouncements, which it might be impossible to find otherwise—at least as clearly. In other words, from a purely logical point of view, our question would follow on from our knowledge about the nature of the Church; but for the theologian, who works from the doctrinal pronouncements of the Church, this question is in its turn also a source of a deeper understanding of the nature of the Church. We see the fundamental importance of our subject precisely in this: that it forces us to develop a deeper-going theology of the Church as a whole.

From what has been said so far, we can already distinguish three questions within the subject under discussion:

I. What does the Encyclical say about the conditions for membership of the Church?

II. What does it say about the possibility of union with Christ through grace for those who, in the sense of the reply to our first question, are not members of the Church?

III. With regard to the Church's nature itself, what further facts, and what indications for further lines of inquiry can be gathered from the answer to the first two questions?

I

We will inquire first of all, then, as to what *conditions* must be fulfilled in a person so that he may be called a *member of the Church.* In formulating a question such as this, we are clearly conscious of the fact that neither the notion of the Church nor the notion of membership of the Church is of itself an unequivocally or clearly defined quantity in the minds of ordinary people today or, for that matter, in theology itself. To begin with, it can be seen without much difficulty that the concept of membership is not of itself clearly determined. From the mere *general* conception of the union of an individual with a community, it is already possible to conceive *a priori* of many different closer or looser ways in which a person may be united with the Church. It goes without saying that the conditions of such closer or looser union of an individual with the Church would be quite different in each case. As it would, however, be completely contrary to the correct theological procedure to construct or even lay down in terminology any special *a-priori* notion of membership of the Church, the only method left open to us in this matter is as follows: We must first of all simply accept, on the Church's teaching authority, who belong as members to the Church and what conditions must be fulfilled in them to constitute such membership. Only in this way can we determine, not only how we must deal with this whole subject objectively, but also what is the Church's own notion of membership of the Church (i.e. this notion as defined in its very terminology by the magisterium of the Church). The same necessary method as follows from the notion of membership of the Church results also from the problematic notion of the Church itself. Here again it cannot be a question of arbitrarily adopting some notion of 'Church' and of then determining logically, in accordance with this notion, who belongs to the Church and who does not. For otherwise we could run the risk of making the full and adequate content of the notion of the Church consist in some merely partial aspect of what is, in reality, her complete nature. If this were to happen, we would deviate in doctrine or at least in terminology from the teaching of the Church, neither of which is permissible; at the very least, the teaching of the Church would be obscured or disfigured.

Hence our method must simply be to start with the Church's doctrinal pronouncements about the conditions of her membership. Here and now, we must simply state the definition of the authoritatively taught notion of the Church, at least as found in present-day ecclesiastical usage. For clearly we cannot treat exhaustively of this notion in these investigations and particularly not at this point. According to the teaching of the Church and the usage adopted by her (and binding also on us), the 'Church' means the Roman Catholic Church, which knows itself to be founded by Christ, even as an external, visibly organized society with the Bishop of Rome at its head, and which as such declares itself to be basically necessary for salvation. That this is the language of the Encyclical needs no special proof for anyone who has read it even once attentively. We do not mean to deny by this that the word 'Church' could of itself have also a wider sense; indeed the history of the proclamation of the Faith, and of Theology, shows that it has in fact had this wider sense as well.[3] Yet the Church is not just the infallible herald of the truths of the Faith; in other words, she does not merely announce the saving realities without error, but has also,

[3] A proper history of Ecclesiology has not yet been written. Such a history would not only need to have as adequate a grasp as possible, and make as complete a collection as possible, of what has been said about the Church in each period, and by the different Fathers–but would also have to give its particular attention to what was uppermost in the Church's consciousness during the different periods. We may mention the following among more recent works: the whole patristic literature as listed by B. Altaner, *Patrology* (Edinburgh-London 1960), pp. 32 *sq.*; J. Cl. Fenton, 'Scholastic Definitions of the Catholic Church', *American Ecclesiastical Review* CXI (1944), pp. 59–69; pp. 131–145; pp. 212–228. M. Ramsauer, 'Die Kirche in den Katechismen', ZKT LXXIII (1951), pp. 129–169; pp. 313–346. A. Mayer-Pfannholz, 'Der Wandel des Kirchenbildes in der Geschichte', *Theologie und Glaube* XXXIII (1941), pp. 22–34; *id.*, 'Das Bild der Mater Ecclesia im Wandel der Geschichte', *Pastor Bonus* LIII (1942), pp. 33–47. S. Tromp, *Corpus Christi, quod est Ecclesia* I (Rome 1937). J. Beumer, 'Die altchristliche Lehre einer präexistenten Kirche und ihre theologische Auswertung', *Wissenschaft und Weisheit* IX (1942), pp. 19–32; *id.*, 'Die Idee einer vorchristlichen Kirche bei Augustinus', *Münchner theol. Zeitschrift* III (1952), pp. 161–175; Y. Congar, *Ecclesia ab Abel; Festschrift für Karl Adam* (Düsseldorf 1952), pp. 79–108; H. de Lubac, *Catholicism* (London, 1950); A. Mitterer, *Geheimnisvoller Leib Christi nach St Thomas von Aquin und nach Papst Pius XII* (Vienna 1950); Th. Strotmann, 'Les membres de l'Eglise', *Irénikon* XXV (1952), pp. 249–262. H. Felderer, 'Der Kirchenbegriff in den Flugschriften des josefinischen Jahrzehnts', ZKT LXXV (1953), pp. 257–330.

for this very purpose, the right to determine usage concerning words and concepts which are employed in this declaration of truth. And therefore, she also has the right to say what she wishes to be understood at the present time by the word 'Church', and to demand that theologians keep to this linguistic usage in order to avoid misunderstandings and errors. Thus, when we ask in this sense what are the conditions for belonging as members to the Church, then we inquire, in accordance with the terminology of *Mystici Corporis*, after the conditions of membership of the Roman Catholic Church, understood as the visibly organized society of believers under the government of the Roman Pontiff. And so, in order to have a proper appreciation of the exact meaning and scope of the teaching of the Encyclical, we must first of all treat of the Church's previous teaching about membership of the Church, and then ask ourselves, secondly, what the Encyclical itself tells us about it.

1. The Church's previous teaching on the conditions of membership of the Church

As already indicated, we are here concerned with the conditions of membership of the visible Roman Catholic Church. This visible character of the Church has, according to her own teaching, itself several dimensions. The Church's teaching[4] itself distinguishes two powers in the Church as a visible society, which constitute it as a '*societas perfecta*': viz. the *potestas iurisdictionis* (under which we may subsume, at least in this present context, the absolute power of enacting binding decisions regarding Faith and Morals),[5] and the *potestas ordinis*.

[4] Cf. e.g. CIC can. 196; 210; 872; 948.

[5] We do not mean to decide by this the controverted question as to whether the powers of teaching, ruling and sanctifying are three specifically distinct powers, or whether there are in fact only two basic powers. The first alternative is the opinion of the majority of ecclesiologists, who explain that the first two of these powers (viz. the powers of teaching and of ruling) are only more closely associated with each other on account of the non-sacramental manner of their transmission; in this way (i.e. as power of jurisdiction—power transmitted in a legal manner) they are more clearly distinguished from the third power than from each other. The other alternative is the opinion of the majority of canonists. For the whole controversy cf. the bibliography in M. Nicholau-J. Salaverri, *Sacrae Theologiae Summa* I² (Madrid 1952), pp. 933–952; J. Salaverri, 'La triple potestad de la Iglesia', *Miscellanea Comillas* XIV (1950), pp. 5–84.

These two powers are together the basis of the visible nature and visible unity of the Church, since authority is the source of the unity, community and consequent visibleness of a *societas perfecta.* These two powers cannot be regarded as two sides of one and the same thing which must always run parallel to each other. It is for instance possible, on the one hand, to have a 'power of jurisdiction' without there being a 'power of orders' (even when it is a power of jurisdiction by divine law, as e.g. that of a legitimately elected Pope, who has however not yet been consecrated Bishop; cf. CIC can. 219); and, on the other hand, there can be cases of a 'power of orders' without a 'power of jurisdiction', and this even in someone who is outside the Church. For the Church's doctrine regarding the validity of the sacraments, as brought out in the third century controversy about baptism by heretics, as well as in her fight against Donatism, shows that even outside the Church—for this was precisely the point at issue—there can be valid administration of the Sacraments and hence a 'power of orders'. Nevertheless, contrary to what might be expected, one must not conclude from this same doctrine that the power of orders can be looked upon as of no account for the constitution of the visible nature of the Church, simply because in certain circumstances this power can be exercised also outside the Church. For the important point to remember in this connection is that baptism is an act of sacramental and not, in itself, of jurisdictional power. Now, the very doctrine under discussion regards baptism basically as the act by which a person becomes a member of the Church, given the various other prerequisite conditions; and it is here quite obviously a question of the membership of the Church considered as a visible, and indeed jurisdictional body. For the Church regards every baptized person as fundamentally under her jurisdiction and obliged by her Canon Law (CIC can. 87). All this makes it quite clear that both the jurisdictional and the sacramental powers of the Church are required as constitutive elements of her visible character. Therefore, when we speak of the membership of the Church in future, we must be understood to refer to membership of the Church under *both* these aspects, since the Church herself when dealing with this membership (as we shall see) does not distinguish between them. We do not mean to prejudge our question about the conditions of the Church's membership by these reflections on the constitutive elements of the Church and of her visibleness. Our intention in this has merely been to call attention, from the very start, to a matter which will have to be taken into consideration when we now come to ask directly what the Church taught about the conditions of membership before the Encyclical was written.

Our procedure will be simply to try to put together, for a start, the pronouncements made by the Church's magisterium, and then to work out the essentials of this question from these various pronouncements.

a. In the first place, it is a *defined Dogma of Faith* that baptism is a necessary condition for belonging in any way to the Church; for baptism is acknowledged as the door through which a person enters the Church,[6] and the Church expressly does not claim any jurisdiction whatsoever over the non-baptized.[7]

It is similarly a defined Dogma that there can be members of the Church who are not in the state of grace, and indeed even such as will not attain salvation.[8]

[6] Third Council of Valence (855) can. 5, Denz 324; Council of Florence, Denz 696; Council of Trent, Denz 895; cf. Denz 869; CIC can. 12; the same is to be found also in the 1st Schema of the *Constitutio de Ecclesia*, cap. 1, submitted to the Vatican Council (*Collectio Lacensis* VII, 567): '*ad hanc vero Mystici Corporis unionem efficiendam Christus Dominus sacrum regenerationis et renovationis instituit lavacrum, quo filii hominum . . . membra essent ad invicem suoque divino Capiti . . . coniuncti.*' Theologians refer to Mt 28.19; Jn 3.5; Ac 2.41; I Cor 12.12 *sq.*; Gal 3.27 *sq.*; Col 2.11 *sq.* For a more detailed statement of the relationship between baptism and membership of the Church, cf. J. Hamer, 'Le baptême et l'Eglise', *Irénikon* XXV (1952), pp. 142–164; pp. 263–275. Further texts in Gasparri-Serédi, *Codicis Iuris Canonici Fontes* II (Rome 1924), n. 394, p. 197.

[7] Denz 895; CIC can. 12; 87.

[8] Denz 424; 485 *sq.*; 588; 627; 629; 631; 838; 1422–1425; 1515. This question of the membership of sinners is emphasized also in the Encyclical (p. 203), and since we will not discuss it any further in what follows, we wish to make at least a very brief reference at this point to the development of this doctrine. On the one hand, the doctrine that in the 'Ark of the Church' and on her 'threshing-floor' there are to be found also 'impure animals' or mere 'chaff', and that the Church is not a Church of saints, is found already in the earliest period of theology. Yet even as late as St Augustine (despite his fight against Donatism), it remained comparatively vague whether these sinners are 'members' of the Church merely supposedly and in the order of external appearances, or whether they really belong to the Church. In other words, the exact meaning of the belonging '*in numero*' to the Church as opposed to the '*merito*' membership of the Church was not made clear. With Bellarmine it is clear that sinners are really members of the Church, and not

It must be qualified as a doctrine clearly taught by the ordinary magisterium of the Church and by Tradition (although admittedly it is not an explicitly defined Dogma), that—notwithstanding their baptism—those baptized persons are no longer members of the Church who have publicly (i.e. by a legally verifiable act) sided against the Church through schism or heresy, and that by a mortally sinful act. For the whole of Tradition, and the practice of the Church concerning readmission of such heretics and schismatics, regards such *formal* heretics as no longer in the Church. Indeed, in the third century and at the time of Donatism, the entire controversy about baptism by heretics already hinged on the question of how baptism and ordination to the priesthood could be valid despite their being administered or received *outside* the Church. In this whole controversy, both opposing parties presupposed as obvious that those who are thus baptized or ordained in heresy, are not in the Church; for the whole theological problem was precisely whether and to what extent the sacrament could, in spite of that fact, still be valid and even fruitful. The same conclusion, viz. that formal heretics do not belong as members to the Church, follows also from the fact that the Church has constantly and emphatically taught (even if not by solemn definition), that she is not made up of the sum of Christian denominations.[9] If, however, public

---

merely apparently members. Yet even he underlines that they are *membra mortua et arida*, and that it is not necessary for membership of the Church that 'Christ should be active in all His members'. The Encyclical, on the other hand, calls sinners 'defiled' and 'sick' members and stresses that they are not deprived of all supernatural life in spite of their loss of sanctifying grace. This, of course, passes over the question of whether this applies also to those who have interiorly lost even supernatural *faith*, since in this context only those are dealt with who have preserved faith and hope. This omission is understandable, since it would otherwise have been necessary to adopt a definite position on the question of whether or not 'occult' heretics are members of the Church, a question with which the Pope obviously did not intend to deal explicitly in this Encyclical. In any case, we recognize in all this a growing tendency to regard the sinner ever more clearly as a member of the Church, and this in the sense that his membership of the Church in the external, juridically and sacramentally visible order is regarded as of consequence also for the inner impulses of grace which are received even by the sinner, and are received by him precisely *as* a member of the Church.

[9] Denz 1685 *sq.*; 1955; 2199. Cf. also the following canon, prepared for the Vatican Council but never actually voted on: '*Si quis dixerit veram Ecclesiam non esse unum in se corpus, sed ex variis dissitisque christiani nominis*

and formal heretics and schismatics were members of the Church, then the one Church would nevertheless in fact be composed of the various Christian groups. For the Church is undoubtedly not to be simply equated with valid baptism as such, but is the people of God and hence a community. If, therefore, all baptized persons belonged as members to the Church simply and solely by the fact of their valid baptism, then the community of the Church would be made up also of those groups of baptized persons who have united together in the other Christian communions. The Church would in that case be objectively the sum total of Christian denominations—a conception which the magisterium of the Church expressly and resolutely rejects. We reach the same conclusion, lastly, from the Church's doctrine about the visible nature of her unity.[10] If formal public heretics and schismatics were also members of the Church, then there could no longer be any question of a visible unity of the Church through oneness of faith and of ecclesiastical jurisdiction, both of which factors are declared by the Church's teaching to be constitutive elements of her visible unity. And so, the Council of Florence[11] regards '*haeretici atque schismatici*' as '*intra Ecclesiam non existentes*'.

For the same reason we must, however, go even further now and state that even those public heretics and schismatics who either cannot be proved to be, or in fact are not, in heresy or schism through formal sin or subjective guilt are outside the Church. In short, even heretics and schismatics in good faith (i.e. merely 'material' heretics or schismatics) do not belong as members to the visible Church.

Of course, as is obvious from the very nature of things, only those are to be considered as (at least) material heretics or schismatics, who —by their own doing, even though through no fault of theirs—have cut themselves off from the Church's communion of belief or allegiance, or have moreover joined a non-Catholic communion. Merely passively received baptism outside the Catholic Church cannot as such

---

societatibus constare, per easque diffusam esse; aut varias societates ab invicem fidei professione dissidentes atque communione seiunctas, tamquam membra vel partes unam et universalem constituere Christi Ecclesiam, A.S.' (*Collectio Lacensis* VII, 577.)

[10] Cf. e.g. Leo XIII, *Satis cognitum*, Denz. 1954 *sqq*.

[11] '*Decretum pro Jacobitis*' (1442) (Denz 714). Cf. also Denz 1641: To deny a defined dogma of faith is '*ab unitate Ecclesiae deficere*'.

(and by itself) make the baptized infant a member of a non-Catholic communion. For baptism, of its whole nature, is in no way ordained to such an effect. And so,[12] those who are baptized outside the Church in infancy, remain members of the true Church until such time as they renounce that membership of the visible Church by their own personal action in the external forum, even though (in certain circumstances) they do so without any personal subjective guilt[13]; thus do they lose that membership of the visible Church which they obtained by baptism in a purely passive manner and without any personal decision on their part, since they were at that stage incapable of receiving it in any other way.

The fact that even merely material heretics and schismatics are not members of the visible Church is proved from the same premises which we used in our proof for the non-membership of formal heretics and schismatics. We cannot, it is true, describe material heretics as heretics or schismatics pure and simple and in the fullest sense, as defined in CIC can. 1325 § 2. For this canon seems to require a *pertinacia*, and hence also a subjective guilt, for heresy or schism in the fullest sense. A Protestant in good faith does not have this.[14] But the

[12] Cf. Denz 324; 696; 895. CIC can. 87 etc. Denz 869–870.

[13] When Benedict XIV says in his '*Breve Singulari nobis*' (1794), §13 (Gasparri, *Codicis Iuris Canonici Fontes* II (Rome 1924, p. 197): '*coopertum est eum, qui baptisma ab Haeretico suscepit, illius vi Ecclesiae Catholicae membrum effici*', nothing more is meant than what we have just indicated For in the following paragraph (14) Benedict emphasizes explicitly that such a baptized person ceases to belong to the one Church and is deprived of all the goods enjoyed by those who 'are in the Church' ('*in Ecclesia versantes*') as soon as he accepts the error of the heresy of the baptizer. No distinction is made here between material and formal heretics. L. Richard is, therefore, wrong in trying to conclude from this text that every baptized person is a member of the Church, although this membership is '*anormale et incomplète*' in the case of material heretics ('*Une thèse fondamentale de l'oecuménisme: le baptême, incorporation visible à l'Eglise*', NRT LXXIV (1952), pp. 485–492). Benedict's teaching does not recognize any 'gradations' of membership, but, on the contrary, is absolutely in agreement in this respect with our interpretation of the teaching of Pius XII. Richard's interpretation (p. 488) of the Encyclical '*Mystici Corporis*' is unacceptable, because it overlooks the fact that it is just not true that heretics '*veram fidem profitentur*', and it is beside the point whether one can or cannot say of them that *they* have severed *themselves* from the bond of the Body.

[14] Cf. already St Augustine, *Epistolae* 43 (PL 33, 160); Chr. Pesch, *Praelectiones dogmaticae* I[5] (Freiburg 1915), n. 395. It goes without saying

Codex Iuris Canonici, it should be noted, must add the factor of *pertinacia* to the notion of heresy or schism. For it is concerned with the question of ecclesiastical *penalties* for heresy and schism, and therefore cannot, in this context, omit the important factor of guilt. Nothing, however, is thereby decided as to whether this factor applies also to the notion of heresy or schism when the question of full membership of the Church is under discussion.

It was the almost universal teaching of theologians [15] even before the Encyclical, and indeed it follows from the very nature of things, that even material heretics and schismatics do not belong as members to the visible Church. For if those who are outside the Church by a non-imputable, but nevertheless public and juridical act, belonged nevertheless to the Church, then the visible Church could no longer be one in respect of her visibleness; nor could conformity of profession of faith and of subjection to the ecclesiastical juridical power be any longer constitutive elements of the unity of the Church.

It might be objected to this doctrine (i.e. that both formal and material public heretics and schismatics no longer belong as members to the Church, despite their baptism), that such heretics and schismatics are nevertheless still basically regarded as under the Church's authority (CIC can. 12). Apart from anything else, this can be quite clearly seen, for instance, by the fact that the ecclesiastical marriage impediments hold good even for heretics and schismatics (CIC can. 1038 § 2). One might say that non-membership of the visible Church and subjection to her laws are mutually exclusive. In reply to this it must be stated that full membership of the Church includes several

---

that even though one cannot do other than use the word 'heresy' when speaking of merely material 'heresy', any suggestion of personal depreciation in this word must, however, be avoided. This word qualifies a doctrine, and not the persons who profess this doctrine in good faith and with unwavering conviction.

[15] A few theologians hold the opposite view. Thus the *Sacrae Theologiae Summa* I[1] (cf. note 5 above), n. 1030 (p. 839) names the following as holding this view: Franzelin, De Groot, d'Herbigny, Capéran, Terrien. The following theologians of the last decades are enumerated in support of the view proposed above in the text: de San, Billot, Straub, Muncunill, van Noort, Zubizarreta, Michelitsch, Dorsch, Lercher, Dieckmann, de Guibert, Fraghi, Stolz, Vellico. The first group includes also A. Malvy (RSR XVII [1927], pp. 29–35), M. Schmaus (*Katholische Dogmatik* III, 1 [Munich 1940], pp. 171 *sq.*) etc., as well as those canonists whom we will mention later on.

factors in its extension as a direct consequence of the complexity of the constitutive elements of the visible nature of the one Church. It follows from this that, even when only one of the factors required for this membership is absent, there is no longer any question of membership of the one Church in its proper and *fullest* sense. However, it does not follow that, even in such a case, there cannot be any consequences of a juridical nature due to some other factor which still survives (and indeed cannot be lost) and which also contributes to the constitution of membership. In other words, the baptized person is formally subject to the Church's authority through baptism—not because he always and *ipso facto* becomes simply a member of the Church through baptism, but precisely because subjection to the Church is an immediate consequence of baptism, quite apart from the fact of whether baptism has actually also given membership of the Church or not.[16]

We will, in the meantime, pass over the various questions controverted among theologians, up to the time of the Encyclical, about full membership or non-membership of the visible Church as far as the so-called *excommunicati vitandi* are concerned. Furthermore, we leave completely to one side the question about the position, in this respect, of those whose baptism is only putatively valid.

There remains, however, one further question of importance for a thorough understanding of the membership of the Church. This is the question about whether those still belong to the Church or not who have *inwardly* abandoned the true Faith, without this apostacy revealing itself in the external forum. This question too has been controverted among theologians up until now. Important theologians, such as Suarez, Billuart, Franzelin, Hurter, Michelitsch, Stolz, Fraghi, Liégé, etc., deny that these occult apostates belong to the Church as members, whereas the great majority of theologians, following Cano, Bellarmine, Palmieri, Mazzella, Billot, Straub and Pesch, affirm their

[16] For a more detailed treatment of the distinction between legal status, the nature of being a subject (*Untertanenschaft*) and membership in the domain of the Church, cf. A. Gommenginger, 'Bedeutet die Exkommunikation Verlust der Kirchengliedschaft?', ZKT LXXIII (1951), pp. 1–71 (and for this particular question, cf. above all pp. 17–25). The difference between membership and subjection to the authority and law of the Church is found clearly expressed as early as, for instance, Benedict XIV ('Breve Singulari nobis', of 1749, §14: Gasparri, *Codicis Iuris Canonici Fontes* II [Rome 1924], p. 197).

membership of the Church.[17] If we leave out of consideration, in the meantime, the question as to whether (and in what direction) the Encyclical may have clarified this issue, then we must, absolutely speaking and for internal reasons, prefer the second of these opinions. For it is impossible to see, for one thing, why such a merely inner unbeliever should belong any less to the Church than other sinners, in whose case it is absolutely certain according to the Church's teaching that they are still in the Church. When Franzelin declares that the Church is the kingdom of truth and that, therefore, someone who denies this truth no longer belongs to the Church, then if this reasoning were correct, we would have to say also that the Church is the kingdom of love and hence an unjustified person could no longer belong to her. Moreover, a bishop or Pope, according to the universal teaching and one which is necessary for the steady and sure continuance of ecclesiastical authority, keeps his ecclesiastical powers even if he is occultly unbelieving in the purely internal forum. But possession of ordinary ecclesiastical authority and non-membership of the visible Church are mutually exclusive notions.[18] Therefore even such occult heretics and schismatics must remain members of the Church. Finally, the opposite opinion is guilty in the last analysis of mixing up two spheres which must be most carefully distinguished, viz. the sphere of the inner and personal moral decision and internal grace, on the one hand—and, on the other hand, the sphere of visible juridical matters

[17] The *Sacrae Theologiae Summa* (cf. note 5 above) gives (on p. 839) the following as examples of further names: Kilber, van Laak, de San, Wilmers, Tanquerey, Muncunill, Felder, Zubizarreta, d'Herbigny, Schultes, Dieckman, Vellico, Parente, Hervé.

[18] It is true that 'having legal authority' in the Church and 'being a member' of the Church are not formally identical notions (cf. Beumer, *Theologie und Glaube* XXXVIII [1947–48], p. 256). But it is contrary to the nature of an *ordinary* sovereign power in a community, that it should be capable of being exercised by a non-member or outsider. For ordinary, enduring exercise of a function proper to the nature of a community does, in fact, constitute membership. This does not mean to say that a merely delegated power, and one which is exercised *per modum actus*, can never be exercised in a particular case even by a non-member. Consider, for instance, the case (if this is really *ad rem* here—which we will leave an open question) of the confessional jurisdiction of an apostate priest in respect of the dying (CIC can. 882). Leo XIII is perfectly justified in saying ('Satis cognitum'): '*... cum absurdum sit opinari, qui extra Ecclesiam est, eum in Ecclesia praeesse.*' Cf. A. Gommenginger, ZKT LXXIII (1951), pp. 51 *sqq*.

and the visible sacramental sign. Sacramental sign, public profession of the truth, external belonging to the order of the Church—on the one hand—and sacramental grace, inner existential ratification of the truth of faith and inner affirmation of the order and unity of the Church through love—on the other hand—are each things which are indeed essentially related to one another. However, they must also be basically distinguished from one another and that to such an extent that, for example, according to the teaching even of the primitive Church, the sacramental sign can be entirely valid without the sacramental grace being actually obtained, and that, conversely, justifying grace can be given without the justifying sacrament. And just as these two spheres are to be clearly distinguished from one another, so also are the constitutive elements of both these spheres different from each other and in the same way as the spheres themselves. Hence, the elements of one sphere can be absent without the elements of the other sphere ceasing thereby to exist. For the same reason, the question about the conditions of membership of the public and juridical communion of belief must not be identified with the question about the conditions of the inner and personal act of faith. The opinion of Suarez and Franzelin does, however, wrongly identify these two questions.

b. With that we come to the *inner organic conception* (*Systematik*) and argument of the statements about who belongs to the Church which we have so far simply collected together in a more *a-posteriori* manner from the doctrinal pronouncements of the Church.

As Leo XIII already argued in '*Satis cognitum*' (1896), the Church is, in conformity with the Hypostatic Union and with the work of salvation in general, both a visible and an invisible structure, a juridically organized, visible society and the inner communion of those who are united in Christ and through the Spirit with the God of the supernatural life. These two dimensions of the Church are essentially related to one another, and this relationship, although it reaches much further in reality, has been thought through most systematically in theology, and has been fought over most explicitly in the history of Dogma, under the heading of the relationship between the sacramental sign and its effect of grace. Now the sacramental sign can be validly posited without there being effected the supernatural reality of grace signified by it. And, conversely, the supernatural reality of grace can, under certain circumstances, be given without the positing of the sacramental sign. In general, then, the question of the conditions for the validity of the positing of the sacramental sign must be clearly distinguished from the question of the conditions for the real happening of the supernatural grace which is signified and normally called into being by this sign. Just as all this is the case, so we must fundamentally observe the same relationship, difference and distinction with regard to the connection between the two dimensions of the Church and with regard to the relationship of the human person to them both.

In this regard it is furthermore essential that we observe the following: when the usage of the Church speaks of 'Sacrament', this term is taken to signify directly the sacramental sign (i.e. the plane of the public historical and tangible proceeding) and only indirectly also the sacramental grace (i.e. in so far as the sign causes the grace), without it being thereby denied that the sacramental sign and the sacramental grace are objectively connected. The same is true of the ecclesiastical usage regarding the term 'Church'. No matter how true it is that grace, inner faith and the union of men with Christ and with each other in the Holy Ghost through grace, belong to the full reality of the Church—and no matter how little true it is that the full objective reality of the nature of 'Church' is accounted for by a legal organization—it is nevertheless a fact that the term 'Church' is employed in the following quite definite sense in ecclesiastical usage. Like the notion of 'Sacrament', the term 'Church' refers in ecclesiastical usage directly to the external, visible and legally structured community of believers. It refers only indirectly to men's inner faith and union with Christ by grace, in so far, namely, as these, both as signs and as tangible realities, are effected and become present in this world through the visible Church. It is true that, to some extent, one may not find this usage too obvious in itself and it is undoubtedly in a certain sense merely a question of a *de facto*, fixed terminology; nevertheless we must take cognizance of this. This fact must be respected by Catholic theology and also in the proclamation of the Faith. It must be fully fathomed if there are not to be continual misunderstandings, and it has undoubtedly (as we shall see later) its own positive and essential importance. Thus when we ask about the membership of the Church, it is a question of the Church as a visible historically tangible unity (for, as we have just pointed out, this is the direct object of inquiry when it is a question of the membership of the 'Church'). Hence this question, to put it in this particular way, is posed on the plane of the sacramental sign and not on the plane of personal attitudes and inner decisions or inner grace. For this reason, therefore, all those and only those points which affect the Church as a visible, public and juridical society are significant and decisive for the question of membership of the Church understood in this precise manner. Since the visibleness and visible unity of the Church are constituted by the sacramental and juridical authority of the Church (which latter includes in its turn the teaching and ruling authority of the Church[19]), all and only those belong to the Church as members who are visibly, i.e. in the external forum, subject to these two powers of the Church. And everyone who, on the social plane, is cut off or has withdrawn himself from one or both of these powers, is not a member of the Church. From this fundamental principle there follow then quite clearly the individual propositions which we have established in the first instance in an *a-posteriori* manner under (a) from the doctrinal pronouncements of the Church and the teaching of theologians. Since the theological note of each individual proposition does not appertain to it as a consequence of a systematic principle, but only according to the manner in which it is presented by the magisterium of the Church, these individual propositions retain their different, theologically gradated notes, as stated under (a).

c. At this point we wish right away to append a few words on the statement of this question as frequently found in Catholic *canonistic literature.* In contrast to dogmatic Ecclesiology, certain canonists very often state our question as if every baptized person necessarily is, and always remains, a member of the Church (taken as a perfect society), in such a way that even a heretic, schismatic or *excommunicatus vitandus* is still a member of the Church, and that only his rights as a member are to a large extent in abeyance. This conception which has become much more common in canonistic writings particularly through the work of A. Hagen,[20] continued to be put forward even after the

[19] Cf. Note 5 above.

[20] A. Hagen, *Die kirchliche Mitgliedschaft* (Rothenburg 1938). Hagen's view is not quite clear. Cf. also note 13 above. A similar view is held by J. B. Haring, *Grundzüge des katholischen Kirchenrechts*[3] (Graz 1924), pp. 38 and 942; G. Ebers, *Grundriss des katholischen Kirchenrechts* (Vienna 1950), pp. 244 and 254; P. Minges, 'Gehören Exkommunizierte und Häretiker noch zur Kirche?', *Passauer Monatsschrift* XII (1902), pp. 339–347; L. Valpertz,

Encyclical, as e.g. by Klaus Mörsdorf.[21] According to Mörsdorf it is through baptism alone that an essential membership is given which cannot be dissolved either by the baptized person himself or by the Church. This he calls 'constitutional membership', and this is the basis for an operative (*tätige*) membership (of an active and passive nature) which activates the legal status, both active and passive, conferred with baptism. Now, according to Mörsdorf, heresy, schism or ecclesiastical penalties give rise to a more or less far-reaching curtailment of membership-*rights*, without the membership proper, i.e. the 'constitutional' membership, being thereby destroyed. This conception bases itself on the following considerations. On the one hand, it considers it impossible to decide anything definite about the conditions of membership of the Church from the allegedly vague notion of the Church's nature as found in Fundamental Theology. On the other hand, it is possible to decide our question definitely (and in the sense of this canonical conception) by means of the declarations of Canon Law, which after all are also significant expressions of the teaching authority. For this they appeal particularly to canon 87 of the CIC (and to its sources), which declares: Baptismate homo constituitur in Ecclesia Christi persona cum omnibus christianorum iuribus et officiis, nisi ad iura quod attinet, obstet obex, ecclesiasticae communionis vinculum impediens, vel lata ab Ecclesia censura. Canon Law seems therefore to acknowledge only baptism as the constitutive element for personal legal status and hence for membership of the Church, so that, with enduring membership in the case of all baptized persons, it can only be a question of how far they possess the rights and duties which in the normal course of events spring from membership of the Church.

To begin with, we can concede without any difficulty that this difference of opinion is *in part* merely a matter of difference in terminology. But even in this respect there remains the objective question as to which conception renders the terminological usage of the Church

---

'Kirchenbann und Kirchenmitgliedschaft', *Theologie und Glaube* XIX (1927), pp. 254–258; N. Hilling, 'Die kirchliche Mitgliedschaft nach der Enzyklika Mystici Corporis Christi und nach dem CIC', *Archiv für das katholische Kirchenrecht* CXXV (1951–52), pp. 122–129.

[21] Kl. Mörsdorf, 'Die Kirchengliedschaft im Lichte der kirchlichen Rechtsordnung', *Theologie und Glaube* (1944), pp. 115–131; *id.*, *Lehrbuch des Kirchenrechts* I[7] (1953), pp. 183 *sqq.*

more exactly. But furthermore, this is after all *not merely* a matter of terminology. For once we presuppose the conception of these canonists, there immediately arises, for example, the still objectively speaking most important question as to whether only the 'constitutional' membership is necessary for salvation according to the Dogma concerned, or whether operative membership is also required for this. There is at least the danger that in this canonistic explanation one regards the constitutional membership alone as necessary for salvation in the sense of Catholic Tradition. But this would undoubtedly be completely contrary to the Church's understanding of the Faith, since she emphasizes even to baptized heretics and schismatics the necessity for salvation of a membership of the Church which they do not possess.

If we now turn to the arguments of the canonists, we will have to state the following (even prescinding for the moment from the Encyclical): To begin with, it is not true to say that the conception of the conditions for Church membership as found in Fundamental Theology proceeds from an absolutely controversial conception of the nature of the Church. For no matter how hotly debated and deeply problematical a 'definition' of the nature of the Church may be, it is quite clear and definite from the Church's doctrinal pronouncements that the Church is an undivided and visible quantity which essentially requires for its constitution the unity of Faith and of Law. And the conception of the ecclesiologists with regard to the prerequired conditions of Church membership follows from this with logical necessity, quite apart from the way in which they may try to capture the sense of the Church's nature more exactly in a definition.

Turning now more in particular to their appeal to can. 87 itself (and to its sources), we can quite readily concede that the formulation of this canon does not take the conception, which we have here proposed as the common (although not defined) teaching of the Church on our question, as much into consideration as might be desirable. One is not, however, forced to say that this canon contradicts this teaching and that it is therefore a final argument in favour of the above-mentioned canonistic conception regarding our question. For one may quite rightly suppose that this canon and its sources have in mind the normal cases of baptism, in other words baptism in the Catholic Church (and particularly such baptism of those who have not yet reached the use of reason). Since, therefore, baptism in these cases does actually make the person a member of the Church by its very inner nature, provided of course that the other prerequired conditions are fulfilled (which can be presumed, since they are in the same line of intention as baptism, the sacrament of faith and love), we may quite safely affirm with the Code that baptismate homo constituitur in Ecclesia Christi persona, without it being necessary to mention explicitly the other conditions of actual membership of the Church. If the canon recognizes over and above this only a limitation of the *rights* of membership, then this must simply mean that it has only those baptized persons in mind who are and remain members of the Church (and who as such experience a limitation of their rights), without wishing to declare itself on the question of whether a loss of the real membership of the Church is possible or not. The opposite interpretation of can. 87 also presupposes, without proving it, that having legal status in the Church, being a subject of the Church and having membership of the Church are all convertible or at least inseparably connected terms. But these notions must be distinguished. And when we do distinguish them, then there is a question of whether can. 87 speaks of proper membership at all, or merely of the legal status and the subject relationship of the baptized person to the Church.[22] Even if we leave this an open question, it still remains true that this canon is not a cogent argument against the traditional doctrine.

Moreover, the very concept of operative membership is itself full of problems. It presupposes that there is such a thing as non-operative membership. Now it is, of course, correct to say that there are greater or lesser degrees of enjoyment, by a member of the Church, of the rights derived from his membership of the Church—but that fact alone would not mean a change in the sort of membership *as such*.

Furthermore, if we give the terms constitutional and operative membership their normal sense, then we mean by these that anyone who, even without operative membership, possesses constitutional membership, is a member of the Church and is not separated from her. According to Mörsdorf, therefore, a baptized schismatic or heretic would still be *in* the Church, because he still has constitutional membership. But the Encyclical states exactly the opposite when it

[22] For the interpretation of this canon cf. A. Gommenginger, *loc. cit.*, ZKT LXXIII (1951), pp. 17 *sqq.*

declares[23] that schism, heresy and apostasy cause *hominem ab Ecclesiae corpore* separari.

Finally, this whole canonistic argumentation jumps to conclusions. For it concludes from the fact of being subject to the legal power of the Church to the subject's membership of the Church. It is, of course, evident that a member of the Church must be subject to her. But that the subject is *ipso facto* a member, is the very thing that has to be proved and cannot be presupposed as self-evident. For the passive object of the legal claim of a community does not for that reason have to be already, without any further conditions having to be fulfilled, a member of that community.

When, quite apart from this, the doctrinal pronouncements of the Church say that a person becomes a member of the Church through baptism, we must explain that such formulations wish to emphasize that baptism is the first and most basic condition of membership of the Church. And such formulations presuppose that normally the other conditions are fulfilled automatically together with baptism, without necessarily implying by this that a person is already a member of the Church in a true and proper sense by baptism *alone*, even apart from his being subject to the authority of the Church. Whenever (as they frequently do) the sources of CIC can. 87 (and, by the way, the Encyclical too; cf. p. 201) explain the belonging to the Church and the incorporation in the Mystical Body of Christ as an effect of

[23] AAS XXXV (1943), p. 203. The same statement is to be found also in the *Catechismus Romanus* (I, 9, 12): '*tria tantummodo hominum genera ab Ecclesia excluduntur, primo infideles, deinde haeretici et schismatici, prostremo excommunicati . . . haeretici et schismatici, quia ab Ecclesia desciverunt, neque enim illi magis ad Ecclesiam spectant, quam transfugae ad exercitum pertineant, a quo defecerunt: non negandum tamen quin in Ecclesia potestate sint, ut qui ab ea in iudicium vocentur, puniantur et anathemate damnentur . . .*'. We already mentioned above that according to the Council of Florence, too, heretics are *not in* the Church (Denz 714). Using Mörsdorf's terminology, however, we would have to say: they are in the Church—only they do not have any active or passive functions of membership (either through their own fault or simply through being barred); for 'just as baptism, once validly administered, may never be repeated, so also is incorporation into the Church irrevocable once it has taken place, i.e. constitutional membership is indissoluble,' (*loc. cit.*, p. 184). But anyone who is irrevocably and indissolubly incorporated into the Church, can never be 'outside' the Church or 'separated' from her. Yet the latter is precisely what the terminology of the Church affirms.

baptism, the following fact must also be borne in mind. It is a universally accepted usage in the theology of the Sacraments to attribute certain effects to certain Sacraments without any further qualification, even if these Sacraments have these effects only under certain conditions which are not always necessarily fulfilled. Although we ascribe, for example, inner rebirth simply to baptism, no one will hold for that reason that it follows from such a statement that this effect will always be present whenever baptism is validly administered. For in fact this rebirth is effected only under certain further conditions, even although these are not explicitly mentioned in such a statement. Thus when the Council of Florence, for example, declares in the *Decretum pro Armenis* that the effect of baptism is membership of Christ in the Body of the Church,[24] it is arbitrary and illegitimate to suppose that this effect in particular is always and immediately brought about, without any further conditions, whenever baptism is valid. Only one of the effects of baptism is 'theologically certainly' caused by every valid baptism, viz. the sacramental character. Now it is indeed true to say that the sacramental character is directed in some way towards membership of the Church—viz. in so far as it is in its nature of *signum configurativum*, *distinctivum* and *dispositivum*—the condition and root of all the other effects of baptism. But just as it is not true that the other effects of baptism are always given and inseparably bound up with the character, so it is also untrue to affirm this as necessary of membership of the Church. If we now conceive *fides* and *communio ecclesiastica* as conditions of baptism received properly in every respect (and this is a completely reasonable conception), then there is no reason why membership of the Church should not be declared a consequence of the character and hence of baptism—with the tacit condition, it is true, that *fides vera* and *communio ecclesiastica* are present—without it being necessary to underline this expressly.[25]

[24] Denz 696. Cf. the 'Decretum pro Jacobitis' (Denz 714) in the same Council: Heretics are '*intra catholicam Ecclesiam non existentes*', they do not remain in the '*ecclesiastica corporis unitas*', but must first of all be rejoined ('*aggregari*') to her.

[25] When Mörsdorf says (in the 6th edition of Eichmann [1947], p. 169, note 2), that the conditions demanded here over and above baptism are on the 'plane of free personal decision', he presumably means to imply by this that the conception which we have advocated here, demands simultaneously completely disparate things for membership of the Church. The following must, therefore, be kept in mind in this connection. On the one hand, even

In rejecting the above canonistic conception, we do not mean to dispute the fact that man can have a closer or looser connection with the Church, even when, as we have established, he has not fulfilled all the conditions of membership of the Church. This looser way of belonging to the Church, however, can come about (although only in an essentially lesser measure) even in the case of a non-baptized person, as e.g. in the case of a non-baptized person who is in the state of grace. It is, therefore, impossible to understand why the canonistic conception wants to situate the step between belonging and non-belonging precisely in baptism, and why it does not want to use the term 'membership' to describe full and complete membership. For there is an alternative. We must either draw the border-line between 'belonging' and 'non-belonging' on the plane of inner personal being, and therefore between the 'justified' and the 'unjustified' person—and in that case we would, on the one hand, have to reckon even non-baptized per-

---

valid baptism is impossible without an 'intention' on the part of the baptizer. But this 'intention' is also on the 'plane of free personal decision', even though it does not need to be a morally good act. (Cf. for this H. Schillebeeckx, *De Sacramentele Heilseconomie* [Antwerp 1952], pp. 457–479.) On the other hand, when we speak of faith and obedience to the Church's authority as relevant to membership of the Church, we do not refer to the moral and supernatural side of this faith and this obedience, but to faith and obedience in so far as they are data of the external forum. After all, it has been explicitly stated that the 'occult' heretic still belongs to the Church. But as data of the external and verifiable legal order, the external profession of faith and the corresponding obedience to the Church's authority are on radically the same plane as the '*professio fidei*' given in baptism—on the same plane as that of the sacramental signs, which are also connected with a 'forum' (*sacramentale*). In the 7th edition of Eichmann (Paderborn 1953, pp. 183 *sq.*), Mörsdorf concedes (for adult Christians) the *three* essential marks of membership of the Church and then distinguishes two 'strata' in this membership, since one of the essential marks depends on God alone, whereas the other two depend on a free and personal decision of the Church member. He then characterizes these two 'strata' once more as 'constitutional membership' and 'operative membership', i.e. he distinguishes two memberships and not two strata of the one membership. And then he finally states once more that 'both (memberships) together form the essence of Church membership for the adult Christian'. I still find that this terminology is unfortunate. For one cannot help asking oneself: is there one membership or are there two? What Mörsdorf describes as 'operative membership' ('the personal realization of the Christ-likeness imprinted on the baptized in a consecratory manner') is not really an active membership, but the activation of membership.

sons as belonging to the Church, and, on the other hand, reckon sinners as no longer belonging to the Church (which is impossible according to the terminology of the Church). Or we must draw this line on the plane of the visible and of what is verifiable in the historical and legal order (and *hence* also then on the plane of the sacramental sign), and then we cannot understand why baptism should have an essential priority (with regard to the constitution of membership of the Church) over the communion with the Church's unity of faith and law; the only way to understand this would be to conceive baptism in a wider and fuller sense as including also an external avowal of the Church's communion of belief and law. But in that case our question would have been pointless from the very start.

d. In conclusion, in order not to give any false impressions, we would like to add the following with regard to what the Church taught before the Encyclical about her membership. When this teaching states that only baptized Catholics belong to the Church, it is not thereby maintained that there is nothing Christian *outside the Catholic Church.* In Part II of this inquiry we will have to treat expressly of the question about the possibility of grace for those who do not belong in the full sense to the Church. But even prescinding from that, the doctrine expounded above does not maintain that Christianity simply ceases at the borders laid down by this doctrine. After all, it is in the first place a Dogma of Faith that even baptism by a heretic is valid and, under usual conditions, also fruitful. And it is a self-evident fact that the Sacrament of baptism is actually administered in this way even outside the Church. This fact necessarily represents not only a part of the grace of Christ in the world, but also a continued embodiment in history and a visible appearance of the divine causality of grace in Christ. Furthermore, there are the Holy Scriptures even outside the Church, as the Word of God—and men who receive the Scriptures as the inspired Word of God in faith and obedience. That too is a part of the continuation in the flesh and in the human word of the visibleness of the eternal Logos in this world. There is still, furthermore, an apostolic succession even outside the Church, especially in the Eastern Churches, at least in respect of the *potestas ordinis* and at least in respect of the material connection of the present-day office of Bishop with the Church of the Apostles. And this apostolic succession in these Churches is not only factually present, but is also affirmed as a necessary and inalienable Christian reality. In this way too is found a part of that reality which even inside the Church belongs to the basic elements of that Church. Even outside the Church the will to Tradition is still alive to a large extent, i.e. the consciousness of being bound in conscience to the truth which Christ brought us and which must be transmitted as his message, with the assistance of the Holy Ghost and from generation to generation. In brief, there is Christian doctrinal truth (even though not in its undiminished fullness and purity) even outside the Church. And conversely, it is perfectly true that the Roman Catholic Church knows itself as the only Church of Christ. And it is perfectly true that she stresses that the one Church of Christ does not still have to be created but is already and always was achieved in her. Yet it is equally true that it is not thereby claimed that the catholic fullness of truth, grace and sanctifying love has already always and everywhere been manifested and represented *actually* and fully in this concrete Catholic Church, or even that this is possible without the return into the Church, as to their father's house, of the separated Christian communions (and even of the pagan peoples). And these must bring with them into the Church that aspect of Christian realization which they alone can achieve in full measure on account of their racial, historical and cultural characteristics. Even the one Catholic Church, therefore, only really attains the realization of the fullness of its *actual* reality and *explicit* development, when these our separated brethren bring it back to where it really belongs and is truly at home. This is true all the more so because the present-day separated Christian communions cannot be simply put on a par with those heretical secessions from the one Church which the Fathers of old and pre-Reformation Tradition had before their eyes and against which they fought. In those days, the Fathers of the Church saw themselves faced with heresies which in relation and comparison to the one Church possessed nothing in terms of actual historical realization apart from heresy, error pure and simple, and (at the most) perhaps also that general truth-impulse towards greater and clearer truth more explicitly unfolded, which can be the real strength even of error. But over and above this these heresies and schisms had nothing. Anything else they possessed, they had brought with them, in precisely the form in which they possessed it, from the Mother Church: law, liturgy, Scriptures, etc. They were in very fact and in every respect only less than the true Church. Today the Church finds itself in quite a different situation. She is faced with Christian communions which have a long history, a history of many hundred years. This history is, however, in this case not *only* the history of error and of a progressive loss of the substance of Christian reality. It is also and, at the same time, always a history of the development of genuinely Christian possibilities. The latter are indeed present in germ and radically in the one true Church and *can* unfold themselves in her. But it is not necessarily certain that they are always and everywhere equally present 'in act' in the Church, in the way in which they are present in the separated Christian communions. That it is also a history of this kind, is a historical fact which we can view without concern, since it is a living witness not, properly speaking, to heresy, but to the power of the one Christian truth and grace even outside the Church, which is a known fact. This is not the place to submit these Christian realizations in the non-Catholic Christian communions for examination and to compare them with the Church. But if there are such factors which, on the one hand, are genuine realizations of the Christian spirit and of Christian grace outside the Church and of which, on the other hand, it is not certain *a priori* that they must already be actually present to the same extent and in the same measure within the Church, then there arises a task for the Church which she did not have towards the heresies and schisms of earlier times. Previously heresy was *nothing more* than the lost Son who brings nothing with him. Today such a Christian communion can bring with it genuine Christian realizations which represent an enrichment of the Church. For this the Church, however, needs to have discernment and needs to be in a receptive preparedness. Men in the Church must not simply identify the present state of Christian realization (in theology, culture, Christian life, etc.) with that Christian reality which the Church has been commissioned to realize; they must be ready to learn in all humility even from those who, while they are outside, possess already (in spite of all the error and loss of Christian reality) part of those riches which we are meant to have, and indeed have already '*in potentia*', but which we do not always and in every respect possess '*actu*' and perhaps never will until everything Christian which has been scattered, has been brought into the one Church of Christ.

2. The teaching of the Encyclical about membership of the Church

We must now look at the teaching of the Encyclical against the above background. We will first of all state this teaching, then give a more detailed explanation of it and finally, estimate its doctrinal significance.

a. The teaching of the Encyclical.

The Encyclical positively determines to begin with who belongs to the Church as a member (AAS 202): Only he is a member of the Church (*Ecclesiae membrum*) who firstly has received baptism, secondly professes the true Faith (*veram fidem profiteri*) and thirdly, has neither severed himself from the bond of the corporate ecclesiastical body (*corporis compago*) nor has been separated from it by the ecclesiastical authority. From this it follows, in the negative sense, that the unbaptized and those who have set themselves in opposition to the Church through a profession of faith different from the Faith of the Church or through a radical rejection of the authority of the Church (*fide vel regimine dividi*), are no longer members of the Church.

b. Indications for a more detailed explanation of the principles laid down by the Encyclical.

Prescinding for the moment from the question of the membership, or respectively non-membership, of the *excommunicatus vitandus*, we can state that these principles of the Encyclical do not mean anything more, either objectively or in formulation, than what we have established under 1) as the general teaching before the Encyclical.

With regard to the necessity of baptism for belonging to the Church, the phrase '*regenerationis lavacrum recepisse*' will no doubt not need to be interpreted as a decision about whether someone's belonging to the Church can be based on a merely putatively valid baptism or not. But it is clear, in any case, that even according to the Encyclical no one is a member of the visible Church who has not positively received sacramental baptism (which is more than '*sacramentum in voto*').

With regard to the second condition for full membership of the Church, viz. the *professio verae fidei*, we think the following must be said: The Encyclical gives nowhere even the slightest indication that it wishes to decide the hitherto controverted question about whether occult heretics are still members of the Church or not. The majority of theologians before the Encyclical had counted such heretics as still belonging to the Church, and one of these theologians was Bellarmine, a classic author in Ecclesiology who is cited in the Encyclical. There is, therefore, no real reason for seeing in the Encyclical a confirmation of the opinion that occult heretics no longer belong to the Church. There is no reason for this even on the grounds of terminology. For '*veram fidem* profiteri' can be understood, without forcing it at all, of the *public* profession of faith, even when prescinding in this from the question of whether the inner and personal decision of faith corresponds to this external profession or not. This does not mean that the Encyclical has by its wording decided the previously controverted question in favour of Bellarmine's view. It simply means that the text of the Encyclical contains nothing which militates against his view.[26]

The Encyclical makes no distinction between material and formal heresy with regard to the fact of being separated in faith as a reason for the lack of membership. We have, therefore, no right to read such a distinction into the wording of the Encyclical and thus to try to understand the '*fide dividi*', which divides someone from the Church, as referring only to formal heresy. This is seen to be all the less admissible when it is realized that we cannot attribute a *professio verae fidei* even to a material heretic, and yet this is an explicitly demanded prerequired condition for belonging to the Church. In the abstract, on the other hand, the doctrinal pronouncement of the Encyclical retains a meaning even if it were understood merely of formal heretics. It no doubt follows from this that even the distinction in theological notes given above under (1), relative to the membership of formal and merely material heretics, is not abolished by the Encyclical. This affirmation has of course no particular significance in practice and objectively speaking. For neither before nor after the Encyclical was it possible, once one had evaluated the various objective reasons correctly, to hold

[26] It must, however, be added, it is true, that the official German version of the Encyclical has not been particularly felicitous in its translation of this *veram fidei profiteri*. For there is a certain difference in the genius of the German language between '*den wahren Glauben bekennen*' ('to profess the true faith'—Tr.), as stated by the Latin text, and '*sich zum wahren Glauben bekennen*' ('to profess oneself an adherent of the true faith'—Tr.), as stated by the German translation. The careless reader might thus get the idea that this '*sich zum wahren Glauben bekennen*' is always and of necessity also a matter of an inner personal faith, so that even the occult heretic or apostate no longer belongs to the Church. This the official text of the Encyclical not only does not state, but evidently also did not wish to state.

that material heretics belong to the Church, in spite of the different opinion of a few isolated theologians.[27]

'Those who have severed themselves from communion with the ecclesiastical body' means of course schismatics. It would be important even objectively speaking to examine at what point and by what means such a separation takes place in the concrete. According to CIC can. 1325 § 2, where the notion of 'schismatic' is more clearly described, this separation from the communion of the Church can apparently take place even without consequent entry into a non-Catholic communion. One would therefore have to inquire into the question of

[27] The following must be noted for the correct appreciation of this sentence. We start from the theological note which was established with regard to the doctrine that formal heretics do not belong to the Church. We determined this Note above in the sense that it is not an explicitly defined dogma of faith, but a dogma which is proposed by the ordinary *magisterium* and by Tradition, that formal heretics do not belong to the Church. Thus Lercher-Schlagenhaufen, for instance, (*Institutiones Theologiae Dogmaticae* I³ [Innsbruck 1939], n. 407), gives *saltem fidei proximum* as the Note of this doctrine; and *Sacrae Theologiae Summa* (cf. note 5 above): *implicite definitum praesertim in Conc. Florentino* (p. 842). But the objective reasons for the non-membership of formal and of material heretics are the same, and also there is no distinction made between them in the Church's dogmatic pronouncements on this question. For the distinction between a formal and a merely material heretic—decisive as it is from a moral point of view—is irrelevant for this question about the visible Church community, since it is quite intangible on this plane. Otherwise even the occult heretic would have to be regarded as outside the Church. Since there is such an immediate inferential connection between the proposition about material heretics and the doctrine about formal heretics, we will have to say that the non-membership of the Church of material heretics may not be disputed. Nothing that has been said here attaches an adverse theological Note to the canonistic view which affirms that all baptized persons belong to the Church or are members of the Church. For this view refers equally to formal and material heretics. And so this canonistic conception is not necessarily affected by the theological Note given with regard to material heretics (viz. 'theologically certain'), to the extent and degree in which such a conception and terminology does not have to be regarded as being necessarily directed against the doctrine of the non-membership of formal heretics (since one may say that it works with a different set of concepts, which objectively do not necessarily express anything contrary to this doctrine). Of course, whether this canonistic view agrees sufficiently with the Church's official usage is quite another question. We have already stated that we do not consider it very felicitous but fear, on the contrary, practically unavoidable misunderstandings as a consequence of this view.

whether the refusal of *communicatio cum membris Ecclesiae* (CIC *loc. cit.*) cannot also be effected in certain circumstances even without an officially registered (*standesamtlichen*) secession from the Church, but simply by a permanent non-participation in practical Catholic life. For such non-participation can in certain circumstances manifest a radical rejection of the *communicatio cum membris Ecclesiae*, even if this non-participation in Catholic life is not a direct and express refusal of obedience to the Roman Pontiff. But we cannot enter any further into this question within the present context. Suffice it simply to add that this question might under certain circumstances be important also from a pastoral point of view.

It is furthermore significant that the Encyclical also recognizes a dissolution of Church membership by a positive act of the ecclesiastical authority itself. The Encyclical does not say what form such an act must take in order to have this effect. If, however, there is to be such an act at all—and in this connection we can safely take it as self-evident that such an act of the ecclesiastical authority is not only radically possible, but is moreover already provided for in practice by the Church's actual law—then we must see this act at least in *that* kind of excommunication by which an explicitly named individual is declared an *excommunicatus vitandus*, and that by an express act of the Apostolic See, valid in law (CIC can. 2258). The question as to whether an *excommunicatus vitandus* is still a member of the Church was controverted up to this time.[28] Hence the Encyclical has here made a decision on this particular point of the controversy, in a manner which under a certain regard is authoritative, although of course not of itself infallible.[29] This particular point is, therefore, the only one which has

[28] Bañez, Gregory of Valencia, Suarez, Guarnieri, and among more recent theologians d'Herbigny, Spacil and Dieckmann (cf. *Sacrae Theologiae Summa* [cf. note 5 above], p. 840), all denied, as is well known, that excommunication can effect a loss of Church membership properly so called.

[29] One may, of course, say that such excommunication with which, according to the declaration of the Church, there is connected an 'e gremio sanctae Dei Ecclesiae penitus eici' (AAS XIV [1922], p. 593), could be in the nature of things simply a '*sententia declaratoria*' regarding an already existing state of separation on account of heresy or schism, quite independently of this sentence—and that this sentence does not effect this exclusion from the Church independently of such heresy or schism. Viewed in this way, even the appeal to Mt 18.15–18 is no longer a compelling argument. Nor is the appeal to the teaching of the ancient Church about

given rise to a certain shift of position regarding the question of membership of the Church. In practice, this particular point is of no great importance; for apart from someone who is guilty of personal assault on the Roman Pontiff (CIC can. 2343 § 1), no one is really

---

penitential excommunication within the whole framework of penitential procedure (the 'binding' of the sinner) to the point here, because this teaching was concerned with quite a different matter. This follows immediately from the fact that according to this teaching *every* person in mortal sin had to be 'bound' in this way. This was, therefore, basically a question of that removal of the sinner to the furthermost limits of the communion of the Church, which still takes place even today in the exclusion from the Eucharist of everyone who is in mortal sin. It will be extremely difficult to name cases in most recent times where someone who was not already a public heretic or schismatic has been declared '*vitandus*' by excommunication. It will also not be easy to find an *a priori* argument which proves that the Church as a society must have the right to exclude someone completely, even when this person who has offended against her has not already cut himself off from her by his very offence. Hence, in view of this situation with regard to the proofs for the aforesaid thesis, one may begin to wonder whether the Encyclical really meant to decide this hitherto controverted question. Perhaps, in the last analysis, it meant merely to establish by this 'ob gravissima admissa a legitima auctoritate sejungi', that such an *excommunicatus vitandus* is *de facto* separated from the Church, in the same sense as (public) heretics and schismatics; and thus it would not necessarily follow from this that the question as to the real, ultimate cause of that separation had actually been decided. One could then say, in this sense, that the Encyclical has not decided whether the cause of separation is the guilt which is established by this excommunication and which must (of necessity) be at the root of the excommunication—or whether it is the sentence of excommunication itself. Even in the first case the Encyclical would still bring with it a certain clarification in regard to the above mentioned view of Bañez, Suarez etc. For it would now at least be certain, as against these authors, that by an excommunication of the severest kind ('*faciens*' or at least declaratory) the Church has in view a real exclusion from the Church, of the same nature as that brought about by heresy and schism even according to these authors. *To that extent* the Encyclical does decide a hitherto controverted matter. It shall here remain an open question whether the Encyclical has also ended controversy in the sense of determining that such an excommunication does not simply legally establish a loss of Church membership, but is actually itself the cause of it. Cf. for this A. Gommenginger's profound work: 'Bedeutet die Exkommunikation Verlust der Kirchengliedschaft?', ZKT LXXIII (1951), pp. 1–71, which comes to a negative conclusion on this question. Similar in matter is V. Morel, NRT LXXX (1948), p. 721.

nowadays declared an *excommunicatus vitandus* except someone like Loisy, for instance, who, quite independently of this declaration, was already no longer a member of the Church, on account of his notorious heresy or manifest schism.

We said just now that at least the *excommunicatus vitandus* is to be counted as one who is severed from the ecclesiastical corporation by the Church's authority itself. By this nothing has been decided of itself, either positively or negatively, about the question of whether or not other kinds of excommunication imply a dissolution of Church membership in the sense of the Encyclical. It is indeed true that every *excommunicatio*, and hence even the kind by which the excommunicated person remains an *excommunicatus toleratus* (CIC can. 2258 § 1), is defined as '*censura, qua quis excluditur a communicatione fidelium*' (CIC can. 2257 § 1). Thus, at least explicitly, Canon Law does not recognize as essential a difference between the excommunication of an *excommunicatus vitandus* and that of a *toleratus*, as there would have to be on the supposition that only the excommunication of the *excommunicatus vitandus* implies a dissolution of the membership of the Church. Yet, on the other hand, we cannot say that Canon Law excludes this essential difference by its definition of these two forms of excommunication and by its combined treatment of them both. When, therefore, in general only the excommunication of the *vitandus* is regarded as dissolution of Church membership, there can be no essential objection to this on the grounds of can. 2257. In fact, this differentiation must be made, since e.g. according to can. 2266 an *excommunicatus non vitandus* retains his ecclesiastical titles and offices and so must obviously still possess membership of the Church. We can here leave it to the Canon Lawyers to determine how and in what sense even such an excommunication (which does not deprive a person of his membership of the Church) can be defined as *exclusio a communione fidelium*.[30]

We would like to draw the reader's attention to two further points, in view of what we will have to say in our summary under (c). Firstly, we would point out that, according to its explicit and immediate wording and sense, the Encyclical's explanation of Church membership is an explanation of the membership of the *Church* (*in* Ecclesiae

[30] Cf. for this the article by A. Gommenginger, which we have already quoted more than once.

autem membris . . .) and not expressly of the conditions for belonging to the *corpus Christi mysticum*. It would certainly not be in the spirit of the Encyclical to overemphasize this nuance in any way, since it is after all the essential endeavour of the Encyclical to show the equivalence of the concepts of 'Church' and '*corpus Christi mysticum*'.[31] Yet at the same time, in the light of later reflections, this nuance does not seem insignificant either. Secondly, we would point out that the Encyclical speaks simply of membership of the Church. It does not give the least hint of any kind of distinction such as, for instance, between constitutional and active membership. Its train of thought runs throughout on the same lines as the traditional thought of Fundamental Theology on this question. We have, therefore, no right to read such a distinction into the text of the Encyclical, nor indeed do we have any reason for doing so. And so, we cannot help thinking that it is rather an arbitrary interpretation of that text for a canonist[32] to say that the Encyclical hints at a constitutional membership by the fact that it does not regard separated Christians as strangers, but as those who come home to their father's house. For those who are not in the home of the Church, are indeed to return to it, but precisely because they are not in fact in their father's house but outside it—in other words, they are not members of the Church. If they did, however retain a constitutional membership, then it would be meaningless to speak of their being outside their father's house—at most it might be said that, while being in their father's house, they cannot exercise all the rights of a child of the house. Since it is here as elsewhere a basic principle for the interpretation of the doctrinal pronouncements of the Church, let us repeat once more that what is decisive, is that the teaching of the Encyclical reproduces so obviously the usual and general doctrine of fundamental theology and of dogmatic theology, as it has been taught by theologians for centuries. It must, therefore, also be interpreted according to this general teaching, even when the conception of certain canonists diverges from that teaching, at least in terminology. The Encyclical knows, therefore, only *one* proper membership, and even baptized persons can lack this, viz. when they are separated from the Church by schism or heresy (or 'total excommunication').

[31] An endeavour which was emphatically underlined once more by the Encyclical '*Humani Generis*' (Denz 3019).
[32] Cf. Mörsdorf, *loc. cit.*, p. 190.

c. Evaluation of the doctrinal significance of this teaching.

If we prescind from the question of the position of the *excommunicatus vitandus*, we can say that the explanation given by the Encyclical of what it means to belong to the Church, does not create a new state of affairs in theology. For what the Encyclical says on this matter had always either been Catholic Dogma or (in the case of the non-membership of material heretics and schismatics) is to be qualified as having always been 'theologically certain' on account of the common and clear teaching of theologians. The Encyclical is indeed an authentic doctrinal pronouncement, and as such it certainly obliges the believer to an internal assent. But it is not of itself an infallible doctrinal pronouncement of the supreme teaching authority of the Church. Hence it has not, in practice, altered the theological notes given to the norms regarding membership of the Church. The teaching of the Encyclical is, therefore, in this respect a confirmation and more recent enforcement of the traditional teaching. But this teaching of the Encyclical has its own significance. For evidently a false notion of the Church appeared to have been more or less clearly presupposed here and there outside the field of specialized theological writings, such as in talks on the union of the Churches, etc. According to this notion even those separated from one another in belief could nevertheless form the one Church together. But such a notion would turn the Church founded by Christ as the visible, one and juridical society with the Roman Pontiff at its head, into a purely inward, pneumatic community of love. This, however, contradicts in its very deepest sense the incarnational principle of Christianity, according to which God was made flesh and attached his grace to the concrete, historical here and now of human realities. And according to this principle, God has not left it to the free choice of man to decide for himself in what concrete form and historically verifiable reality he wishes to find Christ's salvation and the grace of God.

II

What does the Encyclical say about the possibility of *union with Christ* by grace for those who, in the sense of the reply to our first question, are *not members of the Church*? This is the second question which we must pose ourselves.

We have to ask ourselves this, for the whole question of who properly speaking belongs to the Church as a member and who does not, is given its full weight and significance only by the fact that this same Church declares both herself and full belonging to her (understood in the sense explained) as necessary for salvation. This is what happens also in the Encyclical, and it is precisely its statements regarding this matter which have aroused real bewilderment among non-Catholic Christians. The real significance of the question about full belonging to the Church can, therefore, be explained only by confronting this question with the statement to the effect that the Church is necessary for salvation. And only in this way will the question about membership of the Church lead us back from an area of more or less exclusive concern with definitions of terminology to the question about the objective nature of the Church, which we will then have to take up directly in the third part of these investigations.

Since man's salvation is assured, in the last analysis, by the fact of his possessing the Spirit of Christ and grace, the necessity of the Church for salvation cannot be defined merely in the sense of stating that outside the Church there is no salvation. Such a definition must also include the statement that outside the Church it is impossible to possess the justifying grace of the Holy Spirit. Our present question can, therefore, be formulated both as a question about the Church, as necessary for salvation, and as a question about the possibility of grace for those who, according to the definitions of our first part, are not members of the Church. Now the formulae of the Encyclical, which are to be examined as to their meaning and extent in this second part of our reflections, do in fact follow both these directions. Just as in the first part, we will first of all present the previous teaching of the Church on this point, so that we may then look at the pronouncements in question against this background. In this part, even more clearly than in the first, it will be necessary to observe the essential rules of our theological method to which we drew attention at the very beginning of these reflections. We must first of all simply accept the doctrinal pronouncements of the Church, even when these seem to point in completely different directions or even seem to contradict each other at first sight. We must accept them, even if theology has not as yet completely succeeded in deducing them speculatively from one uniform principle, and even if we too may perhaps not succeed absolutely in this.

1. The necessity of membership of the Church for salvation, as found in the Church's teaching before the Encyclical

Before we try to answer this question directly, we must first of all reflect a little on where in practice and in the concrete this question was treated in theology *in the first instance*. In the course of the history of the development of Dogma, this question was posed first of all in the concrete form of the question about the necessity of *baptism* for salvation. This is easily understandable from everything we have said so far. It took this form, not merely because baptism is one of the necessary conditions for belonging to the Church, but also, and above all, because even the other element of membership of the Church, viz. subjection to the juridical authority of the Church, is in its profoundest nature of the same 'sacramental' structure. What is valid of the one, viz. of the element of sacramental incorporation into the Church, with regard to its necessity for salvation, is valid in the same way also of the other, viz. of the element of being subject to the legal power of the Church (as teaching and ruling power). It would be quite wrong to make any distinctions in this respect, as if, for example, baptism were basically more important for belonging to the Church and hence also more necessary for salvation, than the other element. Thus it is a fact that the axiom, '*Extra Ecclesiam nulla salus*', was applied in absolutely the same way both to heretics (and schismatics) and to pagans. Therefore if, in what follows, we reflect more explicitly, although not exclusively, on the necessity of baptism for salvation, in order to discover whether and in what sense membership of the Church is necessary for salvation, everything we say in this connection will be equally valid of the legal element of this membership. Having pointed this out, we can now proceed immediately to the statement of the Church's teaching on her being necessary for salvation.

a. We find statements of the necessity of membership of the Church for salvation, first of all in phrases which are in reality synonymous with the axiom: *Extra Ecclesiam nulla salus*. Thus Innocent III's statement of the Church: *Extra quam neminem salvari credimus*,[33] and: *extra quam nullus omnino salvatur*[34]; or such statements by Boniface VIII as: *Extra quam . . . nec remissio peccatorum*[35], and: *Subesse*

[33] Denz 423. [34] Denz 430. [35] Denz 468.

Romano Pontifici omni humanae creaturae declaramus ... omnino de necessitate salutis[36]; or Clement VI's: *Nullus homo ... extra fidem ipsius Ecclesiae et obedientiam Pontificum Romanorum poterit finaliter salvus esse.*[37] Thus also the Council of Florence: *Nullos intra catholicam Ecclesiam non existentes non solum paganos, sed neque Iudaeos aut haereticos atque schismaticos aeternae vitae fieri posse participes,*[38] where it is expressly added that even the Sacraments avail for salvation only when their recipient remains in the Church. Formulae such as these, and others similar to them,[39] could be further multiplied.[40] This is, indeed, as Pius IX says,[41] a *notissimum catholicum dogma*. The unbending unconditionality itself of these formulae is the very property of the oldest doctrinal proclamations. The Fathers compare the Church—and by this they mean the visible Church—to an organic body, to paradise, to Noah's Ark and to the house of Rahab. And over and over again, beginning with Ignatius of Antioch and right down through Irenaeus, Tertullian, Cyprian, Origen, Augustine, Fulgentius and Gregory the Great, they derive from this the one truth formulated by St Augustine[42] in the following words: *Extra Ecclesiam catholicam*

[36] Denz 469. [37] Denz 570b. [38] Denz 714.

[39] E.g. Denz 1647, 1677, 1717.

[40] Cf. in particular the Tridentine Profession of Faith, Denz 1000. Cf. also: L. Hofmann, 'Die Zugehörigkeit zur Kirche in den Verhandlungen und Entscheidungen des Konzils von Trient', *Trierer theologische Zeitschrift* LX (1951), pp. 218–231. In the same way, Pius XII in his Encyclical '*Humani Generis*' (Denz 3019). On these declarations of '*Humani Generis*' cf. J. Vodopivec, 'Ecclesia catholica romana Corpus Christi mysticum', *Euntes docete* (Rome 1951), pp. 76–98; J. Cl. Fenton, 'The meaning of the Church's necessity for salvation', *American Ecclesiastical Review* CXXIV (1951), pp. 124–143, 203–221, 290–302.

[41] Denz 1677. It was intended to issue the following definition in the Vatican Council: *Fidei catholicae dogma esse definimus extra unam Ecclesiam Christi nullam esse sperandam salutem.* This is the wording of the revised Schema, after the first draft had explicitly mentioned the '*necessitas medii*'. This phrase had then been left out, but with the explicit explanation that the necessity spoken of in the revised Schema is to be understood as a necessity of means (cf. Mansi LIII, pp. 312, 323). Cf. for this: *Sacrae Theologiae Summa* I^2 (Madrid 1952), n. 1095; J. Beumer, 'Die Heilsnotwendigkeit der Kirche nach den Akten des Vatikanischen Konzils', *Theologie und Glaube* XXXVIII (1947–48), pp. 76–86; G. Gonzalez, 'Quintana, El axioma "Extra Ecclesiam nulla salus" segun el esquema De Ecclesia Christi al Concilio Vaticano', *Eccl. Xaver.* (Bogotá) I (1951), pp. 71–90.

[42] PL 43, 695.

totum potest habere (Emeritus) praeter salutem. Potest habere honorem potest habere sacramentum, potest cantare alleluja, potest respondere amen, potest Evangelium tenere, potest in nomine Patris et Filii et Spiritus Sancti fidem et habere et praedicare, sed nusquam nisi in Ecclesia catholica salutem poterit invenire.[43]

b. The necessity of *baptism* for salvation is emphasized just as apodictically.[44] This necessity of baptism for salvation is also more immediately evident in the Scriptures (Jn 3.5) than the explicit doctrine of the necessity of membership of the Church for salvation in general, so that usually the scriptural proof of this general statement is furnished by the scriptural proof of the necessity of baptism for salvation.

c. On the other hand, the *magisterium* of the Church emphasizes, at least in more recent times, that those who live *outside the Church* can also be *saved*. Thus Pius IX says in his Allocutio '*Singulari quadam*' (1854): 'We must hold fast in the Faith that nobody outside the Apostolic Roman Church can be saved; she is the only ark of salvation and everyone who does not enter it must perish in the flood. But we

[43] For further texts, cf. e.g. A. Straub, *De Ecclesia Christi* I (Innsbruck 1912), nos. 365 *sq*: Chr. Pesch, *Praelectiones dogmaticae* I[5] (Freiburg 1915), n. 392; P. Murray, *De Ecclesia Christi* I (Dublin 1860), pp. 737 *sqq*.; A. Seitz, *Die Heilsnotwendigkeit der Kirche nach der ältesten Literatur bis zur Zeit des hl. Augustinus* (Freiburg 1903); M. J. Rouet de Journel, *Enchiridion Patristicum*[17] (Freiburg 1952), series 47, p. 761; L. Capéran, *Le problème du salut des infidèles. Essai historique* (Toulouse 1934); F. Hofmann, *Der Kirchenbegriff des hl. Augustinus* (Munich 1933); J. Beumer, 'Ekklesiologische Probleme der Frühscholastik', *Scholastik* XXVII (1952), pp. 183–209 (esp. pp. 197–203); L. Smit, 'Extra Ecclesiam nulla salus', *Jaarboek 1951 Nederl. Kath. Theologen* (Hilversum 1951), pp. 5–26. Moreover, all the early Protestant Creeds stress the necessity of the Church for salvation in exactly the same way; for texts, cf. e.g. Straub I, n. 368. That it is possible even today to stretch the principle of the necessity of the Church for salvation too far, can be seen from the so-called Boston Heresy Case; for this, cf. C. Goddard-Clarke, *The Loyolas and the Cabots* (Boston 1950); G. Montesi, 'Skandal in Boston', *Wort und Wahrheit* VI (1951), pp. 233 *sq*.; E. Brock, 'The Boston Heresy Case', *Theologische Zeitschrift* (Basle) VIII (1952), pp. 49–59.

[44] Cf. e.g. Denz 348; 482 (*Baptisma . . . credimus esse . . . perfectum remedium ad salutem*); 712; 796; 799 (*Sacramentum fidei sine qua nulli unquam contigit iustificatio*); 861 (*Si quis dixerit, baptismum liberum esse, hoc est, non necessarium ad salutem, anathema sit*); 1470 (*baptismum esse necessarium ad salutem*).

must hold fast just as firmly to the truth that in the eyes of the Lord no one who lives in invincible ignorance of the true religion is stricken with this guilt.'[45] Similarly in his Encyclical '*Quanto conficiamur moerore*' (1863).[46] If we examine these and similar texts closely, we find that they are couched in much more careful terms with regard to the possibility of salvation for someone outside the Church than might appear at first sight. When we submit these and similar texts (to which we will return later on) to an exact analysis, we will find that they actually state only that someone who lives in invincible error about the true religion is naturally not regarded as guilty of this by God. Whether this invincible ignorance of the true religion can actually last for a whole lifetime, and what will be the eternal fate of such a subjectively guiltless person (especially when he has moreover not received baptism)—in other words, whether he will in fact reach *supernatural* salvation—these are questions about which these and similar utterances say practically nothing positive. But one can nevertheless say, first of all, that the Council of Trent evidently[47] recognizes, for all that, a properly supernatural rebirth of man by grace even by the *votum baptismi*. In other words, it recognizes a supernatural justification of man even before the most fundamental condition for belonging to the Church, namely actual baptism, has actually been fulfilled. Basing ourselves on this, we may legitimately give a wider interpretation to the first texts mentioned above about the possibility of salvation for someone outside the Church, and we may thus understand them as extending the possibility and actual, final realization of salvation even to those who never enter the Church. We are entitled to do this, even although, strictly speaking, the Council of Trent does not say anything about whether there actually are cases in this actual order of divine providence of someone having been justified by the *votum baptismi* who never reaches actual baptism and the full membership of the Church during the further course of his life. We may adopt this large-hearted and optimistic interpretation of the texts cited at the beginning without fear of erring and of reading too much into these texts, if only because it corresponds to what has now generally become, with ever decreasing exceptions, the generally accepted view of Catholic theologians, a view never objected to by

[45] Denz 1647. [46] Denz 1677.

[47] Denz 796. Cf. also Denz 1031–1033; 1070 *sq.* (justification is always given with believing love, even before baptism).

the *magisterium* of the Church.[48] But it is undoubtedly true that such positive formulations of the possibility of salvation for those outside the Church had not been given with such clarity and optimism until more recent and indeed most recent times.

And yet it is not as if, even in earlier times, there were no traces of that consciousness in Tradition, which has since then led to such views as have already been allowed, although with very great caution, to leave their clear imprint on the above quoted formulae of Pius IX. Already at the time of St Cyprian, the anonymous author of a writing entitled *De rebaptismate* speaks, with reference to the centurion Cornelius (Ac 10.44 *sqq.*), of a baptism in the Holy Ghost, without water.[49] Well known also is the following expression which St Ambrose used in his funeral oration for the Emperor Valentian who had died without baptism[50]: *Hunc sua pietas abluit et voluntas.* It is possible to establish the doctrine of such a *baptismus flaminis* also from St Augustine, at least from certain periods of his theological development.[51] This doctrine of the possibility of justification and hence of salvation outside the Church solidified then (to put it bluntly and boldly) in the Middle Ages—beginning, for instance, with St Bernard[52] —into the explicit doctrine of the *baptismus flaminis* or *baptismus in voto*, and then settles in the Church's doctrinal pronouncements as the doctrine of the necessity of baptism, at least *in voto*, i.e. under certain circumstances also only *in voto*.[53] On the other hand, we have to admit nevertheless that the testimony of the Fathers, with regard to the

[48] Thus also the Sacred Office, in a declaration of 8th August 1949, seems to count without hesitation on the fact that a *votum implicitum Ecclesiae* suffices for salvation in the case of someone in invincible error. Cf. A. Hoffmann, 'Die Heilsnotwendigkeit der Kirche', *Neue Ordnung* VII (1953), pp. 90–99.

[49] Cyprian, *Opera* III, 75 (Hartel).

[50] PL 16, 1374.

[51] For further reading on this question we would suggest L. Capéran, *Le problème du salut des infidèles, Essai historique* (Toulouse 1934), or A. d'Ales, *Dictionnaire apologétique* II (1924), pp. 819 *sqq.*; F. Hofmann, *Der Kirchenbegriff des hl. Augustinus* (Munich 1930); A. Landgraf, 'Das sacramentum in voto in der Frühscholastik', *Mélanges Mandonnet* II (Paris 1930), pp. 97–143. For the Fathers this problem arose in connection with the question about the eternal salvation of those who had died as catechumens. The biblical example is usually the good thief on Calvary.

[52] PL 182, 1036.

[53] Denz 388; 413; 847 and above all Denz 796: Council of Trent, Session VI, cap. 4; cf. CIC can. 737, §I and Denz 1031. Cf. for this also P. Hörger,

possibility of salvation for someone outside the Church, is very weak. Certainly, even the ancient Church knew[54] that the grace of God can be found also outside the Church and even before Faith.[55] But the view that such divine grace can lead man to his final salvation without leading him first into the visible Church, is something, at any rate, which met with very little approval in the ancient Church. For, with reference to the optimistic views on the salvation of catechumens as found in many of the Fathers, it must be noted that such a candidate for baptism was regarded in some sense or other as already 'Christianus',[56] and also that certain Fathers, such as Gregory Nazianzen[57] and Gregory of Nyssa,[58] seem to deny altogether the justifying power of love or of the desire for baptism. Hence it will be impossible to speak of a *consensus dogmaticus* in the early Church regarding the possibility of salvation for the non-baptized, and especially for someone who is not even a catechumen. In fact, even St Augustine, in his last (anti-pelagian) period, no longer maintained the possibility of a baptism by desire.[59] The hard inflexibility in the formulation of the meaning of '*Extra Ecclesiam nulla salus*', which has, after all, remained the same even in most recent times,[60] can, no doubt, be explained to some extent by the fact that the early Church did not, at the outset, make any very explicit or clear distinction between material and formal guilt. The Church only made this distinction in subsequently admitted, and particular cases. Instead, the early Church during the period of the preaching of the Gospel more or less took it for granted that every pagan remained a pagan through his own fault, and that every heretic and schismatic was a formal heretic or schismatic.[61] But we would not do justice to the theological sense of this ancient formula (which is

---

'Concilii Tridentini de necessitate baptismi doctrina in decreto de iustificatione (sess. VI)', *Antonianum* XVII (1942), pp. 193–222; 269–302.

[54] What Jansenism still denied: Denz 1376, 1377, 1379, 1522.

[55] Cf. e.g. the Council of Orange, Denz 179 *sqq.* etc.

[56] Cf. e.g. the *Canones Hippolyti*, can. 63 *sq.*

[57] Or. 40, 23 (PG 36, 3890).

[58] 'Sermo contra dilationem Baptismi' (PG 46, 424).

[59] Cf. Fr. Hofmann, *Der Kirchenbegriff des hl. Augustinus* (Munich 1933), pp. 221 *sqq.*, 381 *sqq.*, 464 *sqq.*

[60] Cf. Denz 1647.

[61] And thus, for instance, usually regarded baptism among heretics as valid indeed (and hence as incapable of repetition), but did not regard it as

after all formulated in an equally apodictic manner with regard to the necessity of the orthodox faith, for instance, in the Athanasian Creed[62]), if we were to look on it as a formulation of the necessity of the Church for salvation *merely* in so far as it points out that subjective guilt either does not allow full membership of the Church to materialize or dissolves it again. This is clearly shown even by the simple fact that salvation was radically denied even to unbaptized children by appealing to this proposition: '*Extra Ecclesiam nulla salus*'; and in their case there is of course no question of subjective guilt. In other words, even this fact alone shows that the necessity of belonging to the Church asserted by this formula, was of a fundamentally different order from any merely subjective moral obligation to belong to the Church. Having said all that, there still remain two further questions to be dealt with in the light of the Church's teaching before the Encyclical. First of all there is the question as to the way in which theology normally defines this particular necessity of membership of the Church more exactly; and then the question as to how such a necessity can nevertheless be objectively and logically reconciled with what we have just seen, viz. the fact that salvation is possible even for someone who does not in fact actually belong to the visible Church.

d. In order to define more exactly in what way external membership of the visible Church is necessary for salvation, theologians make use of the notions of *necessitas medii* and *necessitas praecepti*.[63] This terminology, it is true, is not yet to be found explicitly in the pronouncements of the *magisterium* of the Church—these speak simply about a necessity for salvation. But this distinction, in its application to our

---

conferring the Holy Ghost;—in fact, this was precisely the presupposition for the development of the doctrine of the sacramental character in St Augustine. Cf. as against this, however, the view of Pope Stephen (Denz 47, note 1), who obviously allows for a certain supernatural effect of baptism even amongst heretics. For the question as to which particular effects Pope Stephen adjudges to heretical baptism and which effects he excludes, cf. my remarks in the article entitled: 'Die Busslehre des hl. Cyprian von Karthago', ZKT LXXIV (1952), pp. 264–271.

[62] Denz 40.

[63] Cf. J. A. de Aldama, 'La necesidad de medio en la Escolástica postridentina', *Archivo Teológico Granadino* VIII (1945), pp. 57–84.

question, has its objective basis in the doctrine of the necessity both of baptism and of faith—or, formulated differently, it is objectively based on the necessity of wiping out original sin and of being in the state of grace in order to enter Heaven. This necessity was in all this always understood by Tradition and the teaching of the Church in the sense that it still applies even to one who, without any fault of his own, cannot comply with this necessity, as is seen most clearly in the case of the necessity of infant baptism.[64] Since the necessity of infant baptism is obviously a case of something necessary for the attainment of justification and salvation which still remains necessary even when the non-reception of baptism is absolutely guiltless, this necessity is therefore a *necessity of means* and not merely of precept. Thus if in fact, as is the almost universal view,[65] the consequences for the infant dying without baptism, even although this happens through no fault of its own, are that it remains in original sin and hence cannot attain justification, then this means that, according to the explicit teaching of the Church, the infant which has died in this way incurs the loss of supernatural beatitude. Consequently, the necessity of baptism for the attainment of the Beatific Vision, at least in these particular circum-

[64] Denz 102; 410; 424; 430; 482; 712.

[65] In most recent times, it is true, there has been renewed theological controversy about this question. Cf. e.g. Ch.-V. Heris, 'Le salut des enfants morts sans baptême', *Maison-Dieu* X (1947), pp. 86–105; G. Mulders, 'Rond het Limbus-Vraagstuk', *Bijdragen* IX (1948), pp. 209–244; N. Sanders, 'Het ongedoopte Kind in het andere leven', *Studia Catholica* (1948), pp. 125–138; E. Boudes, 'Réflexions sur la solidarité des hommes avec le Christ. A l'occasion des limbes des enfants', NRT LXXI (1949), pp. 589–605 (giving a further bibliography); P. Laurenge, 'Esquisse d'une étude sur les enfants morts sans baptême', *L'Année théologique augustinienne 1952*; F. H. Drinkwater, 'The "Baptism invisible" and its extent', *The Downside Review* LXX (January 1953), No. 223, pp. 25–42; for a summarizing account cf. Peter Gumpel, 'Unbaptized infants: May they be saved?', *The Downside Review* No. 230 (1954), pp. 342–457. These attempts to leave a way open even for the *super*natural salvation of infants dying without baptism (without going against the teachings of Scripture, Tradition and the Church's *magisterium*) do not touch directly on our subject and, therefore, we do not need to enter here into a discussion of them. For even these attempts admit that an unbaptized infant is not saved simply because it was not its own fault that it could not receive baptism and hence seek some 'substitute' for baptism. In other words, they all presuppose that the necessity of baptism is a necessity of means (albeit a conditional necessity). And in the final analysis, this is really the only point with which we are *here* concerned.

stances, is more than just a necessity of precept; it is here a question of a necessity of means, since in this case the lack of baptism makes the attainment of the Beatific Vision impossible even although this lack is not due to any guilt. And since, according to what we have stated previously, the necessity of belonging as a member to the Church is of the same kind as the necessity of baptism, we must therefore affirm that the necessity of full membership of the Church is a necessity, not merely of precept, but of means. Accordingly, theologians do in fact teach unanimously that the Church's dogma of the necessity of the Church for salvation is to be understood in the sense of a necessity of means, so that this interpretation of the Church's dogma must be looked upon as itself a theologically certain doctrine. Up to this point the matter is relatively clear and simple, at least if we prescind from the fact that the notional distinction employed in all this is not, in fact, as unproblematical as it might seem. This doctrine, stating that membership of the Church is necessary as a means for salvation, becomes difficult only when we now go on to ask how it can be reconciled with the already explained doctrine of the Church about the possibility of salvation even for someone 'outside' the Church. For if membership of the Church, as defined more precisely in the first part, is required for the attainment of salvation with a 'necessity of means', then this membership is therefore also necessary for all those who through no fault of theirs do not possess it. Hence it would seem that the possibility of salvation is for this very reason denied to every one of these untold people from the very start, and even prescinding from any guilt, simply because they are not members of the Church.

e. It is relatively easy to give a purely formal solution to this difficulty regarding the compatibility of the facts that the visible Church is a necessary means for salvation and that it is possible for someone to be saved who does not belong to the visible Church. For just as Tradition and the *magisterium* of the Church recognize a *baptismus in voto* (a baptism of desire) besides actual baptism, so the same can and must in itself be held regarding full membership of the Church. Besides actual belonging to the visible Church (in the exact way in which this full membership was defined in the first Section), there is then also a membership of the Church *in voto*, a *desire of the full membership of the Church*. This desire in its turn can be conceived either as an explicit desire which as such is known to the person and willed by him (e.g.

when a catechumen is prevented from receiving baptism by purely external circumstances) or as a desire which is present implicitly, i.e. is included in a serious general moral outlook[66] and intention to do everything necessary for salvation. And this intention or readiness can after all be present even when the person concerned does not know explicitly that membership of the Church is one of the objective factors necessary for salvation. When we thus distinguish between real and desired membership of the Church, there is no longer any formal difficulty, at any rate, in reconciling the two principles stating that the visible Church is a necessary means for salvation and that someone who is not actually a member of the Church can be saved. For these two principles are then reconciled by saying that the real full membership of the Church is necessary as a means for salvation in the sense that it can also, under certain circumstances, be supplied for by an (explicitly or implicitly) desired membership of the Church. And in this sense actual full membership of the Church is necessary with a *conditional* necessity of means. Or, to put it even more simply, full membership of the Church is a necessary means for salvation, but the notion of membership in this axiom embraces both actual and desired membership. By formulating it in this way, the possibility of attaining salvation even for someone who does not visibly belong to the Church is then not excluded from the sense of the statement that the Church is the only ark of salvation. And thus the statement, that the visible Church is necessary for salvation, loses its appearance of cruel and haughty severity towards that unnumbered multitude of those who seem to live with good intention outside the Church and beyond Christianity.

f. With the foregoing we have stated at least in outline all that can be affirmed from the explicit teaching of the Church and of theology before the Encyclical. But even before looking at the teaching of the Encyclical itself, it seems appropriate to point out a *further series of theological problems* (*weitere theologische Problematik*) which lie hidden

[66] We naturally cannot enter here into the question concerning the extent and the exact sense in which *Faith*, in its strict theological sense, is necessary for *everyone* without exception as a means for salvation, as part of this ethico-religious attitude which guarantees salvation. Cf. on this point S. Harent, 'Infidèles', DTC VII, pp. 1726–1930; R. Lombardi, *La salvezza di chi non ha la fede* [4](Rome 1949). (E.T. *The Salvation of the Unbeliever*, London, 1956).

behind the apparently slick formal answer given by theology. It will be the task of the third part of these investigations to try at least to approach a solution of these problems. But even at the present stage we must not give the impression that this theological teaching on the necessity of the Church for salvation and on the possibility of salvation outside the Church does not need any further clarification. For this reason we must already at this stage clarify at least to some extent the further problems involved. It will certainly be objectively correct to say, on the one hand, that someone who has come to the use of reason can suffer the loss of supernatural salvation only through his own personal and grave fault. That seems to follow quite simply from the knowledge of the serious and universal salvific Will of God with regard to all men, which is clearly found in the Church's consciousness of Faith. On the other hand it is also true that we may not presume that all those who come to the use of reason (i.e. who have the capacity of making their own moral decisions), but who during their life do not, in fact, reach full and external membership of the visible Church, are kept from this by their own personal grave fault. For no matter how great the tendency may be for us today to be wary once more of conceding a clear conscience, we will hardly be able to suppose, in view of the immense amount of external conditioning of the personal spiritual life of man by disposition, race, upbringing, level of culture, etc., that the unnumbered millions of people, who throughout the Christian period have not come to the Church, were prevented from doing so by their own fault. Nor will we be able to assume, as Billot[67] did a few decades ago, that the majority of these people remained on the infant level with regard to ethico-religious decisions, and that therefore the question about the possibility of their salvation is simply part of the question about God's salvific Will regarding infants. We

[67] Cf. L. Billot, 'La providence de Dieu et le nombre infini d'hommes hors de la voie normale du salut', *Etudes* CLXI (1919), pp. 129–149; CLXII (1920), pp. 129–152; CLXIII (1920), pp. 5–32; CLXIV (1920), pp. 385–404; CLXV (1920), pp. 515–535; CLXVII (1921), pp. 257–279; CLXIX (1921), pp. 385–407; CLXXII (1922), pp. 515–535; CLXXVI (1923), pp. 385–408. For a criticism cf. L. Capéran, *Le problème du salut des infidèles, Essai historique. Essai théologique* (Toulouse 1934) (2nd edition of both works); S. Harent, 'Infidèles', DTC VII, p. 1891; pp. 1898–1912; M. Larivé, 'La providence de Dieu et le salut des infidèles', *Revue Thomiste* XXVIII (1923), pp. 43–73; H. Lange, *De gratia* (Freiburg 1929), n. 694 (with further bibliographical references).

will really, therefore, have to conclude from these two propositions that there are in fact people who attain their supernatural goal without externally belonging to the visible Church. If, and in so far as, these persons have an interior supernatural faith and, rooted in this, a supernatural love of God (how this can be in the case of pagans, is a question which cannot occupy us here), then we certainly can and must say on these presuppositions that such persons have at least implicitly had the desire (*votum*) for external membership of the visible Church. But if one gives these words their plain meaning and understands them exactly and dispassionately, then, by speaking precisely of a *votum* for external membership of the Church, we once more underline by this term itself, that these persons did not actually belong to the visible Church, but merely desired to belong to the Church. And it is no use, with regard to this point, to side-step the issue by suddenly and imperceptibly switching over to some concept of 'Church' other than that of 'visible Church'; the latter was the sole concept of which we spoke in the first part, and it was with this concept alone in mind that we inquired into the conditions of membership. For the axiom of the early Church about the necessity of the Church for salvation seems to state precisely that it is necessary for salvation to belong *actually* to the visible Church. It would seem that, when the early Church explains its teaching of the necessity of the visible Church over and over again by means of such illustrations as 'paradise', 'Noah's ark', 'the House of Rahab' or 'an organic body', we are meant to understand by this that it is here a question of absolute (and not merely conditional) necessity of means. After all, someone saves himself from the raging seas only when he has actually got on board the ship and not when he merely desires to be on the ship—and a member is alive only when it is actually united with the body and not simply when it would like to be united with it. Of course, it is certainly true to say that such comparisons must not be stretched too far. But would these illustrations have any meaning left if they were not meant to indicate the necessity of an actual membership of the Church? It is, after all, precisely the visibleness of the Church and the necessity of actually and fully belonging to this visible Church, which the Fathers wish to underline and explain by these similes; but to belong *in voto* to the Church means precisely that there is in this case no visible membership, and it, therefore, cannot be considered for the constitution of the visibleness of the Church either. Moreover, to solve our question by showing the possibility of a baptism and a Church membership *in voto*, seems to be a confusion of two orders which should be clearly distinguished. The desire for baptism and membership of the Church belongs to the dimension of the inner and personal decisions of man, whereas the actual membership of the visible Church belongs to the dimension of the visible and signifying sacramental actuality which symbolizes and effects saving grace. The inner spiritual attitude of a man (in so far as he is capable of such) is, of course, also of decisive importance for the actual attainment of salvation; this does not, however, imply that this attitude as a personal, spiritual and free human act before God (and which as such lies beyond historical verifiability and the social order), can replace the visibleness of membership of the Church which has the nature of a sacramental sign. If one were to suppose this, however, then one would have to be consistent and say that the cessation of such an inner personal will to membership of the Church would also dissolve this very membership of the Church. But we have already rejected this in the first Section for a very decisive reason, when we showed that someone who disbelieves merely internally, still belongs to the Church. If the *votum baptismi*, merely as an inner subjective human act, were sufficiently constitutive of membership of the Church, considered as a necessary means of salvation—and all the more so if this were true even of a merely implicit *votum*—then, in order to be consistent and logical, we would have to say that it is really the inner spiritual attitude of the adult which is necessary as a means for salvation. And thus it would have to be said that the obligation to belong also externally to the Church is merely implied in this necessity of the inner attitude as a consequence or as added to it, and implied by a *necessitas praecepti*, if it be possible and if one becomes conscious of this precept. But if, in this way, the inner decision of a person were properly speaking and fundamentally the sole necessary factor for salvation, then it is difficult to see why the necessity for salvation of such an inner and freely adopted attitude should and could be any different from the necessity of a moral obligation. For the necessity of a free decision seems of its very nature to be the necessity of a moral demand, i.e. a *necessitas praecepti*. Of course, one might object to this on the grounds that according to all theologians the freely and personally made act of faith is, after all, also an inner, free human act on the one hand, and that, on the other hand, it is nevertheless regarded by all theologians, in accordance with Heb. 11.6, as a necessary means for the salvation of adults. However this merely extends the problem, but does not solve it. For the distinction between what is necessary as a means and what is necessary by precept would in this way seem to be reduced to a point where it can no longer be conceived with any meaning at all. The sole decisive factor for salvation would in this case seem to be merely man's inner attitude. And this attitude, in the form of a *votum baptismi et Ecclesiae* or of an act of faith, would then have to be said to be necessary as a means for salvation, in spite of the fact that, as a free moral act, it can surely imply only a moral obligation for man. And thus the question would arise of how God can demand such an act from an infant dying before reaching the use of reason for the attainment of its salvation, when it is quite incapable of performing this act. If what is strictly necessary as a means of salvation is the inner faith of man—and since God will surely not demand more of the infant than of the grown-up—he would, in that case, seem to demand an act of faith from the infant and not properly speaking actual baptism, since even of the adult he seems to demand actual baptism only by precept. Or conversely, if inner faith is really necessary as a means for salvation (understood in a sense which is more than a necessity of precept), then this faith would have to be demanded of the child as necessary for salvation, even though (according to all appearances) it is incapable of making this act of faith. There would then remain only one way out of this difficulty, viz. to postulate (contrary to all appearances) the possibility, even for a dying infant, of making a free decision of faith (as has still been done most recently by Daniel Feuling,[68] for instance). In this way we could then indeed regard the inner personal decision of faith as necessary, both as means and by precept, for the salvation of all men. But even this would not help us to solve the actual question we have posed ourselves. For this would still leave us only with a demand in the sphere of free personal attitudes and decisions, which is also a necessary means for salvation. However, according to everything that has been said so far, it is more than improbable that whatever is meant by the necessity of the Church for salvation could be found on this level of inner personal decision alone. Is it possible, ultimately, fully to explain the apodictic statements of the Fathers, who flatly deny the possibility of salvation to unbelievers

[68] *Katholische Glaubenslehre* (Salzburg 1937), p. 904.

and schismatics practically without any restrictions (with the few exceptions we pointed out above), merely by the fact that they do not explicitly take into account the distinction between those in good faith and those in bad faith for the simple reason that they always presumed in practice a formal guilt on the part of pagans and heretics? Or is there a still deeper theological reason behind the emphasis on the necessity of the visible Church for salvation, which is to a certain extent clouded by the nowadays usual formulation, according to which actual membership of the visible Church can be supplied for by a purely interior, personal human act? Or to put it more exactly: Is the *votum Ecclesiae*, in fact and in the concrete, a purely spiritual, personal human act in the sphere of a positively extra-sacramental and utterly invisible interiority of grace, and does it *thereby* and in *this* manner replace the visible and, in a certain sense, sacramental way of belonging to the Church, the sign of salvation made incarnationally visible? Or is it necessary to show that the *votum Ecclesiae* has a certain inherent 'visibleness', so that it can *on that account* replace the normal external membership of the visible Church when the need arises, without the sacramental structure of all salvation being thereby suddenly suspended in a special case? Is this the truth of the matter, so that something which is necessary as a means in the dimension of personal decisions does not suddenly supplant or replace something necessary as a means in the dimension of the nature of the sacramental sign?

This brings us to the end of our outline of the teaching of the Church's *magisterium* and of theologians, *before* the Encyclical, about the possibility of grace and salvation for someone, who in the sense of the first Section, does not belong to the visible Church. We have also at least suggested the whole line of problems which still demand further explanation relative to this doctrine. However, before we pursue this task of further explanation, we must examine the teaching of the Encyclical on whether it is possible for someone who does not belong to the visible Church to be saved.

2. The teaching of the Encyclical on the possibility of grace and salvation for those who are not members of the visible Church

a. The texts themselves:

There are three statements in the Encyclical[69] to which we must

[69] AAS XXXV (1943), 203; 243.

now give our attention: (*Spiritus Christi*) *membra . . . a corpore omnino abscissa renuit sanctitatis gratia inhabitare. Qui ad adspectabilem non pertinent catholicae Ecclesiae compagem . . . de sempiterna cuiusque propria salute securi esse non possunt. Qui fide vel regimine invicem dividuntur, in uno eiusmodi corpore atque uno eius divino spiritu vivere nequeunt.*

As can be seen, these sentences also express the necessity of the Church for salvation in the twofold way of which we spoke before: outside the Church there is no certainty of salvation; anyone who does not belong to the Church, does not have the grace of the Holy Ghost, in which salvation consists in the concrete.

b. Some general considerations about the interpretation of these texts:

When we think back over our statement of the previous teaching of the Church's *magisterium* on the necessity of the Church, of baptism, of subjection to the Roman Pontiff, etc., for salvation, we see at once that these three statements of the Encyclical do not add anything new. They in no way differ, either from the point of view of their meaning or of the perspective which gave rise to their expression, from the previous pronouncements made by the *magisterium* on the necessity of the Church for salvation and on the conclusions to be drawn from this. These three statements are simply a reiteration of the dogma of Faith as it had been clearly held even before the Encyclical and indeed from the very beginning of the Church. Hence no one at least who knew the previous unchangeable teaching of the Church will be surprised or astonished at the apparent harshness of these statements.

The Encyclical treats exclusively of the nature of the Church. The particular subject of the Encyclical does indeed include in some way also the necessity of the Church for salvation, therefore, but it is quite obvious, by the same token, that the question about the possibility of salvation for someone who is actually outside the visible Church, is simply viewed in the particular perspective of the necessity of membership of the Church for salvation. It lies, therefore, completely outside the scope of the Encyclical to treat of the question as to what positive possibility of salvation there is for such a person and as to how such a possibility of salvation can be objectively and logically reconciled with the necessity of the visible Church for salvation. If, therefore, we do not receive any information on this question, the reason for this is not to be found in the fact that the present *magisterium* of the Church contests such a possibility of salvation, or tries to push it as far into the background of theological consciousness as possible. The reason for this lack of information will simply be the fact that this question does not pertain to the subject of the Encyclical. It is, therefore, obvious from the outset that all those insights into the possibility of grace and of salvation for non-Catholics, which had been manifested up until then either by the Church's *magisterium* itself or by the universal teaching of theologians, remain rightly intact even after the Encyclical. And this all the more so, since no counter-appeals to all this will arise out of the interpretation of those statements of the Encyclical which are under discussion. Many even of the previously referred to statements by the *magisterium* of the Church about the necessity of the Church for salvation lack those precise qualifications, in their apodictic form, which we have added to them in the spirit of the *magisterium*, of Tradition and of the universal teaching of theologians, when we spoke of the possibility of salvation for those who are outside the visible Church. When the Council of Trent,[70] for example, anathematizes anyone who denies that baptism is necessary for salvation, this canon does not deny (although there is no reference in it to the *votum baptismi*) what the same Council[71] teaches elsewhere, viz. that in certain circumstances even a *votum baptismi* can suffice for justification. In the case of all such statements about the Church and baptism as necessary for salvation, we may rightly, and indeed must, according to the mind of the Church's *magisterium*, add the qualification that this membership of the Church, and baptism, are *conditionally* necessary. Thus the statement about the membership of the Church as a necessary means for salvation may and must be understood as referring to a conditional necessity of means for salvation, so that the actual membership of the visible Church can, with the usual prerequired conditions, be replaced also by the fact of belonging to the Church *in voto*. And this is valid even when this is not expressly added in such statements about the necessity of the Church for grace and salvation.

There are partly objective and partly historical reasons why in such pronouncements by the *magisterium* about the necessity of the Church for salvation this qualification is normally not added. The objective

[70] Denz 861. [71] Denz 796.

reason consists in the fact that it follows immediately from the very nature of things, that the mere *votum Ecclesiae* is not of equal privilege with actual membership of the Church as a means of salvation, but can only supply for this actual membership of the Church in exceptional cases. The historical reason for this traditional way of expression—and probably the more important of the two—lies in the fact that, in respect of our present question, it is clear from the history of the development of the Church's consciousness of the Faith that the knowledge of the necessity of actual membership of the Church came earlier and was more explicit than the reflections about the possibility of salvation for someone who is outside the Church. And, therefore, that knowledge fashioned its dogmatic formulae (which, speaking naturally, have an extraordinary consistency) much more decisively than the only slowly and timidly developing reflections about the possibility of salvation and grace for someone outside the Church. Added to this there is the fact that the proclamation of the Faith as message of salvation has of its very nature an existential character. This means that it is a message which tries to express God's demands of men and man's duty even in its most abstract formulae, a message, in other words, which outlines the existential situation of *man*. But it does not have so much to say, on the same lines, about the sovereign freedom and mercy of *God*, which God reserves to himself and which, precisely in these questions of grace and of eternal salvation, are largely incomprehensible to man's understanding even when enlightened by revelation. And what is valid, in this sense, of the interpretation of these earlier statements by the Church's *magisterium*, can equally well be applied to the statements of the Encyclical. This means that we have from the very start the right to add the qualification of the conditional to its statements about the necessity of the Church for grace and salvation, if they do not already state this qualification explicitly themselves.

c. About the particular interpretation of each of the three statements.

The following points should be made regarding the *first* statement cited above: the starting-point of the interpretation of this statement must be the question as to the exact meaning of the phrase '*membra a corpore omnino abscissa*'. Two conceivable possibilities offer themselves here: The *first* possibility is to understand this phrase about the members separated from the body, simply of all those who, according to the norm given by the Encyclical (p. 202), are not full members of the Church, i.e. of those who are separated from the visible Church by lack of baptism, or by a profession of faith different from that of the Church, or by non-subjection to the ecclesiastical ruling power. Interpreted in this way, the meaning of the statement must be as follows: Anyone who does not possess full membership of the visible Church, does not possess the sanctifying grace of the Spirit of Christ. This statement would in that case be one of those apodictic pronouncements about the necessity of Church membership as a means for justification, which we have already frequently cited from earlier doctrinal utterances by the *magisterium* of the Church. Even although it is not here explicitly stated by the Encyclical, such a statement (as we have seen) permits of the tacit addition: 'unless he be in this state through no fault of his own and also has the *votum Ecclesiae*'.

But there is a *second* possibility for the interpretation of this first statement, and this seems the probable one to us. According to this interpretation, the *membra a corpore omnino abscissa* are not simply all those who are not members of the Church in the full sense in accordance with the norm on p. 202, but only those who are *utterly* and in every respect separated from the Church. For, in spite of its emphasis on the fact that heretics and schismatics are not members of the Church in the proper and strictest sense, the Encyclical nevertheless evidently recognizes explicitly or tacitly some sort of wider reference and manner of belonging to the Church for men. It recognizes an *inscio quodam desiderio ac voto ad mysticum redemptoris corpus ordinari*[72] (p. 243) in the case of those who are not simply speaking members of the Church. It often stresses the natural blood relationship of all men with Christ; it knows that Christ in becoming man became the Head of *all* men and the Saviour of *all* men (even although 'especially' of the faithful). When the Encyclical stresses that those who are not simply speaking members of the Church are deprived of many and great heavenly graces (p. 43), it obviously presupposes that these

[72] Chavasse (NRT LXXX [1948], pp. 697 *sq.*) and Brinktrine (*Theologie und Glaube* XXXVIII [1947–48], p. 292) draw attention to the fact that Bellarmine's '*voto* esse in *Ecclesia*' is most likely intentionally avoided in the Encyclical, which says instead '*desiderio ac voto ad mysticum Redemptoris corpus* ordinari'. In other words, the Encyclical did everything in its power to avoid giving the impression that the yearning for membership is already a 'being-in-the-Church' or a proper actual membership.

people who are separated, are not however deprived of every influence of grace from Christ. The Encyclical also represents the ecclesiological aspect of the Sacraments in great detail. Therefore, since it is self-evident in this connection (for it is Catholic Dogma) that the Sacraments can be valid and effective even outside the Church, this again implies that there is, if we may put it this way, a share of 'attachment to the Church' (*Kirchlichkeit*) even outside the Church, precisely if and because such sacramental visibleness of the saving work of Christ has its proper place basically 'inside' the Church. Again, the Encyclical (p. 242) speaks of the High Priestly Prayer for the members of the Church on the one hand, and, on the other hand, for those who, because they are pagans or heretics and schismatics, are not members of the Church. And in this connection it mentions not only the Souls in Purgatory but also the catechumens in the section on prayer for members of the Church. But according to the previous declarations of the Encyclical, catechumens are not '*reapse*' members of the Church. There must, therefore, be some way of belonging to the Church which is to be distinguished from the notion of full and proper membership and yet is not purely fictitious. All these hints given by the Encyclical are so many indications of the fact that, besides the simple straightforward membership of the Church, there are other lesser and looser ways of belonging to Christ and to the Mystical Body of Our Lord which reaches concrete form in the Church.[73] If this is right, then it is

[73] We wish to remark at once that such a view (of which we will speak more explicitly in Part III) has nothing to do with the distinction between constitutional and operative membership of the Church as advocated by some canonists (cf. note 25 above). For this distinction, as made e.g. by *Mörsdorf*, presupposes that the proper, essential membership is the same in all baptized persons, since it can at most experience an abatement merely in its activation but never in its nature. This distinction also presupposes that the unity of faith and law is less constitutive of the membership of the Church than baptism. Even if 'operative membership' in Mörsdorf's sense were to be explained as 'essential' (since in his sense it too is obligatory), one would still be bound to say that on this supposition the distinction between constitutional and operative membership has a most misleading effect as terminology. For what distinguishes an operative or active membership from an activation of membership? An activation of membership, however, from the very nature of things, cannot be an essential membership, but can at best be only the act of an essential state. But all this has nothing to do with the acknowledgement of the fact that, besides proper and full membership (for which baptism and unity of faith and law are, essentially speaking,

equally important constitutive parts), there are also looser ways of belonging to Christ and to that saving reality which becomes concrete, in an historically and juridically verifiable manner, in what we call 'the Church'. We grant that greater clarity could be achieved on this point both in the Encyclical and amongst theologians, if one were to use a more differentiated terminology. Using the precedent of canonistic terminology, we have already distinguished above between 'legal status in the Church', the 'subject relationship' ('the being-subject') and 'membership', each of which is different from the other and is also constituted in a different way. One might now go on to ask whether 'belonging' (*Zugehörigkeit*) and 'being a member' (*Gliedschaft*) are to be considered as terminologically equivalent or whether they can be distinguished. To the feel of the German language, at least, these two notions are not absolutely equivalent. 'Belonging' seems to be a wider notion which, for instance, embraces also legal status and the subject relationship (or could do so, at least). One could inquire whether, on the presupposition of such a terminological distinction, one should not say that 'being a member' (of the actual kind) is something which does not admit of degrees (one either is or is not a member) whereas 'belonging' does admit of degrees, the highest and fullest of which is precisely membership itself. From there one could go on to ask further, whether the '*ordinari*' towards the Church, of which the Encyclical speaks, is not an *even wider* notion, which does, indeed, include all grades of 'belonging' apart from the highest degree of belonging (i.e. membership), but over and above this applies also in the case where one may no longer speak even of an incomplete 'belonging', as e.g. in the case of a non-baptized pagan of good dispositions. At the same time, the notion of 'belonging' would then find its proper application, in such a context of a more precise terminology, only in cases where one or several (but not all) of the elements are present which, apart from those conditions which can never be missing, are required for full belonging (i.e. membership), such as baptism, for instance, or profession of the true faith (as in the case of a catechumen). Although the individual theologian cannot simply create such a terminology for himself in the hope that its use will then become universal, he can nevertheless try to employ it on his own account and at his own risk. It is in this sense that we speak here of 'belonging', on the one hand, and of 'membership', on the other. Objectively there is no problem about this. For no theologian can deny that even a heretic, while not being a 'member' of the Church, remains nevertheless subject to the Church and, therefore, still 'belongs' to her in this sense, even although one cannot say that he 'belongs as a member' ('*angehört*') to her. Furthermore, the term 'being-in-the-Church' will be reserved for membership. For already in the imagery used by the Fathers (and especially by St Augustine), a heretic is someone who—like the soldier with his army unit or the sheep in its fold—*ought* to be in the Church (and therefore, still 'belongs', in the nature of things, 'to' the army or fold of the Church), but, in fact, simply is no longer 'in' the Church. This manner of belonging to the Church (who is herself visible) without, however, being an (actual) member of the Church, can itself be again either 'visible' (i.e. historically verifiable) or 'invisible'. If it is 'visible', true also that all those and only those can come under the heading of *membra* omnino *abscissa*, who do not even belong to the Church in any of these looser ways. It is, of course, in consequence absolutely and unconditionally true to say of these, that they do not have the Holy Spirit of Christ. But in the concrete this could be said with certainty only of those who, having come to the use of reason, have explicitly or implicitly rejected any union with Christ as their head by their own and subjectively grave fault, and thus have also severed every relationship with his mystical Body.

It follows from all this, however, that objectively speaking both interpretations of the text in question come to the same thing in the end. For one's meaning is ultimately the same, whether one says that heretics and schismatics do not possess the Holy Ghost unless they have a *votum Ecclesiae* (all other conditions being fulfilled), or whether one says that those heretics and schismatics do not have the Holy Ghost, who do not even have the *votum Ecclesiae* (and thus are *membra* omnino *abscissa*). It is therefore quite immaterial which of the two interpretations is formally correct, and hence we also cannot reproach the Encyclical for not having presented this doctrine clearly enough. The first statement under discussion, therefore, does not exclude the possibility that someone possesses justifying grace, who is not a

---

it is constituted either by baptism *or* by the profession of the true faith (in the case of the catechumen), or by baptism and true faith without, however, subjection to the ecclesiastical authority (in the case of the schismatic). If this 'belonging' is 'invisible', it is constituted by the possession of justifying grace (or by infused supernatural faith). Of course, one and the same person may thus 'belong' both visibly and invisibly and yet not be a member. We will have to ask ourselves in the third Part of these investigations whether someone can belong 'invisibly' to the visible Church (without having proper, full membership), i.e. in a manner which has absolutely no quasi-sacramental visibleness and historical tangibility—or whether this is unthinkable. We have not really anticipated this question by the notional distinctions just made. Such a manner of belonging to the visible Church would be termed 'invisible' only *in so far as* it is constituted by grace, which does indeed relate man to the one Church through his social nature and the Holy Ghost, although not in a historically perceptible manner. For an account of similar attempts to evolve a more precise terminology in this matter, cf. M. Nothomb, in *Irénikon* XXV (1952), pp. 241 *sqq*. These attempts originated above all from the French-speaking world, where it is perhaps more difficult to distinguish between *appartenance*, *incorporation* etc.

member of the Church in the full sense of the fundamental norms of the Encyclical (p. 202). For, on the one hand (to repeat our basic reflections once more) we have seen that, according to the traditional ecclesiastical usage and even when this is not expressly stated, the emphasis of the necessity of actual membership of the Church for justification does not exclude the possibility of this 'belonging' being supplied by a desire or *votum* for it, in the case of someone who, without any guilt on his part, is in error or ignorance. And, on the other hand, the Council of Trent (not to mention other arguments which could be adduced) evidently presupposes the possibility of a person's being justified by the mere *votum baptismi*,[74] in which connection it must be noted, however, that such a person, who has not yet received the Sacrament of baptism, is certainly not a member of the Church without any further qualification, in spite of his *votum baptismi.*

The statement quoted by us in *second* place is taken from the *Litterae Apostolicae* of Pius IX, which the latter addressed '*ad omnes Protestantes aliosque Acatholicos*' on 13th September 1868, in order to announce to them the summoning of the Vatican Council and to exhort them to return to the unity of the Church.[75] Let us say at once that this statement about the uncertainty of salvation for those who are separated from the Church, naturally does not mean that Catholics, as opposed to those separated from the Church, have an absolute subjective certitude of their salvation and do not have to 'work out their salvation in fear and trembling'; such an absolute subjective certitude of salvation is not normally granted to anyone.[76] Hence in the statement under discussion it is not directly a question of subjective certainty or uncertainty of salvation in the human consciousness. It is rather a question of the presence or absence of the objective presuppositions for salvation, such as they are normally provided for, prepared and demanded by God in the concrete order. Since membership of the Church is one of these conditions, it is obvious that anyone who is not a member of the Church lacks one of the positive conditions for objective security of salvation. It follows from this that anyone who of his own grave fault rejects this objective condition for salvation which is obligatory for him, thereby also forfeits salvation as long as he persists in this state of mind—and that such a person can in that

[74] Denz 796. [75] *Collectio Lacensis* VII, 8–10.
[76] Cf. Denz 802; 822–825.

sense also not be subjectively certain of salvation. As is emphasized by the Encyclical (p. 243) it is a fact that actual membership brings with it a great abundance of graces, on account of the common life of the faithful in the true faith and on account of their sure direction by the Church, etc. All this is lacking even to someone who is outside the Church through no fault of his own. Taking this fact into consideration, it follows that no one has at hand the same objective aids for his salvific activity as the members of the Church, even though he is in no way responsible for his being separated from the Church. And, therefore, such a person is also objectively in a less secure position than a member of the Church. In this sense it is also true to say of him that, although he is guiltless, he is not as sure of his salvation as a Catholic (but ultimately, of course, all this is rooted in God's free and inscrutable Will of good pleasure, for he distributes his grace as he wills). But the statement in question does not mean that this objective insecurity of salvation, even for someone who is outside the Church through no fault of his own, is such that it is absolutely impossible for him to attain salvation. Indeed it does not even mean that the grace which is included in actual membership of the Church, can never under any circumstances be replaced in God's mercy by some other, more hidden supernatural aids from God. For the rest, we can apply the same to this statement as what was said about the first. In other words, if we understand by uncertainty the insecurity of salvation on account of the lack of absolutely every means for salvation, then this applies only to those who are separated from the Church through their own subjective fault. If we understand this statement as meaning an insecurity of a relative and not of an absolute kind, on account of the lesser although still sufficient[77] degree of objective possibility of salvation (which is still given even by the looser relationship with the Church), then it can and must apply to all who do not actually belong in the fullest sense to the Church. Objectively speak-

[77] On account of his universal salvific Will, God gives every man sufficient grace to work out his salvation, if he does not reject this opportunity through his own fault. Hence, anyone who does not want to maintain that to remain outside the Church throughout one's life is always and in every case a sign of grave subjective guilt, must admit that, on account of God's universal salvific Will, a person can be provided with sufficient opportunity for salvation even when he never actually attains to membership of the Church throughout his whole life.

ing, these two possible interpretations come once more to the same thing in the long run.

We come now to a more particular explanation of the *third* of the statements cited above: *Qui fide vel regimine invicem dividuntur, in uno eiusmodi corpore atque uno eius divino spiritu vivere nequeunt.* In the framework of this second Section of our investigation there is no longer any question of the fact that those who are not subject to the teaching and ruling authority of the Church, no longer belong to the Body of the Church. What we have to discuss here is that interpretation of this statement which goes on to conclude that these same people are moreover neither animated by, nor live in, the divine Spirit of this Church. Objectively, of course, to live by the one divine Spirit of the Church in the fullest sense, means sanctifying grace and, to a lesser degree, possibly even the infused virtues of Faith and Hope. The latter can, according to the Council of Trent, still be present even in someone who has lost justifying grace. To live by the divine Spirit of the Church does not mean a 'spiritual communion of outlook' with the Church, as some have tried to interpret it in order to make things easier for themselves. For in the whole Encyclical the word *spiritus* is never used to mean a spiritual attitude or outlook, or anything else of that nature. On the contrary, it is always used to mean the divine Person of the Holy Spirit, in so far as he is the justifying and sanctifying principle of the members of the Church, together with his created graces.[78] If, therefore, anyone who is not in the fullest sense a member of the Church is nevertheless to be said to be justified, then such justification and sanctification can only be the work of this

[78] I cannot see why the divine Spirit in question should be the 'Spirit who is the Soul of this Body and who above all effects and guarantees the infallibility of the Church' (thus Brinktrine, in *Theologie und Glaube* XXXVIII [1947–48], p. 293, note 24). It is, of course, true that the statement with which we have just been concerned, is the summary and conclusion of the statements about the conditions of Church membership and about the reasons for them. But from this it follows that this Spirit, according to the texts from St Paul (1 Cor. 12.13 and Eph 4.5) quoted by the Encyclical in the very preceding sentence, is the One in Whom we were baptized *at* baptism *into* the one Body animated by this Spirit. Now the whole of Tradition and the whole teaching of the Encyclical take it for granted that one is granted *justification* by being made a member of the one Body of the Church and by thus participating in its Spirit. But where does the Encyclical speak of our participating in this Spirit by baptism precisely in as far as he effects the infallibility of the Church (which, of course, is in fact one of his effects)?

divine Spirit of the Church. But precisely this seems at first sight to be excluded by the statement under discussion. And at least at this point we cannot give the second and more probable interpretation of this text which we used when interpreting the first statement in question. In itself, only those were formally said to be deprived of the Holy Ghost together with his sanctifying grace, in that interpretation, who are no longer in any way united with the Church. But in the third statement the same is said also of those who do not possess full and proper membership of the Church, although their lack of this proper membership is still always compatible with a looser relationship to the Church. As far as the third statement is concerned, therefore, it can only be a question of emphasis on the necessity of full membership of the Church for the possession of grace. However, according to our previous arguments, this necessity of full membership of the Church for the possession of grace is a conditional necessity of means, i.e. a necessity which, in certain circumstances and under appropriate presuppositions, can be fulfilled also by the mere *votum* of full membership of the Church. Our explanations in the first section of the second part have already proved that it is ecclesiastical usage (which is, of course, based on the nature of things) to predicate this necessity of the visible Church for grace also of full membership of the Church, without mentioning always also that it is possible for this form of belonging to the Church (which is a necessary means for salvation) to be supplied for by the *votum Ecclesiae*. We have also shown already that we are not prevented from understanding this necessity of belonging to the Church as a means to salvation in the sense of a conditional necessity, by the fact that it is formulated apodictically. This usage of the Church is completely justified by the fact that the *votum Ecclesiae*, which, if need be, can be sufficient in certain extreme cases, merely re-emphasizes of its very nature the necessity of the Church for salvation. For the possibility of salvation provided by the mere *votum Ecclesiae* is not really founded directly on the objective nature of things. It is founded rather on the inadequacy (even although guiltless) of the circumstances and of the understanding of the person who finds grace and salvation by reason of the *votum Ecclesiae* alone. For, if it is in this way understood correctly, the possibility of salvation provided by the *votum Ecclesiae* does not mean a separate possibility of salvation which would take its place with equal rights beside that other possibility of salvation provided by full actual membership of the Church. And this is true, no matter how much more decisively important the *votum Ecclesiae* may be, in practice, in innumerable cases. Hence, even in the case of this third statement, we may tacitly but objectively add that anyone who is divided from the Church by faith or government, cannot possess its divine Spirit, unless he be in good faith and has the *votum Ecclesiae*.

We conclude this Section with two quotations which, although quite independent of the Encyclical, seem to us to reiterate and to summarize well the material contents of the problems with which we have been concerned in this Section. The first passage to be quoted consists of the 6th and 7th Chapter of the *Schema constitutionis dogmaticae de Ecclesia Christi Patrum examini propositum*, submitted for the Vatican Council.[79] Albeit this *Schema*, as seen from the point of view of the *magisterium*, is a purely private work of theologians, it is nevertheless a good summary of the Church's teaching on the necessity of the visible Church for salvation and on the possibility of salvation for those who are divided from the Church. Moreover, it has not really been surpassed by any theological work since the Vatican Council. It reads as follows:

> The Church is a society which is utterly necessary for the attainment of salvation. Hence everyone should understand exactly how necessary the Church of Christ is as a society for the attainment of salvation. For she is as necessary as the unity and union with Christ, the Head, and with his Mystical Body. Apart from her there is no other community which he nourishes and cares for as his Church, which alone He has loved and for which He has given himself so as to sanctify her, by purifying her through the waters of baptism in the Word of Life, in order to render her unspeakably exquisite to himself, without spot or wrinkle or anything of that kind, but rather holy and without blemish. We therefore teach: The Church is not a society with regard to which man may please himself, as if knowledge or ignorance of her, entry into her or leaving her be quite indifferent for salvation. On the contrary, she is utterly necessary for this, and this not only by the necessity of the Lord's precept, by which the Saviour prescribed entry into her for all peoples. She is also necessary for this by the necessity of means, since in the factual order of saving providence, the communi-

[79] *Collectio Lacensis* VII, 569.

cation of the Holy Ghost, and the participation in Truth and Life are only obtained within the Church and through the Church of which Christ is the Head. Furthermore, it is a Dogma of Faith that outside the Church no one can be saved. And yet no one who is in invincible error regarding Christ and his Church, will have to be declared deserving of eternal punishment on account of such error. For such a person is in no way involved in guilt in this respect before the eyes of the Lord. God desires that all men should be saved and should attain to the knowledge of the Truth, and He will not deny to anyone who does what is in his power, the grace for being able to attain justification and eternal life. But no one will attain eternal life who passes out of this life separated from the unity of faith or from the community of the Church, through his own fault. Anyone who is not in this Ark will perish in the raging floods. Therefore we reject and abhor the doctrine of religious indifferentism, which is both a godless doctrine and one which is, in fact, contrary to reason. We mean the doctrine according to which the children of this world annul the difference between truth and error and then declare that one religion is as good as the other for reaching the haven of eternal life. Or they maintain that one can have only more or less probable opinions about the truth of a religion, but never certitude. We equally condemn the godlessness of those who close the kingdom of heaven to men, by maintaining on false pretexts that it is unbecoming and quite unnecessary for salvation to change from the religion in which one was born or brought up, even if that religion be false. We condemn the godlessness of those who reproach the Church for declaring herself to be the only true religion and for rejecting and condemning all other religious communions and sects which are separated from her communion—as if righteousness and godlessness had anything to do with each other, or light and darkness had anything in common; as if Christ and Belial could speak with one voice.

The other text is taken from Pius IX's Allocution '*Singulari quadam*' of 9th December 1854[80]:

Another error, equally destructive, has taken hold of some parts of the Catholic World, as we see to our sorrow. It has sunk deep

[80] Cf. Denz 1646 *sq*. (English Translation: *The Church Teaches* [St Louis and London 1955], nos 173–174).

into the minds of those Catholics principally who think there is good hope for the eternal salvation of all those who in no wise live in the true Church of Christ. Therefore, they are in the habit of frequently asking what will be the future lot and condition after death of those who in no way have given adherence to the Catholic faith. Advancing the flimsiest of arguments, they expect a reply that will support this erroneous opinion. Far be it from Us, Venerable Brethren, to dare set limits to the divine mercy, which is infinite. Far be it from Us to want to penetrate the secret plans and judgements of God, which are a great abyss, impenetrable to human thought. But according to Our apostolic office, We want your episcopal care and vigilance to be on the alert to keep away from men's minds, with all possible effort, that opinion which is as unholy as it is deadly. We mean the opinion that a way of eternal salvation can be found in any religion whatever. With all the learning and ingenuity that is yours, teach the people entrusted to your care that the dogmas of the Catholic faith are not in the slightest opposed to the mercy and justice of God. It must, of course, be held as a matter of faith that outside the apostolic Roman Church no one can be saved, that the Church is the only ark of salvation, and that whoever does not enter it will perish in the flood. On the other hand, it must likewise be held as certain that those who are affected by ignorance of the true religion, if it is invincible ignorance, are not subject to any guilt in this matter before the eyes of the Lord. Now, then, who could presume in himself an ability to set the boundaries of such ignorance, taking into consideration the natural differences of peoples, lands, native talents, and so many other factors? Only when we have been released from the bonds of this body and see God just as he is shall we really understand how close and beautiful a bond joins divine mercy with divine justice. But as long as we dwell on earth, encumbered with this soul-dulling, mortal body, let us tenaciously cling to the Catholic doctrine that there is one God, one faith, one baptism. To proceed with further investigation is wrong.

3. Summary and supplementary remarks to Part II

a. The Encyclical says nothing beyond what was already and always, quite apart from the Encyclical, obligatory theological doctrine in the Church, with regard to a person's membership of the true Church of

Christ and the necessity of this Church for salvation and grace, and regarding the possibility of salvation for someone who is not a member of the Church in the fullest sense of ecclesiastical terminology. It stresses, on the one hand, the real necessity of strict membership of the Church for salvation, without excluding, on the other hand, the possibility of justification and salvation for those who through no fault of their own do not belong to the Church as members in the strict and full sense. The terminology of the Encyclical also moves along traditional lines with regard to the formulae expressing the necessity of the Church for salvation, without laying any more stress than had been traditional usage on the positive possibility of salvation even without full actual membership of the Church.

b. In what concerns our questions, the only peculiarity of the Encyclical is that it employs the terms 'Church' and '*corpus Christi mysticum*' synonymously, in a much more definite fashion than had perhaps been the custom up to then in respect of man here below, i.e. in the dimension of the *Ecclesia militans*. In proceeding in this way, the Encyclical is obviously imbued with the urgent desire to remove a theological error from the scene which evidently still prevails today in certain quarters in the discussions on union between Catholics and non-Catholics. We refer to that error according to which a man, or at least a Christian, may belong to the Church, or at least to the Mystical Body of Christ, no matter how he stands in relationship to the Roman Catholic Church. By identifying in practice the Church on this earth, which is also a visible, juridical society under the authority of the Roman Pontiff, with the Mystical Body of Christ, the Encyclical obviously wishes to free the theological consciousness of today from the danger, even in the field of terminology, of distinguishing these two notions in such a way that the uniqueness, visibleness and necessity of the visible Church for salvation are at least in danger of being obscured.

c. On the other hand, it is true to say that the Encyclical as a whole makes the visible *Church* on this earth and not the *corpus Christi mysticum* the subject of its declarations. Taken as a whole, the notion of *corpus Christi mysticum* remains in the Encyclical a notion which is predicated *of* the Church. It is of course equally true that Tradition also recognizes a wider concept of the *corpus Christi mysticum*, which, for instance, embraces also the just who lived before Christ's coming or all those who are justified even if they are not in the full sense members of the visible Church, or which includes also the peaceful unity between Church and State.[81] Thus, in view of both these facts, it will not be necessary to regard this terminological identification by the Encyclical of 'Church' and '*corpus mysticum*' as theologically obligatory in *such* a way that it would, in principle, no longer be permissible to use the term '*corpus Christi mysticum*' in a terminologically wider sense. One should, however, be very careful in future, when using this wider notion, not to conjure up again the misunderstandings and errors indicated above. Even when making a *terminological* distinction between the two notions, which is '*in itself*' possible, it would at all events have to remain clear that the 'Mystical Body of Christ and the Roman Catholic Church' are 'one and the same thing',[82] in the sense that one cannot belong to the former if, and in so far as, one does not belong to the latter. It seems to us, however, that this doctrine of the two Encyclicals *Mystici Corporis Christi* and *Humani Generis* does not require us to make the assertion, from the historical point of view, that both notions have always and everywhere been identical in theology. For one would find it difficult to make this assertion. Indeed, a careful differentiation of the two notions will even in future not be impossible, as long as one observes what has been said before. For, although it would in itself be possible for these Encyclicals to determine the *terminology* of this matter (and this is something which has frequently happened in the course of the history of Dogma[83]), which would prohibit the further employment of the previous usage, they do not say anything about intending to do so directly. Thus it will, for example, still be possible to prefer to say that the just of pre-Christian times belong to the Mystical Body, rather than to say that they belong to the Roman Catholic Church.[84] In other words, the identity of the

[81] Cf. S. Tromp, *Corpus Christi, quod est Ecclesia* I (Rome 1937).

[82] '*Humani Generis*', Denz 3019.

[83] As, for instance, the restrictive determination of the sense of '*physis*' in Christology. This is a case of a determined terminology which can now be looked upon as absolutely obligatory. For otherwise there would only be misunderstandings and confusions (if nothing worse), without there being any rational reason for resurrecting an earlier phase in the development of dogmatic terminology.

[84] Indeed, it must not be forgotten that the notion of the '*Church*', too, has had, and can have, a narrower and a wider sense in history. Cf. for this

two terms, as taught by these Encyclicals, is valid in as far as they relate to the time of salvation after Christ. And, moreover, it is a material and not a formal identity, i.e. the two notions regard the same thing in so far as they relate to the Church considered as the juridical foundation of Christ for the time after Christ—yet this same reality is, and can be, looked at by these two notions from different points of view, since it has several dimensions, etc.

d. The Encyclical calls the Holy Ghost the soul of the Church (p. 220). But it emphasizes most explicitly that this justifying and divinizing Spirit is the 'soul' of the *visible* Church and hence can properly speaking be found in her alone. For this precise reason, it does not seem to be in line with the Encyclical's direction of thought simply to say (as e.g. Dieckmann still does), that those who are not members of the Church in the strict and full sense but are nevertheless justified, do not indeed belong to the Body of the Church, but do, however,

---

the bibliography given above on p. 5, Note 3, and the examples collected together from the works of St Thomas and Suarez in the *Sacrae Theologiae Summa* I[2] (Madrid 1952), no. 1060 *sqq.* The Church is, for instance, constituted 'in the wide sense' (a modern qualification) of all men, beginning with Adam; the Patriarchs belong to her by faith, as we do; all those who have *fides informis* (i.e. the infused virtue which can also be in a heretic), are her members, it is the same Church before and after Christ etc. But one cannot simply make the above question easy for oneself by saying: just as the notion of the 'Mystical Body of Christ' can have a manifold, narrower and wider meaning, so also in the case of the word 'Church',—thus these two notions are still identical in every respect. For '*Humani Generis*' does not speak of a simple identity of notion between 'Church' and 'Mystical Body of Christ', but between the latter and the 'Roman Catholic Church'. This last expression is, however, identical merely with the notion of 'Church in the narrower sense'. And so the question arises as to how *this* identification is to be understood. And to this we have just answered: *this* identification refers to the two quantities only in the order of salvation after Christ and on this earth,—and their identity is merely a material, not a formal identity. We, therefore, do not conflict in any way with the Encyclical '*Humani Generis*'. The *Sacrae Theologiae Summa* I[2] (Madrid 1952), no. 1007, nota 30 is therefore incorrect in counting us among those who cast doubt on the traditional teaching about the identity of the two notions. This teaching is in no way disputed, but simply more precisely determined in its meaning and extent. Cf. also M. Nothomb, 'L'Eglise et le Corps du Christ. Dernières Encycliques et doctrine de Saint Thomas', *Irénikon* XXV (1952), pp. 226–248.

belong to the Soul of the Church.[85] What is, of course, correct about this manner of speaking, is precisely what the Encyclical itself also teaches explicitly, viz. that non-Catholics cannot be simply called members of the Church without any further qualification. But it would nevertheless be misleading and contrary to the ultimate intention of the Encyclical, although very natural, to understand such a mode of expression to mean that there can be a relation to the Spirit of the Church by grace, without this having *anything whatever* to do with her visible Body. Even although the Encyclical does not in any way enter directly into this question, one may nevertheless say that it gives us to understand that there is in some way or other a further reference, relation and connection with the *visible* Body of the Church for everyone who is justified. And we may say that in this way the Encyclical somehow points out that each and every grace of God has, in a certain sense, an incarnational, sacramental and ecclesiological structure. The Encyclical, to be sure, leaves the further theological elucidation of this question to the work of theologians. We will have to return to this question in our third part.

e. In the work for union between the Churches, apparent solutions and the obscuring of differences of dogmatic teaching are neither in the

[85] The same opinion is held e.g. by B. J. Beumer (in *Theologie und Glaube* XXXVIII [1947–48], p. 84; compare this also with: J. Beumer, 'Der Heilige Geist "Seele der Kirche"', *Theologie und Glaube* XXXIX [1949], pp. 249–267). J. Brinktrine (*loc. cit.*, p. 294), on the other hand, is of the opinion that the distinction between Body and Soul of the Church, if properly interpreted, is unobjectionable and reconcilable with the Encyclical when applied to someone's belonging or not belonging to the Church. This distinction can pass, if it is understood *correctly*. But the real question is whether it must not almost necessarily be misunderstood. Brinktrine's interpretation identifies 'belonging to the Soul' with 'belonging invisibly to the Church', and 'belonging to the Body' with 'belonging in an external, visible manner to the visible communion of the Catholic Church'. But is this 'invisible belonging' an invisible belonging to the visible Church (even *qua* visible), or is it merely an invisible belonging to some invisible element of the Church? This is precisely the question which must not be left open—but this distinction does leave it open. And then: can one belong to the visible Church, precisely as visible, in a way which is utterly and in every respect 'invisible', i.e. without any tangible historical expression whatsoever, but simply grounded in the pure interiority of a personal act? This question, too, clamours for an answer. It will be treated explicitly in the third part of the present chapter.

interest of truth nor in the interest of charity. If, therefore, the Encyclical draws attention to ecclesiological truths which belong to the Church's inalienable deposit of faith and which, with the best intentions in the world, had perhaps here and there not been clearly enough stated or professed before separated Christians, then this is not meant to arrest properly understood efforts for union but rather to further them. Union, such as Christ wills it, can only mean the unity of Christians in the Church such as Christ has willed her, and such as, according to her nature and constitution founded by Christ, she has always actually existed, and still does actually exist, in the Roman Catholic Church. Even the clearest and strongest emphasis on the uniqueness, visibleness and necessity for salvation of the true Church, i.e. the Roman Catholic Church, does not imply that one presumes in any way to judge the good faith and the grace of separated Christians. Nor does it in any way mean a denial of the great treasure of Christian reality in their teaching, in their faithfulness to Holy Scripture and in their sacramental life. It also does not mean a denial of the fact that the true Church herself would be enriched in Christian reality (in so far as this is to be realized in men according to their national, historical and psychological characteristics), if these Christians returned to the home which, in the words of the Encyclical (p. 243), is not strange to them but is their own father's home.

III

The third question which we intended to ask ourselves in our consideration, asks: With regard to the *Church's nature* itself, what *further facts*, and what *indications for further lines of inquiry* can be gathered from the answer to the first two questions? We intend to take our starting-point for this task from two problems which have been raised rather than solved by our answer to the first two questions in the light both of previous teaching and of the Encyclical. The first problem arises out of the notion of the Church which is at the root of the Encyclical's teaching on man's belonging to the Church, i.e. the problem which in practice arises out of the answer to our first question. The second problem arises out of the question about the objective compatibility of the doctrine of the visible Church as a necessary means for salvation, and of the doctrine of the possibility of salvation for someone outside the Church, i.e. the problem which in practice arises out of our second question.

1. We said in the first Part of our considerations that, according to Tradition and the Encyclical, only those, and yet all those, who are distinguished by baptism, by external profession of the faith of the Church and by subjection to the legal authority of the Church, belong as members to the Church. The consequence of such a definition of Church membership is that, on the one hand, e.g. some people who are justified and in the state of grace do not belong as members in this strict sense to the Church, whereas, on the other hand, some people who are not in the state of grace, are still members of the Church. This conclusion, drawn from the definition of membership of the Church, is not in itself surprising so long as one does not think of the Church as anything but an external, juridically organized society confessing one faith. For such a notion of 'Church' it is naturally self-evident that the internal possession or non-possession of grace, which is an intangible factor for the external forum, cannot be of any consequence for membership of the Church. Indeed, one will have to say at first sight that this definition of Church membership cannot but proceed from such a notion of the Church and that it, therefore, has this notion as its only legitimate basis. For if, as we have shown, this definition of Church membership is at least a theologically certain doctrine, and if the notion of the nature of the Church just mentioned is unequivocally and clearly the logical presupposition to this theologically certain doctrine, then that notion of the Church's nature must also be said to be a theologically certain doctrine. We would, therefore, have to consider it a theologically certain doctrine that the Church's nature lies exclusively in the visible and juridically verifiable sphere. For only on this condition, as we have said, can all those (and only those) circumstances of membership (*Zugehörigkeit*) of the Church be taken into account, which are to be found in this sphere. However, the Encyclical (p. 197) declares that it would be a rationalistic error to see nothing more in the Church of Christ than a purely juridical and social unity. And Leo XIII had already characterized this particular notion of the Church very profoundly as ecclesiological Nestorianism in his Encyclical *Satis cognitum* of 29th June 1896. The Church is more than just a juridical organization, even one founded by

Christ himself. She is the Body of Christ, animated and sanctified by the Spirit of Christ, she is the Communion of Saints; the grace of Christ, the Holy Ghost and the interior union of men with Christ as their head by an inner god-likeness and assimilation to Christ, all manifestly belong to the reality of the Church. Thus we seem to be faced with a dilemma: the definition of the conditions for Church membership knows only one notion of the Church for which the Church, whose membership is under discussion, can only be an external juridical organization; and yet precisely this notion of the Church seems to be rejected by Tradition, and also by our Encyclical, as nestorian rationalism in Ecclesiology. The solution of this apparent contradiction between various declarations of one and the same Encyclical, which is something on which the Encyclical itself does not explicitly reflect, provides us with a first possibility of acquiring a somewhat better grasp of the nature of the Church.

We have already pointed out earlier on that the theological clarification of the *notion of Sacrament* is very fruitful and important for Ecclesiology.[86] This assertion may also find verification in our present question. A Sacrament is a sign which confers grace. It does not only subsequently symbolize the internal event of the sanctifying meeting between God and man by grace. Rather this event takes place under and through this sign. The nature of a Sacrament as an external liturgical rite can only, therefore, be comprehended by having regard to that event which happens behind and through it in the form of the hidden mystery of grace. If we were to separate this reality of grace which takes place behind the sacramental rite from the latter, or even merely attempt to comprehend the sacramental rite separately from its

[86] I have already discussed some of the points required for an understanding of the notion of Sacrament (which we are here trying to clarify) in *Die vielen Messen und das eine Opfer* (Freiburg 1951), and in 'Personal and sacramental piety', theological reflections on 'spiritual Communion' and similar matters, cf. pp. 109–134 below. Certain facts concerning the historical background of the conception of the relation between the sacramental sign and the signified reality of grace, which underlies our present considerations, become clear in the Essay: 'La doctrine d'Origène sur la pénitence', RSR XXXVII (1950), pp. 47–49; 252–286; 422–456. Cf. also the treatise on 'Guilt and its remission' in the *present* volume. Furthermore: H. Schillebeeckx, *De sacramentele Heilseconomie. Theologische bezinning op S. Thomas' sacramentenleer in het licht van de traditie en van het hedendaagse sacramentsproblematiek* (Antwerp 1952).

effect of grace, then the Sacrament would lose all its meaning and significance. The Church's fight against a Protestant kind of conception of Sacrament,[87] which latter ultimately and basically transposed the event of the reception of grace exclusively into the purely internal and subjective sphere of fiduciary faith and of the interior experience of justification, is sufficiently clear proof of the way in which the Church has never given its consent to the rending of the natural bond between sacramental rite and inward grace. Yet, in spite of this, it is equally a truth of faith that there are cases when the Sacraments are validly conferred but do not actually effect this grace. The third-century controversy about baptism by heretics and the fight against Donatism were not simply wrangles about the existence of sacramental events outside the Church. These controversies were at least equally also a fight for the truth that, in spite of the essential reference of the sacramental rite to the inner event of grace, there could be real and valid sacramental events which are not fulfilled by the reality of grace necessarily symbolized and, of itself, effected by these events. Two questions must, therefore, be clearly and essentially distinguished in connection with the Sacraments. Firstly, there is the question about the necessary and unalterable conditions for the sacramental sign as a real and valid visible act of Christ and the Church effected on man. And secondly, there is the question of what conditions are necessary so that this visible action of Christ and the Church on man can actually attain what it symbolizes. And in accordance with this it is, in fact, essentially and inevitably possible (and not just something due to the indifferent notions employed), to give a twofold description of the nature of a Sacrament. Thus, on the one hand, one can give a definition of a Sacrament which includes exclusively only what belongs to the constitution of a *valid* sacramental sign. And, on the other hand, one can give a description of the nature of a Sacrament which also includes that reality in its notion for which the external sacramental event is essentially intended and without which it would ultimately lose its meaning. Both these notions of Sacrament, if we may put it this way, are necessary and indispensable, neither can replace the other; they must not be played off one against the other. One may not even regard the full notion of Sacrament as the only valid one, to the detriment of the other notion of Sacrament on the plane of the sacramental sign.

[87] Cf. e.g. Denz 848 *sqq*.

For the fact that there can be a valid but unfruitful Sacrament shows that a genuine and decisive Christian reality can exist on the visible, and sacramentally and juridically verifiable plane, without always being, in fact, an immediately effective expression and manifestation of an actual event of grace. Indeed, one will have to go further and say that this notion of Sacrament which is concerned solely with the visible and juridically verifiable dimension, must be the one which strikes man first and foremost, as he does not and cannot, in the last resort, grasp or determine the interior event of grace. When one asks about a 'Sacrament', one's question is in the first place concerned with what man himself must do and achieve in the externality of his necessarily self-averted consciousness. In other words, one asks first of all about the sacramental happening as such, in as far as this must be essentially distinguished, although not really separated, from sacramental grace as such.

Now these facts of the particular domain of the Sacraments are, however, only a particular instance of the general structure of Christian reality. Just as in Christ himself the divine nature and the human nature are as much unmixed and necessarily to be distinguished as they are unseparated, so it is also in the case of the Sacraments and elsewhere in Christian reality. And precisely this fact manifests itself now also in the nature of the Church. The Church is in a certain sense the Proto-Sacrament[88]; this means, however, that she is, in her whole concrete, visible and juridically verifiable appearance, a real sign and embodiment of the salvific will of God and of the grace of Christ. That is, she has a bodily nature which as such possesses an unmistakable, fully determined and juridically determinable form, and which actually causes the grace which it renders present in the historical here and now; and yet that bodily nature remains essentially different from this divine grace which will always be the sovereign mystery of God's freedom and can never be subdued by man. Hence there can be, as in the case of the Sacraments, a *twofold notion of the Church* which is due, not to the vagueness of notions or inaccuracy of terminology, but to the very nature of things. Thus, on the one hand, there is the notion of the Church as incarnate presence of Christ and his grace, *together*

[88] Cf. about this e.g. O. Semmelroth, 'Die Kirche als "sichtbare Gestalt der unsichtbaren Gnade"', *Scholastik* XXVIII (1953), pp. 23–39; *id., Die Kirche als Ursakrament* (Frankfurt 1953), together with its review by H. Zeller in ZKT LXXVI (1954), pp. 94–99.

with Christ and his grace, and, on the other hand, the notion of the Church in as far as she must be essentially *distinguished* from this grace and inner divine union, without ceasing, however, to be even in this way a still valid Christian reality; in other words, Church as parallel notion to Sacrament, understood as sign *and* grace, or Church as parallel notion to Sacrament, taken as the valid sacramental sign, even in as far as this can be thought of, and indeed can exist, without an effect of grace.[89] We will have to say in this connection also that this second notion of the Church (i.e. in the historical, juridically verifiable and humanly clearly determinable dimension) is the most striking, but for that very reason also the more introductory notion, just as in the case of the corresponding notion of the sacramental sign. And, therefore, the Encyclical, together with more recent theology, simply denotes by the term 'Church', as we pointed out previously, the external and juridical community directly.

As a result of these reflections, the dilemma with which we began, now gradually solves itself. When the Encyclical defines the conditions of Church membership exclusively on the basis of the external social structure of the Church, this means that it proceeds from this second notion of 'Church'. And since this notion is fully valid, and to mix up

[89] One could also say: Church as '*res et sacramentum*' (or even as '*res sacramenti*') and Church as '*sacramentum* (*tantum*)'. The history of the notion of the Church is in great part a history of the transition or change of accent from the first to the second of these notions of the Church. With St Thomas, for example, the first notion still holds supreme sway: the 'Church' is humanity united with Christ in grace and faith. And this was even more truly the dominant notion before his time. The external, sacramental and juridical form of this Church was not, of course, denied; but nevertheless, the constituting cause of this external form as a Church was above all the Spirit. Thus it could, for instance, remain quite clear right up to the later Middle Ages, that the sin of the Christian sinner changes also his relationship to the Church; the whole history of Penance bears witness to that fact in the formation of the rites of this Sacrament. Cf. also for the early Middle Ages: A. Landgraf, 'Sünde und Trennung von der Kirche in der Frühscholastik', *Scholastik* V (1930), pp. 210–247; and P. Anciaux, *Le Sacrement de Pénitence au XIIᵉ siècle* (Louvain 1949), *passim*. All this is also brought out by the fact that even St Augustine, in spite of his fight against Donatism, still struggled with the difficulty of admitting that sinners belong really and not merely apparently to the Church. Hence we also find in St Augustine the conception that the Sacraments administered outside the Church are 'valid' indeed, but that they do not on that account bestow the Spirit, since the latter can, in fact, be obtained only within the Church.

the two notions would merely expose us to the danger of obscuring the objectively existing multidimensional structure of the Church's reality, the definition of the conditions for membership of the Church is also valid. This definition, to express it in terms of sacramental theology, is the definition of valid but not necessarily fruitful membership of the Church, and of the necessary conditions for the full constitution of the *visible nature* of the union with Christ through grace. But it does not define those conditions in so far as this visibleness is actually imbued with the 'grace-full' reality which it signifies and, in itself, renders present in the here and now of the finite space of man's life on this earth. On the other hand, in view of what has been said, the comprehensive notion of the Church, which includes also the divine interiority of the Church, remains also fully valid. For the whole earthly reality which we call Church (in the other sense of that word) does, in fact, have a meaning only as the effective sign of the unity of the world with God through grace. Hence, without coming into conflict with the doctrine of faith that sinners too are members of the Church, one may rightly ask also about the nature of the conditions for a membership of the Church *by grace*. For full membership of the Church by grace in this sense, we would then have to add all those conditions to the conditions for external membership of the Church, which are required for the justification and sanctification of man (into which, of course, we do not need to inquire here). It is equally clear with regard to the full notion of the Church as giving grace, that the sinner does not belong to the Church to the same extent and in the same sense as the justified member of the Church. Thus, for instance, the ancient Church right up to the later Middle Ages was clearly conscious of the fact that the sacramental reconciliation of man with God by Penance is also a reconciliation with the Church, and that every grave sin is a 'separation' from the Church as a reality full of grace. And in keeping with this consciousness, the proceedings of the Sacrament of Penance were opened in the ancient Church by making this 'separation' visible also in the external forum of the Church. All this is proof of the fact that the Church fully appreciated that the sinner is no longer related to the Church by a fully fruitful membership, although his membership is still valid.[90]

[90] Cf. apart from the bibliography given above, p. 74, note 89, the bibliography given in my article 'Forgotten truths about the Sacrament of Penance', pp. 135 *sqq.* below.

The ultimate reason for this distinction of the two notions of 'Church'[91] is easy to understand: only if there are Sacraments which really cause grace, can there be a genuinely 'incarnational' presence of God and of his grace in the world of man here below where he is imprisoned in space and time and in the 'flesh'. Only if there are (in principle) also merely valid Sacraments which really are Sacraments and yet are empty of grace, can the grace of God remain free and beyond the ravishing grasp of man which would turn it into magic; only in this way can the grace of God remain the mystery of the unfathomable God, without this having, at the same time, the effect that God and the salvation he gives disappear into the nowhere of his infinity. In the mystery of the valid Sacraments which nevertheless are actually empty of grace there moreover reveals itself once more the mystery of the crucified God: the God-emptiness becomes a real form of God's appearance in the world. The same as is true of the Sacraments is also true of the Church: she is the real, permanent and ever valid presence of God in the world. And this remains true even when she is the Church of the sinner; the presence of God is in her in a manner which leaves the mystery of God and the incomprehensibleness of his grace and free love intact. And just as with the Church, so also with the membership of the Church: in a certain sense, viz. in its external juridical verifiability, this membership is the basic sacramental sign of the sanctification of the individual man. And since this membership is still valid even when it has lost grace, it leaves the grace of God in respect of the individual human being with that mystery which must be respected even by the man of the Church, who must always renounce all ultimate certainty about this.

2. If the reflections on the problems of the first Part of our considerations have thus given us a somewhat deeper understanding of the unseparated and unmixed divine and human natures of the Church, the reflections on the problems of the second Part will lead us to the

[91] It is to be noted that it is here a question of two *notions* of the Church and not of two Churches. By distinguishing between a valid and a fruitful Sacrament, one arrives at two notions but does not thereby distinguish two Sacraments; no more do two notions of the Church imply the assertion of two Churches of which it might then be asked how far they 'coincide' or do not coincide with one another.

realization of a *stratification within the nature of the Church as sacramental sign.* The visible nature of God's grace which we call Church is itself composed of several realities. In what follows we must try to clarify what exactly is meant by this.

The consideration of *the necessity of the Church for salvation* in the second Part led us to the question as to the possibility of salvation for someone who does not belong in the legal sense to the Church. Our answer was that the necessity of the Church as a means for salvation does not deny the possibility of salvation for someone with the *votum Ecclesiae* and is, therefore, to be conceived as a *conditional necessity of means.* The necessity of the Church for salvation and the possibility of salvation for someone outside the Church were, therefore, logically reconciled with one another in this notion of the conditional necessity of the Church as a means for salvation, but only in a formal notional manner. For there remained the question as to what is left objectively of the necessity of the visible Church as a means for salvation, if man can attain God's grace even without the sacramental medium of the visible 'historical' Church, but simply by the pure interiority and spirituality of his own personal decision. For the ancient Church's conception of the necessity of the Church for salvation meant precisely the Church as something visible and distinct from the subjective attitude or 'good will' of man. There seems to remain nothing of this conception, if man can under certain conditions find salvation also by his 'good will', even if this be the will for the Church. Therefore, on the one hand, the practical possibility of justification by the mere *votum Ecclesiae* cannot be denied and, on the other hand, the objective significance of the dogma that a visible Church is necessary for salvation must be more clearly understood than is commonly the case in the ordinary explanation of the *votum Ecclesiae.* Since this is so, it will obviously only be possible to attain this clearer understanding by a more exact theological reflection which will show how even a mere *votum Ecclesiae*, as long as it is really present, has a *quasi-sacramental visible aspect* in the concrete, which can and must also be included in the visible nature of the Church. We must now develop what is postulated by this from a different angle.

The *human race is a unity.* This unity manifests itself right away in the common descent of all men from Adam.[92] The human species is

[92] Cf. Denz 3028. '*Humani Generis*' draws attention to the fact that the unity of descent of the human race is no theologically indifferent conception.

In a metaphysical anthropology, the unity of the human species would have to be considered even more exactly. Scholastic Ontology recognizes properly speaking and explicitly only that '*species*' which is the purely logical comprehension of many individuals which are the same, the ontological substratum of this unity being merely the repeated sameness of 'nature' in many. This leaves out of consideration the question as to what is meant by the historical unity of many, who are the same by oneness of origin, and also the question as to how far specific unity is based on such a unity of origin and history. One cannot *a priori* point to the 'specific' sameness of inorganic things in objection to this. For in the first place, it would be necessary to look more closely into the merely analogous nature of the individuality and difference of the 'individuals' on both of these levels of being, before one could assert that the unity of origin is irrelevant to the specific unity of living beings. And secondly, one would have to inquire into whether the 'individual' (particle) in the inorganic world does not have essentially less determined limits and less independence in contrast to the 'field' (of force) etc., than is analogously the case in the organic world. And one would then have to ask whether the unity of origin and the consequent unity of history in the organic world is not perhaps in some way the 'homologue' in this world of the unity of the field in which the inorganic 'individual' exists as a moment of this field, outside of which it cannot even be thought. These reflections are simply meant to show that the unity of origin of the human species has more to do with its specific unity and hence with the possibility of a common determination of all men and of a common goal, than might appear to a more superficial view. One should in any case ask oneself seriously whether the unity of origin of the human race (i.e. 'monogenism' in its specific theological sense) is not also a datum of a deeper-going philosophy of Nature—and whether modern theologians have not 'beat the retreat' in the wrong place by regarding this monogenism as a truth which can be known only from revelation and as a fact which is simply and necessarily based on the Creator's free decree. Moreover, one need not be afraid that this monogenism might appear as a theological distortion of the hypothesis of a real connection between human life and the animal kingdom. For, on the contrary, both theses (i.e. the thesis of the anthropological theory of descent *and* that of monogenism) arise from the *same* metaphysical principle of economy: i.e. the intervention of the divine, world-transcendent cause can be postulated only where, and only in as far as and as often as, terrestrial forces are insufficient for the explanation of a certain phenomenon—in fact, only where something really and irreducibly new appears and in so far as it does appear. It is no doubt unnecessary to explain further that a polygenism (which still wanted to recognize the irreducible novelty of man) is contrary to this metaphysical principle of economy in the case of a man who can beget his like, and that it turns the miracle of the one creation of man by the divine cause behind the world into an oft-repeated miracle of a demiurge in the world. Cf. for all this, Vol. I of the present work, pp. 229–296 ('Theological reflexions on Monogenism').

regarded and treated by God as a concrete unity, not only in the natural order but also in the order of salvation, as is seen in the fact of original sin and in the fact of the radical and universal redemption of the human race by Christ. This unity can here be presupposed as a fact, without our having to enter into the ontological question as to how this unity is to be more exactly established and conceived metaphysically. It cannot, therefore, concern us here whether this unity is established more exactly in a platonic or aristotelian manner, more from the point of view of the unity of the Idea of 'Man' or more from the point of view of the infraspiritual unity of the one materiality (in the sense of the thomistic *materia prima*); nor whether it be more clearly established from that openness of man to the personal community of spirits, based on his spiritual nature, or from something else. Whatever may be the more exact explanation, there is, in fact, such a natural unity of all men, which is the underlying *potentia oboedientialis* of God's saving work with regard to humanity—in the sense that humanity is not merely the subsequent, purely conceptual summation of the many human individuals. The inclusion of the individual man within this unity is also, therefore, a reality presupposed by his free personal activity. And he necessarily takes up position relative to this reality in his activity in as far as it is the prerequired condition which makes this activity possible. Moreover, he consciously helps to consummate this unity by his action as a person, since it is part of his 'nature'. This oneness with humanity, in so far as it is presupposed as a part of Nature by man as an acting person, belongs to the *visible nature* of man, in so far as we understand by this everything concrete in the spatio-temporal sense which the freedom of man as a personal being presupposes as the preceding and determining condition of action and which, as a reality stamped by the personal decision of man, is the substance of the gradual revelation of man in history as an intelligible free being.

For by reason of his twofold nature of spirit and matter, we must distinguish between man as intelligible person and man as 'nature'. By person[93] we mean man in so far as he can be, and is, freely in

[93] The terms 'person' and 'nature' are, of course, used here in a modern sense which must not be confused with the sense which these terms have, for instance, in the scholastic exposition of the doctrines of the Trinity or of the Hypostatic Union. But if one is careful, it will not be too difficult to keep these meanings apart. In any case, the modern usage is also already fore-

command of himself (as nature). By nature we mean here everything which, as condition for its possibility, precedes this free activity of man as a person and signifies a norm which sets bounds to the autonomous sovereignty of his freedom. In conformity with the general structure of human activity, which is that of a spirit in matter, we must also distinguish two strata in man's existential determination of himself.[94] We refer to the initial intelligible free human act as such and its necessary materialization in what are commonly known as man's actions, actions which are always necessarily also activation and activity of the 'nature' of man. These two 'strata' in the free activity of man are, on the one hand, always inseparable one from the other. This means that man's free action is never absolutely creative (in the terms of pure existentialism), but is always also subjected to the laws of the matter of free activity (i.e. to man's 'nature'—to his 'corporeity' in the metaphysical sense—to the 'world'). On the other hand, the initial intelligible act of free will and its materialization must also never be identified, just as the 'spirit' of man is never absorbed by the soul, and just as (in scholastic terminology) the *anima intellectualis* is never *merely* the *forma corporis* (no matter how much it is this form also *qua* spirit). With this there is given a peculiar but real dialectic between what is freely willed as such and what is freely done. Because it is necessary for the action of freedom, that which is carried out by the person into the dimension of nature, is the expression and revelation of that decision of freedom in the spatio-temporal materiality of

---

shadowed by the old scholastic terminology, as when the latter for example distinguishes in its exposition of the doctrine of original sin between '*peccatum naturae*' and '*peccatum personae*' (*personale*). Hence it may not be said that the modern conceptualization endangers the clarity and unambiguous preciseness of scholastic terminology. Regarding the concepts concerned, cf. also chap. 11 ('The theological concept of concupiscentia') in the first Volume of the present work, pp. 347–382; and: *Würde und Freiheit des Menschen: Kirche in neuer Zeit. Reden und Erklärungen des Österreichischen Katholikentags* 1952 (Innsbruck 1952), pp. 9–43.

[94] For what follows cf. also (apart from the essays mentioned in the preceding note) e.g. W. Brugger, 'Die Verleiblichung des Wollens', *Scholastik* XXV (1950), pp. 248–253; K. Rahner, 'Guilt and its remission: the borderland between theology and psychotherapy', chap. 9 below, pp. 265–281; *id.*, *Geist in Welt* (Innsbruck 1939); *id.*, *Hörer des Wortes. Zur Grundlegung einer Religionsphilosophie* (Munich 1941), esp. chaps 10 *sqq.*, pp. 150 *sqq.*

man, i.e. in his 'visibleness'. But at the same time, because it is different from the initial freedom, it also throws a veil over this initial act of freedom as such, i.e. the revelation of the personal decision of man in man's spatio-temporal appearance can be mere empty appearance. In so far as the finite freedom of man presupposes nature as its condition of possibility, the expression of man's act of freedom in his historical visible nature implies always essentially an acceptance of 'impressions'. It means that what is his very own always reveals itself essentially also by accepting what is alien, by accepting the imposed determination of his nature.

The real unity of the human race, of which we spoke previously and which we saw must be considered as a natural dimension of man's personal decision, to be accepted by the free act of man, is determined in the concrete also by the *Incarnation* of the Word of God. By the fact that God the Son became man of the Virgin Mary, a member of this one human race, the Word of God became himself a member of this one Adamite humanity and, conversely, the one human race became thereby fundamentally and radically called to share the life of God supernaturally. This calling to share supernaturally in the life of the triune God is fundamentally already given as a real fact in the world (and not merely as God's 'intention' and 'law'), by the simple fact of the Incarnation of the Word. And so this calling is, on the one hand, a reality which precedes man's personal decision. And, on the other hand, because it is a reality accomplished by the fact that the Word of God became *flesh*, it is a reality which belongs to the historical and visible dimension and a reality which, as a factual determination of the human race as a whole, is also a real ontological determination of the nature of each human being. Hence, if man as a spiritual person accomplishes his 'nature' by the total decision about himself, then he must in the concrete, by this decision, always and inevitably take position for or against man's supernatural calling to a participation in the life of the triune God himself.[95]

[95] The thesis enunciated in this sentence would, of course, require further elaboration. This would be the only way to prove it sufficiently and to incorporate it properly into the whole context of theology. Indeed, only further development would define this thesis in such a way as to avoid misunderstandings, and in this way, too, all its consequences would be fully unfolded. However, we will confine ourselves here to two observations. Firstly, if this thesis is not to appear unbelievable from the very start, the

Taking up position in this way, considered as happening with and in man's 'nature', the reality presupposed by man's freedom and regulating it, is, on the one hand, the expression of what a man wants to be personally and, on the other hand, the visible historical aspect of the salvific Will of God which man accepts by his personal decision.

Let us try to clarify still further the objective content of what we have just stated on the metaphysical plane of abstraction. By the fact that the Word of God became man, humanity has already in advance become ontologically the real sanctification of individual men by grace and also the people of the children of God. Nowhere that men exist,

---

following must be taken into consideration: every free human act takes place essentially and necessarily within the dynamism of the spirit, which is directed to the good as such. This means that it takes place within the unlimited intentional transcendence of the free spirit, so that the individual good can be freely willed only in as far as man is (always and inevitably) 'set on' Being and the good as such. But this means that each free decision of the will is an act directed into what lies beyond its range of vision; and this is so not only in fact and in everyday life, but always and essentially (as proceeding from the nature of finite freedom which realizes itself in the individual object). Such an act is always essentially either a surrender or a refusal of oneself in face of the uncontrollable and the unpredictable—either (blind) obedience or disobedience—readiness or refusal to put oneself at the disposal of some greater unknown Force. Seen in this light, it is clear that we may not say that the question of the unknown as such (meaning what is not known as something given objectively and consciously), cannot enter into the discussion of the quality of a free and responsible action, when the latter is considered simply *as* such. It can merely be said that something which is itself simply and utterly finite cannot be of any significance for this free act as such, if it be unknown (even although the free act may have further consequences in the dimension of finite unforeseen realities). But such an unknown, finite reality does *not*, in fact, belong to that which, in its incomprehensible immensity itself, is the real object of the act of free will exercised on finite realities. And so this is quite different from the case under discussion here: obedience to God in his infinite incomprehensibility as found in every good act of freedom may, even as such, very well be determined by a reality which, although finite and concrete, is nevertheless the reality of *God himself*. Secondly, the thesis enunciated in the above sentence does not come to the same thing as the doctrine of Ripalda who holds that every morally good, free act is also a supernaturally elevated, saving act. For our statement leaves it still quite open whether according to God's free decree such a saving act requires also faith, with a definitely determined content of faith settled by a revelation coming from without, and whether and in what way this may be lacking in a particular case.

are they in the concrete simply 'mere men' in the abstract sense of the aristotelian-scholastic concept of the essence of man. In as far as mankind, thus 'consecrated', is a real unity from the very start, there already exists a '*people of God*' which extends as far as humanity itself, even before any social and juridical organization of mankind as a supernatural unity in a Church. This people of God exists before its juridical and social organization into what we call 'Church', somewhat as a definite historical people exists before its organization into a State on the plane of this world. This real determination of the one humanity as the people of God is a real fact and no mere abstract idea of what ought to be, for it is based on the two coinciding facts of the natural unity of the human race and of the real Incarnation of the Word of God. It is, indeed, a reality which even as such belongs to the historically visible dimension of human nature, for God became man as Jesus of Nazareth, in a historical here and now, in the 'flesh'. On the other hand, this real and historical actuality of the people of God, which precedes the Church as a juridical and social body, is however such that it can, and according to the Will of God had to be made more concrete on the social and juridical plane, in what we, in fact, call the Church. For no matter how much the setting up of such social and juridical bodies in their concrete determination depends on the free design of man or God, these bodies can at the same time be the concretion and elucidation of a reality presupposed by the freedom of man. Thus, for instance, every actual State is always set up by a free historical decision, and yet it implies at the same time a taking over and a recognition of something which was given before this free, instituting decision and which enforces itself through this decision. If we may settle for this terminology (i.e. 'people of God') to express the reality referred to, without entering into the question as to whether this or another term taken from traditional usage is the most apt, we must say that there exists, therefore, a peculiar relationship between the 'people of God' and the Church. Both of them, from the point of view of the individual man as a person, lie on the visible historical plane of a reality which precedes the free decision of each man. They are both the expression of God's loving salvific Will in this world, for even the assuming of a human nature into the unity of the Person of the Logos is, as such, once more merely the expression and visible manifestation of this salvific Will of God which means the union of all men as persons in grace and glory with God. And in all this the

Church is meant to be a further expression (freely founded, indeed, by Christ, but nevertheless natural) of the very fact that in Christ the human race is the people of God. Hence, in view of these relations it is not surprising, for example, that Tradition (at least to some extent when using terms in a wider sense) gives the name of Church even to humanity consecrated by the Incarnation, i.e. to the 'people of God', and thus has the fundamental foundation of the Church taking place already in the fact of God becoming man. The people of God has a real relation to the Church as a social and juridical body, even although that relation comes into being by way of a free decision made by the God-Man. Therefore, where there is, and to the extent in which there is the people of God, there already is radically also the Church, and that independently of the will of the individual man. Hence wherever, and in so far as, there is the personal will to the people of God, there is also grasped to that extent a reality which has a real tendency to become more concrete on the social and juridical plane in the Church. But, according to what has been said, membership of the people of God is one of the determining factors of a concrete human nature, since every human being is necessarily and indissolubly a member of the one human race which really became the people of God by the divine Incarnation. Therefore, when someone totally accepts his concrete human nature by his decision of free will (the question as to the conditions required for this need not detain us in this context), and thus turns his concrete nature into an expression of every one of his free decisions for God, his free action gains an expression which is at the same time also an expression of the proper, supernatural salvific Will of God. For this decision in freedom necessarily consents also to that membership of the people of God which, in continuance of God's Will of the Incarnation of his Word, constitutes an historically verifiable expression of the Will of God for the inner bestowal of grace on man as a person. Hence, whensoever man as a person accepts the concrete reality of his nature totally, in the free act of a *supernatural* justification by faith and love, the *membership of the people of God* becomes *the expression of this justifying act.* The act of justification itself, therefore, finds expression in something really different from itself, viz. in membership of the people of God which, in its turn, is in reality ordained to membership of the Church in the proper sense.

When the justifying act is thus understood as the *votum Ecclesiae*, then it is not merely an act which aims in intention at the Church as its implicit object. It is, thus understood, a spiritual and personal act which, in fact and of necessity, already comprises something of the Church, since it is the ratification, in an ontologically real sense, of the membership of the people of God. The act of justification, *qua* act of faith and of love, is the deed of a spiritual person; *qua* act of man in the concrete as a member of the one human race which was consecrated by the Incarnation, it necessarily possesses at the same time a reality which is different from, although the expression of, the personal action and which, as membership of the people of God, has a quasi-sacramental nature. Precisely because man as a concrete, bodily human being is a blood-relation of Christ, the *votum Ecclesiae* does not at all take place in a purely extra-sacramental and invisible interiority of grace. Rather it is essentially, as an act of the concrete human being, an acceptance of the quasi-sacramental structure which by reason of the divine Incarnation is necessarily proper to humanity and hence to the individual human being, considered as the people of God or member of this people respectively. The *votum Ecclesiae*, therefore, does not replace real membership of the Church by being 'good will' towards the Church. It replaces it by being the personal acceptance of that membership of the people of God which is already a fact on the historical and visible plane and in which is already given a real reference to membership of the Church as an established society. Real membership of the Church is, therefore, a merely conditionally necessary means, not because it could be replaced by a supernatural moral act of man in so far as it is a moral quantity, but because this act itself already reaches necessarily into the dimension of the visibleness of salvation in which the Church in the proper sense also finds itself. Or conversely, the proposition about the Church as necessary means for salvation suffers no exception through the possibility of justification by the *votum Ecclesiae*, in so far as that necessity of the Church for salvation always does and must mean—by 'Church'—*at least* what we have called 'people of God'—and, indeed, always can mean this. Because 'people of God' has an objective reference to the Church in the proper sense (a reference which is not left to the discretion of the individual human being), the proposition of the necessity of belonging to the people of God for salvation does not impair the proposition of the necessity of the Church in the proper sense for salvation. For whenever man is consciously and freely guilty of excluding this membership of the Church in the proper sense from his intention, he opposes himself to his membership of the people of God, so that even the latter no longer profits him for salvation but only for damnation. We cannot enter here into the question why the mere membership of the people of God does (or respectively does not) also, like the membership of the Church proper by baptism, bring about grace and supernatural salvation for those who are not capable of a personal act.[96] In the event of it being feasible to assume that this presupposition of incapacity of free decision is not actually valid even in the case of those who die as infants, this problem would in fact dissolve itself from the very outset as being merely an apparent one.

These arguments have been given merely as scanty suggestions with the simple intention of showing one thing: the whole series of factual problems connected with the compatibility of the fact of the necessity of the Church as a means for salvation with the fact of the possibility of salvation for someone outside the Church points in the direction of our having to assume a certain stratification in the reality of the Church. And this does not, in this case, refer to the fact that both the juridical and social organization (called 'Church') and also man's union with God by grace belong to the full notion of the Church. The stratification referred to here is to be understood in the sense that the Church, as something visible and as sign of the union with God by grace, must itself be composed of a further twofold reality, viz. Church as an established juridical organization in the sacred order[97] and 'Church as humanity consecrated by the Incarnation'. Any question about belonging to the Church as necessary means for salvation must distinguish between these two strata in the being of the Church, the Sacrament of salvation. It will then certainly be easier to reconcile the necessity of the Church as a means of salvation (although this has to be affirmed of both strata of the Church's nature) with the statement of the possibility of salvation for someone outside the Church, without the former principle evaporating into mere verbalism.

[96] Cf. for this the literature quoted on this question above, p. 43, note 65, which might be afforded a deeper insight by the points of view indicated here.

[97] As such a juridical organization she has then, furthermore, the three dimensions of unity of faith under the authoritative *magisterium*, visibility of grace in virtue of the Sacraments (above all in Baptism and the Eucharist) and united action under the direction of the ecclesiastical ruling authority—in other words, the three dimensions to which correspond the three conditions for strict membership of the Church.

We must now, therefore, answer in the negative to the question we asked earlier on[98] about whether there can be a belonging to the visible Church (i.e. not yet membership) which is *merely* 'invisible', because merely constituted by the metahistorical possession of grace and by the necessary justifying human acts for this in an unbaptized person, *considered as* merely personal acts. For basically every personal act finds also a historical expression (a constitutive sign[99]) for the fact of its being a *votum Ecclesiae*[100] in the concrete nature of man and in its incarnate act. Hence, the justified person who belongs (or is 'referred') to the Church without being a member of it, belongs 'invisibly' to the visible Church by grace *and* has a 'visible' relation to this Church, even when this relation is not constituted by baptism or by an externally verifiable profession of the true faith (as in the case of the catechumen). In other words, there is a lowest limit, in a certain sense, below which man's state of grace and its quasi-sacramental tangibility can no longer be separated from each other, as if the former could exist without the latter. Only the reverse is possible, i.e. there can in some cases be the sign-aspect of grace without there being also the personally and freely accepted grace.[101] But there always is grace in the sense that it is always offered—since everyone belongs indissolubly to the people of God—and in the sense that it is always also visible in this offer.

[98] Cf. above, p. 68, Note 85 (not Note 78, as stated in the German text.—*Tr.*).

[99] Cf. for this expression: K. Rahner, *Die vielen Messen und das eine Opfer* (Freiburg 1951), pp. 8 *sqq*.

[100] This does not necessarily mean that this characteristic of being '*votum Ecclesiae*' must be capable of being deciphered in such a moral act of free will by everyone and from every possible point of view. 'Expression' and 'sign' refer to an ontological quality of the human act in its relation to grace and to the Church,—they do not refer to a quality of knowability for any and every power of understanding.

[101] This is not surprising, since the expression of personal acceptance of grace (which expression can be given without acceptance) is nothing other than the (accepted) expression of the grace offered by God. This offer, however, is directed to *all* men. It is not merely a juridical, transcendental, 'abstract-unhistorical' reality existing only in the other-worldly 'intention' of God, and communicated only by the revelation of the Word. On the contrary, this offer is really present in the world and in history through the Incarnation of the Word in a humanity which is really one. In view of this, it is therefore evident that the expression of acceptance is always already given

even before there is any personal acceptance of grace (i.e. before there is any 'invisible' belonging to the Church), and that the reverse is quite impossible. For the reverse would mean that man assents to a grace which is not at all offered to him, or that this offer has no incarnational presence in the world and in the history of the one human race—in short, that it would be an offer of the 'grace of *God*' which would not be essentially also the 'grace of *Christ*'.

2

FREEDOM IN THE CHURCH

IT is not at all surprising that freedom is so much talked about at the present time. In this world where things last only for a time and then perish, a world in which things are put to the test, we frequently discover values only after they have disappeared or when they seem to be dying. We invoke the values which we lack. And so we speak of freedom and need not wonder at that fact.

But—freedom in the Church: this would seem a somewhat surprising subject for discussion. St Paul spoke of the freedom of the Christian. After that, this particular topic was no longer mentioned very much. Luther turned this theme into a reformational battle-cry against the Roman Church, and yet at the same time he denied man, this same man, his freedom before God. He thought to extol grace by stressing the impotence of the human will to choose between God and the Devil. As against this, the old Church preached the duty of obedience to the teaching and command of the Hierarchy, as well as the freedom of the will before God and in face of his grace. Then there came the period of the liberalistic conception of freedom—when people became preoccupied with liberating man from social and economic restrictions and with the defence of the freedom of conscience, of speech and of the press. However, we do not seem to have got very far with this since 1789. For the proletarians do not find that they have become free. And the various freedoms of speech, etc., have been in the end simply monopolized once more by the Ministries of Propaganda and similar institutions. During this time of Liberalism, the Church preached about the law and authority, about order and obligation. And when she spoke of freedom, she meant the freedom which she claimed for herself against those who wanted to overpower the Church with their omnipotence of the State (always in the name of freedom, of course, and as Liberals), so that she might no more be tempted to threaten the freedom of modern times. And so, since the time of St Paul there was really not much talk in the Catholic Church of freedom *in* the Church. Was this subject overlooked, because it is insignificant or because it was dangerous, or because we do not need to speak much about what we possess as a matter of course? Or was it spoken of in other terms? Who can say for sure?

At any rate we must speak of it at the present time. For in times when there is no freedom, we search anxiously for it in whatever place we still hope to find it; and today people are listening more thoughtfully once again to the message of the Faith, especially such as it issued originally from the pages of the New Testament. We must speak of this subject nowadays, because one has become sensitive and delicate about transgressions against the holy spirit of freedom in the Church, since one does not at any cost wish to confuse the Church with a totalitarian collectivity.

It must be understood that important points of view on this much unnoticed subject may perhaps even here be overlooked in what we shall have to say about it. However, two matters will be the subject of discussion in what follows: 1. the Church, considered in its role of sacramental sign of freedom, and 2. freedom in the Church.

I

There is a freedom which in Christian philosophy is called psychological freedom of choice. This freedom is the presupposition of what is called responsibility, and it characterizes what is meant by person in the modern sense of the word. The Scriptures and Christian consciousness regarded it as self-evident that man is in this sense a free responsible person, even in his relationships with God. This means that they looked on man as a person who is continually and repeatedly called upon to make decisions and choices, who holds himself and his fate in his own hands, who disposes of himself either for good or for evil and thus can be the subject of good and evil actions and of moral reward or punishment. All this is so very obvious in the Scriptures and to Christian consciousness that men never reflected explicitly on it except in times when this permanent and unchangeable basic structure of human existence was called into doubt, as it was, for instance, by Gnosticism, etc., in the second century. *This* freedom is lived in the Scriptures rather than made the object of theoretical reflection. When the Scriptures, and especially St Paul, speak of the freedom which the

Christian message does not regard as its obvious presupposition in man but as something which Christianity brings with it for the first time, then it is a question of a different kind of freedom. It is this freedom which we must first of all determine in its nature and then show why and how it has something to do with the Church. In this way it will then become clear that what we are above all concerned with here is the fact that the Church is the tangible sacramental sign of this freedom.

We obviously cannot give even a brief account here of the history of the Graeco-western notion of freedom, no matter how useful this might be for our purpose. Freedom was regarded at the beginning as freedom from social, economic and political coercion. It was, therefore, looked upon as the antithesis of slavery, servitude, etc. Thus it is in the first instance a property of the citizen of an independent *polis* who is concerned in the supporting and ordering of the State. After that, this notion took on a more individual and inward character. The free man now comes to be thought of as the man who has *ἀυτοπραξία*, who can do what he likes. And this freedom towards himself, as not being bound by any forces which would alienate the individual from himself, is now regarded more and more as confined to the interior life, where man always is and can be really himself. Thus, if man takes this upon himself and if he recognizes and fully appreciates this unassailable precinct of his inner spiritual nature as the very region of his proper human existence, then he is and can be free at least in *this* sphere. Here and there it was apparently thought that man can also free himself from the dimensions of his being which are different from this sublime inner Ego, and from their governing forces (such as the forces of Nature, of the State, etc.), simply by abandoning all opposition to them and withdrawing himself from them as being, in his esteem, indifferent. Man was regarded as becoming free by detaching and freeing himself from these forces, having seen through them and recognized them as inessential in themselves and as insignificant for himself. The remarkable thing about all this seems to be that, until it is seen in the light of Christianity, one cannot have any clear understanding even of real freedom of choice, i.e. of the freedom which consists not merely in the fact that man is not coerced from without, but also in the further fact that a free decision about himself is demanded of him—a freedom, therefore, which is rather a requirement and commission than freedom. For only in the Christian context—in

God's personal love for man—is everyone a unique individual with eternal value and someone who must attain his fulfilment in complete responsibility for himself and hence in freedom.

Be that as it may, the message of Christianity tells man above all: you, together with the freedom in which you have all along taken possession of yourself, are precisely as such the one to be freed, the one to be saved. You have, of course, the formally unfilled capacity of self-mastery and of freedom, you can act in this way or that, not only towards and with the things which constitute your surroundings, but also with regard to yourself. You yourself are the one who disposes of himself. You are not simply one who develops in accordance with a law which has determined your place and role, even if this law were conceived as the most individual of all. You deal with yourself in freedom, forming yourself for eternity through an act which cannot adequately be dissolved into something merely provisional, and which decides precisely what you yourself finally want to be—through an act which you yourself really posit, which does not merely happen to you, an act which is your deed and not your fate.

But all this does not yet make you by any means simply free in the true and ultimate sense of the word. Finite freedom of choice, in spite of its true autonomy, is always choice arising out of a given situation. It is a choice which is imposed on us without our being able to choose it ourselves. It is a choice, imposed without choice, which can itself be the least free of all if the scope given to it, and within which it is exercised, is itself already a prison of bondage in the wrong place—somewhat as if one were to say to someone sitting in a prison-cell that he is free, because he can choose in which corner of his dungeon he wishes to sit. Everything depends on the object of one's freedom. Now one might think that this situation, which limits in advance the capacity of choosing, should of itself include what is right and good for salvation among its possibilities, in so far as the choice has a moral character and is said to be the cause of good and evil. In other words, one might think that if man is the one who, essentially as man, must dispose of himself for salvation or damnation by his freedom of choice, then his salvation must be part of his nature from the very start, as a possibility which, although it can be thrown away, can also, at any rate, be achieved and attained by him of his own power. It would seem that man, being free to choose, must have free and autonomous access to his salvation; his salvation must, therefore, ultimately be himself.

But it is precisely this that is false. The conception of the consummation of human existence, which presupposes and affirms this, is the most abysmal falsehood of all. And the freedom which is understood in this way, not only as a call but as something of itself capable of achieving what it is called to, is the most radically false freedom. For the very fact that man would withdraw himself into his own unassailable interior being, into that dimension in which he would be himself alone and cut off from anything else, would mean that he is not free, but a prisoner and one banished into that inescapable limitation of his nature which is all the more apparent in this freedom. For precisely such a mode of existence, freed from everything else, would be something empty and senseless, and merely the point at which freedom is turned into a state of radical abandonment and into futility. Freedom would thus become sheer negation—in other words, a hell or a freedom which holds itself aloof from everything, because it must fear everything as being alien and oppressive. But if freedom, even in its own most proper sphere, does not of itself have what could be regarded as its liberating or saving realization, where then is the freedom of freedom, i.e. where is the object of freedom which does not cause the very ruin of freedom but, on the contrary, brings about its realization? Where, indeed, is this freedom of freedom, if freedom, delivered up to the finite as such and realized in it, becomes captive freedom, since freedom is to be had only when the finite is recognized as such and because freedom, in spite of the fact that it is essentially referred to the finite for its self-realization, nevertheless *consumes* itself in the finite or must retreat into the empty infinities of its own mere possibilities? In short, where is this freedom of freedom, if there is the oppressive and the enslaving?

To answer that it is in God, is the true answer but also the most dangerous one. For then, if what we are saying is not to be a downright lie and the worst sin, we must mean by this *the One* whom we (in order to be free) do not *have* but who gives or withholds himself, who is not conquered but always remains a grace. God must not be just another word for the splendour of our self-disposing freedom, any more than for the sublimity of our knowledge (called Transcendence). God must be God, the One whom we need, but who does not need us and for whom we remain unnecessary even when we already exist. If God, however, is to be in this way the very object of our freedom which alone makes this freedom free, then this freedom would neither consume itself infernally in its own emptiness when it witholds itself, nor would it deliver itself to the slavery of the finite when it gives itself. Considered in the abstract, then, He can be this liberating reality in *two* ways: by refusing himself and by declaring himself, by remaining afar off and by drawing near. Even the first way would be a consummation of freedom which would give it meaning: to be before God, the unattainable; adoration of the infinitely distant; remaining open to him in the knowledge of his glory as experienced in the blessedness of the painful flame of yearning; the most obedient will to listen attentively to his silence which *also* reveals him; the acceptance of his decrees which is in any case always blessed and more fulfilling than if man wanted to pass God by. But God did not want to be the distant One, which *we* should always be prepared to let him be and, indeed, must be prepared to let him be in order to understand and grasp his gift (and in so far as we do). He wanted to be the God who is near to us, the One who gives himself as a gift in love, who communicates himself and who realizes our freedom in its (very) freedom. He is the freedom of our freedom by the grace of his self-communication, without which our free will could only choose bondage no matter what choice it might make. And he is this freedom of our freedom by way of communication and not of refusal. God's communication of himself, which is the liberating *terminus ad quem* of our freedom, is called by us grace of justification and sanctification, or sanctifying grace, and the Bible calls it also 'divine *pneuma*'. We may say, therefore, that the divine *pneuma* is the liberating freedom of our freedom; our freedom is saved by it from the dilemma of being either a freedom given up to the finiteness of the chosen finite possibilities and thus enslaved, or a freedom preserved but starving to death on account of its own emptiness—in short, it saves it from the dilemma of being either an exhausted freedom or a starved freedom.

The freedom of freedom, in as far as it is that which is offered by God in grace and is thus thought of as preceding its free acceptance, is the decisive factor in the *situation* of our freedom. It can be given or refused by God. Hence it can be made to depend on certain conditions which are outwith and previous to the decision of the freedom proper to each one of us as an individual. And thus there is a *community* of *situation* which applies to the freedom of all men, in spite of the fact that each particular act of freedom can be executed only by the individual himself and cannot be performed for him by any one else. This community of situation is the basic reason for the fact that, by God's decree, the *offer* made to us of the liberating freedom of freedom (called sanctifying grace), was dependent on the acceptance of the offer made to the first man, which offer was *de facto* refused. And so man is the slave of what we call original sin, in as far as this offer of the freedom of freedom made to us in that way through the first man no longer persists, and in as far as man has, therefore, from *that* point of view, lost the freedom of freedom. This means that, as someone who has his origin in the first man, he no longer finds himself on a plane where his exercise of freedom remains free simply on account of an offered self-communication by God. And so, in as far as the *pneuma* of God, which makes freedom free, is offered gratuitously to *this* man of the Adamite community of guilt (which by this fact has become the Christian community of redemption), the freedom of freedom given gratuitously through the *pneuma* is now properly speaking a redemptive freedom from the slavery of guilt. This is all the more so the case if, and in so far as, the individual human being, who has been robbed of the freedom of God by original sin, has willed himself by personal guilt to be in this state without *pneuma*, and if he has tried to remain free while remaining without grace. Thus he might want to do the work of the world by himself in his finiteness and redeem himself in this way, possibly believing himself to be justified by this even before God. Or he might believe that by retreating into his own transcendence, he has already found his redeeming freedom there within himself. This attempt to achieve freedom in the finite, either by laying hold of it or by withdrawing from it, will to a greater or lesser degree become a slavery to the finite. In so far as it does, and to the extent in which the objects of such an enslaved freedom are in their respective orders under the power of personal agencies (called angels or, if evil, devils), this particular kind of slavery is objectively slavery under diabolic powers. The freedom of freedom given by the *pneuma* is, therefore, the redemption from such powers, in so far as these strive to be the *confining* boundary of the situation of man's freedom.

That the *pneuma* is gratuitously given to us as the redemptive freedom of freedom which had fallen into culpable bondage in Adam and in us, is no mere abstract theory or ideological postulate, nor is it an always necessarily valid truth or (merely) a datum of our mystical experience. On the contrary, this spiritual freedom of our freedom is established by the very act of God freely present in the flesh of Christ himself as a sign in this world, and is grasped and made our own as present in this sign. In so far as God freely gives himself in Christ in a tangible and irrevocable manner, the freedom of our freedom (as offered) is really established and present in this world—in the historical, tangible reality of the flesh of Christ. In so far as he became present in the world by his birth as the presence of God himself and remained the Son of God in death and made this even more tangible in his resurrection, Christ is the real and, indeed, tangible and visible fact of the free opening out of the world into God. The fact that there is a *pneuma*, which is the freedom of freedom, has its source, is made accessible and is applied to us in Jesus, the Word of the Father in flesh of Adam, the Crucified and the risen Christ.

Now the Church is nothing other than the visible, socially composed communion of men with Jesus, the source of sanctifying grace; she is the community which, in its historico-social form, its tangible liturgical actions, its word of truth and its life, is the continuation of the historically tangible reality of Christ. And hence she is the community which continues to exercise the function of this historical tangibility, viz. to render the *pneuma* of freedom effectively and actually present in the world and to signify that fact. As the continuation of *the* Sacrament which is Christ, the Church is, therefore, the tangible and original sacramental sign of the *pneuma* which is the freedom of our freedom, i.e. she, and with her also the community, signifies and effects that we have this freedom of God.

We are now in a position to have a somewhat clearer understanding of certain New Testament phrases which state in short formulae what we have up until now tried to set forth in a rather systematic train of thought.

The love of the Father, the ἀλήθεια, which has been revealed in the Son (Jn 8.36), Who became flesh, sets us free (Jn 8.32), because where the *pneuma* is, there is freedom (2 Cor 3.17), since it is for freedom that Christ has made us free (Gal 5.1). This freedom is a freedom from sin (Rom 6.18–23; Jn 8.31–36), from the law (Rom. 7.3 *sq.*; 8.2; Gal 2.4; 4.21–31; 5.1, 13) and from death (Rom 6.21 *sq.*; 8.21): from sin, in so far as this is in a thousand different ways the assertion of self freely accomplished both within oneself and in the world, without being open to the love of God as proceeding both from him and to him; from the law, in so far as this, although the holy will of God, (whether infringed or self-complacently accomplished in deed) merely becomes a stimulus for man without grace to assert himself against or before God; from death, in so far as this is merely the manifestation of guilt. Man appropriates this freedom, which Christ is and gives, by obeying the call to this freedom (Gal 5.13) and by submitting himself in faith and in its tangible sign, i.e. baptism, to the event which breaks open the prison of this world, viz. the Incarnation, death and resurrection of the Son.

We cannot enter more closely into all this here. What is important, however, is that we should in some measure substantiate also the connection of this liberation of freedom with the Church from the Scriptures. Even that can be done only in brief outline. Suffice it to give the following four catch-words which establish the fact of the connection between the Church and Christian freedom from Scripture; Call, baptism, *Pneuma*, the New Law. The Church is the ἐκκλησία, the congregation convoked from those who have received their call, having been called into God's light out of the world of sin and death. But this call is at the same time the call to freedom (Gal 5.13). Baptism establishes the Church (Eph 5.25 *sqq.*, etc) and is at the same time the event through which we enter into freedom (Rom 6.16 *sqq*). The *Pneuma* is the principle of freedom (Rom 8.2; 8.15; 2 Cor 3.17) and the animating entelechy of the Church (Jn 3.5; 1 Cor 3.16; 1 Cor 12.13; Eph 4.4, etc.). Christianity (in contrast to the Law of the Old Testament) is simply characterized by the Law of freedom in the New Testament (Jam 1.25; 2.12), which does not consider it as an idea or a *Weltanschauung* but only as the Church in the concrete. The Epistle to the Galatians accordingly tells us in summary that the Church (as the new, heavenly Jerusalem in contrast to the Old Testament) is the free woman, and that we are not children of bondage but children of the free woman (Gal 4.21–31).

One should now, of course, go on to prove more exactly why, and above all how, the Church is the quasi-sacramental tangible element and the historically visible factor of the redemptive liberation of the freedom of man. In so far as she is, or rather has, the *pneuma* of God, she is or has freedom, and to her alone can we strictly apply the text: *Where* the Lord's spirit is, there is freedom. She is the 'where' of spiritual freedom. In so far as she is different from the *Pneuma* living and ruling within her, the Church is the historical quasi-sacramental sign of this *pneuma*, and hence also of freedom, by which the 'pneumatic' freedom is signified and made present. One should now go on to inquire into the way in which the Church is the effective sign of this spiritual freedom in her being, her Word, her sacramental action and in her history. First of all, she *proclaims* this freedom in her *Word* which is the message of Christ. She does not do this by teaching subsequently *about* freedom which would exist even without this teaching; but, on the contrary, she renders freedom present *by* proclaiming it. She gives man this freedom by effectively obtaining the divine *pneuma* or freedom for him in the *Sacraments*. Her *life* is a *sign* of this freedom, in so far as she lives the love of God and neighbour in her sanctified members. And love, precisely to the extent in which it forgets itself, relinquishes self-assertion and serves others—for the sake of others it even lets itself be bounded by many an earthly and legal limitation. Love frees man from himself. It makes him free for the boundlessness of God and of his eternal life. But even this can unfortunately only be briefly outlined here.

One thing, at any rate, must be firmly borne in mind from what has been said: the reality and the notion of freedom is not merely something which belongs to man's natural being, which the Church, as the guardian even of the natural order, would then in addition defend and regulate in its ordered exercise and in the different fields in which such freedom is lawful. Freedom is rather a proper theological notion which expresses a reality belonging strictly to the order of grace, and much more than this psychological freedom of choice and freedom as a right of the person. Freedom is a theological notion expressing a reality which in the strictest sense of identity *is* itself the gift of salvation, rather than being merely a presupposition for salvation. For the real, true and ultimate freedom, which must be gifted to our freedom to free it from guilt, law and death, is the sacred *pneuma* of God itself and of his Christ. Hence the Church is the indispensable, existential place of this freedom, in so far as and because this *pneuma* can be had only in the Church, since it is her inner reality and she its external sign.

II

Everything we have seen so far is not only in itself more important than anything we are going to treat of now, but is important also precisely for what follows. We are now going to speak of the freedom in the Church. This subject leaves out of consideration everything signified by the question of the religious or civil tolerance of the

Church or a Christian State towards other Christians and towards non-Christians.

We intend, therefore, to inquire only into the freedom which the Catholic Christian as such enjoys in and vis-à-vis his Church. This is a question which must be posed. The Church is a legally established society with laws, regulations, authorities and subjects etc.—and this will always be so, as long as she is still on pilgrimage towards the final return of Christ and as long as she lives in this world and is still *in via* between Adam and Christ in her members. All this, although determined by the will of Christ, belongs to the transience of the present aeon. It is all encircled and supported by the love of the divine Spirit, Who is freedom; this whole order of things can ultimately be respected and accomplished by Christians only out of this love, which does not seek its own and which, freed for the freedom of God, does not need to flee anxiously before earthly ties and obligations built up by this love. All this does and indeed must exist in the Church in the aeon of this world. And so also the question arises as to where exactly lies the balance between these bonds and freedom. This question has, however, its own proper weight in theology, precisely because the Church, as sign of the presence of the divine freedom in this world, must also unquestionably fashion its earthly tangible form in such a way as not to obscure her reality as a sign of the divine freedom. And in this age of totalitarian systems the Church has the additional duty not even to give the impression, either to her own or to outsiders, of being a clerical, religiously camouflaged kind of totalitarian system herself. Her objective nature is not that of a totalitarian system, because the dignity of man, the directness of man's relationship to God and freedom are part and parcel of the basic principles which are proclaimed by her and which have been constitutively established in her very being. Moreover, the Church, and she alone, has been given God's promise (and this is the decisive fact distinguishing her from every other society in danger of totalitarianism), that she will be preserved by his grace until the end of time from every essential defection from this her true nature, to which it also belongs that she must respect the genuine rights of human freedom in this world. However, since the Church is always also a Church made up of sinful men, even as far as the holders of her authority are concerned, she can also in her individual actions offend against her own principles and against the freedom of the individual both within and without. This has happened often enough in the course of history. It can happen even today. And this is what the Church must guard against, for today more than ever she must be the champion of true freedom. But even by such individual offences she does not become a totalitarian system. For she acts in these cases against her own proclaimed and practised principles, whereas a really totalitarian system does not recognize such principles of the freedom and dignity of the individual either expressly or tacitly, but on the contrary idolizes the collectivity and degrades the individual. But the Church must reckon with the real danger of giving the scandal of an apparent totalitarianism. This is particularly the case because, no matter how clear her ultimate basic principles may be, there can be, and in fact there has been, a subjective development of the Church's consciousness in articulating and applying more particular and proximate principles with exactitude and sureness. And this also explains how it is possible for the Church to violate the legitimate claims of freedom both from within and from without, particularly in cases where she does not become clearly conscious of such a violation.

Authority, law, norm, command—all these are to be found in the Church, as well as the reaction of the Church against violations of such norms, which take the form of exhortation, censure, penalty. And there must of necessity be such realities in the Church. After all, she must by the Lord's commission preserve, explain, develop and teach divine revelation authoritatively in its unchangeableness as divine truth and as it terminated with the Apostles. She must maintain and guard the nature given to her by her founder in respect of her form of government, the administration of the Sacraments, etc. She has the duty to promulgate the abiding moral norms of the Natural Law and of the divine positive Law, and to apply them to the changing historical situations. She has, therefore, also the right and obligation to decide by her teaching- and pastoral-authority and in a manner binding on the conscience of her children, whether this or that particular, actual behaviour of individuals or social groups can be objectively reconciled with God's moral law or not. The Church, therefore, has the right and duty not just to lay down general norms of a material or even merely formal kind, as if everything else must then be left on principle to the individual and to his conscience and as if he alone must decide on every occasion whether the general norms promulgated by the Church apply to his case and situation or not. No, more than this, the Church has the right and the duty, as part of her teaching office and especially of her pastoral office, to enact over and above this such norms binding *in concreto* as will make it clear that in consequence certain definite actions fall outside the objective sphere of morally good conduct, both on principle and in every case. Hence, without passing final judgment on the subjective conscience, she can also proceed in her Church law against those who by their conduct place themselves outside this field of action negatively determined by ecclesiastical authority. All this limits the Christian's scope of freedom within the world. It would be wrong to blind oneself to this fact or to try to dispute it by appealing to the pauline doctrine of the Christian's freedom from the law. For according to St Paul, this freedom of the Christian is freedom from the law understood as something divorced from grace, which makes demands from without and thus incites to sin; it is the freedom of man from himself and from his egoistical self-assertion against or before God, and thus it is a freedom for the infinity of communion with God in love. It is not, however, a freedom from the holy Will of God, in so far as this Will can and ought to become the inner law of our heart under the *pneuma* of God, and in so far as this Will of God can and will also become a completely concrete demand in the form of definite and individual material commandments right down to the particular norms of the natural moral law. This freedom is moreover not an emancipation from the teaching and pastoral authority of the Church, of which Christ spoke when He said: 'He who hears you, hears me.'

With reference to this indisputable limitation of the scope of the freedom of Church members, which is absolutely compatible with the pauline doctrine of freedom, three points must be borne in mind:

(a) Freedom, in this intramundane sense of the psychological and moral capacity to decide to act in this way or that, receives its meaning and value ultimately from the object for which and upon which one decides. It is true that freedom as such, i.e. freedom of exercise and not merely freedom in what is done, belongs to the absolute dignity of a person, so that to deprive someone completely of any scope for freedom, even in a case where the object would still be attainable even without this concession of scope for freedom, would still amount to a degrading of the person. This means, therefore, that to deprive someone of the very scope itself for making even morally wrong decisions, cannot be the business of any man or of any human society vis-à-vis other men. For such an unconditioned refusal of the possibility of an objectively and morally wrong decision would amount to a suppression of the very scope for freedom itself. But it nevertheless remains true to say that the objective and moral justification for an individual free act is essentially co-determined by the object of this act. If the latter does not furnish an objective and moral justification, then such justification can also be denied to the free act *qua* individual act. There can, therefore, be no question of a real right to choose error or to decide on some objectively wrong moral conduct, although it is quite a different question whether and to what limited extent someone may have the right to be given room for freedom, within which the possibility of choosing error or what is morally wrong remains open to him. Seen from this point of view, the authority of the Church, her laws and the decisions of her teaching authority cannot be regarded as an infringement or curtailment of a genuine right to freedom. She merely keeps man away from objects which of themselves either cannot be the object of a true exercise of freedom or at least are not a necessary object of such an exercise which receives its dignity from the object and not by a merely arbitrary choice.

(b) It must not be forgotten that the norms promulgated by the Church in limiting the scope of freedom oblige, in as far as they are ecclesiastical norms, only those who, by the free decision of their conscience, have acknowledged the Church as a divine institution, and who acknowledge the authority of this Church as legitimatized by God. The conscientious heeding of an authority acknowledged in freedom can never be objectively contrary to this freedom. And the Church clearly refuses to allow anyone to be physically forced to accept the faith or to receive baptism.

(c) A further point is to be noted. We spoke just now about the fact that the Church is not simply the authoritative teacher of abstract or even merely formal religious and ethical norms, but has also the right and the duty to condemn certain concrete forms of behaviour by the Christian as incompatible with these norms, and thus to delimit the scope of morally possible freedom of action in a negative way. This applies to the Christian even if in a particular case he can no longer fathom the objective reasons for the binding force of the ecclesiastical norm nor understand the application of this norm to life in the concrete, but must simply be satisfied with the fact that, although this is beyond his comprehension, the legitimate authority of the Church has declared this or that to be incompatible with the moral law. But all this does not mean that the freedom of the Christian in the decisions of his life consists simply in the fact that he has acknowledged the Church's authority once and for all by a free decision, and that from this moment onwards nothing is left to him but to receive orders and to carry out commands which determine even the most minute details of his life. Nor does it mean that in those cases in which the Church does not issue the Christian with any such detailed command, it can only be a question of matters which are unimportant from a religious or moral point of view. The true picture is quite different. For when the Church goes beyond proclaiming general norms by her teaching authority and draws concrete conclusions in her pastoral office which are obligatory for the practical conduct of her members, her function is in itself and fundamentally of a negative kind. She sets limits, without thereby ascribing to herself the duty, or even the ability, to say fundamentally in each case what exactly the individual must do here and now in this particular situation and within the bounds set by her in the religious and moral fields, in order to ensure that his action is right both in this world and before God.

For it is wrong to think that the concrete reality of our deeds and omissions corresponds in every respect to God's will and hence to what is fully moral, simply because it does not run into conflict with the general norms which can be formally stated in a proposition. For such an opinion is ultimately based on the platonic conviction that the individual and concrete thing or case is nothing more than the negative limitation of the universal. But if there is a concrete and particular reality which cannot be adequately reduced to the universal (and which, therefore, is not expressible in a formal proposition and thus cannot be dealt with by the authority of a community), then there is an ethics and Christian morality which, for the want of a better word and in spite of possible misunderstandings, we may call 'existential' ethics and Christian 'existential' morality. Such an ethics and morality must not be disregarded, in spite of the fact that one can give only formal and general laws for it.[1] In the concrete, this means that when I am faced with a decision in my private or public life, certain possibilities of action will—basically speaking—be eliminated as being incapable of a Christian or moral realization, since they conflict with this or that formal or material universal norm promulgated by the Church as

[1] Cf. below: 'On the question of a formal existential Ethics'. In this connection cf. also: K. Rahner, *Gefahren im heutigen Katholizismus* (Einsiedeln 1950), pp. 9–30: 'Der Einzelne in der Kirche'.

being objectively right and prohibiting this or that manner of conduct. But this does not basically provide man with a clear positive imperative as to what is to be done here and now in this concrete situation. Such a negative procedure of sifting moral possibilities may, of course, in many cases lead in fact and in practice to an unmistakable conclusion concerning the question as to what is to be done here and now. But this is not necessarily so. In the nature of things there will always still remain several possibilities which could all be realized without coming thereby demonstrably into conflict with any definite material norms of morality. And yet only one of these possibilities can be the morally correct one, because it alone corresponds to the actual demands of the case and of the will of God.

We cannot concern ourselves here with the question of how the concrete imperative for the fulfilment of my actual individual task in a particular situation can be found beyond the analysis of the situation and its confrontation with the universal moral norms. However, it should be immediately evident that this individual norm is not only not settled for me authoritatively by the Church authority, but also that the latter is unable to do this. The Church cannot, for example, tell me what career I must choose, or whether I in particular—this concrete and unique individual—am to marry or not, and whether I should choose this or that marriage partner. The Church can, indeed, promulgate this or that important and very 'practical' social norm; she can also reject this or that actual economic system as being incompatible with Christian standards. But she cannot tell the individual statesman, in the particular concrete situation in which he is placed, which among the Christianly possible social and economic constitutions he in particular is to bring about. She cannot do this, although we cannot say that the choice of a definite form from among the different abstract Christian possibilities is a morally and religiously indifferent matter, simply because all these possibilities proposed for selection are of themselves reconcilable with Christian truth and morality. Precisely this choice from among the abstract Christian possibilities can in many cases be an important matter from the point of view of the situation in this world. Not only that, but for this very reason such a choice can also be a moral decision of the highest order, for which the person concerned is responsible before God, although the Church's authority cannot say in the concrete what is right and the Holy Will of God for him here and now. It therefore follows from this, that fundamentally all moral decisions which have to be made by the Christian—and all his decisions have a moral and Christian side to them—have also a concrete and individual dimension which of itself and directly cannot be covered at all by the authority of the Church. This, therefore, provides a zone of freedom, but not of freedom to act simply as one chooses, as if anything were indifferent before God. This is a zone of freedom where the Church leaves the individual Christian to himself, to his conscience and the guidance of the Holy Spirit, and to his own *charisma* given him by this Spirit. And the Church does so to such an extent that the individual cannot at all transfer the burden and responsibility of this freedom to the Church. The Church is made up of individuals who can never hide themselves under the anonymity and irresponsibility of an ecclesiastical mass. The ecclesiastical and the concrete ecclesiastical reality, on the one hand, and what is Christian and what is justified before God, the Creator of the universal *and* the individual, on the other hand, never coincide completely.

Even in the Church there is to be found an application of the principle of subsidiary function in respect of the functioning of her hierarchically constructed authorities, without prejudice to her basic God-given constitution and the direct origin of her fundamental authority and powers in her divine founder. This means that even in the Church every individual, community and authority must, indeed, be fitted into the whole structure of the Church and subordinated to the highest authority of the Church; but this does not mean that the members of the Church (both individuals and communities), which are thus incorporated and subordinated, cannot and ought not to have their own relatively independent functions; it does not mean that the life of the Church is directed by an omnipotent central body of bureaucrats, and that all others have merely the duty to receive orders passively, without any responsibility or initiative of their own. Even in positive Canon Law (which is not unchangeable) changes can take place in the boundary between freedom and compulsion and in the distribution of duties and rights. The Canon Law obtaining at any particular moment in time does not need to be regarded as something immutable. Because someone does not have a divine right in a certain respect and in a particular case, this does not mean that the Church herself may not invest him with this right in the form of a *ius humanum*, which can be a true right and not merely a privilege. Thus it is conceivable that in this respect the rights of lay people might be further extended or re-extended, since in the long run this is the only way in which the layman can be brought to a consciousness of his duties in and on behalf of the Church.

Even within her life of religion, the Church must combat the tendency among her own members of taking refuge in the mass and taking flight into a merely collective religious life, as is manifested by too great a dependence on others, by the fact of shying away from personal responsibility or waiting for ecclesiastical directives from above in the wrong circumstances, or by the opinion that everything is morally as it should be merely by the fact that the Church has not issued an explicit and detailed verdict, and by the dwindling of a *personal* private life of piety both of the individual and in families, in spite of their participation in the official liturgy, etc.

If, in conclusion, we are to give some indication of certain concrete instances where room should be left for freedom *inside* the Church particularly at the present time, then the following must be said:

(a) Even within the Church there should be room and toleration for the expression of opinion, i.e. Public Opinion.[2] Pius XII himself pointed this out and stated that the absence of such public opinion in the Church would be a fault for which both the pastors and the flock would have to take the blame. The following are the Holy Father's actual words (*Osservatore Romano*, 18th February 1950):

> Public opinion is the natural portion of every normal society composed of human beings. . . . Whenever there is no manifest expression of public opinion at all, and above all whenever one must admit that public opinion does not at all exist, this lack must be regarded as a fault, a weakness and a disease in the life of that society. . . . In conclusion, We wish to add a few words about public opinion within the pale of the Church (in respect of those matters, of course, which are left to free discussion). Only those will be surprised at this who do not know the Catholic Church, or at least know her only badly. For, after all, she too is a living body, and there would be something lacking in her life if there were no public opinion in the Church—a lack for which the pastors as well as the faithful would be to blame. . . .

[2] Cf. Karl Rahner, *Free Speech in the Church* (London 1960).

(b) There must be room in theology for research, for different schools and directions of thought, for experiments and progress, within the framework of actual dogmas and any other really obligatory doctrines.

(c) There is, if we may express our meaning in so profane a manner, a lawful 'freedom of association' for Christians within the ecclesiastical sphere. Even in this sphere is it a valid rule that higher forms of organization must not be allowed to suppress, in favour of a kind of 'State Socialism' which organizes things in a bureaucratic manner from above, the spontaneous individual life of fellowships which grow up within the Church from below. Such methods would be more convenient and would make it easier to survey everything, but they would not be more successful in the long run and would, in fact, mean the death of any true Church life. An exaggerated principle of parochial and natural social groupings offends against the rightful freedom of the Christian in his religious life.

(d) Side by side with the official function which is transmitted in a juridical manner, there is and must also be the charismatic and the prophetic in the Church which cannot be officially organized right from the start but must, in all patience and humility, be given sufficient room for growth, even though its bearers are sometimes rather 'inconvenient'. It is written: 'Do not extinguish the Spirit.'

3

PERSONAL AND SACRAMENTAL PIETY

I. INTRODUCTION TO THE PROBLEM

1. The Question

THE question about the particular place which the reception of the sacraments, and especially the sacrament of the altar, should occupy in our daily spiritual life will always go on being discussed. Years ago people argued about the relationship between 'ontic' piety and subjective piety. Since that time, everyone has no doubt realized that the reception of the sacraments is not meant to dispense us from the efforts of self-discipline nor, therefore, from personal co-operation when receiving the Holy Eucharist. Consequently, the important question for us in our present discussion will lie in a different direction. What we will ask ourselves is whether a 'Spiritual Communion', for example, can be a valid substitute for the actual reception of the Eucharist—without loss of benefits—and whether it is of the same value and has the same effects for salvation. Can examination of conscience and contrition mean the same as a sacramental 'Confession of devotion'? Have there not been times when the reception of the particular sacrament—be it the Eucharist or Penance—was rather infrequent, without it being possible to assume lightly that there was less piety and less love of God among the pious in those days?

2. Insufficient Answers

To begin with, one cannot simply dismiss this question merely by stating that in fact, since the sacrament is effective *ex opere operato*, a sacrament gives grace of its own power, and that one does not receive this grace without a *sacramental* reception of the sacrament. For *firstly*: A sacrament, even when received worthily, does not simply increase grace with absolute certainty and necessity in arithmetical proportion to the number of times it is received. Even although such a conception is the tacit basis of a fairly widespread popular opinion about the sacraments and their efficacy, this view falls down in face of the clear doctrine that the sacraments increase in efficacy (i.e. in the efficacy peculiar to them) in proportion to the dispositions of the recipient. These dispositions are, according to the Council of Trent (Denz 799), the measure (although not the cause) of the sacrament's factual growth in efficacy. And even these dispositions themselves do not grow simply in proportion to the frequency of the reception of the sacrament. Otherwise it would be impossible to explain ultimately why, for instance, the Church allows the Eucharist to be received only once per day.

And *secondly*: Are there 'sacramental' graces which can be received only through the sacrament? There are, of course, *effects* of the sacraments which cannot be received otherwise than through the sacraments, such as our alloted place in the order of the hierarchico-visible Church, given to us by Baptism, Confirmation and Holy Orders, or the sacramental character, and the marriage bond. But our question is not concerned with such matters. The question is rather: is there some *grace* which can be acquired only through a sacrament, be it the grace of the state of justification and sanctification and its growth, or be it (actual) grace to help us to continue in the truly Christian life of oneness with Christ and to fight against sin, face the trial of death, profess the Faith, fulfil our vocation to the priesthood, matrimony, etc.? This may well be doubted. For when we speak in sacramental theology of the peculiar grace of each individual sacrament, which pertains to the particular sacrament in accordance with the particular characteristics and purpose of the sacrament concerned, nothing more is meant by this than that the sacraments differ *from each other* in this way in their effect and not merely in their outward rite. Such a statement does not, however, imply that the sacraments give a grace which otherwise could not be obtained in any way. In reality, sanctifying grace is increased through the whole Christian life—through prayer, penance, the carrying out of one's duties, the keeping of the Commandments, through sufferings undergone in faith, through a Christian dying. Who is going to doubt that the priest obtains further graces by his prayer and by the faithful exercise of his office to help him in the fulfilment of his priestly task, and similarly also in the case of the partners in a marriage? Who is going to deny that penance, prayer, etc. obtain graces for avoiding further sins and for the removal of the consequences of sin which still remain after guilt has been remitted—graces, in short, which are 'peculiar' to the *sacrament* of Penance?

It is also not sufficient to say that God has *de facto* instituted the sacraments as the means for grace and that he therefore wants them to be used, so that anyone who culpably neglects these ordinary means of grace may not count on obtaining this grace by some other means. This may well be correct. But the real question is: *when* does one 'neglect' the sacraments? To judge by the divine or ecclesiastical commandments, the required frequency of reception of the sacraments is not very great. Can someone who takes this frequency as his norm be accused of 'neglect' of the sacraments; could he not expect to receive the necessary helps for a very holy life, merely presupposing (and this must certainly be presupposed) that he uses the other means of grace, such as prayer, penance, etc., most zealously? If one already sees tepidity, and therefore non-disposition for a rich aid of grace, simply in a relatively rare reception of the sacraments itself, then one tacitly presupposes precisely what has to be proved. For, in fact, such conduct, simply considered in itself, is 'lukewarm' only if the person concerned throws away chances of grace in this way, because he cannot merit them in any other way. But this is just what is in question.

One can, of course, pose the following counter-question: What reason could one have for receiving the sacraments (in which Christ applies the power of his grace to us) less frequently than the nature of the sacraments and the demanding circumstances of life and of its situations permit? One might add that a frequent reception of the sacraments is not detrimental to 'subjective' piety but, on the contrary, encourages it. And so, both frequent reception of the sacraments and subjective asceticism and piety together must at any rate be richer in blessings than if one were to be satisfied with the merely 'subjective' way of perfection of the Christian life. Hence, the fact of a rare reception of the sacraments must after all be due to a certain tepidity, i.e. to an indifference towards the divine assistance of grace. This may in fact often be the case. For it is quite right to say that, at least in general, the Christian who really believes in the Incarnation of the divine Logos with a vital faith, feels the urge to meet God's action on himself in the most tangible and human manner possible—and that means in the sacraments. There will, of course, be an upper (albeit fluid) limit to this frequency for practical and essential reasons. But one would surely not be justified in saying that, prescinding from border-line and individual cases, this limit is exceeded by the present-day tradition of frequency in receiving the sacraments, as found amongst zealous Christians in the world, as well as amongst the clergy and in the life of the Religious. Such a frequency in the reception of the sacraments need not, therefore, arouse any suspicions of being exaggerated or superfluous. This is true especially because one's spiritual life, if it is genuine and hence also in accord with the mind of the Church, will fit itself quite simply and trustfully into the life of the Church as established in one's day—and, therefore, nowadays into a life of an increasingly sacramental piety. In this way one can be confident that one lives the sort of life which the Spirit of God, who ultimately disposes sovereignly of men and of the Church, wishes us to lead in his Church at this particular period in time. For after all it is he who in the final analysis brings in the ages of the Church and determines which aspects of the abundance of Christian existence (i.e. of the life of Christ) will be particularly marked here and now. Such accentuations fall under the law of the guidance of the Holy Ghost in the Church, and cannot be entirely deduced from theoretical considerations in theology. But does such an answer say everything that is to be said? What about the question with which we started, viz.: is it possible to receive the effect of a sacrament (the *res sacramenti*) even without receiving the sacrament itself?

II. A POSITIVE ATTEMPT AT A SOLUTION: THE INNER UNITY OF FAITH AND SACRAMENT

It seems that, in order to clarify fully the obscurities which have come to light both in the question itself and in the usual answers, we must inquire somewhat more deeply into the more exact relation obtaining between subjective activity and the sacraments. For, once their inner unity and correlation has become clearer, our original question will answer itself. For if it turns out (as we hope to show) that in the case of subjective activity and sacramental happening it is not at all a question of 'two ways' to the same goal (viz. the reception and increase of God's grace), but merely of two moments or phases of one and the same event, then it no longer makes any sense to ask whether one should take one way *or* the other.

1. The teaching of current sacramental theology about the 'two ways' of justification and of the increase of grace

The whole of the present-day theology of the sacraments is unfortunately directed in its outlook towards encouraging the conception of 'two ways' of justification and increase of grace which meet only (but then entirely) in their final result. Various trains of thought have contributed to this outlook.

When one speaks of sacraments in general and—as it were—constructs the formal model of a sacrament, one instinctively envisages infant baptism as one's example, with the unspoken thought in the back of one's mind that the pure essence of a sacrament can best be represented *in the case where* man's personal activity of faith and love is completely out of the question. As far as the other sacraments (e.g. Penance and Extreme Unction) are concerned, one would probably represent the normal case as follows: one supposes a disposition such that the effect of the sacrament (the *res sacramenti*: remission of sin, justification) does not come about without the sacrament. And one then regards this case as typical (merely imperfect contrition as sufficient disposition) and as the one which should, therefore, give us the clearest idea of the nature and effect of that particular sacrament. Hence, in the case of sacraments which demand a greater disposition (viz. the 'sacraments of the living'), one accordingly regards this disposition merely as a moral demand on the part of God for the *de facto* reception of the *effect* of the sacrament, i.e. as something which remains completely outside the sacramental event as such.

And conversely, when one speaks of the subjective way of justification and increase of grace, one thinks of a purely 'subjective' event. One knows, of course, that such an event (understood in this way) is possible only with the support of the grace of Christ. But one does not, in this connection, bring out the christological and ecclesiological aspects of this grace. There are whole tracts 'De gratia Christi' in which for all practical purposes, and seen as a whole, the word '*Christus*' appears only in the title. These tracts simply presuppose as self-evident, or mention only briefly, that this grace is 'merited' precisely by Christ himself. The word 'Church' just does not appear at all in these treatises. And yet every grace has analogously the same structure as its source, viz. the structure of the Word become *man*, and all grace is grace of the *Church*, i.e. all grace has an ecclesiological structure. The outcome of all this is that in the sacraments, seen now also from the angle of the subjective way of justification, man's personal action in faith and love is conceived as a disposition which remains external to the sacramental happening as such. And furthermore, the ecclesiological aspect of the personal action of the believer (and with that every *inner* reference to the Church as the sphere of the sacramental happening) is then left completely out of consideration (even although it is not explicitly denied).

Against the background of such trends of thought, there must quite instinctively arise the conception of two different ways and manners of justification, and of two sometimes independent and self-sufficient causes of the same effect. This dualism is only barely bridged by the doctrine (in itself quite correct) that even in the case where the subjective way has been taken (such as baptism of desire or perfect contrition) and has borne fruit, the sacrament is nevertheless of obligation and necessary as a means for salvation, and that therefore the merely subjective manner of justification must include a *votum sacramenti* (which in fact it always does). At the same time this doctrine also underlines expressly in this connection that it is not the '*votum*' but charity which justifies, so that no one may possibly get the impression that these two ways could be allowed to fuse into one.

2. Critique of the doctrine of the 'two ways of salvation', by showing the inner unity of faith and sacrament

We naturally do not mean to dispute the correctness of the *starting*-points of this doctrine of the two ways (which doctrine itself is never explicitly expressed, but is all the more effective for that very reason[1]): there is an effective infant baptism, there is a sacramental justification of the person who approaches the sacrament only with attrition or imperfect contrition,[2] there is a justifying *votum baptismi*, etc. But

[1] This doctrine is not at all explicitly expressed, because each of the two ways is even treated in different scholastic tractates, so that the 'danger' of any contact arising between them is avoided from the very start.

[2] It is, however, also true that present-day theology, frequently in contrast to St Thomas, presupposes too easily, by appealing to a very questionable experience, that the dispositions do *not* change under the influence of the sacramental happening, so that the dispositions sufficient for the reception of the Sacrament and the dispositions sufficient for the reception of the *effect* of the Sacrament are presumed to be one and the same thing.

these facts do not at all force us to hold the external dualism which they are intended to justify. This will become clear by the fact that they can be just as easily derived from, or integrated into, a conception of the sacraments which does not contain this dualism. It will now be our task to develop the latter conception and to prove it, in so far as this is possible within the limits of a short article.

It might first of all be said that even on the metaphysical plane it is altogether impossible that *one* effect should have *two formally* different causes in the strict sense. If and when there are, therefore, two *materially* different causes for the same effect (as when one can, for instance, knock a nail into the wall by using either a stone or a hammer), one would at least be obliged to work out the formal identity of the causes as such for this one effect, a unity which must ontologically precede the sameness of the effect. But such very correct metaphysical considerations are not usually very convincing in practice. Nevertheless, they do at least give an indication of methodology: the more a theory of causality succeeds in explaining the same effect by the sameness of its cause, the greater will be its chances of being the right theory. Plurality must be proved, for it, and not unity, is ontologically the more questionable.

Now, in Scripture, justification (and increase of grace, union with Christ, salvation, eternal life, etc.) is sometimes ascribed to a sacrament (baptism, Eucharist), and at other times to faith (and to charity, conversion, etc.). The necessity of *both* sides is stressed. The Scriptures do not reflect on the internal harmony of these two assertions. But they also do not 'make it easier' for us to solve this question which they pose for us, i.e. the Scriptures do not reckon with cases in which the subjective action of man (to which they ascribe justification) would not be sufficient and in which the sacrament would then be the sole means of salvation. The Scriptures speak neither of a justification by reason of a merely imperfect contrition, nor do they speak of infant baptism. Of course, these cases are not thereby excluded. And yet theological speculation is thereby given a different direction, if it is to grasp the unity of the subjective and the sacramental sides of justification. Scripture recognizes beyond this also the possibility of a justification by faith in anticipation of the sacramental happening. It thus gives a hint, indeed, that theological speculation must begin with this point of the 'subjective' happening in order to arrive from there at the sacramental event. It hints, therefore, that wherever precisely this subjective activity of man leads to justification, it must in the present dispensation of salvation lead to the sacraments (and not only in the case of merely imperfect contrition).

It is not possible here to give a theological history of the conception of the relation between *opus operatum* and *opus operantis*. This would lead us too far afield, and the analyses required would be too far-flung, especially since these conceptions are not completely uniform and many attempts have been made to understand these two facts of revelation in their internal harmony.

This question arose already in Tertullian's theology of baptism. It found various and varying answers with Augustine in the course of his life. At this stage (and already with St Ambrose) our question poses itself under the heading of the possibility of a baptism by desire, which question itself was not uniformly answered. Our question appears again later on at the end of the patristic period under the guise of the question as to whether a contrite person who dies without being reconciled with the Church will be saved. In the early Middle Ages it becomes absolutely clear that there is a baptism of desire; it is now explicitly recognized that in the normal course of events a sinner, who has been justified by contrition 'alone', does reach reconciliation with the Church—indeed it was still taught at that time that this is in itself required of him. The patristic teaching is now developed into the explicit doctrine of 'Spiritual Communion'. From the twelfth century onwards the question arises as to what happens in the case where someone comes to the sacrament of Penance with a good will indeed, but with a merely supposedly justifying contrition; and it is admitted (although only very gradually and hesitatingly and with various explanations) that the sacrament becomes effective even in such a case. The case of infant baptism is considered. However much one attributed a cleansing from original sin to it (this question had been decided by Augustine's fight against Pelagianism), one was still very far from understanding clearly whether such a baptism gives also sanctifying grace and the infused virtues. Even the Council of Vienne, in the final analysis, left this question open. It was felt that the question as to where faith is to be found in such a case is a difficulty, for after all according to Scripture faith is absolutely necessary for salvation. The average theology of today probably underestimates the weight of this question.

One can say, in any case, that theology until well into the thirteenth century had a clearer consciousness of the fact that both aspects of the process of justification belong together than theology has today. It is also clear that in those days the case of a sacrament having a saving effect by reason of merely imperfect contrition was not considered as the classical test case for the study of the real nature of the sacrament.

St Thomas still considered it an important doctrinal part of the teaching about the sacraments, that the sacraments are '*protestationes fidei*' and hence also render the faith of the recipient truly visible in the public forum of the Church. Indeed, in his teaching on the sacrament of Penance he develops a theory about the interlacement and mutual dependence of subjective and sacramental events which is far removed from any theory of two ways of justification. The very contrition with which the penitent approaches the sacrament and which in itself he must contribute *qua* justifying contrition, already comes about in virtue of an ecclesiastico-'sacramental' grace (of the 'power of the keys') before the actual reception of the sacrament. And conversely, the conversion of the sinner, rendering itself truly concrete in and before the Church and her authority by the contrite confession of the penitent, enters as a constitutive part into the sacramental happening as such and becomes, together with the absolution given by the priest, the sacramentally efficacious sign and an intrinsic element of the *opus operatum* itself. Thus there is a dialogue between the contrite human person and the Church in which Christ's saving activity becomes really historically tangible in space and time and in the particular 'Now' of each individual existence. In St Thomas' view, it is precisely this dialogue in its unity which reacts *ex opere operato* on the inner attitude of the penitent and on his personal fulfilment of *metanoia*, and really completes it properly. Indeed, in the exceptional case of someone approaching the sacrament in good faith with merely imperfect contrition, it is only at this very moment that this personal fulfilment receives its *justifying* power. Of course, in the normal case (according to St Thomas) the personal activity of the penitent would already have this justifying power even before this moment, by virtue of *the very* grace which had continued to flow towards him from the Church,[3]

[3] This conception will not seem strange to anyone who bears in mind that the Sacraments operate as signs of a human kind, and that it cannot, therefore, in itself be reasonably demanded that their constituent factors should be physically or chronologically simultaneous. This is also the way in which one must understand what current theology usually calls the 'reviviscence'

precisely because (and not although) justification before reception of the sacrament is the normal case. And so, in the case of the sacrament of Penance, the personal supernatural activity of the subject is embodied sacramentally in the visible dimension of the Church, because this activity had itself already been borne along by the grace of the Church. Only in this way does that activity attain the fullness of its existence, which corresponds to the fullness of existence—in the flesh and in the space-time of the empirical world—of Christ the God-Man, the source of this grace, and also to the fullness of existence of the visible-invisible Church, the Proto-Sacrament.

We do not mean to imply by this brief reference to St Thomas' teaching on Penance either that he himself would wish to see the here-developed structure of this sacrament applied to *all* the sacraments in exactly the same way, or that he himself had already thought this theory through to the very last question, or that this theory should or could still be maintained in all its details.[4] But one thing may undoubtedly be claimed by appealing to the authority of St Thomas: the nature of a sacrament as an *opus operatum* is in no way contradicted by the indicated interlacement between the *opus operantis* and the *opus operatum*, which are immediately mutually and internally related by reason of their very natures and not merely by a *votum sacramenti* on account of a purely positive decree of God.

For the sake of brevity we must here refrain from indicating other elements of the sacramental theology of St Thomas which reinforce and clarify this conception further. The view set forth previously, which on the whole is also the usual view on the relationship between

---

of the Sacraments. This is not a question of the reviviscence of a dead Sacrament, but refers to a more extended chronological separation in time of the constituent elements of the Sacrament and the dispositions. In such a conception it will be necessary to dig more deeply than is usual in order to prove the necessity of a disposition being present during (chronologically) the actual positing of the sacramental sign—but it will not be impossible to find a reason for this necessity. To take another example: at the Last Supper, the *consecrated* elements of bread and wine will undoubtedly never have been present at chronologically the same time, although the representation of the Sacrifice of the Cross requires both of them, so that the Sacrifice of the Mass cannot be celebrated under one kind only.

[4] Thus e.g. someone who *explicitly* acknowledges himself to have merely imperfect contrition, may not be excluded from the reception of the Sacrament.

opus operatum and *opus operantis* held in current theology, did not originate until after St Thomas' time. This view has the advantage of being easy to handle in a concise and 'clear' manner, but it does not have the same depth, nor does it exhaust and use all the riches and elements of a comprehensive doctrine of the sacraments as given in Tradition. It is not possible here to attest these elements from Tradition by a *positive* theological investigation. We must content ourselves with giving a brief and more synthetic and speculative outline of the basic theory which would arise from these elements. Using such a procedure, it is inevitable that certain questions cannot be explicitly tackled, and hence that certain things will remain obscure. We will simply try to get a rough idea of the relationship between *opus operatum* and *opus operantis* to the extent in which this is required for answering the particular question of this essay as objectively as possible. The particular question of this essay, let us remind ourselves, concerns the mutual relationship of ascetic endeavours and sacramental events in our day to day spiritual life, and whether there are two different ways for the attainment of salvation, simply to be followed for some reason which is not quite clear, or whether these are only two aspects or phases of what is ultimately one and the same process, viz. an always personal–'sacramental' way of acting which sometimes, and even often (but not always), grows and develops into such an explicit and tangible activity that it is then to be called reception of the sacraments in the strict sense.

3. Theologico-speculative clarification

The supernatural grace of salvation is grace of Christ. It is not merely 'merited' by him, but bears also something of the distinctive trait of him who as God-*Man* has introduced it in a definite manner into the world and has earned it by his act of salvation on the Cross, so that it becomes the legal property of his brethren according to the flesh. This grace, if we may put it this way, has an incarnational tendency. It has not merely a dynamic directed to the inner life of God in which it makes us participate (and this indeed constitutes its nature, but, as it were, its abstract nature which prescinds from the order of Christ). It has also a dynamic directed towards the world, by which it causes the man whom it saves to be comprised within the redeeming and transfiguring descent of the Word of the Father into the world, and in which HE gives this world his Holy Ghost. The grace of Christ is, therefore, also the source of the transfiguration of the body and thence of the transfiguration of the world as a whole. Similarly, it is the basic principle of the slow moral integration of human nature into the theocentric orientation of the sanctified person, i.e. the slow and, in the meantime, piecemeal recovery of the paradisean grace of man's original state in which the psychophysical 'nature' of man was completely docile to the supernaturalized human personality. Hence this grace should and wants to spread itself according to its proper nature over the *whole* stratified being of man, right down to his corporeal nature itself—forming, transforming and elevating, and sanctifying it. This grace is, therefore, not merely the principle of a merely transcendental 'interiority' of man, uniting him with God. It is meant to be rather the sanctifying formative principle of the whole body-soul life of man, coming right down into his concrete, tangible daily life, where it therefore receives its 'expression' and takes on its corporality.

Now grace—seen ontologically—*always* becomes externalized in this sense. For, although ethics may legitimately distinguish from an empirical standpoint between 'internal' and 'external' human acts, there are no purely internal acts from a metaphysical and theological point of view. For even in the most sublime interiority of his spiritual acts man still acts as *man*, i.e. as a *body*-soul being, so that even the most spiritual acts still have extension in that corporeal nature by which human beings, even as spiritual persons, are in touch with one another in a real material spatio-temporal unity. This is a real unity, no matter how difficult it may be to define it in a category. To put it somewhat crudely: even the most sublime stirring of a most supernatural love for God in the innermost depth of the spiritual person still depends on (and at the same time changes) electro-physical processes in the brain, which belong to the one totality of the material world in which everything depends on everything else and everything helps to determine everything else. It would be to the point to apply even here what was said once by a modern physicist: When a child throws its doll out of the cradle, Sirius itself will shake.

Grace, as the principle of a higher order, i.e. of the absolute divine order, transforms and elevates the moral act *qua* spiritual act; the latter however rests on, and at the same time externalizes itself in, an act in the material world (or rather: in an inner moment of the one whole act which diffuses itself through all the dimensions of human existence). And so grace finds its living expression in every act (just as the body is the act and outward manifestation of the 'soul', albeit not adequately), and finds it in the spatio-temporal dimension and hence (still in a general sense) also in history. Every existing supernatural grace has, therefore, its own historical externalization in which (when accepted) it renders itself present and comes to appear. It renders itself present *in* making itself appear: analogously to the way in which the soul 'becomes' and 'is' by endowing matter with a living form and thus in-forming itself into matter, and hence cannot be thought of as preceding this act of in-forming. Grace, therefore, has of its very nature and from its very source a quasi-sacramental structure in the present incarnational order of Christ and of man.

This grace is essentially the action of God on man and cannot be thought of in any way apart from the free personal mercy of God, by which he gives himself as a gift to man. Hence the quasi-sacramental, spatio-temporal and incarnate nature of this grace is to that extent not only the manifestation in which the spiritual-existential act of the *human* person expresses itself at the very first, but also the 'outward appearance' of *God's* action on man and of *his* redeeming love for man. And so the union and relationship constituting the saving dialogue between God and man (which of itself is spiritual and transcendent), becomes present in the spatio-temporal tangible nature of every supernatural-moral act, i.e. it manifests itself in the dimension of the historical situation and existence of each human individual. One cannot object to this that (at least in general) the *empirico*-moral side of human acts for salvation belongs *only* to the domain of natural morality and that it cannot, therefore, be the 'outward appearance' of supernatural grace, since that side is possible even without saving grace. For, prescinding from everything else which is essential and which we pass over simply for the sake of brevity, even the divine assistance which we require for the factual achievement of natural moral acts is willed by God in the present order of salvation as an integral part of the one single new order which is conceived and willed precisely *as* comprehended in Christ and as projecting (and indeed assumed) in him and through him into the inner life of God. And so, in the last analysis, even this divine help is *gratia Christi* (wherever, at the very least, it finds a response). This is why even the actually achieved moral fulfilment of the natural law is already a manifestation of the divine will of grace *in Christo*, especially when it is transformed and elevated by supernatural divinizing grace and is thus orientated to the goal of direct communion with God in eternal life, and when it is modified by this elevation even in its *per se* natural condition.

Over and above all this, the following should be borne in mind: the grace of Christ is intended for humanity as a whole; it reaches the individual in so far as he is a member of the one community of damnation and salvation which represents the human race as a unity. And Christ not only wanted to become man in this community, but to be man as a member of the one humanity, 'born of a woman'. Those who are being sanctified and he who sanctifies are of one race. His grace has, therefore, a social structure. Even in the history of personal salvation there is no isolated individual; there are indeed individuals but no individualists. Indeed, the culminating point of the process of becoming a person, which takes place through the grace of a most direct relationship to God, signifies the highest form of the communion of persons who have become in this way most personal in the one eternal kingdom of God—the highest form of the eternal communion of all saints. 'Individual' and 'community' in this sense are not realities which are opposed to each other or compete against each other. On the contrary, they are two sides of the one reality of achieved and redeemed persons which can only increase or decrease together and to the same degree.

But in accordance with the characteristics of human nature, such a communion of persons, who are justified and share in the divine life, is not willed by God merely as an invisible kingdom of inner and transcendent union by grace. Rather, God wills it as a communion which as such creates its own expression for itself in the visible and spatio-temporal dimension of history, or rather receives this expression in its institution by Christ. God's holy people of the redeemed takes on the form of the Body of Christ and of the Church, which is the combined product of the interior mutual union of the redeemed by grace and of the historical, visible form of this transcendent interior union which consists in the united profession of truth and a social union through one hierarchical order and its functions. Just as on the natural plane a people renders itself historically tangible and capable of concerted action by forming a State, so the communion of the redeemed becomes historically tangible in the Church. By the impulse of the ultimate and inmost principle of her unity—the grace of *Christ*, the Holy Ghost—this communion becomes a corporate and socially constituted body. Yet this process must not be thought of as a kind of process of nature. It must not be thought of as a process which by-passes free voluntary decision and historical action. Rather it must be thought of as a process which is accomplished primarily by the will of the divine-*human* founder of the Church, and then secondarily by the will of the Church herself, who by her own institutions renders the communion of grace and salvation (which she is) even more tangible and historically manifest.

In accordance with the nature of man which develops and unfolds itself in time, the tangibility and historical character of the Church, the people of God historically constituted, must not be thought of as something merely static which as such alone would give historical expression to the grace uniting the redeemed even amongst themselves in the closest communion. The Church carries this grace into effect and lets it appear in its *deeds*. Thus grace appears as truth in her continually renewed and progressive teaching which introduces men more and more into the fullness of the truth of Christ according to the particular character of their mental, historical position. This grace appears also as the demand made on man by her pastoral office in her law and commandments—as the sanctification of men in her sacraments—as surrender to God in the Sacrifice which she celebrates daily. There where the Church, in her action on the individual, renders grace historically manifest as the sanctifying principle on the level of her supernatural social life according to the will of her founder, she dispenses her sacraments. *By* giving this sanctifying grace a historically tangible form in such basic social acts, in accordance with the commission given her by Christ, the Church renders this grace really actual and present as well as effective in the here and now of her individual members. The Church effects grace *by* signifying it. The sacrament effects grace *because* it is its sign—a sign, in other words, which, as externalization (*Leibhaftigwerdung*) of grace, renders grace present—in short, a sacrament is a constitutive sign. In other words, it is not only true that the sacraments are signs of grace because they are its cause, but essentially the converse is just as true: they are causes because they are signs.

This category of causality *per modum signi* must not, however, be forced into other familiar *a priori* categories of natural causality, for otherwise the peculiarity of this particular category would suffer or at least be overlooked. The relation between the outward bodily aspect of a spiritual act and that act itself is probably the closest analogy we can find. The spiritual act posits itself and is caused by taking on an outward bodily form.[5] The spiritual person, superior in its origin to the corporeal, posits its spiritual act by interpenetrating the corporeal principle formatively from this its superior position; it gains its proper achievement from its opposite, material pole.

It is somewhat similar with the activity of the Church; by positing the material, outward sign and expression of grace in space and time through her ritual action, which is the action of Christ, she obtains a really efficacious mode of presence for the grace thus signified in this historical moment of time. By the fact that Christ acts on man through the Church by giving his grace the form of a constitutive sign, it is *he* who renders his grace inwardly efficacious in man, and not his servant nor the recipient of the sacrament. This is the meaning of the term '*opus operatum*', which has therefore nothing to do with the imagination of any kind of physical effectiveness of a material occurrence which would appertain to this occurrence independently from its nature as a sign, so that this occurrence would only be 'incidentally' 'also' a sign of grace.[6] The gestures of Christ which he performs through the Church, one might simply say, are gestures meant in earnest; he on his part really effects by them what he expresses by them, simply because he performs them. If these gestures of the Church are understood from the outset (as they must be) as Christ's gestures, as the real physical appearance of his action, then it will be quite easy to understand that there is no sense in asking oneself whether and how they 'act on' the divine (and divine-human) Agent of grace, and that there is no sense in trying to solve the problem of the causality of the sacraments in that direction.

Now, whenever man really receives the grace of a sacrament as its effect, he must provide a disposition, to the extent to which he is capable of a personal act. This disposition is, however, necessarily

[5] One might think here of Pascal's profound remark to the effect that one must perform external humble acts in order to become humble.

[6] Hence the intention of the human minister of the Sacrament is also required, since without it the sign would just not be a sign, i.e. a human expression. And conversely: whenever one ascribes a really physical efficacy to the Sacrament, one can no longer explain properly why the intention of the minister is necessary even for the mere existence of the Sacrament.

borne by grace which, as already pointed out, is, on the one hand, grace of Christ and of the Church, and, on the other hand, finds its outward bodily expression in the space and time of history by this activity of man. For after all this disposition is not merely something 'interior'; for man must desire to receive the sacrament visibly and he must manifest this desire—he lets the sacrament be administered to him and this fact of letting it happen to himself is as much a historical act as any other. Thus the sacrament takes place in a historical dialogue between Christ in the Church, on the one hand, and man on the other. And seen from both sides, this dialogue is the constitutive sign of the one grace of Christ and of his Church, which is effective at this moment.[7] A sacrament takes place, therefore (in the case we are considering), as a dialogic unity of the personal acts of God and of man in the visible sphere of the Church's essential (i.e. given to her directly by Christ himself) sanctifying ministration. The 'incarnation' of grace, and grace's process of becoming tangibly historical, reaches its climax in the sacraments. Grace is not only incarnated in the personal supernaturalized activity of man, but also in the acts of the Church as such: not only in the activity of a member of God's people, but in the essential activity of the *historically constituted* people of God, i.e. in the essential activity of the *Church* in her own public, social sphere.

There is, indeed, no saving human act which in its historical spatio-temporal nature does not experience an embodying of grace or which falls outside the fundamental law of incarnation applicable to Christian salvation as such. But this process of embodiment has its own definite variability. This is somewhat similar to what happens in an ordered society, where there are acts, performed by and on the individual, of a

[7] This does not necessarily involve a denial of the fact that in general, and especially on account of the case of valid and fruitful administration of the Sacraments to infants, only that part of the dialogue which the Church actively posits can be called 'Sacrament' in the strict sense. But this fact in its turn need not exclude the other fact that the totality of the dialogue is externalization (*Leibhaftwerdung*) of grace. This grace, proceeding from Christ present in the Church, seizes hold of man, becomes 'flesh' in his activity which brings him to the Church (i.e. in the words and gestures of man vis-à-vis the Church) and then receives a further tangible expression (*Leibhaftigkeit*) in the active response of the Church, precisely *as* tangible response of the Church, and this is an expression of grace precisely *qua* grace *of the Church*. And so, in this way the full 'truth' of grace now appears and carries itself into effect.

more or less official or public nature. Everything a man does is done by him in some degree or other as a member of his people; it has to a greater or lesser extent an effect on this people and is some kind of expression of the life of this people, and hence is an act of this people, no matter how 'private' it may be—this is after all the reason why there is not only a history of States and of wars, but also a history of cultures. But there are acts of the human individual and of the people which take place in a qualified public sphere, in which the act of the people as such manifests itself and the act of the individual has its full validity only when it is done in the properly qualified public forum and is replied to by the act of the people through the action of its public authorities; thus, for instance, a marriage contracted before the registrar, a contract drawn up by a notary, a testament attested before a notary, the confirmation of property-rights by a judge, etc. So also the sanctifying word of Christ to man, which is uttered in the depths of conscience and which in any case becomes outwardly present in the world in the active assent of man, can receive a properly qualified embodiment through the Church in her public forum; it can then become sacramental in the strict sense of the word. And in view of the incarnational structure of Christian salvation and of the ecclesiastical constitution of the people of God, it is easily understandable that the Lord of grace should *wish* and (to various degrees) demand this qualified outward form of his word of grace to man wherever it is a question of the *basic* effecting of the event and acceptance of His grace.

It would lead us too far afield for our present purpose if we were to take a detailed look at the organized body of the seven sacraments in the light of what we have just seen. For the seven sacraments are the seven basic embodiments of the occurrence and appropriation of grace. What is important *in the present context* is simply to note clearly that grace does not occur merely internally and subjectively (as it were outside the visible form of the Church) at certain times, and in the form of sacraments at other times. No, presupposing the corresponding subject, grace always occurs both subjectively *and* in the Church, interiorly *and* outwardly, existentially *and* collectively, although in varying degrees of one or other of these elements.

This variability is in the nature of things: not every occurrence in a community which is brought about by the individual and is also borne at the same time by this community, can have the same degree of explicitness and be of the same official public nature in the social framework of this community. The more basic and significant an act is for the individual and the community, the greater must be the public explicitness demanded of this act. The more humdrum an act is, the less will be demanded of it in the way of public and official outward expression; this is true to such an extent that it becomes practically imperceptible that even in this case the community still helps to condition such an act. The exact dividing line between these two kinds of act cannot, of course, be simply deduced *a priori*. This is a matter which is determined legally by the authority which has the right to give intentional determination to the constitution and law of the particular constituted community. It can, therefore, also happen that it is left to the free decision of the individual whether he will perform an act in this or that form—take, for instance, the different forms of wills and contracts, or the case of a valid but clandestine contract of marriage, etc. So it is also in the visibly constituted community of the people of God—in the Church. The application of all this does not require any further detailed explanation here.

III. CONCLUSION: ONE WAY OF SALVATION BY FAITH AND THE SACRAMENTS

We can now approach our particular question from what we have seen above. What happens in fact when, for example, a Christian repents of his sins in the quiet of his own little chamber in one case and at other times makes a 'Confession of devotion'? Does he follow a different way to the same goal in each case, or else what happens? Can one say: take the first way, for the effect is the same and you can spare yourself the second way? Or should one say: in the first case you are merely concerned with yourself and everything is merely 'subjective', whereas in the second case the grace of God is having an effect on you . . . ? Or should one merely say: do both, for after all two is better than one . . . ? And similarly in the case of Spiritual and Sacramental Communion?

1. The quasi-sacramental visible appearance of the workings of God's grace in Faith and Love

God's action on man occurs even in the 'subjective' way, and even the 'subjective' way occurs in the Church. Here, too, there is a dialogue of grace between God and man, an effective action of God which really and truly fills and transforms the heart of man more and more with his Holy Spirit. Here, too, there occurs not merely a disposition of repentance, but God also gives his word of forgiveness to man. Even in this case there is not merely an intellectual and affective reference of man to Christ, but a true deepening of the real union with Christ in the Holy Spirit. In this case, too, these forces pour forth upon man because he is incorporated into the Body of Christ which is the Church, and because this Church prays, sacrifices and loves for him. Here, too, the life of the one Body of Christ goes on, and everything is embraced and supported by the visible-spiritual unity of the Church, which is not an ideological but a real unity, preceding the individual man's subjective will for union. And when man acts in this way in the quiet and seclusion of his closet, it is not only his own dispositions which are expressed in his actions (his praying, kneeling, etc.), but God's grace in him and that through his freedom. When he reflects on his actions and looks at them as it were from the outside, he can say: God acted there, and in this hour of my life he became tangible and visible in the intangible workings of his grace. The life of Jesus, which pervades all spaces and times, has advanced another little step further. His hand has rested upon me and his own word has gone straight to my heart; the life-streams of his Church have risen out of the hidden depths of his Heart, in which the Holy Ghost is poured out, and have risen to the surface of my life where they become accessible to my everyday consciousness.

2. Grace and Love, inspirited and embodied in the visibleness of the Sacraments

Why does such a person nevertheless receive a sacrament even in cases where he is not obliged to do so? Is this merely a help for the weak in faith who would otherwise not comprehend what happens in and to them even without this sacrament, when they simply believe and have faith? Or does the recipient of the sacrament suddenly do something quite different now from what he did before, because this also is blessed? Neither is true. On the contrary, reception of the sacrament continues the life of faith and lets this identical faith grow up into the fullness of its being and thus gather strength. *Ceteris paribus*, i.e. presupposing his 'subjective' act as also accomplished in the sacrament, he does the same now as what he did or let be done to him before in the silent room of his secluded prayer. Only now he does it in a more tangible fashion, and hence more intensely to himself, and lets it happen to him in a more tangible and hence more intense manner by his co-operation. Christ's deed and the vitality of the Church take shape in him in a tangible and express manner. Christ's gesture towards man becomes more emphatic: Christ's word of absolution is clearly set off against man's word of contrition (although the latter was never possible other than as a *response* in which Christ's word took effect). And Christ's word is here addressed to him explicitly and powerfully. Christ's body is received as a palpable pledge of the fact that a profounder union is taking place here and now with the living Lord in the Holy Ghost. Explicit expression is given now to the relationship all grace has to the *Church*, by the fact that the Church takes a visible part by her tangible action. In short, what had already been happening previously, now becomes a qualified tangible event and appears *publicly* in the form of a means of grace which had already sustained the previous events and which is the Church. However, this qualified, higher objectivity of the constitutive sign of the grace of Christ, considered as rendering man's action tangible, means (*ceteris paribus*) an intensification of man's own supernatural fulfilment of life (*opus operantis*); and when considered as the tangible aspect of the action of Christ, it means a new actualization of grace (the *opus operatum* in the sacrament). Hence no *new* path is taken. Rather the one way of salvation and of grace is pursued right to the end. The final phase follows from the first phase, and the latter is completed by the former. These two phases of the one process depend on one another; in both of them the same powers are at work: Christ, the Church, and the human person as recipient of grace.

The whole process can be compared to the life shared in common by two lovers. Everything they do is sustained and transformed by this love and is its—very discreet, almost imperceptible—expression, even the insignificant, ordinary things which seem to have quite a different meaning and purpose from love and which would have to be done even if there were no love between these two persons. And yet, sometimes, and even often, they must tell each other their love openly, in words and by gestures which are nothing but the expression of love—of a love which was already finding expression in everything they do. It is as if the hidden law of the whole of their two lives united together must continually bring forth new formal, outward expressions (*Gestaltwerdungen*) of their love, in which this love, which after all is always there, realizes itself ever more fully and in ever new forms. These are only gestures, not love itself—gestures 'which do not really seem to matter' compared with the proving of one's love in deed and in truth; and yet love lives by them. Love would die if it were not for these expressions which are not love itself at all and which those not in love consider superfluous 'formalities'. There is a connection between the proofs of one's love in deed and in life (i.e. of the real love which really matters) and these gestures; yet in the ultimate analysis this connection cannot be formulated in rules but must always be discovered anew. It is impossible to lay down hard and fast rules for everyone and for each individual, telling him in what rhythm and proportion both of these factors belong to the one life of love and in what way the one love lives by both. But the everyday course of love will always go on concentrating itself in such gestures and love itself will always draw new life from them.

This comparison is merely a—comparison. But it may illustrate the fact that there can be no real competition in the spiritual life between the *opus operatum* and the *opus operantis*. Not only because the *opus operatum* also demands in some small measure the *opus operantis*, if the sacrament is to be in any way fruitful. But because the *opus operantis* reaches its proper climax in the *opus operatum*, i.e. its climax of outward, corporeal expression which corresponds to its proper and always given nature. And the *opus operantis* attains in this way the highest fulfilment of its own inner existential intensity which is in itself possible here and now,[8] because this intensity itself (other things

[8] It is important to note the terms 'in itself' and 'possible here and now'. For otherwise this part of the statement would be an exaggeration. To take an example: a martyr for the Faith has received the Sacrament of the Altar with great devotion—before being sentenced to death; now, supposing that —after sentence of death has been passed—he places his life in his hands for whom he sacrifices it, and that he does so out of the freest, believing love. There is no difficulty on theological grounds (on the contrary; remember the patristic teaching about baptism of blood) in assuming that in the second, i.e. the non-sacramental act, the existential acceptance of his sharing in the fate of the Lord—the '*res*' of the celebration of the death of the Lord—is more intense than in the first act. Nor is there any difficulty on theological grounds in accepting that more happens in the line of the supernatural and of grace in the second act than in the first. The constitutive *sign* of one and

being equal) does not in fact grow merely through this increased intensity of its expression (by giving rise to the latter), but grows also through the grace of the sacrament itself which comes out to meet it. For the event of this grace does not merely mean an increase of a purely inactive state of grace. It also effects this increase through and by way of an intensification of the personal activity to which it responds. It would be a merely superficial empiricism to try to deny this statement by appealing to a contrary 'experience' on the occasion of a pious reception of the sacraments. One would in that case confound certain verifiable feelings of consolation, uplift, etc., which are accessible to direct internal experience, with more profound spiritual-supernatural acts which can become more interior, personal and 'existential' without this fact being necessarily verifiable by ordinary internal experience.

3. Consequences of the foregoing for determining the frequency of the reception of the sacraments

The foregoing again does not mean that we may simply lay down the principle that the greater number of times the sacraments are received, the better the recipient's spiritual life will be. Such a somewhat wild repetition of the reception of the sacraments does not only go beyond the limits of what is possible in practice or according to the law of the Church, but it would be senseless even apart from that. It is simply a fact that, if life is to remain healthy, then those spiritual acts which are done with great explicitness and solemnity must be relatively rarer and more unusual than the more humble and ordinary actions of everyday life. So also in the case of the sacraments. Let us put this more precisely and explain this matter factually, judging it by the finite, spiritual and moral possibilities of a human being which are conditioned by the level of his spiritual development, his personal characteristics, his external circumstances, etc. Now, there can be cases where, seen and judged in this light, it cannot really be

---

the same reality present in both acts (viz. the participation in the death of Christ) is greater and has a higher excellence in the first act (i.e. in the reception of the Body of Christ, which is the sign and not the signified thing or effect of the Eucharist); but the '*res sacramenti*' is more intensely and really present in the second act, even though this act takes place without the *sacramentum*.

expected that a more frequent reception of the sacraments would mean any marked increase in the intensity of the existential accomplishment of the reception of the sacraments (even remembering that this must not be confused with certain very devout sentiments and emotions). In such cases any further increase in the reception of the sacraments will be senseless, even though such further acts of receiving the sacraments would still have to be characterized as 'fruitful' '*in the abstract*', i.e. purely in accordance with the norms of the general moral theology of the sacraments. In the normal case of the average Christian, there would be no sense, for instance, in his wanting to keep on going to Holy Communion several times successively each day, or in his wanting to get absolution from the priest several times in uninterrupted succession, even if the law of the Church had not placed any limit on this (in the former case). The reason for this is quite simply the fact that it is the 'dispositions' which are the measure (not the cause) of the sacramental effect. If, in a particular case, these dispositions cannot actually increase any further to any marked extent either before or through the reception of the sacrament (for reasons which lie beyond the sacrament and the good will of man), then the sacrament, too, cannot achieve any further marked increase of its effect. Two kisses of love—to use the language of our previous illustration—are not always more than one.

This principle in no way permits us to criticize and to combat as exaggerated what, for example, Canon Law (can. 863; 595, 2) as well as the Encyclical '*Mediator Dei*' (C.T.S., London, no. 127) and the rules and customs of Religious Orders regard as the normal frequency of reception of the sacraments for a devout Christian of today. For one must take it absolutely for granted that in the normal case the dispositions required in present-day practice (before and through the reception of the sacraments) are possible for anyone who has the good will, and that, therefore, the now normal frequency does make sense. But the aforesaid principle, even if it does not permit deduction of any hard and fast numerical rules, can be useful for recognizing in practice that a certain freedom of the children of God is justified in what concerns greater or lesser frequency, and the upper and lower limits of frequency in the reception of the sacraments. We will not, for instance, smile at a Saint (such as Francis Borgia) because he receives the sacrament of Penance daily, nor look on him as a noteworthy oddity on that account. Nor will we immediately have suspicions of tepidity about a mature priest, in whose life examination of conscience and contrition are firmly established (quite apart from the rules of the Order), but who only goes to Confession every four weeks. Seen in this light, it is also absolutely understandable that the most authoritative moralists count with the fact that a priest may on occasion not offer the sacrifice of the Mass and not receive the Holy Eucharist, without thereby missing an opportunity for growth in grace.

4. The inner unity of personal and sacramental piety

One may not, therefore, say that 'Spiritual Communion' is 'just as good' and as profitable as sacramental Communion, or that the mere examination of conscience and contrition achieve 'the same thing' as sacramental Confession. This is so, not because these acts of one's private spiritual life are so to speak only an 'as if', but because, in the incarnational order of Christ and of our flesh and as long as we remain dependent on the shadows and signs of our world even in our relationship to God, these acts of our everyday spiritual life only attain their proper essential climax precisely in the sacraments. Faith (itself) realizes itself most really and intensely, of its very nature,[9] in the sacrament of faith. The unity and union with Christ, which takes place through love, appears and realizes itself with the greatest intensity in the sacrament of the Body of Christ. The forgiving grace of God reaches its clearest and most efficacious expression in the sacrament of Penance.

[9] I.e. if faith in its existential profundity were to correspond fully to the unsurpassable dignity of the sign as such. We have already said that this is often quite different in actual fact, even in the providence of God—i.e. that it can happen that the *res sacramenti* is acquired in greater measure outside the Sacrament (cf. note 8 above, pp. 130 *sq.*). This, however, is no argument against the principle just formulated; for in this principle it is merely a question of the highest degree of acquisition of the *res sacramenti* attainable here and now (i.e. in a case where one can receive a Sacrament, the Sacrament is offered, and its reception has sense according to the principle just formulated). In such a case, to abstain from the Sacrament would also mean renouncing the chance to increase one's personal exercise of faith and love. One could imagine a sort of 'case of conflict' only where a sacramental occurrence and another act of virtue apparently compete simultaneously with one another, as e.g. if one could help Christ in a poor person 'now' and only now during the time of Mass. In such a case one must, of course, choose the act of greater and more selfless love, even if under certain circumstances it were 'only' a spiritual Communion included in the act of love of one's neighbour.

4

FORGOTTEN TRUTHS CONCERNING THE SACRAMENT OF PENANCE[1]

THE phrase, 'forgotten truths', in the title of this article, must naturally be taken with a grain of salt. The Church's consciousness in faith always stores up more in her memory, as her lasting property, than is 'present' to it at any particular moment in time which we may arbitrarily mark off. For the past and Tradition belong to this consciousness. But there will also be 'forgotten truths' if it is true that the Scriptures and Tradition must be the ever new and inexhaustible source of theology—the source from which theology must always draw anew and without which it would become sterile[2] (i.e. if it were to believe that it conceives everything adequately 'now', which it possesses in the memory of its Tradition but which it must also always awaken and raise again by ever new efforts). Such truths do not necessarily need to have been 'defined' or to be truths found in 'Denzinger'. For if this were necessary, then the study of 'Denzinger', and 'Denzinger' itself, could make the Scriptures and Tradition, as well as the ever renewed delving into them, superfluous. That truths are 'forgotten', also does not imply that no one knows these truths. Indeed, it is often almost comical (and yet really quite natural) how this shows itself in theology. Thus, when someone exclaims: 'This is something you have forgotten (you theologians, preachers, catechists), you never mention this!', then the accused parties take notice and

[1] I was somewhat grieved to notice—only after having finished this article—that I had overlooked an article by M. Schmaus ('Reich Gottes und Busssakrament', *Münchner Theologische Zeitschrift* I [1950], pp. 20–36), in which much of what I have said here has been anticipated (besides treating other things which are not mentioned in the present article). In referring the reader to this excellent article, I hope, however, not to have worked completely in vain. Cf. also on this whole subject: K. Rahner, 'Beichtprobleme', *Geist und Leben* XXVII (1954), pp. 435–446.

[2] Cf. Pius XII, '*Humani generis*' (Denz 3014).

retort somewhat indignantly: 'You are wrong, that is something we have always known and indeed have always stated in such and such a place. For have we not always known, with Augustine, Thomas, Suarez (where the point which has been passed over in silence, is to be found), what you are now affirming?' One knows these truths—they seem familiar and (more or less) self-evident, when one is reminded of them, and yet one may have forgotten them. When we speak in what follows about such truths concerning the sacrament of Penance, we do not mean to imply by this that all of these 'forgotten' propositions have always the highest degree of theological certitude. We are satisfied (without making it an object of inquiry or defending it), if a reasonable theological justification can be given for these propositions and if they are supported by the views of authoritative theologians. Nor do we mean to maintain that these 'forgotten truths' are more important than those which are always and everywhere explicitly preached about and meditated upon. When one states that in the sacrament of Penance God forgives us our guilt by the grace of Christ and through the word of the Church, one has undoubtedly stated the most important facts that are to be stated about this sacrament. However, the works of God are in fact too rich in their reality to allow these riches to be rendered adequately by a short formula, no matter how clear and powerful the latter may be. Sober exactness and lucid abstractness, although good in themselves, may also lead to spiritual impoverishment in theology. We have no right, whether it be in theology or in our spirituality, simply to select arbitrarily according to our own particular tastes; rather we have the duty to penetrate more and more, and in ever new ways, into the infinite breadth and depth of divine truth.[3]

1. Consideration of sin as sin against the Church

Sin is opposition to the holy will of the eternal God; it is opposition to the love which he offers us and in which he wants to give and communicate himself more and more, so that we might participate, or increase our participation, 'in the divine nature'. The offence against

[3] The bibliographical references given here and there in this essay do not claim to be exhaustive. Moreover, no attempt has been made in the notes to furnish scientific proofs for every proposition and every remark on the history of dogmas.

this God is the very essence of sin. Over and above this, sin is however not only an offence against the nature of man and against his supernatural calling to grace, and against the growth and ever deeper personal acceptance of this grace. Sin is also an offence against the holy communion of the redeemed, which is the Church. For the divine will of love and the supernatural calling of man, against which man offends by sin, are not realities which concern man only as an isolated individual or existent. The Christian who is baptized meets the holy God of grace as a member of the Church. The baptized Christian belongs both to the visible and invisible reality of the Body of Christ. His visible belonging to the Church, which is based on the sacramental character of baptism, is the 'proto-sacrament' which gives him a constant and effective title to justification and sanctification in the Holy Spirit. He ought to contribute his share by his life of walking in the Spirit, so that the Church, whose member he is, will be the 'holy Church' even in a 'moral' sense and thus bear witness to the fact that God's mercy and grace have really come into the world both validly and invincibly.[4] The holiness of the *Church* (*her* Spirit) is given to the Christian as his own, because he is her member—and he is to give his holiness (his life in the Spirit) to the Church, so that she will be the holy one. The Christian who sins offends, therefore, against his own attachment to the Church (which is essential to him as a Christian) and against the Church herself. Not that he is simply severed from her by (grave) sin, as lack of baptism, heresy and schism separate a person from the Church on the level of her historical visibleness and tangibility. Nor is it that sin (if it is not schism or heresy) is of no account for the Church and for the Christian's membership function in the Church. Just how sin affects the Christian's *belonging* to the Church is something we will have to deal with more explicitly in the next section. The main thing to realize at this point is that the baptized sinner becomes guilty in regard to the Church by his sin. He offends against *her* Spirit, against her mission and against the unquestioning obedience he owes to her. He for his part renders the Church herself sinful in a certain regard.[5]

This ecclesiological aspect of sin can already be clearly perceived in Holy Scripture—even although we cannot enter more deeply into

[4] Cf. e.g. 1st Vatican Council, sess. 3, cap. 3 (Denz 1794).

[5] Cf. on this: K. Rahner, *Die Kirche der Sünder* (Freiburg 1948), (also in *Stimmen der Zeit* CXL [1947], pp. 163–177).

this here. The Holy Spirit and the Body of Christ belong together in the one Church. Anyone who belongs to her, has her Spirit and is sanctified by belonging to her and by having her Spirit through her mediation. Anyone who belongs to her is holy in this sense, so that his holy life (his living by the Spirit) is the incumbent *consequence*, and not the original cause, of this holiness in the Spirit of God. Anyone, therefore, who as a Christian becomes once more a child of disobedience through sin, upon whom comes the wrath of God (Eph 5.5 *sqq.*)—anyone who gives way again to the lusts of the flesh when, incorporated into the Body of Christ, he could and should instead be spiritual (Gal 5.13–21)—whoever is dead and worse than an unbeliever (1 Tim 5.6–8)—such a person contradicts his membership of the Church and the nature of the Church, which is the sanctified communion of the members of God's household, the communion of Saints (Eph 2.19; 5.26 *sq.*; 1 Cor 12.13). The early Church knew this not only in some theoretical way, but she also really lived this in her day to day existence. One cannot understand the whole ancient penitential discipline of the Church properly, if one does not keep this ecclesiological aspect of sin constantly and vividly before one's eye, as did the early Church.[6] The fact that the early Church—as we will see more explicitly in the next section—took public action against the sinner (and this in principle even when his sin was occult), is based on the consciousness that the sinner has transgressed even against the Church. The early Church, in her penitential discipline, is not only the representative of God who helps the sinner to get rid of his guilt against God—as we are 'forgetfully' inclined to think nowadays—but she is also the representative of God who reacts against the injustice which has been done to *her*—although she reacts, of course, with a strictness which is the manifestation of the curative mercy of God.

It cannot be maintained that this idea is valid only in the case of those sins which 'exclude from the kingdom of God'[7]—in other

[6] Cf. B. Poschmann, *Paenitentia Secunda* (Bonn 1940); *id.*, *Busse und Letzte Ölung* (*Handbuch der Dogmengeschichte* IV, 3) (Freiburg 1951); K. Rahner, 'Zur Theologie der Busse bei Tertullian: Abhandlungen über Theologie und Kirche', *Festschrift für Karl Adam* (Düsseldorf 1952), pp. 139–167; *id.*, 'Die Busslehre des hl. Cyprian', ZKT XIV (1952), pp. 257–276; 381–483; *id.*, 'La doctrine d'Origène sur la Pénitence', RSR XXXVII (1950), pp. 47–97, 252–286, 422–456; *id.*, 'Busslehre und Busspraxis in der Didascalia Apostolorum', ZKT LXXII (1950), pp. 257–281.

[7] Cf. 1 Cor 5.6–13; 6.9–10; Gal 5.19–21; Eph 5.5.

words, only in the case of (objectively and subjectively) grave sins. Certainly, *these* are the sins for which the sacrament of Penance exists principally. Mortal and venial sin are not only different in degree—they differ essentially, so that they are only 'analogously' covered by the one notion. But just as venial sin—although in an essentially different qualitative manner—represents an offence against the will of God analogously to mortal sin, so it is also in the same analogous measure an opposition to the Church. Since venial sins form an obstacle to the actualization of God's love in man, they simply diminish, by that very fact alone, the depth and power of God's love which should be found in a holier Church—quite apart from all the tangible social damage done to the Church by the majority of venial sins. They contribute to a lowering of 'standards' in the Church. Superficiality, tepidity, great or small egoism, obstinacy, want of prayer and penance—such and other 'venial' sins are, therefore, an offence against the Church, and this not only in those cases where we can perceive this diminution of the life and salvific power of the Church through such 'venial' sins (because, for example, they offend directly against certain official ecclesiastical duties).

Would it not be well if, when receiving the sacrament of Penance, we took to heart—somewhat less forgetfully—the truth that we have also sinned against the Church, that we are coming to the *very* grace of the Church against which we have offended and that she, too, has something to forgive us? It has been said that the man of today is almost incapable of the thought of being happy or of reaching heaven without bearing his neighbour and his fate along with him—that he does not wish for any happiness if it does not also include that of others. If this is so, then it ought to lie heavily on our soul that we have been guilty of offences against our neighbour, even if only in our most secret thoughts, and that to some extent the field of our disloyalty and of our failure is spread over the whole Church (and beyond her). No one lives for himself alone. And so no one sins for himself alone. In the darkness of the world, in its stifling sinfulness, in the mental indolence of the Church of which we complain so often—as if we did not bear any responsibility for it—our own guilt looks us in the face. Anyone who understands this, will recognize that the most truly Christian revolt against sin in the Church is—to accuse oneself of one's own guilt before the Church, in the face of which one has oneself been guilty by one's own sins, both great and small. Since the time when the divine Logos himself became man and in his Holy Spirit permanently united himself with the congregation of the sanctified redeemed, the '*tibi soli peccavi*' of the psalm 'Miserere' no longer has the sound of a lonely individualism. It does not express the thought that my relationship to God, both in good and evil, concerns myself and God alone, and no one else. This does concern me and God. But therefore it concerns everybody. 'I confess to God . . . to all the Saints and to you, brethren, that I have sinned.' We could not and would not need to confess to the brethren if we had not sinned against them also, by every sin we have to acknowledge.

2. 'Binding'

It is a well known fact that the early Church appealed more to Mt 16.18 and 18.18 than to Jn 20 for the scriptural proof of her sacramental power to forgive sins.[8] The reasons for this fact (which may at first seem strange to us today[9]) need not be examined here. The said fact alone already shows us that remission of guilt by the Church in the sacrament of Penance—to formulate it quite cautiously and vaguely to begin with—has something to do with 'binding and loosing'. If we now go on to ask what exactly this means, and especially what is meant by this 'binding', then we discover once more that this also is a 'forgotten' truth in the theology of the sacrament of Penance. For if we inquire into the ordinary interpretation of these words current in scholastic theology today, we do not receive a really satisfactory answer. 'Binding' (and the corresponding 'retaining' in Jn 20), in so far as it regards the administration of the sacrament of Penance, means, we are told, the 'refusal of absolution' to someone who by a self-accusation has surrendered himself as a sinner to the penitential tribunal of the Church.[10] Theology, in opposition to the

[8] Cf. e.g. H. Bruders, 'Mt 16.19; 18.18 und Joh 20, 22.23 in frühchristlicher Auslegung', ZKT XXXIV (1910), pp. 659–677; XXXV (1911), pp. 79–111; 292–346; 466–481; 690–713. Also instructive in this respect would be a look into P. Anciaux, *La théologie du Sacrament de Pénitence au XIIe siècle* (Louvain 1949); cf. the Index of this work, p. 619.

[9] The Council of Trent, sess. 14, cap. 1; can. 3 (Denz 894; 913), refers only to Jn 20.22 *sq*., although with the restriction that our Lord instituted the sacrament '*praecipue*' on the occasion referred to by Jn 20. Recourse to other texts is therefore not forbidden.

[10] Cf. e.g. J. B. Umberg, 'Die richterliche Bussgewalt nach Joh 20,23', ZKT L (1926), pp. 337–370; P. Galtier, *De Paenitentia tractatus dogmatico-historicus* (new edition, Rome 1950), nos 125–141.

theology of the Reformers, tries to prove the *judicial* nature of the Church's power of forgiveness over the baptized sinner precisely by the *dual* power of binding *or* loosing. And so a great deal of formal juridical acumen is often summoned up in order to show that such a refusal of absolution—as opposed, e.g. to the refusal of baptism to a sinner or unbeliever—represents a truly positive judicial act which creates a new legal situation. Thus, for instance, the sinner is obliged in such a case to deliver himself up once more to the penitential tribunal of the Church, and the state of sin which had to some extent become liable to forgiveness through the accusation, has been re-confirmed through the refusal of absolution, etc.

We need not here go into the *internal* difficulties of this explanation of the meaning of the term 'binding'. All these difficulties arise ultimately from the same fact, viz. that, objectively speaking, a refusal of absolution, no matter how cleverly it may be explained, cannot be any more than the (in certain circumstances) obligatory omission and refusal of an act—no more than this can be said of a refusal of baptism (which does not involve any judicial decision on the part of the Church). Such a refusal cannot be an independent act with its own, new legal consequences, which is, after all, precisely what the above explanation must presuppose. Much more decisive is the fact[11] that 'binding', in the language of the New Testament and in the view of the early Church, means something different (which also makes the 'retaining' in Jn 20 fully understandable, if this is taken in the same sense); its meaning there is 'to put under the ban'. It is important to stress from the outset that we must not be too hasty in making a mental connection between this meaning and the modern canonical concept of 'excommunication'. The latter is a proper ecclesiastical

[11] Cf. K. Adam, 'Zum ausserkanonischen und kanonischen Sprachgebrauch von Binden und Lösen', TQ XCVI (1914), pp. 49–64; 161–197 (also in: K. Adam, *Gesammelte Aufsätze* [Augsburg 1936], pp. 17–52); Strack-Billerbeck I, pp. 738–747; 792 *sq.*; IV, I pp. 293–333; Kittel, *Theol. Wörterbuch* II, pp. 59 *sq.*; III, pp. 749–753; V. Brander, '"Binden und Lösen" in der altsyrischen Kirche', *Der Katholik* XCV, I (1916), pp. 220–232; 287–304; V. Brander, 'Ist Binden und Lösen bei Mt 16.19 und 18.18 ein rabbinischer Schulausdruck?', *Der Katholik* XCIV, 2 (1914), pp. 116–132; B. Poschmann, *De Paenitentia Secunda* (Bonn 1940), pp. 4–9. Also Paul F. Palmer, *Sources of Christian Theology* II: 'Sacraments and Forgiveness' (London 1960), p. 3 (on this particular point), and the whole work for the present chapter in general —*Tr.*

penalty which is imposed in a fixed manner for certain crimes committed within the Church. In order to understand what is meant by this 'binding' banishment in the New Testament and in the early Church, we must remember what we have already said about the ecclesiological aspect of (grave) guilt. A baptized person in mortal sin still belongs to the Church, he is still 'inside'. But this very fact of his continuing to belong to the Church is robbed of its real meaning by his guilt. It should be a permanent, quasi-sacramental visible sign of his possession of the Spirit.[12] His belonging to the Church in the visible dimension of the Church (i.e. in the sphere of the historically and juridically tangible, of the tangibility of the profession of faith, etc.), becomes a lie in the case of the sinner. It becomes in a sense a 'merely valid' but not 'efficacious' continuous reception of the Proto-sacrament which the belonging to the Church represents. The first thing, therefore, the Church must do (precisely in order to save the sinner), consists in exposing this guilty and mendacious state of the sinner even in the external visible sphere. In short, the Church must first of all unmask the outward appearances—i.e. she banishes or 'binds' the sinner. She establishes the true facts even in the historical tangible sphere: you are precisely as a member of the Church not at all the person you appear to be by your visible membership; you have the appearance of being alive (simply because you belong to the communion of the living in the Body of Christ which is filled with the life-giving Spirit), but in reality you are dead. The Church, in judging, distinguishes and separates in accordance with the twofold meaning of the word *κρίνειν* (*κρίσις*).[13]

It follows from this also that 'binding' and 'loosing' are not two sides of an alternative, but two phases of the one reaction whereby the Holy Church answers the sin of one of her members. At least this is so in the intention of the Church. When she binds, she binds in order to be able to loose. Only once the truth, which is covered up by the outward appearances[14] of the belonging to the Church, has been

[12] Cf. e.g. O. Semmelroth, 'Die Kirche als "sichtbare Gestalt der unsichtbaren Gnade"', *Scholastik* XXVIII (1953), pp. 23–39; K. Rahner, 'Membership of the Church according to the teaching of Pius XII's Encyclical *Mystici Corporis Christi*', see above pp. 1–88 (esp. pp. 69–88).

[13] Cf. e.g. 1 Cor 5.3 *sqq*.

[14] The sinner's belonging to the Church is not 'outward appearance' in the sense that he no longer belongs to her, but in the sense that his continuing state of belonging (both according to its true sense and its demon-

brought to light on the visible plane of the Church, can the guilt towards the Church and God be lifted or 'loosed' again on the same plane, i.e. on the sacramental plane. Nothing is altered in this regard even in a case where the obduracy and impenitence of the sinner make it impossible to proceed beyond the 'binding' stage. The second stage of the one process (i.e. the loosing) depends on the repentance of the sinner. But the binding already aims at the loosing, and the latter presupposes the former. This is the way in which the early Church always understood it.[15] She always stressed the fact that the Christian who is weighed down with grave guilt must be bound so that he might be effectively loosed. And she never regarded this binding, this segregation of the sinful Christian from the full enjoyment of her communion, as an additional penalty of merely external Church discipline, which could only be imposed in certain cases. On the contrary, she always regarded this binding as a reaction incumbent on the Church in the face of every sin (in principle) which 'excludes a person from the kingdom of God'. It is significant in this respect[16] to note the identical nature of the pauline catalogue of depravities, i.e. of sins which exclude from the kingdom of God (in other words, of mortal sins, in our terminology) and the pauline catalogue of those sins which the Church (congregation) must answer by expelling the sinner from its midst. Thus it remained also in the theology and discipline of the early Church. In our present context, we cannot give a more detailed consideration to the exact form taken by this 'ban'—the connatural reaction of the Church to the grave sin of her member—in the actual practice of the early Church's penitential discipline; and it could, of course, take on a variety of forms there. One thing is clear everywhere and this is the theologically deciding factor: the sinner was at least excluded from the precinct of the Church's innermost life. He was excluded from her central *mysterium*, the source of all salvation—from the Lord's Supper and Sacrifice. Of course, he was excluded because

---

strative character) gives a false appearance of something which should be there but no longer is there, viz. the sharing in the holy Spirit of the Church.

[15] Cf. among others the literature cited above, p. 138, note 6.

[16] Cf. on the one hand 1 Cor. 5.1–8; 5.11; 2 Ths 3.6; 2 Tim 3.2–5; 1 Tim 1.19 *sq.*; Ac 8.20 *sqq.*; Ap 2.2; 2.14 *sq.*; 2.20 *sq.* (lists or cases of a 'ban', 'avoidance' etc.), and on the other hand Gal 5.19–21; Eph 5.5; 1 Cor 6.9 *sq.*; Col 3.5–8 (lists of sins which exclude from the eschatological kingdom of God).

he had excluded himself from it by his guilt. But precisely this culpable self-separation from the precinct of the Church's innermost life which takes place in the depths of conscience, is given its tangible character and bodily reality on the plane of the visible Church[17] by the 'binding' of the sinner on the part of the Church. The plane of the visible Church does not necessarily mean the '*forum externum*', in the sense in which this term is used in modern Canon Law. For, in itself, it is here a question simply of the visible plane on which are found also, for instance, the sacraments.

Now, it might be said that this interpretation of the 'binding' as an inner and necessary moment in the sacramental process of forgiveness (as the so-called 'public' 'excommunication'-penance in the early Church), must be false or, at the most, can have a merely historical, antiquarian interest for us. For, firstly, this expulsive binding is surely no longer to be found in the present-day administration of the sacrament of Penance; and, secondly, this whole 'construction' surely cannot be applied to the 'Confession of devotion', and yet the latter is nevertheless a dispensation of a sacrament. The examination of these objections will show us that we have uncovered a forgotten truth in this question of 'binding', which is still significant for us today and which will enable us later on to see the Church's propitiatory 'loosing' also under a 'forgotten' aspect.

The first objection states that this 'binding', such as it has been explained and defined to the exclusion of the proper ecclesiastical penalty of excommunication as found in present-day Canon Law, no longer exists today. In order to see the falsehood of this statement, we

[17] N.B.: This lies on the same plane as the 'loosing' and 'forgiving' in *every* possible or thinkable interpretation of the 'binding' (on earth) or of the 'retaining'. Now in every Catholic exegesis and dogmatic theology, this 'loosing' or 'remitting' is, however, a *sacramental* process and therefore one which essentially has a historical tangibility in the visible Church as such. In other words, it is a process which is enacted in a '*forum*', even though this '*forum*' must be called 'internum seu conscientiae sacramentale' (CIC can. 196, 1047, 2314 § 2) compared with the external dimension of the Church in which those processes are enacted which affect the Church as a merely external society and her 'bonum commune' as such. Events which take place in the sacramental forum effect directly happenings in the 'sphere of conscience' (as simply all sacraments do). They do not, however, take place only in the 'private' sphere of internal conscience, but in the visible Church. The same must, therefore, be said in any case also of the 'binding'.

will first of all make a little thought-experiment before we start talking more 'theologically'. Let us think of a very zealous little Christian parish of today, in which everybody knows everybody else even as ordinary 'citizens'. Let us suppose that *all* the members of this congregation meet together on Sundays for the celebration of the Eucharist and that, under the necessary presuppositions, they all receive during it the Body of the Lord as a matter of course. Let us suppose furthermore (without wishing, of course, to recommend such a practice) that these zealous Christians have—as in the early Church—the seemingly strange custom for us of merely submitting those sins committed by them to the sacramental tribunal of Penance which are objectively *and* subjectively grave, but that they do nevertheless go to Confession in the manner to which we are nowadays accustomed, viz. by queuing up before the Confessional on Saturday afternoons. All these hypotheses are conceivable even today, even without making the slightest alteration in the present Canon Law. The people of this parish need only act in this way. No one could oblige them to act in a contrary manner—one could at the most encourage them to do so. What form would the life of this parish take under these presuppositions? With only slight modifications in the theological or practical sense and without any new canonical measures being taken, there would immediately and visibly appear again in such a parish what could be called 'the public ecclesiastical penance' or 'excommunication-penance'. If someone in such a community committed a mortal sin and consequently does not (as he must not) receive Holy Communion on the Sunday, or (as he is equally obliged to do) queues up before the Confessional on the Saturday, then he would publicly confess himself to be in mortal sin[18] and he would be in the '*ordo*

[18] It will not be very easy to prove that the Church, in the said hypotheses, has the strict duty to modify the external apparatus of the sacrament of Penance in such a way as to prevent anyone, even in these circumstances, betraying himself in practice to be in mortal sin. At any rate, the Fathers of the Church demanded a public ecclesiastical penance even for occult (mortal) sins (cf. e.g. B. Kurtscheid, Das *Beichtsiegel* [Freiburg 1912], pp. 16–23; Öffentliche Busse für geheime Sünden). Although this naturally did not signify a public *Confession* of guilt in the proper sense, the sinner did nevertheless inevitably reveal, in the then absence of a Confession of devotion and on account of the public nature of penance, that he had been guilty of grave sin. By such considerations it also becomes clear, incidentally, what pastoral difficulties would necessarily arise if the tendency of those who

paenitentium' even in the public sphere of the Church (even although the exact nature of his mortal sin would be known only to the Confessor through his Confession, as was also the case, by the way, in the early Church). It would not make any real difference whether such a sinner has his assigned place at the very back of the church on Sunday, as was the case in the early Church, or whether he inevitably attracts attention by remaining alone in his usual place (as would be the case in our little congregation); he would in either case inevitably avow himself 'publicly' to be a sinner. And the parish priest of this congregation could also preach just as publicly about the 'queue' which stands outside his Confessional on a Saturday evening: '*abundant hic paenitentes*; *quando illis imponitur manus*, *fit ordo longissimus*' (innumerable are the penitents among us; there is a long queue at the time when the hand is imposed on them. Sermo CCXXXII, 7). With St Augustine, he could say of these penitents: '*proprie vocantur paenitentes remoti etiam a sacramento altaris participando*, *nec accipiendo indigne iudicium sibi manducent et bibant*' (penitents in the proper sense are also excluded from participation in the Sacrament of the Altar, so that they may not eat and drink judgement to themselves by partaking unworthily of it. Sermo CCCLII, 3.8). He, too, could preach with St Augustine: '*illi enim*, *quos vidistis agere paenitentiam* (i.e. 'who stand outside the Confessional'), *scelera commiserunt*, *aut adulteria aut aliqua facta immania; inde agunt paenitentiam. Nam si levia peccata ipsorum essent*, *ad haec quotidiana oratio delenda sufficeret*' (those whom you see doing penance, have committed crimes, either adultery or some other terrible crime; this is why they are now doing penance. If they had only venial sins, daily prayer would be sufficient to blot these out. *De Symbolo* VII, 15). It can also not be said that in our case the 'public nature' of this penance is only a factual one, without being constituted by a proper act of the Church. For these people are also excluded from the sacramental centre of the visible supernatural life of the Church by an act of the Church herself. Their sin forces them (under our presuppositions) to do 'public penance', because they are also excluded

---

oppose the practice of the 'Confession of devotion' (or wish to push it into the background as far as possible) were to succeed. If these tendencies were once to prevail, it would in practice be impossible to get those who have committed mortal sins to go to Confession except on their death-bed (just as at the time of Caesarius of Arles and during the succeeding centuries).

from the Eucharist by a legal enactment of the Church, which falls upon everyone in mortal sin (and yet is not an excommunication in the modern sense of the word)—and because a commandment of the Church obliges them to receive the sacrament of Penance at least once a year, to which those who have not committed mortal sins are not obliged. Nothing is fundamentally changed in this by the fact that this ecclesiastical act is not nowadays enacted for every individual in particular and as such (as was the practice in the early Church): nothing is basically changed, in other words, by the fact that this act is nowadays to some extent '*latae sententiae*' and not '*ferendae sententiae*'. Even today, the Church still 'binds' everyone in mortal sin, just as she did before, by isolating such a sinner even by her own legal enactment from the circle of those members of the Church who enjoy free access to her highest *mysterium*. And this activity of 'binding', which isolates, could at any time and by purely factual changes assume again the tangible and distinct character which we find in connection with the act of 'binding' in the early Church and which we (unlike the early Church) qualify nowadays as the 'public nature' of penance.[19] The act of 'binding', considered as the first stage of the Church's reaction to the mortal sin of the Christian, is, therefore, to be found today just as in the early Church. It is merely covered up, and hence 'forgotten' by us today, because it does not attract attention. But it does not attract attention because in fact many of those who would have the right, unfortunately do not receive the Eucharist; and many, fortunately, go to Confession who are not obliged to do so.

This whole matter can be expressed somewhat more briefly and in a somewhat more theological form in the following terms. The Church 'binds' the Christian who has sinned gravely. This is still true in so far as the Church excludes such a Christian by her own act (CIC can. 856) from the Eucharist, the greatest *mysterium* of the Church's life and the communion of Christians with each other in the Church (even although this is nowadays done in a somewhat abbreviated form, as was indeed the case already here and there in the early Church[20]). It is

[19] The early Church did not, after all, qualify ecclesiastical penance as 'public' in contrast to a 'private' *sacramental* penance, but in contrast to *non*-sacramental penance for venial sins (by prayer, fasting, almsgiving etc.).

[20] We would refer the reader, for instance, to the abolition, under Nestorius of Constantinople, of the office of priest-penitentiary, who had to deal in an inquisitorial fashion with those who had rendered themselves

true also in so far as the Church has laid down[21] (over and above the divine commandment) that such sinners are obliged to surrender themselves to the tribunal of Penance at least once a year. And this 'binding' of the Christian in mortal sin by the Church takes place in the dimension of the visible Church, which differs indeed from the '*forum externum*' but which nevertheless is really a sphere of the visible order, because it is precisely that dimension of the Church in which the sacraments are effected as 'visible' signs of grace. The fact that this visible (and hence 'public') process of 'binding' is not noticed in our present-day practice, is due to accidental circumstances which lie outside the nature of this matter. Because it does not attract notice, we are inclined to overlook and 'forget' this aspect of 'binding', yet this does not in any way mean that it no longer exists.

Would it not be better if we did not forget this 'binding'? The separation from God and his grace, and the binding by guilt before God himself is, of course, the last and greatest awfulness of sin. But this very separation is brought out of the hidden depths of conscience to the surface of man's existence through the 'binding' by the Church. Anyone who has met people (and there are such people) who suffer from this banishment from the innermost sacramental sphere of the Church, will be able to imagine what this 'binding' can mean in a person's religious life. St Paul saw it as a handing-over to the power of Satan.[22] And how could man not fear this banishment, when he cannot take refuge in the very precinct of the Church in which the incarnate Mercy itself is present as the power of life over sin, death and diabolical passions? How could a man 'bound' in this way not feel abandoned and lonely in the fullest sense, when he is shut out from the *mysterium* in which is given the closest communion of men with one another? Because there is one bread, we who are many form one

---

unworthy of partaking of the Holy Eucharist. By this abolition, the decision in each *concrete* case, as to whether one is in fact in a state of unworthiness, was left to the individual, and thus the Church contented herself with laying down the general principle (considered, however, as a principle laid down by herself and not merely announced by her). In so far as, for instance, St Augustine too expected that the secret sinner would present himself spontaneously before the Church and abstain voluntarily from the Eucharist, he too really presupposes such an exclusion from the Eucharist '*latae sententiae*'.

[21] CIC can. 901, 906.

[22] Cf. 1 Cor 5.5; 1 Tim 1.20.

Body; for the one bread is shared by all, says St Paul (1 Cor 10.17). How must these words affect someone who is excluded from partaking of this bread?

At this point it might be said—and with this we come to the second of the above mentioned difficulties—that the fact that there is no possibility of a 'binding' in the case of a 'Confession of devotion', which is nevertheless a sacramental forgiveness of sin, shows that the 'binding' does not after all belong to the essence of the Church's penitential procedure.[23] 'Binding', one might therefore object, is not a necessary first stage in the judicial and saving reaction of the Church to the sin of her member, or at least this aspect does not enter into a 'Confession of devotion'. This does, of course, represent a certain difficulty which must plainly be admitted. But it must be recognized, first of all, that this difficulty exists just as much in the usual explanation of 'binding' and 'loosing' ('retaining' and 'forgiving') mentioned at the beginning of this section. For this theory tries to prove the judicial character of the sacrament of Penance precisely by the alternative dual power of binding *or* loosing, with legal consequences in both cases. It must then be admitted, however, that even in this theory there can be no question of a true 'binding' in the strict sense with regard to merely venial sins. For the wiping out of venial sins is simply not dependent (not even by obligation) on the sacramental judicial intervention of the Church in the same sense as is true in the case of mortal sin. In addition, even in the usual theory, it is only by making superfluous and objectively most problematical assumptions that one can imagine a case in which someone confesses a venial sin in a mere 'Confession of devotion' which he has not already had forgiven

[23] N.B. we do not say: 'to the proper essence of the *sacrament of Penance* as such'. The *sacramental* power in the strict sense is, in *every* view, merely *part* of a judicial (binding and loosing) power of the keys which Our Lord has given to the Church with regard to sinners. It is, therefore, justified and unobjectionable to distinguish between the nature of the (whole) penitential procedure and the nature of the particular phase of this procedure which must (and can alone) be designated in a more restricted sense as 'the sacrament'. For the 'binding' as such retains its meaning and significance even in the case of the sinner who remains impenitent, but it is not, of course, of a sacramental nature in this case at any rate. And this sacramental nature should not, therefore, be attributed to it either in the case when, in accordance with what is properly and originally meant by it (cf. 'ἵνα' in 1 Cor 5.5), the 'binding' in fact 'resolves' itself into 'loosing'.

before he comes to the sacrament.[24] Venial sins cannot properly speaking be 'bound' or 'retained' in the strict sense, *no matter how* one may interpret these two words expressive of the full authority of Christ, which are the scriptural foundation for the sacrament of Penance. It follows from this that the above mentioned difficulty is one which affects every theory, and not merely our own particular explanation of 'binding'. For *every* theory must recognize, on the one hand, that the sacrament of Penance is geared in its whole structure to the wiping out of mortal sin, and, on the other hand, every theory knows from the practice and teaching of the Church that in a secondary and derived sense it can nevertheless also be a sacramental means for the cleansing from venial sins.

Presupposing these preparatory reflections for a '*retorqueo*', we may say that venial sin, *analogously* to mortal sin (i.e. in a really similar way or with *merely* small differences), is also an offence against the holy Church and against the functions of membership to which a Christian is obliged in the Church. Venial sin does not, indeed, exclude the sinner from the inner life of the Church which is the 'vessel of the Spirit' (as Irenaeus would say), but does, however, hold him back from the full unhindered exercise of the life issuing from this inner vital principle of the Church. As St Thomas would say, venial sin does not exclude the virtue of *caritas*, but impedes the act and *fervor caritatis*[25]; however, caritas must not be understood here as the merely subjective disposition, or merely as the individualistically conceived 'infused' virtuous habit, but as the divine love which pours forth continuously in our direction from the Church: Ecclesiae *caritas, quae per Spiritum Sanctum diffunditur in cordibus nostris* (the Church's love which is poured into our hearts by the Holy Spirit, Augustine, *In Joan.* tract CXXI, 4). By venial sin man places a distance between himself and this fiery fervour of love which issues from the Church and from her divine principle, seeking to grip man ever more fully and jealously—to this fire he consciously opposes himself. This is first of all enacted in his own private sphere, perhaps even only in the hidden

[24] As to the reason why the reception of the sacrament does nevertheless not become meaningless, this has been sufficiently discussed in two of my articles: 'Vom Sinn der heutigen Andachtsbeicht', *Zeitschrift für Aszese und Mystik* IX (1934), pp. 323–336, and 'Personal and Sacramental Piety', cf. above, pp. 109–133.

[25] *De malo* q. 7, a. 2; I.II q. 89, a. 1.

depths of his conscience. And he himself *can* also terminate and repair this culpable resistance to the stirrings of the Spirit in these dimensions of his existence, viz. by 'private' penance, prayer and reception of the Eucharist which is after all the very sacrament of the 'fervor caritatis' according to St Thomas.[26] But the case which really concerns us here is when the sinner comes to the Church and deplores, and accuses himself of, his remissness and contrariety, and when the Church in her official representatives accepts this accusation and takes it seriously, confirming by seriously listening to this confession that this is not merely the expression of a sensitive soul, which is concerned with its private individual blamelessness, but a confession of guilt through which the Church herself must join in suffering and expiating. In such a case even the hidden separation of man from the fullness of life and vital energy of the Church, which is implied by venial sin, is in fact given a visible character in the sacramental forum of the Church. And this visible character is analogous to the visibleness which arises through the binding of a person in mortal sin (especially since even *such* a person does still remain a member of the Church). The confession of venial guilt, consisting in the declaration by the sinner and the acceptance by the Church, renders this guilt, and the separation from the Church caused by it, 'present' in the particular public sphere of the Church (no matter how discreetly this is nowadays constituted) which, distinct from the *forum externum*, is precisely the sphere in which the Spirit and Body of the Church permeate one another most intimately. The fact that the distance of the sinner from the Church's fullness of life becomes perceptible as a result of the Church's action and not merely by the action of the sinner, makes it quite legitimate to call this action of the Church a 'binding', analogous to the 'binding' by which the Church responds to the mortal sin of a Christian.

Again, anyone who reflects properly on this will not say that these are theological subtleties which cannot be of any importance for man's religious life in practice. There is no sin by which we do not also become guilty against our neighbour; this is only too obvious in the case of most sins, including venial sins. Take a priest who kneels in the Confessional and confesses his sins. Suppose he confesses 'merely' venial sins: his gruff manner, his formalistic performance of his

[26] III. q. 79, a. 4 etc.

priestly functions, his lack of penance and deficiency in the spirit of prayer, his haughtiness and his egoism, his cowardice in carrying out his mission. How much has he not in reality fallen short, both visibly and imperceptibly, in his duty towards others—how much is he not guilty towards the children, the poor, towards those who look for the Church and cannot recognize it in him, towards all those whose soul God will demand of him on the day of judgement? When this priest now confesses his sins, his 'merely' venial sins, in this way, then this is not (or should not be) only the unavoidable presupposition for his getting rid of these sins. This Confession has its own weight (after all, he could cleanse himself of these sins even without this Confession); it says: Oh my God, I, the most reverend gentleman, Your anointed and ordained priest, the representative of holy Church—I am a poor sinner and no better than those before whom I am meant to walk as a good shepherd on the paths of salvation. How great a gulf there is between what I am and should be as a priest and what I am as a poor sinner! And how this disparity weighs heavily upon me! How am I to confess it, how destroy the false appearance and the lie which spread around the truth of my priesthood by my guilt! I cannot kneel down before my parishioners to beg them to forgive me my guilt towards them, so that God in heaven may forgive me. And, therefore, I confess at least to another priest, to my own brother—in the place of God and God's holy congregation whom I have offended—my fault, my grievous fault. . . . Do not take me for an exalted saint but regard me rather as what I am through my guilt: a poor sinner. Through this Confession, by showing myself before the Church and thereby before all against whom I have sinned to be far from what I should be and seem to be, I can hope that God, by the love of his Spirit Whom he bestows, will also place me again where he has placed me by Ordination. By the fact that I show my fetters, he relieves me of them. This is merely an example. It could be made to apply to the case of the person in public life, of the father who has to watch over the salvation of his children's souls, of the mother who should be an example to her family of what is meant by being a true Christian, of the poor and lonely who should draw grace for others out of their own bitterness, of those who live in a monastery which should be a radiant city set on a hill. . . . All of these should try to gain an existential realization of their being bound before and by the Church, before they let themselves be loosed from their venial sins by and before the Church.

3. The 'Matter' of the Sacrament of Penance

Anyone who has at some time or other studied theology, will recall (probably with feelings of weariness and disinterest) a 'scholastic controversy' about the question of what is the 'matter' of the sacrament of Penance. He will probably regard this controversy as an exceedingly empty wrangle about words, which is utterly unimportant in practice and for our spiritual life. He will probably regard it as a controversy which drags on in the textbooks simply because theologians have taken it into their heads to distinguish between matter and form even in the case of the sacrament of Penance, although (in his opinion) this distinction which is clearly understandable in the case of other sacraments (such as baptism), can be applied to the sacrament of Penance only by dint of artificial subtleties. And so one gets the impression that the Thomists will go on calling the 'acts of the penitent' the matter of the sacrament of Penance, the Scotists (who deny this) will go on regarding these acts as merely necessary conditions for this sacrament, and that in the last resort both opinions come to the same thing. And yet this whole matter is a bit different in reality. This question is important, and not only because the Reformers disputed the proper sacramentality of ecclesiastical Penance partly by maintaining precisely that there is no '*res*' in this case, i.e. no 'matter' (as there is in the case of baptism and of the Lord's Supper), but merely 'words' (*verba*). And, they maintained, since these words stand on their own, there is no question here of a sacrament, but rather of something belonging to the efficacious preaching of the Gospel of forgiveness. We prescind here from the significance of the scholastic controversy in this particular respect. Even apart from this, once we presuppose the thomistic view as well founded and as the now more common opinion in theology, we can discover a 'forgotten' truth in this question discussed in the schools, which is not without some significance for our religious life.

We will come closer to the proper meaning of this thomistic doctrine, if we try to discover how it originated. The application of the notions of 'matter' and 'form' to the sacraments as a whole was not made until the first decades of the thirteenth century, partially replacing the older notions of '*res*' (*elementum*) and '*verbum*'. Now, before the question as to what is the matter and form in the sacrament of Penance was first asked in the thirteenth century, there had already been a question (in the twelfth century) as to what in general is the sacramental *sign* of this sacrament, in contradistinction to the effect as such. The almost universal answer[27] given to this question during the whole of the twelfth century was, however, that the external penitential acts of the penitent are the sacramental sign, and above all his confession or the imposed penance. It should be noted, in parenthesis, that if, here and there,[28] the absolution given by the priest was already regarded as the sacramental sign, this opinion is only apparently identical with the Church's present-day teaching. For practically nowhere in the twelfth and thirteenth century (up to the time of St Thomas), did speculative theology regard Absolution as the sacramental process which *effects* the cleansing from guilt as such before God. Speculative theology attributed other, even though supernatural, effects to Absolution, and regarded the contrition of the penitent (caused in him by grace) as the sole cause, even in the sacrament, of the cleansing from guilt in the strict sense. But to return to the then prevalent explanation of the sacramental sign: we should not be surprised at this explanation. Both in the practice and in the theology of the early Middle Ages, the personal doing of penance by the sinner through contrition, confession and satisfaction (all done, indeed, before, and under the direction of, the Church) stood so much in the foreground of consciousness, that theology until the time of St Thomas saw the proper cause of forgiveness of guilt in this personal penance and in this love given by God. All that remained then to be attributed to the priestly absolution (the necessity of which was never disputed) were other effects, such as, for instance, the forgiveness of the *punishment* due to sin, etc. If it was asked from this point of view as to which is the sacramental sign of the sacrament of Penance, the answer could in consequence merely lie in—the acts of the penitent. And so, when, in the middle of the thirteenth century, theologians turned slowly and hesitatingly to the question of how they could distinguish between matter and form in the sacramental sign of the sacrament of Penance (because they were trying to apply this distinction to all the sacraments), the answers necessarily took on very different and undecided forms in view of the above situation, viz. the

[27] The materials for this will be found in B. Poschmann, *Die abendländische Kirchenbusse im frühen Mittelalter* (Breslau 1930); P. Anciaux, *La Théologie du Sacrement de Pénitence au XIIe siècle* (Louvain 1949).

[28] Cf. Anciaux, pp. 146 *sq.*, 376, 382.

general opinion that the acts of the penitent are the sign and that the Absolution has no causal effect on the cleansing from guilt as such. We do not need to enter here into the theory propounded by High Scholasticism before the middle of the thirteenth century on this question.

At this time (shortly before St Thomas and through St Thomas himself) the original and early tradition of the Church was successfully given a clear formulation in the new set of concepts. This was achieved first of all with regard to the sacramental causality towards guilt as such: Absolution by the Church exercises a sacramental causality on the cleansing from guilt as such. This is the decisive step forward which was taken by the theologians of this period (William of Auvergne, Hugh of St Cher, William of Meliton, Bonaventure, Thomas Aquinas)[29] in the clarification of the theology of Penance; we are not, however, concerned with this here. But this very step forward also made it clear that the Absolution, which cleanses from guilt, *is* therefore also necessarily the sacramental sign, or at least belongs to it as a necessary and constitutive moment. Now St Thomas, being the conservative and harmonizing genius which he is everywhere in his theology, could not and would not simply discard the theological thesis, traditional for one and a half centuries and still current in his day, according to which the acts of the penitent are the sacramental sign in the sacrament of Penance. The two notions of matter and form give him the possibility of working the traditional thesis and the newly won understanding into a harmonious synthesis. Thus, the acts of the penitent belong to the sacramental sign (this is where the older view is right); they are the matter, the one element in the sacramental sign which must be formed and further determined, and which signifies and calls forth the divine forgiveness. But the absolution given by the priest also belongs to this sacramental sign (this is where the new view is right); it is the form, the determining element in the totality of the sacramental sign which puts the final stamp on the acts of the penitent, and by which alone these acts are given their ultimate meaning. The (moral, not physical) union in meaning of the tangible penance done by man before the visible Church and the forgiving,

[29] Cf. for the above mentioned theologians: Valens Heynck, 'Zur Busslehre des hl. Bonaventura', *Franziskanische Studien* XXXVI (1954), pp. 1–81; for St Thomas: III, q. 84, a. 1 corp., ad 1, ad 2, ad 3; a. 3; a. 4, ad 3; a. 7 corp.; q. 86, a. 6 corp.; q. 89, a. 1, ad 2.

authoritative discharge given by the Church forms the unity of a sign, which signifies the divine forgiveness and which, by signifying it, effects it, i.e. allows it to become an actual happening.

Within this totality of the sign (and only thus), the priestly absolution (understood as 'form') is, for St Thomas, the decisive element as regards the causal *effect*[30]; the acts of the penitent, however, are the more important element as far as the *sign*-function as such is concerned.[31] These two elements of the one sign, in so far as they are ordained to one another by their very nature, can together also form the unity of the one signifying and effective sign.

It can be seen from this that St Thomas does not arrive at the theory, that the acts of the penitent are the matter of the sacramental sign, by the consideration that the judicial verdict of the Church requires a 'matter' (as has often been done since, in order to try to 'prove' his thesis[32]). Indeed, such a proof would merely show objectively that there must be an object for the Church's pronouncement of a sentence, to which it can refer, and so this would not go beyond the Scotist theory. St. Thomas' sole proof (which, it should be remembered, he does not at all work out fully and on which he does not at all reflect) is rather the usual scholastic doctrine which was held before his time, viz. that within the one totality of the ecclesiastical process of penance, the personal act of the penitent has an effective influence on the cleansing from guilt and is not merely an extrinsic *conditio sine qua non* for the latter, as it is in the case of baptism (according to St Thomas). One could even say that this teaching of St Thomas was inspired by his deep theological instinct which urges him to let the personal and sacramental moments in the process of justification permeate one another as intimately as possible. This instinct does not allow him to recognize two separate 'ways' of justification, but urges him to regard the personal and sacramental elements—both of them in and before the Church—as two sides or phases of the one process, which demand and condition each other.[33] The reason why he was able to carry this basic theological conception through, particularly in

[30] III, q. 86, a. 6 corp. [31] In IV Sent. dist. 22, q. 2, sol. 2.

[32] Cf. e.g. Chr. Pesch, *Praelectiones dogmaticae* VII 4–5 (Freiburg 1920), no. 79.

[33] Cf. on this: K. Rahner, 'Personal and Sacramental Piety', pp. 109–133 above; H. Schillebeeckx, O.P., *De Sakramenteele Heilseconomie* (Antwerp 1952).

the case of the sacrament of Penance (and more clearly there than in the case of other sacraments), lies, it is true, in the peculiar situation of the theology of Penance at his time, which moved the acts of the penitent to an even more central position in the sacrament of Penance than in the other sacraments.

It would be most superficial to attempt to see in this thomistic theory merely a clever verbal harmonization of objectively quite different points of view, and to admit in this way that Scotus[34] was right after all. Scotus, taking his departure precisely from this newly won position of St Thomas, transposed the sacramentality of the whole process of Penance exclusively into the priestly absolution, because this is ordained authoritatively and effectively to the cleansing from guilt itself, which St Thomas had been the first to make theologians see. With St Thomas it is a question (it seems to us), not merely of including in his theory an opinion of the schools which has existed before him, but of conceptually working into that theory a *genuine* tradition from the time of the Fathers. We can give only a very brief indication here of the proof of this statement, without going into the various pieces of evidence. The Fathers see first of all an essential difference between baptism and ecclesiastical Penance.[35] Baptism is forgiveness by free favour, a new creation, simply remission, sheer direct action of the Blood of Christ. Penance (even as a sacrament) is laborious atonement, baptism in one's own tears, not rebirth of a sudden kind, but a slow bitter cure by one's own efforts (even though these must be supported by the grace of God). And the Fathers refer this difference not merely to the cleansing from the temporal *punishment* due to sins but to the remission of guilt itself.[36] They see this difference not merely in the relation of baptism to the cleansing from sin after baptism which takes place extra-sacramentally, but in the

[34] Cf. N. Krautwig, *Die Grundlagen der Busslehre des J. Duns Skotus* (Freiburg 1938), pp. 133 *sq.*

[35] Cf. e.g. B. Poschmann, *Paenitentia secunda*, pp. 161, 239, 241 *sq.*, 285, 287 *sq.*, 400 *sq.*, 409, 413, 427–435; B. Poschmann, 'Die kirchliche Vermittlung der Sündenvergebung nach Augustinus', ZKT XLV (1921), pp. 208–228 etc. (esp. pp. 210–214); K. Rahner: RSR XXXVII (1950), pp. 52–69, 73–79, 96 *sq.*

[36] This (objectively correct) distinction which was as yet foreign to the Fathers, must not be arbitrarily introduced into their teaching to the effect that the sinner after baptism must get rid of his *sins* differently from the candidate for baptism.

relation of baptism to the cleansing from sin which constitutes the penitential process regulated by the Church terminating in the reconciliation with and by the Church. If personal penance were only an extrinsic *conditio sine qua non* even in the sacrament of Penance,[37] then this difference between the two sacraments as such could not be maintained, or at least could be maintained only with regard to the temporal *punishment* due to sins. In view of this difference between the two sacraments, it is also not possible to hold that subjective penance has an effect on the cleansing from sin precisely in so far as these acts are *meritorious*. It is true that they are meritorious. But that is true also of the personal preparation for baptism (in so far as this normally includes faith, contrition and love), and so this circumstance does not constitute a difference between the two sacraments. This difference can, therefore, lie only in the fact that in contrast to baptism, subjective penance, done before and in the Church, is itself an intrinsic co-constitutive element of the sacramental happening and hence of the positing of the sacramental sign.[38] However, the act of the Church, her forgiveness, also belongs to this very happening, for it also is effectively ordained to the cleansing from sin. Hence both of these facts cannot be true at the same time unless the subjective and ecclesi-

[37] As it is in the case of baptism, which fact is emphasized also by the Fathers: cf. P. Galtier, *L'Eglise et la rémission des péchés* (Paris 1932), pp. 51 *sqq.*

[38] The *inner* reason for this difference is understandable: the baptized sinner is still a member of the Church. His actions in and before the Church are, therefore, an expression of the life of the Church (in contrast to the actions of the unbaptized), and can, therefore, more easily have the character of a sacramental (even though merely partial) sign than the activity of an unbaptized person. This does not imply that an unbaptized person must in every case be incapable of positing a sacramental sign (an unbaptized person can at least baptize, after all). Such exceptions are based on the historical and free nature of the divine institution of the sacraments; they do not prove that the sacraments are not intended by their nature to be posited by members of the Church and as deeds of the Church. Added to this, in our case, is the fact that the sins of the unbaptized are sins which do not incriminate the Church considered as the visible saving community. It is different in the case of the baptized. He does penance, therefore, as a member of the Church. His penance as *such* is, therefore, an expression of the life of the Church as such. The fact that *this* penance, in contrast to that of the candidate for baptism, is included in the sacramental sign-nature of the sacrament, has thereby its meaning (even though perhaps not its strict necessity) from the very nature of things.

astical penance of the sinner and the Church's word of forgiveness combine (before there is any question of the effect) in one unified sign of the interior event of grace which is the remission of guilt, and constitute together the one sign of forgiveness. St Thomas is, therefore, absolutely right in calling the 'acts of the penitent' the *matter*, and the priestly absolution the *form* of the sacrament. He merely states in scholastic terms what had always been the conviction of the Fathers.

If we try to get a clearer idea of what is contained in this thomistic thesis, by approaching it in a somewhat less abstract and scholastic form, it will perhaps become clear why we think that there is a 'forgotten truth' hidden in it. We can do this even if someone were of the opinion that the theological proof for the thomistic thesis is not beyond all doubt. For we have the right, even under this presupposition, to entrust ourselves without fear to the authority of the 'Prince of the schools'.

To begin with: if the thomistic thesis is correct (and is really understood), then the penitent sinner co-posits the sacramental sign and hence is also a subordinate cause (of a sacramental-instrumental kind) of the sacramental grace. He is not only the passive recipient of this grace but is the one who, together with the priest, actively celebrates the sacred *mysterium* itself which is the sacramental cause of the grace which he receives. Matrimony, or, for instance, the priest's Communion in his own Sacrifice, provide us with similar cases. We may not on this account, it is true, call the penitent the 'minister' of the sacrament of Penance in the proper sense, for he does not give the absolution but only receives it, and his own penitential act does not presuppose any new authorization of an official kind in the proper sense. But it remains true to say that, in the thomistic theory, the penitent is an associate cause of the sacramental sign and hence of the sacramental grace, with the causality of an instrument and of a sign. By his confession and request for forgiveness, the penitent lends his interior penitential disposition a concrete form and a tangible character in the ecclesiastical sphere (i.e. in the public forum of the Church, no matter how discreetly a public form this may take) and in the presence of the Church—he incarnates that disposition, so to speak, historically. By doing so, he creates a reality in the dimension of the Church which, given the response and the transformation by the forgiving answer of the Church, becomes the sign of the effective presence of God's forgiving grace.

In a sacred process of mystery, he himself—the sinner, that is—provides God's pressing will of forgiveness in the Church with its matter in which this forgiveness becomes concrete and thus effective in this particular sinner. He who has ratified the black godlessness of the world by his guilt and has increased it in his own person, is permitted to prepare the means himself by which the invisible grace of God comes to shine out even in a concrete historical manner. The readiness of the sinner to accept God's grace (if it should come to him by free favour), which occurs and manifests itself within the sphere of the Church, becomes itself, under the response of the Church and with her forgiveness, the sacred sign *of the fact that* this grace really comes to pass here and now. His 'Come' is transformed into a 'Here I am'; man's cry becomes itself part of God's answer. If the carrying out of the sacraments is 'liturgy' in the proper sense of the word, then the confessing sinner celebrates a part of the Church's liturgy and does not merely receive the effect of someone else's liturgical action. In him, too, the Church acts and executes her liturgy. A staggering liturgy this, the liturgy of the Church of sinners, the solemnly regulated appearance of the Church of sinners before the seat of grace of the Father Who holds the Cross of the Son; the liturgy of the prodigal son which consists in man's confessing himself before the holy God to be what he is of himself, namely a sinner; the sacrifice of praise by the lips which God himself must open, even if it is 'merely' a question of preventing them from denying one's own sinfulness as a result of being both proud and cowardly at the same time; the prize of grace in the confession of guilt. The early Church celebrated this terrible and healing liturgy of the Church of sinners most 'solemnly' (if we may say so) in her penitential discipline.[39] The 'celebrant' of this liturgy wore a special vestment for this, viz. the penitential robe; he fasted and wept; over and over again during the long period of penance he let the representative of Christ impose hands upon him, in prayer and in exorcism of the powers of darkness; the whole congregation celebrated with him, praying and interceding on his behalf. This liturgy took place in the presence of the whole saintly congregation; the distance from the pure bliss of the Altar, which was both punishment and healing, was clearly brought out. The priest (bishop) took

[39] Cf. J. A. Jungmann, *Die lateinischen Bussriten in ihrer geschichtlichen Entwicklung* (Innsbruck 1932).

part in the prayer and fasting. He made his grace-giving word of forgiveness still more tangible and clear by his imposition of the hand (which was probably done ever since the time of the Apostles: 1 Tim 5.20–22).[40] Today this liturgy is quite sober—indeed, it is often mistaken for a primitive psycho-therapeutic consultation of hideous profanity; it is the liturgy of the Confessional. But perhaps this liturgy is in its kind most expressive for anyone who can see by faith, just because it is so sober: the liturgy of poor little sinners, of the mediocre and the weak, who are too poor and feeble to say and do more than what is absolutely necessary. Perhaps the liturgy thus expresses even better today what man is: a poor being which is just able to call for the mercy of God in a weak, almost dying whisper, and whose little lamentation is already enveloped by the loud, powerful utterance of mercy which fills all spaces: ego te absolvo. Christian Pesch is right when he says in sober theological language: 'If someone denies that the *acts* of the *penitent* cause grace *ex opere operato*, then he is objectively on the side of Scotus, even if he says that these acts are the "matter" and "parts" of the sacrament of Penance.'[41] What we have just stated, therefore, gives a completely true interpretation of the meaning of the thomistic conception. No one will be able to dispute the fact that we usually forget this significance of the personal acts in the sacrament of Penance, even if the tradition of the thomistic conception is carried on in the textbooks.

Why and how can the 'penitential' deed of the sinner in the dimension of the Church be itself, even though only together with the priestly absolution, the sign of the effective presence of God's grace of forgiveness? First of all we must reflect on the fact that the penitent sinner is a Christian. The grace of Christ in the Church, therefore, does not flow towards him as towards someone who is 'outside' (as in the case of a candidate for baptism). He is himself already a member of the Church, his penitential activity (unlike that of someone to be baptized) is already based on the character of baptism and on the historical tangibility of his belonging to the Church. Hence whenever that activity takes place before the Church (as in this case) and wherever it is directed towards her sacramental action of grace, it takes place *as* act of the *member* of the Church in the sacramental public

[40] Cf. P. Galtier, *Aux origines du sacrement de pénitence* (Rome 1951).
[41] *Praelectiones dogmaticae* VII 4/5 (Freiburg 1920), no. 74.

forum of the Church, no matter how unobtrusively it may be done in the obscurity of the Confessional; it has, therefore, an ecclesiological explicitness; it is itself *ecclesiastical*. Since this activity is, however, necessarily supported and caused by the anticipatory and supernatural saving grace of God, and since it thus renders its own divine basis tangible in the historical here and now (which is done by any effect for its cause), the penitential activity of the Christian is also the sign of the anticipatory effectiveness of *divine* grace in the sinner. In so far as this very grace is grace of the Church, since all grace is grace of the Body of Christ (i.e. from this Body and directed towards it), and in so far as it is given as a gift to this baptized sinner *qua* member of the Church (as her vital force), the personal penance of the baptized person is a manifestation of grace both as divine and as of the Church. Hence, the personal doing of penance by the baptized Christian is, in so far as he comes to the Church, already a sign and appearance of further divine and ecclesiastical grace in the dimension of the official and sacramental public forum of the Church. This personal penance of the baptized is not yet simply by that fact and by itself alone an *ex opere operato effective* sign of the sacramental remission of guilt—for this it is required that the priestly absolution, the response of the Church, be joined up with it. But it is easily seen from what has been said, that the personal penance done by the baptized before the Church is in itself *suited* to cooperate in constituting this one effective sacramental sign of divine forgiveness and that it is also orientated *to* the Church's forgiveness together with which it is meant to constitute the one sacramental sign.

4. The Prayer of the Church

When the priest exercises his office of messenger of the effective word of reconciliation, he says the *Misereatur* . . . and the *Indulgentiam* . . . before he pronounces the *Ego te absolvo*. But how often does he not say these words thoughtlessly and hurriedly, if he does not omit them altogether because he must hurry as there are many waiting outside his Confessional and these little prayers really do not belong to the necessary '*forma sacramenti*'. The penitent, in his turn, will only too often wait eagerly until these prayers are past and he hears the longed for '*Ego te absolvo*' which he understands much better. In most cases he will not know or notice at all that what the priest whispers between the giving of the penance and the *Ego te absolvo* is already familiar to him from the prayers at the foot of the altar at the beginning of Holy Mass. But even in the Mass he will seldom come to 'experience' that in such a request and intercessory prayer for liberation from guilt this freeing from guilt can become a real event; he is too much caught up in the constricting impression that such a thing happens simply in Confession and that such prayers are merely pious wishes which, if they are fulfilled, realize themselves, in the normal course of events (indeed, almost exclusively), in Confession. How many priests and faithful have the concrete experience—such as they have sometimes experienced in Confession—that even a truly genuine *Confiteor* . . . can be a grace-giving event of real forgiveness of sin on the part of God,[42] so that they begin the Sacrifice of the Mass as different persons from what they were when they gathered round the altar for the preparatory prayers?

What exactly is the meaning of these little wishes expressed before the absolution? They can no longer be called 'prayer', strictly speaking, since they do not address God at all but the penitent. They are a small relic of that part of the old penitential liturgy in which the Church made intercession for her member and prayed with him since she suffered with her member in his guilt. But what does this intercessory prayer of the old penitential liturgy mean? When we speak of the sacrament of Penance, our regard is more often than not strangely confined to seeing only the particular event which alone can be called 'sacrament' in the strict sense and, in fact, can be distinguished as a sacrament from other sacraments. And we moreover attach importance in this only to what is absolutely required—and sufficient—for the constitution of this sacrament. In this way we isolate the sacrament

[42] Even though, naturally, not of a sacramental kind. We may mention in passing that in a sober theological treatment one would have to be careful in maintaining that such a remission is 'surer' in the sacrament than outside it where it happens merely '*ex opere operantis*'. For, given the corresponding necessary personal disposition, then it is possible to have the certainty even outside the sacrament which can be attained in the sacrament, because the success even of the sacrament depends on this disposition. If one wished to insist on the fact that 'imperfect contrition' suffices in the sacrament, whereas 'perfect contrition' is required outside the sacrament, then it must be remembered that the 'difficulty' of 'perfect contrition' consists precisely in something which is also required for 'imperfect contrition', viz. in the honest renunciation of sin considered as an offence against God. If this, however, is truly present, it is hard to see what special and new difficulty should be presented by contrition out of *love* for God.

from the totality of human and Church life, from the whole penance of man and the Church in which the sacrament is embedded and which leads to it and springs forth from it. We know all this, it is true, but we forget it. We need only ask ourselves some time what has all happened already in terms of supernatural events when a Christian stands outside the Confessional. Augustine[43] would say: he has already been raised by the word and grace of Christ from the tomb of sin like a Lazarus (not that he necessarily has already obtained the remission of guilt which is freely given to him by his being loosed by the Church); he has already begun to live, he needs 'only' now to be loosed by the Apostles from the fetters of sin. But the tomb *is* already open and the power of Christ, which is life, has already taken hold of him. Indeed, consider, in the light of the simplest principles of the Faith, what must already have happened before Confession and absolution! There has been a miracle of grace. For only in that way does a man come to that repentance without which the sacrament would be a sacrilege. There is no contrition of any significance for salvation unless God's gratuitous grace has already anticipated man *so that* he may be able to repent and actually does repent, since the capacity and the actual doing are God's grace. But this miracle of grace does not simply fall from heaven. It too has an incarnational nature: it is the miracle of the grace *of Christ*. It is conditioned by the historical event of Christ and of his Cross, by the preaching of the Word of God in the Church; it may depend on the example and word of another Christian which in the last analysis does also originate again in the grace of God; it is given as a gift to man, because and in so far as he is baptized and a member of the Church. Even before the *Ego te absolvo* there has already taken place a miracle of grace in the *Church*. And this miracle is also sustained by the intercessory prayer of the Church. We already find testimony of this intercessory prayer of the Church for sinners in the New Testament—it is so important there, that its refusal to certain sinners constitutes the gravest rebuff imaginable to a sinner by the Church: 1 Jn 5.16, and also in the Didache,[44] in Tertullian[45] and from then

[43] E.g. *In Joan. tract.* XLIX,24; XXII,7; Sermo LXVII 1,2; Sermo CCXCV 3,2; Sermo CCCLII 3,8 (and not 38, as stated in the German text. *Tr.*). Cf. B. Poschmann: ZKT XLV (1921), pp. 214 *sqq.*

[44] *Didache* 8, 2.3; 14, 1.

[45] *De paenit.* 10,5 *sq.* Cf. K. Rahner, 'Zur Theologie der Busse bei Tertullian' (cf. above, note 6, p. 138), pp. 152–154.

onwards over and over again in the Fathers.[46] Christ prays in the Church for the penitent, and this prayer is gladly granted, says Tertullian. The Fathers of the Church emphasize over and over again that the sinner is freed from his burden by the 'prayer' of the Church and above all of her episcopal representatives—especially when, liturgically speaking, the intercessory prayer of the *whole* congregation in *direct* conjunction with the penitential process had receded into the background. And by this 'prayer' must not be understood here merely the 'absolution'; it really refers (also) to the intercession made by the Church for the sinner. Because the Church prays and does penance in her Saints and justified members, God anticipates the sinner with his grace and leads him to the conversion without which no absolution is of any avail and which itself leads to salvation, in a case of necessity, even without priestly absolution. (It is obvious, of course, that this intercession and penance of the Church springs itself again from nothing other than the grace of God and the power of the Cross. But this itself again does not rule out the fact that such a deed done by someone is significant for the salvation of others.) When the penitent Christian comes to the Church's sacrament, the Church does not only not start her work on him, but she even *has* already done her greater work on him. For his interior conversion is also already the work of the praying Church.

In earlier times the Church included this work more tangibly and in a more developed form in the sacramental liturgy of the remission of sins: the bishop imposed hands (and this quite frequently during the period of penance) with prayers and exorcisms, the congregation assisted in this prayer and there was a proper penitential liturgy joined to the Eucharistic Sacrifice.[47] In the early Middle Ages the priest and penitent knelt before the altar and said long prayers together; the priest had to fast before he administered the sacrament, etc.[48]

[46] Cf. e.g. St Augustine, sermo CCCXCII,3 (*agite paenitentiam, qualis agitur in ecclesia, ut oret pro vobis ecclesia*); St Ambrose, *De paenit.* I. 15, 80; St Jerome, *Dial. contra Lucif.* V; Epist. LXXVII,4 *sq.*; St Pacian, *Parenesis* X (*exoratricem Ecclesiam deprecari*); St Leo the Great, Epist. CVIII,2 (Denz 146: . . . *supplicationibus sacerdotum* . . .); Sozomen, *Hist. Eccl.* VII, 16. Cf. also B. Poschmann, *Der Ablass im Licht der Bussgeschichte* (Bonn 1948), pp. 10–13.

[47] Cf. above all J. A. Jungmann, *Die lateinischen Bussriten* (Innsbruck 1932).

[48] Cf. e.g. apart from Jungmann, the different 'Ordines paenitentiae' in H. J. Schmitz, *Die Busskirche und die Bussdisziplin der Kirche* I (Mainz 1883),

Today all that has diminished and has become much more unobtrusive: a short expression of the desire to forgive, addressed directly to the penitent. But it should remind us of what is still true and actual today when we come to the Church to beg for forgiveness: she has already borne our guilt together with us, suffering by it and helping to atone for it when we became hardened in this guilt; she already sought us in her prayers when we were still obstructing the reign of her Spirit in us; she had already met us with her love when we were still indifferent to it; we came to her because she has sought us out. And when she now completes the work of reconciliation in us by the authority of Christ, she can do this because she had already begun it a long time ago in her prayer.

5. Loosing on earth and in heaven

When we read in the Scriptures about the power given to the Apostles to 'loose' sins in such a way that they are loosed also in heaven, we think instinctively and as it were naturally of the power of according the sinner forgiveness of his sins, in the name of God and by commission of Christ Our Lord, in such a way that the annihilation of his guilt through God's grace of forgiveness becomes an event in him here and now in a sacramental process (similar to that of baptism), and all this precisely on account of these words addressed to the Apostles. To understand the Bible text in this way is absolutely correct (especially with a view also to the commission given by Christ in Jn 20), and indeed we can recognize this immediately and historically as being the interpretation already given to the text by the early Church from the third century onwards. But if we think that we have thereby exhausted the meaning of these words, then a more careful exegesis, and the mind of the early Church, will show us that we have not done full justice to the content of this text and have overlooked part of it. Not the essential and decisive part, certainly. For all that matters ultimately is that God forgives us our trespasses and that precisely *this*

pp. 75 *sqq.*, 87 *sqq.*, 98 *sqq.*, 239 *sqq.*, 397 *sqq.*, 471 *sqq.* These Ordines are still alive today—at least in writing—in the Pontificale Romanum, which still contain a solemn episcopal liturgy of penance for Ash Wednesday and Holy Thursday.

forgiveness is given a tangible sacramental form and an effective presence in our life by the word of the Church. And yet it is not as if the further content of truth and reality of these words regarding the earthly and heavenly loosing of sins could remain indifferent to us, simply because we have understood the decisive and most important thing properly and have let it become a reality in the Church in the sacrament of Penance.

We are already partially prepared to grasp what more there is in these words, by what we said above about the 'binding on earth'. For the meaning both of 'binding' and 'loosing' obviously becomes clearer by the antithetical nature of these terms. And what is even more important (and something which is not taken into consideration by the customary view about the meaning of 'binding' which we mentioned above) is that we can surmise from the very outset that the loosing by the Church to which Mt 16 and 18 refer, does not simply represent an alternative for binding but refers to the very binding undertaken by the Church—in other words, that the person to be loosed is loosed precisely from the ban imposed by the Church. This is the most obvious thought purely linguistically, simply because in this context there is no question whatsoever of any other restraint which could be loosed. If, therefore, any kind of meaning can be gathered from the text in this particular direction, it must be preferred to other meanings. Now we saw that 'to bind on earth' means the showing forth, by the official authority of the Church, of the distance which has arisen in the public sacramental sphere and through man's fault, not only between God and the sinner but also between the Church and the sinful member of the Church. It is to be noted that this 'binding' contains a twofold element of 'distancing', viz. the one which arises through man's guilt itself, and the one which is set up by the Church's act and by the Church herself. These two moments are to each other as nature is to connatural manifestation, or as a thing is to its constitutive expression. It therefore followed from this also that, in the case of grave sin, this expression (the 'binding') *must* in principle ensue on the part of the Church and before the Church, and that the Church's first reaction to the guilt of her members is always a 'binding'. The first element itself is again insolubly bound up with the guilt before God. Precisely because and in so far as this guilt is present, the person has (by that very fact) put himself at a distance also from holy Church, and so the Church must (in the case of grave sin) put herself at a distance from the sinner by binding and banning him. She can, therefore, lift her ban (*Bindung*) only when she knows that the guilt is also forgiven before God 'in heaven' and that the sinner is also loosed in heaven. Now the words of our Lord state, however, that this very thing happens *by the fact that* the Church looses the sinner 'on earth', i.e. looses him from the ban imposed by her and (since this cannot have meaning or be possible in any other way) looses him also from the cause of this ban, i.e. from the ecclesiological side of his guilt. This means, therefore, that the remission of guilt in heaven is not simply and solely a presupposition for the loosing on earth but is also, moreover, its *effect*. It means, therefore, that if and because you loose something on earth, it will be loosed also in heaven—however much the effective loosing on earth naturally presupposed the repentant return of man to God, and however much the change in the relationship of man to God and to the Church which comes about through the loosing in heaven and on earth, represents basically only the two sides of the one unified process.

What meaning, and what increase of meaning, is given then to these texts beyond the meaning given to them by the usual, correct but inadequate interpretation? These texts now signify: when you have bound a sinner on account of his guilt in the face of God and against the holy Church ('on earth', i.e. in the visible sphere of holy Church) and when you then—on the sinner's repentant return—loose *these* bonds (his officially manifested distance from the Church) in the perceptible sphere of the Church by your sovereign act, forgiving him thereby his ecclesiological guilt, then he is also loosed *by* and *through* this from his state of guilt before God (from his 'bound state in heaven') and then he is also recognized once more 'in heaven' as a free member of the Congregation of Christ, animated by his Spirit, with all the rights and graces of such a member. The Church grants the sinner peace with God in granting him the gift of *her* peace and by once more according him her spiritual love in an authoritative manner.[49]

This is also how the Fathers understood this text. By receiving the peace of the Church, we receive the Spirit of the Father, says Cyprian (Epist. LVII, 4). By the fact that they (the sinners) are restored to

[49] Cf. 2 Cor 2. 5–11: the sinner is once more granted access to the agape of the Church in due form (cf. Kittel, *Theol. Wörterbuch* III, pp. 1098 *sq.*).

peace with the Church, they receive the pledge of life (Epist. LV, 13). Peace with the Church remits sins, estrangement from the peace of the Church retains sins, says Augustine (*De bapt. contra Donat.* III, 18.23). Or St Augustine again in another place: 'The *Church's* love which is poured out into men's hearts by the Holy Spirit, remits the sins of those who participate in this love, and retains the sins of those who have no participation in it' (*In Joan.* tract. CXXI, 4). 'The City of God renders man guiltless by receiving him into herself' (*Contra Cresc.* II, 16).

Elsewhere too—however little the remission of guilt before God was overlooked, indeed as clearly as this final outcome was kept in view—the final result of the whole penitential process is characterized above all and before all else as 'peace with the Church', 'communion' (with the Church), 'reconciliation with the Altar', full 'return into the tower of the Church', 'reincorporation into the Church', etc. Even during the early Middle Ages, indeed until right into the thirteenth century,[50] there still persists the clear consciousness of the fact that absolution given by the priest is a 'being received into the Church as someone healed',[51] an introduction into the Church of Christ,[52] etc. This is true, even although it was perhaps no longer so clear in this connection that all this is not only *one* effect of the priest's absolution *among* others, but the first effect in the objective, ontological order *through* which the other effects—especially the remission of guilt before God—are attained. Indeed St Bonaventure still says that Confession was directly instituted so that man could be reconciled again with the Church and so that his reconciliation with (through) God might thus become manifest (In IV Sent. dist. 17, q. 3, a. 2, fund. 2). And St Thomas says that, by the sacrament, man must be reconciled not only with God but also with the Church (IV Sent. dist. 17, q. 3, a. 3, qc. 5, ad 3).[53] The decisive factor for this testimony of

[50] Cf. e.g. Anciaux, *loc. cit.*, pp. 277, 290, 320, 321, 344, 350, 453, 496, 499, 503, 504, 516. A. Landgraf, 'Sünde und Trennung von der Kirche in der Frühscholastik', *Scholastik* V (1930), pp. 210–247. Cf. also V. Heynck, *loc. cit.*, pp. 14, 17, 34[93], 40, 45 (Lombard), 52[160] (Hugh Ripelin of Strasbourg).

[51] Anciaux, p. 170[1].

[52] Richard of St Victor (PL 196, 1172).

[53] When St Thomas says about venial sin (in opposition to mortal sin) that '*nec indiget reconciliatione ad Ecclesiam*' (IV Sent. dist. 17, q.3, a.3, sol.3), the stress is on the *indiget*; it does not, therefore, need to be denied

the Fathers is, however, the practice of the early Church (and the Fathers' explanation of this practice). The 'public' penance is as such the sacrament of Penance; it is not merely a disciplinary measure taken by the Church and running concurrently with the sacrament, i.e. a 'censure' in the current canonical sense. This is why the Fathers (e.g. Tertullian, Cyprian, Origen) keep emphasizing the fact that the sinner must first of all be 'bound' (at least through the exclusion from the Eucharist) in order to be capable of being loosed. One cannot really explain why the whole process of sacramental remission of sins as such took the particular form it actually did take in the early Church, if one does not realize that the early Church clearly and consciously recognized an ecclesiological aspect in this sacramental process as such. We mean by this that she saw sin as an offence against the Church and looked on forgiveness also as a remission of the guilt of such an offence against the *Church*, as a reconciliation with the Church. And so, in accordance with the Scriptures, she regarded this very reconciliation with the Church as the means to reconciliation with God. We must—one could say in the spirit of Cyprian— be reconciled again with our Mother the Church in order to be in a position to have God for our Father once more. Even though, given the present-day external structure of the sacrament of Penance, this aspect has receded more into the background in the case of a 'Confession of devotion', it is nevertheless still there even today. This needs no further proof after what has been said above about mortal sin considered as an exclusion from the Eucharist and even venial sin as an offence against the Church, and about Confession and its acceptance considered as the distance of the sinner from the Church becoming officially and publicly visible. But these truths should become less 'forgotten' truths.

The following would be a brief exposition in scholastic concepts of what has been said: The state of being reconciled again with the Church is the '*res et sacramentum*' of the sacrament of Penance. As is well known, we make a distinction with regard to the sacraments between the sacramental sign (*sacramentum*), the effect of grace which is the ultimate object of the sign-causality of the sacrament (*res*

---

that when venial sins are confessed, the absolution has, as in the case of mortal sins (even according to St. Thomas), the character of an (analogous) reconciliation with the Church.

sacramenti) and an intermediary reality between these two which has both the character of the sign with reference to the 'res sacramenti' and also the character of the effect in relation to the sacramental sign, and is, therefore, called the '*res et sacramentum*'. A more precise analysis of those sacraments in which such an intermediate factor between sign and effect is most clearly perceptible, shows that this factor always has an ecclesiological character. Thus: the character of baptism which means that a person is permanently directed to the Church as her member, the character of Holy Orders which is the appointed mandate of one's station in the Church—and the deeper incorporation into the Mystical Body of Christ through communal reception of his Body in the Eucharist.

Now in the High Middle Ages, the 'internal disposition of penance' was designated the '*res et sacramentum*' of the sacrament of Penance in so far as it is the effect and not merely the presupposition of the sacrament; in modern theology, thinking in terms of purely formal, legal niceties, it is 'the right to the grace of the sacrament' which is held to be the '*res et sacramentum*' of this sacrament. For reasons which we cannot explain just now, these explanations do not satisfy. If one does not wish to abandon altogether (as is in part the case today) any attempt to find such an intermediate reality between sign and effect in this sacrament, the most meaningful answer, historically and objectively, is that in the sacrament of Penance the forgivingness of the Church towards the sinner is the '*res et sacramentum*'. This no more endangers the character of the *opus operatum* in the sacrament of Penance than is the case in the sacrament of baptism. In the latter case this intermediate reality is made to consist in the character of baptism considered as the first incorporation into the Church; the intermediate reality in this case is regarded as that real right which gives the recipient a claim to the actual reception of the grace of justification in baptism, as long as there is no obstacle placed in its way by the unbelief or the impenitence of the recipient of baptism. In so far as man, therefore, through the process of reconciliation with the Church (*sacramentum*: loosing on earth), enters once more into the state of being fully reconciled with the Church (res et sacramentum: *pax et communio cum Ecclesia*), he necessarily receives a (new or more profound) share in her Spirit which forgives guilt and justifies before God (*res sacramenti*: peace with God). This intermediate reality does not always require to be stressed in baptism (and is not, in fact, stressed in the formula of baptism, and very rarely and slightly in the old Tradition[54]). Instead, the proceedings of baptism are directly connected in the explicit formulation with the final effect of baptism (baptism for forgiveness of sin, for the gift of the Holy Spirit), although there certainly is a character of baptism which constitutes that intermediate reality. Similarly, this intermediate reality does not always require to be stressed in the case of the sacrament of Penance (neither in the words of its form nor throughout its theological description), and yet it must not be denied objectively. The basic conception of the nature of the Church points in the same direction, when it is again emphasized more strongly today that the Church is the 'Proto-sacrament'. In fact, this old doctrine about the *pax cum Ecclesia* as '*res et sacramentum*', which is old in substance if not in its explicit formulation, gains more and more adherents in modern times.[55] It does not really matter so very much in the end about the formulation; what matters is the very essence of the facts. And these facts, it seems to us, are at any rate given in the forgotten truth: '*non . . . adhuc* Ecclesiae *reconciliatus est . . . nisi prius sacerdote absolvatur*' (unless the priest absolves him first, he is not yet reconciled with the Church), as St Thomas puts it.

If we stop there, this does not mean that we have even touched on all the 'forgotten' truths in the theology of the sacrament of Penance. There still remains a lot to be said. We will end by simply mentioning a few things at random.

Theologians speak about the penance imposed by the Church in the sacrament (i.e. the satisfaction) as belonging to the sacramental sign itself (even though not as an essentially necessary part, yet as an integral part), and thus as participating *ex opere operato* in the sacramental causality. Do we have too poor an opinion of ourselves and of other Christians if we maintain that such a doctrine is to be found only in books, but is not 'realized' in our religious life? I am afraid

[54] Much less than in the case of the sacrament of Penance, since reflection on the baptismal character, considered as the sign of belonging to the flock of Christ, only began with St Augustine.

[55] Cf. B. Xiberta, *Clavis Ecclesiae* (Rome 1922); B. Poschmann, 'Die innere Struktur des Busssakraments', *Münchener Theologische Zeitschrift* I (1950), pp. 12–30; H. de Lubac, *Catholicism* (London 1958), pp. 37 *sq.*; M. de la Taille, *Mysterium Fidei* (Paris 1931), p. 581; M. Schmaus, *Katholische Dogmatik* IV, I4/5 (Munich 1951), pp. 527 *sqq.* (cf. also the article by M. Schmaus cited in note 1 on p. 135 above).

that this question cannot be answered in the affirmative. One 'says one's penance' simply because this is part of the proceedings. Moreover, the penance is usually too insignificant to make us really and strongly conscious of the fact that we are doing penance. How could it then be recognized that the sacred *Liturgy* of the sacrament of Penance is not yet completed when we leave the Confessional? But this is after all what is meant when it is said that the sacramental satisfaction belongs still to the sacramental sign and indeed fuses, without ceasing itself to be sacramental, with the whole of one's life in so far as this is penance. For the penitent who has been absolved is told at the end that all his actions and sufferings are to avail him unto the forgiveness of sin.[56]

The fact that the sacrament of Penance is based on the baptized condition of the Christian, i.e. on his baptismal character, could be brought more explicitly into consciousness. Not merely in the formal juridical sense that only a baptized person can receive other sacraments. Rather, the baptized person activates, develops and carries through afresh in his life the conversion which was begun in baptism; he acts in the sacrament of Penance as a member of the Church, which he is by baptism; his sin has a peculiarity about it which does not belong to the sins committed by 'those who are outside'; he has a judgement passed on him which can be passed only on members of the Church (1 Cor 5.12 *sq.*). The negotiation of redemptive grace which takes place in the sacrament of Penance is a release of the (formal) efficacy

[56] A good number of theologians are indeed of the opinion that the prayerful wish expressed by the '*Passio Domini . . .*' is intended to urge the penitent to regard his whole life, in all its hardness, as a continuation and expansion of the penance imposed. *This* is the reason why according to this opinion the confessor (in the expectation that this stimulus will be followed up) gives only a mild penance, and why the 'penance of one's life' receives by this mutual intention also a *sacramental* efficacy of satisfaction. Cf. St Thomas, *Quodlibet* III, a. 28 (cf. also III, q. 84, a. 8 and a. 9); Pesch, *loc. cit.*, no. 253; P. Galtier, *De Paenitentia* (Rome 1950), no. 511. This, at any rate, is—even from a historical point of view—the meaning and intention of this concluding wish, which is found in the penitential liturgy at least in spirit since the thirteenth century (in the *Poenitentiale Vallicellanum II* in F. G. H. Wasserschleben, *Die Bussordnungen der abendländischen Kirche* [Halle 1851], pp. 550–557) and which later on appears more and more often in that same liturgy (cf. Jungmann, *Bussriten*, pp. 199, 237, 262). It can also be concluded from St Thomas' *Quodlibet* III, a. 28 that this terminating formula was still quite new in his day and not quite universally used as yet.

of the baptismal character,[57] as was already seen clearly by St Augustine.[58]

We should above all consider and apply to the sacrament of Penance what St Thomas—in full accord with the old Tradition—says about the sacraments in general: viz. that they refer back in their signs to the mysteries of the life and death of Christ and point ahead to the end of the whole history of salvation. For it is true that there occurs in this sacrament, taken as a visible ritual *mysterium*, a dying to sin first of all in the mortification of the flesh, and hence (because happening by Christ's grace) a sacramental manifestation of the death of Christ, a submission of oneself to the judgement of God which on the Cross condemned sin in the flesh of the Son (Rom. 8.3). And this judgement points in advance to the judgement at the end of life and of time in which grace will triumph.[59]

[57] Cf. pp. 21–25 of the article by B. Poschmann cited in note 55 on p. 172 above; M. Scheeben, *The Mysteries of Christianity* (St Louis and London 1947), pp. 576 *sqq.*; H. Oswald, *Die dogmatische Lehre von den Sakramenten* II[5] (Münster 1894), pp. 11 *sqq.*, 310 *sqq.*

[58] Texts in Poschmann, *loc. cit.*, p. 24.

[59] III q. 60, a. 3. See the profound commentary on this by H. Schillebeeckx, *loc. cit.*, pp. 143–183.

5

REMARKS ON THE THEOLOGY OF INDULGENCES

We may sometimes get the impression nowadays that there are truths in the Church which, although they are not indeed disputed in their explicit ('*in thesi*') formulation, are being silenced to death by the fact that no one takes any notice of them any longer in the practice of their religious life.[1] They are to be found in the Catechism, but they are not inscribed 'in our hearts on tables of flesh'. Of course, we know that such a process, which threatens to kill some particular truth in the Church, cannot lead to the real death of this truth—at least not in the case of those truths which really belong to the deposit of Faith. But this does not dispense theology from reflecting on the reasons for any such 'shrinking' processes which it observes. These reasons are not always and exclusively to be found necessarily in the spirit of the age, bad faith, or heretical hardening of the heart against a truth of the Church. The reason may also lie in the fact that a changed age really finds it difficult to understand these truths 'in the form' in which they had been expressed up to this time. Theology is not trying very hard to make them understandable. And so the poor Christian, who is not a theologian and therefore cannot resist this process himself, often cannot do very much else but let such an uncomprehended truth rest in the files of the *fides implicita* where it lies buried. He has the feeling that no doubt there is a truth here and that there is no doubt something in it, but that he himself cannot 'do anything with it'; and so he feels he just has to let the matter rest there, especially since there are after all enough other things and truths in Christianity which are for the moment more 'real' to him. It is not, of course, as if such (uncomprehended) truths

1 Cf. for this also K. Rahner, 'Der Gestaltwandel der Haeresie', *Wort und Wahrheit* IV (1949), pp. 881–891. Included also in K. Rahner, *Gefahren im heutigen Katholizismus* (Einsiedeln 1953²), pp. 63–80.

are in danger of disappearing all at once and everywhere, and for everyone simultaneously. After all, contemporaries live only apparently in the same age, and a truth can still be very much alive and be put into practice in certain quarters when elsewhere it gives the impression of being almost dead; it can be coming to life again somewhere, while elsewhere people have not even noticed yet how dead it has been in their hearts. Regarding such truths, the following should also be taken into account: they often cannot in any way be enjoined as a necessary part of men's lives—not even in the case of a member of the Church and not even by the threat of an anathema on such a member. How could anything like this be done with reference to the certain doctrine of the profit and blessing of the Confession of devotion or of the private devotion to Our Lady or of the private Sacred Heart devotions? The Church can proclaim the truth of the profit to be gained by such things; she can hope that this proclamation will move her hearers to action, but she cannot enforce the 'realization' of such truths as it were by strictly binding regulations. And no doubt it is not absolutely certain that the assistance of the Holy Spirit, which is assured to the Church, always guarantees in the respectively desired measure that such exhortations to the realization of such truths will bear much fruit. In such cases, too, it will, therefore, sometimes be useful to reflect on the reason why so little success is granted to such efforts not merely to state certain truths in the children's catechism class or in a sermon (so that it has been said and the preacher can then speak of something else with a clear conscience), but also to make them really enter into the life of the Christian: whether it is not because the proclamation itself has not quite understood the truth in question in such a way that it can be easily 'assimilated' and 'realized'.

Is not, for instance, Christ's descent into 'hell' such a truth? Who has ever heard a sermon on this since the time he heard it stated during the children's catechesis? Is this not strange in the case of one of the articles of the Apostles' Creed? It has recently been said that the doctrine of hell is beginning to be a truth which no longer has any existential meaning for Christians—even though they still hold it in a theoretical way. Is that not also true of indulgences and the doctrine of indulgences? There are indeed many indulgences actually in existence and it is not very long since the latest edition of the list of indulgences was published. In every treatment of dogmatic theology, and even in Canon Law, can be found what is necessary to know about all this. But it is surely no false suspicion and no pessimism in the pedagogical and pastoral religious field to advance the conjecture that—at least in Central Europe—the interest expressed by the average Christian in indulgences and in gaining them has very much decreased compared with earlier, i.e. pre-reformation *and* post-tridentine, times. People still like to make pilgrimages to Rome or other sacred places during the Holy Year or on other similar occasions, and even for religious motives—and they do, perhaps, in the process gain also the corresponding indulgences—because this is simply part of these exercises. But it will be difficult to maintain nowadays that the promised plenary indulgence is the decisive motive for these pilgrimages of the Christian masses, and that the indulgence once gained is for them the most precious effect they carry home with them. Indeed, how could anyone think in this way when an indulgence, even a plenary one, can be gained 'more cheaply' and at any time by saying a little prayer after Holy Communion, for instance. It cannot, after all, be said that the plenary indulgence of a pilgrimage (in its present-day form!) is more certain than some other indulgence. Contrition for sin is equally difficult in both cases. And the prescribed works for the indulgence, the conditions on which it is granted, are, according to the common teaching of theologians, merely an 'extrinsic condition' laid down on the part of the Church and by her authority alone for the granting of an indulgence. Whether this condition be great or small, difficult or easy, does not alter anything as regards the certainty and amount of the indulgence gained. Why should one, therefore, gain it precisely by a pilgrimage to Rome? There are many good reasons for making such a pilgrimage. However, that the indulgence is one of them, is not so easily seen. Whatever may be the truth of all these considerations, it is perhaps possible already to see that the interest in indulgences, and in gaining them, has undoubtedly decreased. And perhaps some of the blame for this must be attributed to the obscurities in the doctrine of indulgences which were less noticeable to earlier ages, but which today—even if we do not reflect on this at all—act as psychological repressions for the religious realization of an indulgence. It is, however, not completely superfluous—even looking at this from a religious and not merely scientific point of view—to strive for the greater clarification of the theology of indulgences. We may regret the falling-off of interest in indulgences or we may be inclined to accept it as a possible and, in itself, harmless change in the history of piety (because not only are there such changes, but they are quite legitimate). But only a clear and deepened theology of indulgences will enable us to understand whether there is something to be regretted in this state of affairs or merely something to be observed, and, if the former, how we can make indulgences become something vital again for men today. The latter undertaking will not be very easy. How are we to get to grips with a Christian who declares that he accepts the teaching of the Council of Trent that the Church has the power to grant indulgences and that to gain them is useful and salutary (Denz 989), but for the rest declares himself not to be very interested in them in his own religious practice? For he himself, he says, has the impression that his religious life in the present day and age, and in the unavoidable narrowness of his consciousness, has more important things to think about and to live for. This is so also because he has moreover the faint feeling—without being able or willing to state it so clearly—that the complete wiping out of his sins with all their consequences can, in fact, be achieved more surely and honestly in other ways.

We must, at any rate, welcome gratefully every attempt at gaining a better theological understanding of the nature and mode of operation of indulgences, especially any attempt which will do this in such a way that the man of today can more easily overcome the undeniable repressions he has developed with regard to this matter. For it is not immediately certain that the repressions are due merely to the nature of this matter.

A great deal of work would have to be done in this connection in the history of dogma and in dogmatic theology. In the field of the history of Dogma we do indeed possess the great and scholarly work of N. Paulus. But no matter how great the industry shown and how important the material results achieved in this work, it has nevertheless been written in the spirit and mentality of an age which wrote history in order to understand how it had evolved and not in order to understand what would still develop in the future. Applying this to theology, this means that the theological position which is the goal and norm of historical research, forms in the case of works of history of theology of this kind the reassured theological knowledge of the present which itself is not questioned and is regarded as complete and properly terminated without any inner dynamic. History, in such a perspective, naturally teaches also only what has been transmitted to us as theological inheritance from the most recent past. And at the end of all this historical work, which has often been carried out with admirable industry and acumen, we know more about the history of the question, but not really more about the question itself. Because these historians had basically no new questions to pose, history also does not volunteer any new answers about such matters. Hence, even after having studied the weighty volumes of Paulus, we know no more about the nature of indulgences than what we could have gathered even before that from an ordinary textbook. And so it is also not in the least surprising that these manuals themselves simply refer to such historical works in a single line of the bibliography given in small print, and that otherwise everything remains as it was before.

And yet so much remains still to be done on this question. So much remains to be done in a theological way and not primarily in the manner of the history of dogmas. Or to be more precise, it must be done in the historical field of Dogma but by a dogmatic theologian who has the courage to pose questions and who does, in fact, pose them, quite unconcerned about whether he is also immediately capable of answering them adequately. A beginning to this work has undoubtedly been made by the not very bulky but important work[2] on which we wish to make a few comments in this chapter. If in this way our own contribution to the understanding of the doctrine of indulgences is only very small, this should be taken as an indication of the fact that we think this work should go on and must not come to a standstill simply because this subject is rather tricky and dogmatic theologians, too, do not like to skate on thin ice.

B. Poschmann, the well-known researcher into the ancient and early medieval history of penance, investigates in this work[3] the *nature* of

[2] Bernhard Poschmann, *Der Ablass im Licht der Bussgeschichte* (Theophaneia IV; Bonn 1948, Hanstein). For the history of this question cf. also Paul F. Palmer, *Sources of Christian Theology* II: 'Sacraments and Forgiveness' (London 1960), pp. 321–368; 398–401.—*Tr.*

[3] The book has unfortunately, as far as I know, not met with the interest it deserved. So far Poschmann's theses on this question have not yet been very closely investigated. Karl Adam has given his assent to them (at least this is the impression one gets): TQ CXXIX (1949), pp. 242–245. H. Weisweiler declines, politely and gently, to accept them: *Scholastik* XX—XXIV (1949), pp. 591–594. The position he adopts shows indeed (even though we do not consider it as the correct position as far as its ultimate verdict is concerned) that—as we, too, shall emphasize—the question which

indulgences in the light of the history of penance. His intention, therefore, is not in the last analysis a purely historico-dogmatic one, but a dogmatic one. He wishes to show, on the one hand, how the doctrine of indulgences evolves naturally out of the development of the Church's penitential practice, and, on the other hand, he wishes to clarify in this way the nature of indulgences by going beyond the position commonly adopted in theology today—an endeavour which in fact is seldom pursued and achieved in the field of the history of Catholic dogmas. In this endeavour, he traces the development of the practice and doctrine of indulgences up to the High Middle Ages—that is to say, until the last significant change in the theory of indulgences up till now. As P. himself says (in the Preface), he takes the materials for his historical expositions in this book from his own researches into the history of penance, from J. A. Jungmann's treatise on the Latin penitential rites and above all from Nikolaus Paulus' great work on indulgences and their history. Even as a mere summary of these researches, P.'s new work deserves our gratitude. But even in its historical aspect, this work is more than just a precise and concise summary of the conclusions of those other works. For he makes certain small critical corrections even in the work of N. Paulus (cf. e.g. p. 58, note 287; p. 85, note 401). The accent, too, even in the dogmatic point of view, is shifted quite significantly, in the sense that the meaning of the early medieval 'Absolutions' (both outside and in the sacrament of Penance), as seen in their significance for the development and the nature of indulgences, is brought out much more than had been the case in Paulus' work—in spite of the abundance of his material on this question.

It is not possible here to recapitulate P.'s survey of the origin and development of indulgences which is in itself already very concise. We

---

Poschmann poses himself can surely not be answered conclusively from history alone. P. Galtier seems in the last analysis to agree with Poschmann (although he bases himself on somewhat different reasons), at least in what concerns the factual uncertainty of the effect of the indulgence grant on the individual. Cf. his discussion of Poschmann's work: 'Les indulgences, origine et nature', *Gregorianum* XXXI (1950), pp. 258–274. Galtier does not, at any rate, raise any conclusive objections against Poschmann from the point of view of any binding doctrine of the Church. That is already a great deal. Especially since Galtier has frequently and resolutely contradicted the conceptions of Poschmann elsewhere in questions of the history of penance.

wish simply to give a few brief indications which are necessary for the understanding of the dogmatic conclusions of this book. P. first of all exposes those elements of the early Church's teaching on penance which are important for indulgences later on (pp. 1–14): the necessity of subjective penance for post-baptismal sins as a cleansing factor in respect of sin, without distinguishing in this between guilt and punishment; the support given to this subjective penance by the co-operation of the Church (congregation, martyrs, 'pneumatics', etc.) and above all by the intercessory prayer of the priest which is to be distinguished from the act proper of reconciliation (with the Church and thereby also with God) and which must not be conceived as absolution (in the modern sense) in a deprecative form (p. 11). P. then (pp. 15–36) treats in detail of the nature, forms and modes of operation of the early medieval 'absolutions' outside (this is the earlier element, beginning already with St Gregory the Great) and within (from the tenth century onwards) the sacraments of Penance. These 'absolutions' are (at first independently from the imposition of an ecclesiastical penance) the genuine continuation of the priestly intercessory prayer for the penitent; and, in spite of the continually recurring appeal in this to an apostolic authority and the power of the keys, these 'absolutions' must be conceived as an *intercessory* (though authoritative) prayer of the Church for full forgiveness (hence embracing also the *punishment* for sin) of the penitent's sins—and not as a jurisdictional and hence infallible act of absolution from the temporal punishment due to sin. This follows from the fact of their taking place (even earlier) outside the sacrament (especially also in the case of 'general absolutions'), from their style and their restrictive clauses, and from the early scholastic theories about the nature and extent of the priestly activity in the sacrament of Penance. P. then (pp. 36–43) describes the historical and theoretical presuppositions in penitential matters which lead to the origin of indulgences: the change of the penitential institution from public to private penance and the placing of the reconciliation before the fulfilment of the ecclesiastical penance leads to the reflex differentiation between the guilt of sin and the punishment due to sin; thus subjective penance is now related more clearly to the payment of the debt of temporal *punishment* for sins, and the 'absolutions' are now appraised as helps of the Church for the payment of these same *punishments*, without there being as yet any question of a relaxation in the imposition of ecclesiastical penances as well. Then there follows (pp. 43–62) an analysis of the first indulgences in the proper sense. They appear in the eleventh century in France, whereas the remissions of penances, granted to pilgrims to Rome since the ninth century, must (contrary to N. Paulus' view) be held to be still graciously-granted redemptions. The essence of the new indulgences consists in the fact that, on account of the hoped-for effect before God of the intercessory absolutions on the payment of temporal punishment due to sin, the penitent is made a gift also of part of the ecclesiastical penance imposed. Thus, in these indulgences in the proper sense, a jurisdictional element is now added to the previous 'absolution', in so far as the 'absolution' now regards also the ecclesiastical penance imposed and naturally has a legal character relative to this imposition. Side by side with these indulgences in the proper sense, simple 'absolutions' in the old sense continue to exist for a long time. The beginnings of indulgences, therefore, are found in a *practice* which develops without being conscious of being something new. The Church had all along claimed the right to accommodate the amount of ecclesiastical penance imposed to the concrete circumstances and capabilities of the penitent. This was already the case in the first centuries, and in the early Middle Ages this practice was merely extended by various commutations and redemptions. The Church claimed this right although the sinner himself had to pay the temporal punishment due to his sins before God, even although with assistance from the Church and her authoritative intercession. And so such an 'absolution' could be granted the penitent to help him with his own penitential efforts, in view of some good work which made him particularly worthy of this 'absolution'. It was then possible to remit a part of his ecclesiastical penance, because the ultimate purpose of the latter was thought to be achieved by the 'absolving' intercession of the Church. There follows then (pp. 63–99) an account of the judgement and theory of this practice of indulgences by the theologians of the early and High Middle Ages. Abelard completely rejects the then still new practice of indulgences (this is the first known declaration of theological attitude; Peter of Poitiers takes up essentially the same position, although in somewhat more moderate terms). Abelard was censured because he denied not merely that bishops were able to grant a *judicial* release from temporal *punishment* for sin before God, but also that they have the power of the keys in general (except in regard to ecclesiastical penances). From the end of the twelfth century onwards, the practice of indulgences becomes gradually clarified and recognized in theology, but only after many vacillations and obscurities; for this the practice itself is used at first as the main argument for its justification, and its objective justification is found in the *communio suffragiorum*. With Huguccio (†1210), the notion of indulgences appears fairly clearly for the first time as a *jurisdictional* release from temporal punishment before God. But it still remains obscure for a long time why the *suffragia* of the Church are a sufficient substitute for the non-occurrence of the heavenly effect of the remitted ecclesiastical penance. And it is not clear for some time yet what is the role of the good work required for the gaining of the indulgence with regard to the effect: whether it is to be regarded as a redemption or merely as a condition for an effect which as such originates exclusively from the power of the keys. However, before the actual high scholastic period, it seems to have been the more general opinion that an indulgence does not have its transcendent effect on account of a direct power of absolution on the part of the Church, but only *per modum suffragii* (pp. 81 *sq.*). Through the explicitly developed doctrine of the 'Treasury of the Church' (already to be found in Hugh of St Cher, 1230), a new phase begins in the development of the doctrine of indulgences. It was possible to point out more clearly now the factor in which the remitted penance finds its substitute. And when it was then added that the Church has a legal claim to this 'Treasury of the Church', and one which can be applied in a jurisdictional manner, all the previous difficulties seemed to be solved. It was now possible to develop the doctrine of indulgences which is still familiar to us today: the remission of temporal punishment due to sin (for which, until this time, the Church had simply interceded, with the result that the ecclesiastical penance imposed was remitted) could now be seen as taking place by means of a jurisdictional act which disposes of this Treasury of the Church authoritatively (as does the owner with regard to his property) and hence with infallible effect (St Albert, St Bonaventure, St Thomas). Once this stage was reached, the reference of indulgences to the remission of an ecclesiastical penance imposed could become increasingly loose, until at least some theologians (like Billot) exclude this reference completely from the nature of indulgences. For the same reasons, the granting of indulgences (beginning with St Thomas) came to be more and more independent of the sacrament of Penance. It came to be something reserved to the Pope, because only the Pope (or someone else dependently on him) can dispose of the Treasury of the Church in a legal manner: whereas before—since it had been essentially a question also (but not merely!) of the remission of an ecclesiastical penance—all those who imposed such penances (confessors or at least bishops) could grant indulgences by their own power. On the other hand, if the Church can dispose of the Treasury of the Church in a legal manner, it becomes again more difficult to solve the question why, and to what extent, a good work is required as a necessary condition for an indulgence—for basically this can be understood only in relation to the more primitive commutations and redemptions of penances, and not in the new theory.

As already stated, these merely suggestive and fragmentary references to the outline of this history of the practice and theory of penance as given by P. are meant merely as a preparation for the understanding of the question which really matters to P. (pp. 99–122) and to us, viz. how are we to conceive the nature of indulgences theologically in the light of this history of indulgences? And this is what is really new in P.'s treatment. What conclusions does he come to concerning the nature of indulgences?

The Church has always known that in the Communion of Saints, in the Body of Christ, the individual Christian is assisted in getting rid of his sins by the whole Church on earth and in heaven, and she has translated this knowledge into action in many different ways. In the case of indulgences, what was new at first was the fact that the knowledge about the 'Treasury of the Church', when carried into intercessory action, gave rise to the conclusion that the sinner could be granted remission also of a part of the *ecclesiastical* penance by a jurisdictional act. Thus an indulgence has an effect in heaven and an effect on earth. Everything is clear and comprehensible up to this point, and P. believes that even the pronouncements of the Church's *magisterium* about indulgences do not contain anything more as of obligation. The theological interpretation of the doctrine of indulgences, however, goes beyond the bounds of what is true and what can be proved, when it now adds to this the notion that in the case of indulgences the *jurisdictional* act as such refers not only to the Church-imposed penance as such but also directly to the very punishment for sin in the next world. This means that in this interpretation a 'plenary' indulgence, for instance, results (simply on condition of repentance for the sins concerned) in the *full* remission of all temporal punishment due to these sins, and does so with the certitude due to the effect of a jurisdictional act (as in the sacrament of Penance with regard to guilt). That this goes beyond what is true and what can be proved to be true, is clear on several grounds. Thus, indulgences (in so far as they refer to the arrest of punishment before God) grew out of the old 'absolutions'. The latter, however, were explicitly not intended to be an infallible means of a judicial remission of punishment, but were explicitly intended as an *intercessory* aid to the penance of the sinner, even though we may attribute a particularly powerful effect to this intercession, on account of the authority of the intercessor. The appeal to Mt 16 and 18, and to Jn 20, is not telling, because it proves too much (p. 101). For it would then be immediately and unconditionally possible to loose also from temporal punishment due to sin in the sacrament of Penance. And why go to the bother of proving the power to grant indulgences by reference to the Treasury of the Church, when the Church has from the very start been given a legal power over temporal punishment due to sin as well as over guilt itself? Guilt can be remitted by the Church for the simple reason that she has been given the power to do this by Christ (and this precisely in Mt 16, etc.), without having to look for any further explanation for this. In the usual theory of indulgences, the true doctrine of the 'Treasury of the Church' has been turned overmuch into the notion of a sort of 'exchequer', and has been given a legal connotation such as is possible only in the case of *material* goods (*nihil aliud*—says Billot, for instance, about indulgences—*quam solutio ex publico aerario pro debitis privatorum*). But once we see clearly that the reality of the Treasury of the Church simply means that God can gratuitously and freely grant a remission of temporal punishment in view of the Sacrifice of Christ, and the sanctity of the Saints supported by that Sacrifice, then the Church's right to dispose of this 'treasury' depends entirely on the free will of God, and the fact, as well as the manner, of such a disposal must be completely derived from the positive dispositions made by God. There is no proof of the fact that God has granted the Church a *legal* power of disposal with regard to the temporal punishment due to sin, and the assertion of such a concession meets with quite a few difficulties even apart from this. The Church certainly has, however, a moral right to this 'Treasury', i.e. the Church, in her intercessory action for sinners before God, calls upon the merits of Christ and of his Saints, whose ready support she may presuppose as the fruit of her prayers. For God, in and despite the freedom of his dispensation of grace, is undoubtedly especially ready to listen to the Church as a body and to her authorized prayer.

From all this follows naturally the understanding of P.'s determination of the nature of indulgences. An indulgence is a combination of the old 'absolutions' from temporal punishment—which are effective as a *prayer* of the *Church*—and of a jurisdictional remission of ecclesiastical penances. Even in the case of a plenary indulgence, the Church aims merely at a relaxation of all temporal punishment; she cannot guarantee with absolute certitude that God will completely remit these punishments. In this conception of indulgences many other phenomena of the practice of indulgences also explain themselves better: the fact that indulgences still continue to be determined quantitatively by the old rates of penance; the necessity of a *causa proportionata* for the granting of an indulgence, and of a good work for the gaining of it, by which the recipient of the indulgence also disposes himself in a special way for a favourable response to the special intercession made by the Church; the factual uncertainty of the success of an indulgence on which the Church herself counts, etc.

What is to be said about this Theology of Indulgences? First of all, it should not be overlooked from the very beginning in the further discussion of this thesis propounded by P. that this thesis is not so different in its objective, ultimate conclusion from the traditional theory of indulgences as might seem at first sight. For, a thoughtful theology which really and truly reckons with the seriousness of the consequences of sin and knows something about the non-transferable character of a personal deed in spite of the whole reality of the community of guilt and its consequences, will not at all doubt that, in fact, the 'gained' indulgences do not have exactly the effect which is ascribed to them *in se*. Thus far, therefore, P.'s thesis in itself simply transfers the always-given element of factual uncertainty to a somewhat different point than is the case in the usual theory. For the rest, however, we seriously mean to defend the view here that P.'s thesis is right, although one part of the proof which P. gives does not seem to be absolutely watertight, and another part of the proof would seem to be open to still further development and deeper study. It should be mentioned that the whole of this defence is, of course, subject to the results of further theological discussion and to further precisions of the thesis, as well as to the obvious right of the Church's *magisterium*.

P.'s main argument is in fact the one based on the history of indulgences: indulgences grew out of the old 'absolutions', the only really new element being the remission of a penance imposed by the *Church*. But, although the 'absolution' undoubtedly had an effect on the punishment in the life to come, it did not, however, have a judicial but an intercessory character in its regard. Ergo. . . . Now, the *historical* connection between 'absolution' and 'indulgence' has certainly been correctly perceived and worked out. And we shall have to agree with P., that this 'absolution' is the continuation, with an intercessory character, of the penitential intercessions made by the priest in the early Church, which intercessions may not be simply and formally identified with the reconciliation proper. And it is right that the 'absolutions' within and without the sacrament were regarded as such a continuation at the time of their growth and flowering. But will not the dogmatic theologian who wishes to hold on to the current common theory of indulgences, object to the above that this historical connection (in a less empirical conception of the development of dogmas) does not exclude the possibility that the Church came to see only slowly in the course of all this, that her authoritative prayer has the efficaciousness of a jurisdictional enactment[4]? And this all the more so since the authoritative character of this prayer had always been very clearly in the forefront of consciousness, as P.'s description itself shows. And a 'prayer' of an authoritative kind need not necessarily lack the efficacy of an *opus operatum* (remember the 'prayer' of the anointing of the sick). Such a dogmatic theologian could reverse P.'s appeal to the fact that the 'absolutions' before the time of indulgences could not have been more than intercessory prayers because the early medieval theories about the efficacy of the sacrament of Penance for the cleansing from guilt hardly ascribe any more to the 'keys'. He could say that this proves precisely that, both in the first and in the second case, the clear theoretical recognition of an *ex opere operato* efficacy had first to break through, and that this clarification is equally compelling in both cases. He will, in other words, point to the fact that the same development took place also in the case of the deprecative form of absolution from the guilt of sin itself. He will point out that, with regard to its transcendent and certain effect, the jurisdictional character of the deprecative formula employed in the sacrament

[4] The remarks of Weisweiler, for instance, run along the same lines as this objection.

of Penance was also recognized only slowly, and yet that the early obscurities must not be used against the later clarified teaching. P. does indeed give pointers to suggest that this parallel must itself be interpreted differently (p. 11). But this retort depends in its turn on the whole of his interpretation of penance in the *early* Church (*pax cum Ecclesia* as the *res et sacramentum* of the forgiveness of guilt before God, so that the intercessory formula does not at all formally represent the act of reconciliation as such[5]). The present author does indeed agree with this interpretation, but it is an interpretation which has not yet by any means won the day among dogmatic theologians as a whole. If we are in this sense not quite as convinced as P. of the full force of the historical argument for the essence of indulgences based on the nature of the early medieval 'absolution', this does not mean that we do not recognize the importance of this argument. For it

[5] We might get the impression from this work (cf. e.g. p. 20) that P. regards this doctrine of the early Church, concerning the pax cum Ecclesia as *res et sacramentum* of the reconciliation with God in the sacrament of Penance, simply as a theorem of an earlier theology which has now been left behind. This impression is not correct. P. is, on the contrary, convinced of the fact that this doctrine is still correct today and it is still important for a deeper understanding of the sacrament of Penance. Cf. for this, his article: 'Die innere Struktur des Busssakraments', *Münchner Theologische Zeitschrift* I (1950), pp. 12–30. This theory, which can also appeal to de la Taille, de Lubac and Xiberta for support among present-day theologians (and which also seems the correct one to ourselves, cf. the previous chapter in the present volume), is of great significance for the theory of indulgences. For it explains easily why the Church can indeed remit the guilt but not the punishment of sin by a juridical act, although a remission of guilt is in fact more difficult than a remission of punishment, and it would therefore appear that whoever is capable of the greater is capable also of doing the lesser. If the legal power of the Church employed in the sacrament of Penance consists precisely in the fact that man is thereby incorporated into the Church's inner means of grace and hence obtains the grace of God, which is the cleansing from sin, then it becomes immediately intelligible that the Church, by a legal act of reconciliation and reincorporation into the Church *qua* bearer of the Spirit of God, can forgive everything (and only that) which is inconsistent with this reincorporation. Man can, however, be justified in the grace of God and yet, in the nature of things, be burdened with what we nowadays call the debt of punishment (in a somewhat colourless, formalistic and legal jargon). It follows, therefore, immediately from this that the legal power of the Church, when it forgives guilt by such an incorporation into, and reconciliation with, the Church, does not necessarily apply itself also to the punishment due to sin.

shows that the burden of proof for the usual theory of efficacy rests with those who advocate this theory, because they assert more than can be gathered immediately from the origins of indulgences. One may, however, get the impression that theologians have not lost a great deal of sleep over this proof. And even if we presuppose as self-evident that there is a dogmatic proof *ex consensu theologorum*, it is nevertheless doubtful whether such a proof can be gathered in this case from a relative unanimity of theologians regarding the jurisdictional nature of indulgences (*qua* forgiveness of temporal punishment due to sin). For closer scrutiny shows that this unanimity is not as great as it might seem at first sight.[6] The initial verbal unanimity soon turns into

[6] One need only enter more closely into the question as to what sort of uncertainty is supposed by theologians as regards the effective gaining of indulgences, and how they explain this uncertainty, which after all is presupposed in the practice of the faithful. Galtier (*loc. cit.*) maintains that, even in the common opinion, indulgences do not imply a real absolution (with regard to sin's temporal punishment before God), but a '*solutio*' granted by the Church, i.e. the Church places the 'Treasury of the Church' at the disposal of one of the faithful (in a juridical manner), so that *he* may then use it to pay his debt of punishment. Hence, he maintains, the extent to which God accepts this form of payment remains indeterminate (in spite of the juridical character of the '*solutio*'). Now, this explanation does, perhaps, preserve the currently common interpretation of the doctrine of indulgences ('against' Poschmann) as far as terminology is concerned, but objectively it says exactly the same thing as Poschmann. Every theological theory about the nature of indulgences must be prepared to allow itself to be faced with the following question (to be answered clearly by a 'yes' or a 'no'): if a man is in the state of grace, has repented of his sins and has fulfilled the work prescribed by the indulgence grant (and is a *homo viator*), is it *certain* then, under these presuppositions, that in fact all his temporal punishment due to sin is remitted if a plenary indulgence was attached to his prescribed work? Is this objectively certain in this case, and is the doctrine stating that this is so objectively, a theologically certain and binding doctrine? Any theologian who cannot answer these two questions with an unhesitating 'yes', must let Poschmann's theory pass as at least theologically unobjectionable for the time being. Anyone, however, who dares to answer this question with an unconditional 'yes', must not only be prepared to allow himself to be asked as to what sufficient reason he can give for his 'yes'. He must also be prepared to face the following questions: Does his 'yes' fully satisfy the seriousness of the divine justice? Why then cannot practically everyone be preserved right away from Purgatory by a simple jurisdictional act of the Pope? Why do theologians, generally speaking, nevertheless demand a *causa proportionata* for the validity of the granting of an indulgence on the part of the Church? Why does the normal Christian, with the true instinct

an objective difference of opinion, once we demand more precise information regarding particular questions.

There is another argument for his thesis which seems more telling in P.'s work than the proof from the history of 'absolution' taken by itself. Only that argument seems a little bit too brief and too historical in P. For it is not, after all, merely the *early* Church's theory of penance (which seems to be somewhat too much in the foreground with P.) but also the dogmatically binding teaching of the Council of Trent (Denz 807; 904; 922), that the Church does not always and necessarily absolve from all temporal punishment due to sin in the sacrament of Penance. However, this proposition, which has the whole of the ancient teaching on penance behind it, makes sense only if it is not merely a fact that in practice the Church does not remit this punishment by her jurisdictional act exercised in the sacrament, but also that she *cannot* remit it (with certainty based on this act as such). For, on the one hand, no more is demanded on the part of the penitent for such a remission according to the usual doctrine of indulgences) than for the remission of the guilt itself. And, on the other hand, the sacrament is simply orientated in every respect towards the cleansing from sin. And so it is impossible to see why the Church would not remit by her jurisdictional act in the sacrament what she could remit. If, however, the Church cannot do this with the efficacy of a jurisdictional act *in* the sacrament, then she cannot do it either outside the sacrament. Otherwise she would be able to do more outside the sacrament—at least in one respect—than in the sacrament, and indeed in respect of an object to which the sacrament is ordained. For in the last analysis the sacrament is also ordained to the blotting out of the temporal punishment due to sin, as is shown even by the imposition of a penance which is included in the *opus operatum*. It is necessary to state all this, and all the more so since theologians appeal to the same scriptural texts to prove the power to grant indulgences as they do when proving the power to forgive sins in the sacrament.[7] If this proof proved anything,

---

of the faith, nevertheless regard a plenary indulgence, gained by the performance of a very small good work prescribed, as more uncertain than another indulgence gained, for instance, by a fatiguing pilgrimage? etc.

[7] Cf. e.g. Ch. Pesch, *Praelectiones dogmaticae* VII, no. 492; F. Diekamp, *Katholische Dogmatik* III[8], p. 315; J. Pohle-M. Gierens, *Lehrbuch der Dogmatik* III[8], p. 506; M. Schmaus, *Katholische Dogmatik* IV, 1[4], p. 541.

it would be that the full power of a jurisdictional (and as such certainly efficacious) freeing from temporal punishment due to sin is an *intrinsic* moment of *the particular* sacramental power which is given in these texts. It is, therefore, impossible to prove from these texts the jurisdictional nature of the power of granting indulgence *and* to deny at the same time that this power can be exercised in the sacrament of Penance *qua* sacrament (which is instituted or promised in these texts). If, however, this proof from Mt 16 and 18 is abandoned, then there is absolutely no scriptural proof left for a jurisdictional power of the Church with regard to temporal punishment due to sin. However, there is not only no proof for this, but also the very object of such a proof is immediately excluded by the teaching of the Church to the effect that she does not forgive temporal punishment in the sacrament *ex opere operato* simply as she pleases (and hence also *cannot* thus forgive it). For it is absolutely impossible to find any reason why the Church should not be able to do *in* the sacrament (which is there for the purpose of cleansing from the whole sin, including the debt of punishment) what (*ex supposito*) she is able to do outside the sacrament.

To put all this in a different way: if the reasons for the uncertainty of the success of an indulgence (which uncertainty is ultimately admitted by every theologian and good Christian) were to be found, as in the sacrament, merely on the side of the subjective disposition of the penitent, and were the same as in the case of the sacrament (as the usual indulgence-theory maintains), then the effective cause of this objectively infallible result would have to be, as in the case of the sacrament, a legal act, even if not already a formally sacramental act. For only such an act (we prescind from a physical act) can be infallible in its effect and yet be hindered from achieving this effect by merely subjective conditions in the line of the aim of the act. But then this legal act could be distinguished merely formally (or as a part of the whole) from the legal act exercised in the sacrament of Penance; it would, at any rate, no longer be possible to see why it could and should not be posited in any case also within the sacrament, especially since it is supposed to be included in the sacramental power given in Mt 16 and Jn 20. It would in this case be possible at the most to show that this act, in so far as it refers only to temporal punishment, may also be posited outside the sacrament, in accordance with the principle; qui potest plus, potest et minus. In order to avoid this whole conclusion, it would be necessary to adopt the despairing subterfuge of saying that the Church *can* indeed exercise this legal power of forgiveness in the sacrament of Penance with regard to temporal punishment, since it is included in the sacrament, but that she does not do so on account of a self-imposed limitation of what is itself a greater power. To this it would then have to be replied that the Church cannot suppress in such an arbitrary manner the greater power given to her, *ex supposito*, by Christ. It is also impossible to give a really intelligible reason in the usual theory about indulgences for the fact that the Church requires a *legitima causa* for the granting of an indulgence over and above the need of the sinner for complete cleansing from his sin. For such a power of a legal kind (included in the sacramental power of Mt 16 and 18, from which it is after all derived) would be given precisely for the sake of that complete purgation of man. And so, no more than the power to forgive guilt as such could it be made dependent on any other conditions than the need of the sinner and his dispositions.

Let us elucidate these reflections further by a few observations taken from some of the most recent treatments in dogmatic theology[8] on the question of the sacrament of Penance and indulgences. Galtier refutes the theory which holds that by an indulgence the Church simply 'makes a present of' the punishment due to sin by means of a simple remission on her part, by pointing out that indulgences would in this case be more efficacious in regard to temporal punishment due to sin than the sacrament of Penance. This theory attacked by him '*ascribit concessioni indulgentiae efficacitatem ex opere operato veriorem et maiorem, quam quae sacramentali absolutione agnoscitur*'. For the sacrament does indeed also effect a (partial) remission of temporal punishment due to sin *ex opere operato*, but only in the measure of the subjective dispositions of the penitent. But under the presupposition opposed by him, the indulgence is effective *ex opere operato* (presupposing simply contrition), purely and simply in the measure of the amount of indulgence determined by the one who grants the indulgence. In accordance with this view, the Pope could, by a mere act of his will, remove something which is binding (the debt of punishment), which he could not do as the minister of the sacrament and by virtue of the sacrament. This consideration put forward by Galtier is, in our opinion, conclusive. But this is precisely why we cannot understand how Galtier can nevertheless teach before this, that indulgences are

[8] P. Galtier, *De paenitentia*, (new edition, Rome 1950), no. 613.

effective *ex opere operato*,[9] and indeed in such a way that their effect, in contrast to the sacrament of Penance, '*independens est a subjectiva dispositione et proportionatur tantum voluntati concedentis indulgentiam*' (no. 610). This seems to us to be in utter contradiction to what Galtier says a few pages further on concerning the fight against the theory of indulgences for punishment due to sin *per modum absolutionis*. It cannot be said that this contradiction disappears by the fact that Galtier rejects the infallibility in the form of '*absolutio*' and admits it in the form of '*solutio*'. Given that the '*solutio*' is really infallibly effective even in its *end*-effect, independently of the dispositions of the recipient, then Galtier's objection holds true also against the '*solutio*': its effect is surer and greater than the effect of the sacrament. If, however, this '*solutio*' is to be taken as meaning that the Church does indeed (in certain circumstances) place her 'Treasury'—in a jurisdictional act—completely at the disposal of the penitent by a plenary indulgence for the payment of the debt of temporal punishment due to sins but that it is an open question whether, and in what measure, God is prepared to accept this supplied payment in any particular case (that he has, therefore, not bound himself in this case—contrary to what is true of the sacrament, as far as the guilt of sin is concerned), and acts in this case (in what concerns the debt of punishment) exactly as he does in the sacrament: then this is saying the same thing, in a more complicated terminology, as what Poschmann holds. For with regard to the end-effect, which consists in the effective payment of the debt of punishment, the jurisdictional process of placing the Treasury of the Church at the disposal of the faithful has exactly the same value as an intercessory prayer of the Church. Such a prayer is addressed to God in the form of an appeal to the merits of Christ and the Saints, i.e. the 'Treasury of the Church'. Galtier himself, it should

[9] *Loc. cit.*, no. 609. It should be mentioned that this doctrine is proved merely by an appeal to the teaching of St Thomas (*Suppl.*, q. 25, a. 2). The conceptual background of this proof, however, is the idea that the Treasury of the Church is inexhaustible, and that the Church can draw on it and apply it in an authoritative manner. *If* she can do this, it is indeed correct to say that in this case the effect of the indulgence is not dependent on the dispositions of the one gaining the indulgence, and hence that indulgences '*tantum valent quantum praedicantur*' (St Thomas, *loc. cit.*). But how can we prove this presupposition if the Church does not only not acknowledge herself to have such a power even in the sacrament, but explicitly denies having it?

be noted, remarks quite rightly about this 'Treasury' (no. 600), by appealing to Lehmkuhl, that it must not be imagined as something which is divided out quantitatively and bit by bit—and hence with the danger of being exhausted—but that it must be thought of rather as the undivided totality of the moral works of Christ and of all men who are in his grace, in view of which God grants grace and forgiveness to other men.

It may be maintained that this argument, which is merely hinted at by Poschmann, is more convincing and objectively more conclusive and that, considering that P.'s aim lies in the field of dogma rather than purely in the field of the history of dogmas, it should therefore have been developed further than the purely historical argument from 'absolution'. In the case of the latter argument we have constantly to ask ourselves whether it is not tacitly based on too positivistic and empirical a notion of the history of dogmas, i.e. on the conviction that the Church cannot even come gradually to the consciousness of a power of which she had not always been aware and which she had not always employed from the very beginning.

Naturally this main consideration, which we have even here merely indicated, should be deepened even further. It would be necessary above all to go into the question of how we can explain and make intelligible the fact (which at first sight seems a surprising one) that the Church can indeed wipe out the greater by a legal act, viz. the guilt before God, but not the smaller, viz. the debt of punishment. If we do not want to answer this question merely by appealing to a positive divine decree, made intelligible by means of such considerations as are contained in Denz 904, then we can only answer this question in a more profound manner if we enter more closely and comprehensively into the nature of the punishment due to sin than is usual in current theology. Current theology sees this punishment too exclusively as something which is extrinsically imposed on man by the justice of God, conceived merely as something vindictive. A practically necessary presupposition for a deeper study of this question would be to examine the doctrine of temporal punishment due to sin in the light of the *history* of dogmas, in such a way that this examination would also further the *dogmatic theology* of this doctrine. It is to be hoped that someone will soon write us such a history. Only a more profound doctrine about temporal punishment can offer any prospect of our being able to break down, even in this direction, the objections and prejudices of Protestant and Eastern Christians against the Catholic teaching on punishment due to sin, satisfaction and indulgences.

The doctrine, and the history of the doctrine, of temporal punishment due to sin is a much more difficult Chapter than the average textbook of dogmatic theology would lead us to believe. For the Church did not get a clear consciousness of a debt (*reat*) of punishment really separable from the 'debt' (*reat*) of guilt until the moment when the practice of the Church (for very practical reasons) brought about a temporal link-up between the absolution in the sacrament of Penance and the commencement of penance. Thus the performance of the penance (which in the Fathers was concerned with the cleansing from sin in general, without any distinction between the 'debt' of guilt and that of punishment) had to have a really distinguishable effect from the reconciliation which had now already taken place in the sacrament by means of contrition and absolution. And so we would have to inquire exactly as to what doctrine of the 'debt' of punishment really does arise (and what does not) from *such* a starting-point. It would then be necessary to inquire further as to what exactly was meant originally by the Fathers' demanding a long period of subjective penance for post-baptismal sins in contrast to the cleansing from sin in baptism. Was the real 'living basis' of this demand the conviction that the sinner has incurred temporal punishment in the next life which he must pay for already in this life (why, by the way, already in this life?)—a payment to which he must be constrained under pain of refusal of reconciliation? (It is well known that even Scotus felt uneasy about the logical clarity of these considerations.[10]) Or is this patristric theory about the difference between the forgiveness granted by baptism and that granted by post-baptismal penance already a theory (which does not mean that it must be false) constructed to explain and support a practice whose basis lay elsewhere, viz. in the conviction that a baptized person who has relapsed into sin must be examined much more closely and critically than a catechumen, before being readmitted into full communion with the Church? And if this is the real starting-point of the practice in the early Church[11] which gave

[10] Cf. J. Lechner, *Die Sakramentenlehre des Richard von Mediavilla* (Munich 1925), pp. 321 *sq*.

[11] Cf. on this K. Rahner, 'Die Busslehre des hl. Cyprian von Karthago' ZKT LXXIV (1952), pp. 257–276; 381–438, esp. 395–403.

rise to the theological theory, what results from this as far as this theory itself is concerned? This theory does not at all need to be false. But perhaps we could circumscribe its contents much more precisely and carefully once we think this theory through, starting from the point indicated. Would this—we may at least *inquire*—lead us to a doctrine of temporal punishment due to sin which is a little less juridical in the formal sense than the present common doctrine? Would it lead us to a doctrine which could bring more understanding to the Greeks (Origen at their head[12]) than the Latin doctrine of the punishment due to sin and of Purgatory has done hitherto? An examination of the real nature of punishment due to sin would practically have to bring in, and set in motion, the whole of theology. Is there really, from and on God's side (in distinction to an earthly lawgiver), an objective distinction between vindictive and medicinal punishment? St Thomas, to be consistent with his deepest intuitions, would have to deny this. *Non esset perpetua poena animarum quae damnantur, si possent mutare voluntatem in melius, quia iniquum esset quod ex quo bonam voluntatem haberent, perpetuo punirentur* (*Summa contra Gentiles* IV, 93). Could we not also omit the '*perpetuo*'? In other words, can we not say that man and the world (including the realities beyond) have been constituted by God in such a way that sin punishes itself? Is it not true that wherever the connatural consequence of sin is accepted and endured to the bitter end, sin becomes of itself the temporal and medicinal punishment (no matter how much this punishment is a manifestation of the justice of God and is in this sense *also* vindictive)? And is it not true that whenever the will, in permanent obduracy, refuses definitively to acknowledge the most profound meaning of the attitude of sin, sin becomes of itself an eternal punishment? Such a conception would not in the least need to dispute that there are 'external' punishments due to sin. It would not at all have to conclude that, in as far as the divine punishments are concerned, these consist merely in 'sorrow', 'feelings of remorse', and similar 'inner' punitive consequences of sin. With the principle of the nature of divine punishments due to sin thus envisaged, it would not at all be denied but, on the contrary, even demanded, that there are 'external punishments for sin'. To see this, we would simply need to base ourselves on a deeper Ontology of the nature of the spiritual (human)

[12] Cf. on this K. Rahner, 'La doctrine d'Origène sur la pénitence', RSR XXXVII (1950), pp. 47–97, esp. 79–97; 252–286; 422–456.

person and its surroundings. For the human person is spirit in materiality, which itself is again a part of a uniform and (in its continuity) indissoluble world of a material kind. Whenever, therefore, some act of spiritual freedom is exercised, this act embodies itself necessarily in the 'exterior' of the being—which is not simply identical with the personal core of this act—and it does so right into the materiality of this exterior. In this 'embodiment', the actual physio-psychical corporeality of man consists much more in the most exterior stratum and in the index both of the stratification and of the outward-directed construction of man, than that this should simply be identical with 'what is different from the personal nucleus of man' and hence be no longer present in any way after death. Now, such 'incarnations' of man's personal decision of freedom in the 'exterior' of the person (and, beyond this, in his surroundings) are not simply cancelled out again, once they have taken place, by a change of disposition in the spiritual nucleus of the person through contrition, etc. Of themselves, these 'incarnations' remain and can in certain cases be changed, and work themselves off, only by a slow process in time which may last much longer than the free conversion in the centre of the person. The person, who has himself caused these 'exteriorizations' of his own guilt in his 'exterior' and his surroundings, inevitably experiences them as something causing him affliction, as a connatural punishment. Although this punishment arises out of the guilt itself, by the collision of the guilty act with the given structures of the 'exterior' established by God into which the guilt engraves itself, it must nevertheless be called an 'external' punishment. For this punishment is not simply the conscious reflection of guilt in the consciousness of the guilty person, which must disappear again together with the annihilation of the guilt. Any attempt to understand the nature of the punishment due to sin in the sense indicated must then, of course, also conceive the payment of the debt of punishment in a somewhat less juridical and formalistic manner than is usually the case. The payment of a punishment of this kind could in this case be conceived only as a maturing process of the person, through which, though gradually, all the powers of the human being become slowly integrated into the basic decision of the free person. This does not at all necessarily mean that the soul after death is still capable of meriting supernaturally an actual growth in grace. The profundity of the '*option fondamentale*' which has been made during life can no longer grow in the life beyond. But this, in its turn, does not exclude the possibility of conceiving man as still really maturing in the purgatory condition of 'Purgatory'. We are not, at any rate, in any way compelled by the dogma of the Church to think of 'Purgatory' as a purely passive endurance of vindictive punishments, which, when they have been 'paid for' in this sense, release man in exactly the same condition in which he commenced this state of purification. For not every 'change' or 'process of maturing' must necessarily be already what is theologically described as growth in grace, increase of merit, advance in the degree of glory. Such a change of condition in the degree of maturity can just as well be conceived as an integration of the whole stratified human reality into that free decision and grace which, having been made and won in this life, is in itself definitive. Certainly such a conception of sin's temporal punishment in the life beyond requires implicitly also a certain modification of the conception as to the manner in which these punishments can be 'remitted'. In the common, purely formal-legal and 'extrinsicist' conception according to which these punishments have a purely vindictive character, and according to which they are connected with sin only by a juridical decree of God and are added by a divine intervention exercised purely 'ad hoc', these punishments due to sin can obviously be 'remitted' by a simple remission which merely consists in God *not* adding them and in the fact that God refrains from the tormenting action on the 'Holy Souls'. In the conception of temporal punishment proposed for discussion above, it would not be possible to conceive the remission of punishment as a mere abstention from punishing. This occurrence would have to be conceived rather in the sense that the process of painful integration of the whole of man's stratified being into the definitive decision about his life, taken under the grace of God, happens more quickly and intensively and therefore also less painfully. That this is possible can be seen from our life on this earth. Thus, depending on circumstances, aids offered, etc., the same living 'process of working out' a moral problem can proceed easily and quickly or painfully and slowly. We cannot indeed picture to ourselves *how* in particular such a process of maturing can develop in different ways in the life after death; but *that* such a thing is conceivable will be very difficult to dispute *a priori*. In other words, a 'remission' is conceivable even in the conception of temporal punishment suggested above, even although this remission does not in this case consist simply in the mere omission of punishment.

Such and many other questions would have to be considered if we really wished to work out an adequate theory of indulgences understood as the remission of temporal punishment due to sin. These questions are enumerated here, not in order to give an answer to them, but merely to show how much would still have to be done to clarify the questions which Poschmann has tried to solve.

Even apart from this, P.'s theory of indulgences would, of course, require to be proved and developed more closely. What is the exact nature of an *authoritative* prayer of the *Church* in distinction to a private intercessory prayer? Where is such a prayer to be found in the present-day granting of indulgences? If we adopt P.'s theory of indulgences, is it still possible to make the distinction between indulgences for the living and those for the dead sufficiently intelligible? For surely this is a distinction which goes further than the fact that after death the soul can no longer be absolved from a penance imposed by the Church? Why does not the Church return to the simple 'absolutions' (to use P.'s terminology), since the imposition of an *ecclesiastical* penance, from which we are also freed by an indulgence, is after all purely hypothetical nowadays? Why do we, strictly speaking, still need to appeal in *this* theory of indulgences to the Treasury of the Church, which is part and parcel of the Church's doctrine of indulgences, when elsewhere (e.g. in the case of the Sacramentals) the theological explanation of the intercessory prayer of the Church, no matter how authoritative this prayer may be, does not, as far as I know, fall back (at least not *explicitly*) on the Treasury of the Church? What is the meaning, in Poschmann's theory taken as a whole, of the good work with which the Church connects the granting of an indulgence? (Schmaus[13] gives a good explanation: the good work is a sign of the incorporation into the outlook of Christ and of the Saints to which the Church appeals in her intercessory stand on behalf of the person who gains the indulgence.) How and why is there still a concrete and factual difference in this theory between a plenary and a partial indulgence in respect of temporal punishment before God? In other words, is there any intelligible sense in which the authoritative prayer of the Church (in the case of an indulgence) can be intended to relate only to a *part* of the punishment due to sin which is to be remitted by a partial indulgence? Moreover, can what

[13] Cf. M. Schmaus, *Katholische Dogmatik* IV, 1 3/4 (Munich 1952), p. 548.

is contained in the Church's doctrinal pronouncements regarding indulgences be fully reconciled, after thorough analysis, with P.'s theory? Poschmann affirms that it can and gives good reasons for maintaining this. P. certainly does not come into conflict with anything really defined in the matter of indulgences. As to whether this his theory is absolutely compatible with other, if not defined yet theologically binding explanations by the Church of indulgences, is something which would require still closer investigation; it is true, of course, that even such an investigation would have to bear in mind that the expression of such a doctrine taught by the *magisterium* of the Church might possibily be conditioned by some particular age. The references in P. to the explanations given by the Church seem to me to be rather scanty, but of course this question does not really belong to his particular theme.

If we may be allowed to summarize P.'s thesis once more (in terms which do not actually occur in his own formulation of it), we would say that: an indulgence is the sacramental of the remission of sin's temporal punishment before God, and this in conjunction with a jurisdictional remission of an (at least hypothetically) imposed ecclesiastical penance. Being a sacramental, it operates *ex opere operantis* (*orantis*) *Ecclesia*, and not *ex opere operato* as most theologians teach nowadays, even although, for historical reasons,[14] it is connected with a

[14] Galtier, *De Paenitentia*, (new edition, Rome 1950), nos. 612–615 also declares that the 'definition' of an indulgence (contained also in the CIC) which regards indulgences as a remission of temporal punishment due to sin '*per modum absolutionis*', is nothing more now than a historical reminiscence which no longer has any real meaning in the present-day practice of indulgences. This means (in Galtier's sense) that we speak of an '*absolutio*' in contradistinction to a '*solutio*', only in regard to the ecclesiastical penances which were imposed in the past, but not in regard to sin's temporal punishment before God. Since, however, such unperformed penances imposed by the Church, which could be remitted ('absolved') in this way, no longer exist at all in the present-day practice, the expression '*per modum absolutionis*' is merely a reference nowadays to a *former* practice. We do not mean by this to claim Galtier as an advocate (in every detail) of the definition of an indulgence proposed by us above. But his arguments prove at least that we may not adduce the definition given in CIC can. 911 to prove that it is a question here of a jurisdictional act of the Church as the '*per modum absolutionis*' appears in opposition to the '*per modum suffragii*' of the indulgences for the dead. As to whether the '*per modum solutionis*', which Galtier (appealing to Cajetan and Billot) declares to be the real essence of

jurisdictional act of the Church which is concerned with the remission of an ecclesiastical penance and produces a sure effect in this regard.[15] We are inclined to think that this thesis is correct and that the reasons adduced in support of it are worthy of consideration. If indulgences are to be found not only in textbooks but also in the practical life of the man of today, and if they are to be the means of blessings in practical life, then the Church's doctrine of indulgences must be thought through anew and in a living manner by theologians. Poschmann has made a good start in this direction, for which everyone ought to be grateful to him.

---

the indulgence grant (i.e. the placing of the Treasury of the Church at the disposal of the believer so that he may as it were clear off or 'pay' the debt of punishment from it), is a proper jurisdictional act and one which causes '*ex opere operato*' (as Galtier maintains), that is a different question again; and it is, at any rate, a theory which has only as much weight as the reasons adduced in support of it, since it is not taught directly and with binding force in the Church's doctrinal pronouncements. How far we today are in this respect from the old practice which still actually presupposed ecclesiastical punishments which were remitted by indulgences, can be seen also from the following observation: the Council of Trent was still afraid that too liberal a granting of indulgences by the Church could bring about a weakening of ecclesiastical discipline. Today, indulgences have become so much separated from, and independent of Church discipline as a whole, that they can neither further nor endanger it. We do not mean to imply by this that the objective content of the exhortation delivered by the Council has lost its object or need no longer be taken to heart. Galtier, too, (*Gregorianum* XXXI [1950], pp. 273 *sq.*) makes it clear, in appealing to the words of Bellarmine, that this warning given by the Council seems still very real in his opinion.

[15] Our 'definition' is cited by M. Schmaus, *Katholische Dogmatik* IV, 1[4] (Munich 1952), pp. 548 *sq.*, who seems to assent to Poschmann's theory. The same is true of L. Ott, *Fundamentals of Catholic Dogma* (Cork 1960), p. 442: 'The Church Authority possesses the right to dispose of this spiritual treasury, though not strictly judicially . . . In the granting of an Indulgence, the Church appeals to the mercy of God . . . The prayer of the Church requires the gracious acceptance of God, but . . . a hearing can, with moral certainty, be counted on'.

6

THE RESURRECTION OF THE BODY

If we look at things honestly, we must notice that divine revelation—and how could it be otherwise—always overtaxes man in a certain respect. We recognize this also by the fact that certain truths of God's revelation are always in danger of becoming 'un-existential' in the everyday practical life of man. And this not only in the case of those why deny these truths, i.e. 'heretics', but also in the case of good, orthodox Christians. This may be true of almost everyone belonging to a certain period (although it should be noted that not all those who live at the same chronological time are contemporaries), or it may be true of all those who belong to a certain stratum of society, as e.g. the 'educated' (how many of these, for instance, gain indulgences nowadays?). These people do not deny the truth concerned. They perhaps even know the truth quite well. They will perhaps even protest vehemently when such a truth is explicitly denied in some quarter. Nevertheless, such truths are 'believed' in a somewhat similar manner as when we buy something 'along with' something else which we really want, simply because there is no other way of obtaining that other thing we really want. We take cognizance of these truths and then push them (not on reflection, of course, but instinctively) to one side a little, to the periphery of thought and life, into the subconscious (as we would say nowadays), or into the sphere of the *fides implicita* (as they used to say). At any rate, we occupy ourselves with such a truth at the most only on the fringe of our religious consciousness (or not at all), compared with the 'existential' interest shown by us for other truths of the same Faith.

When you ask the orthodox Christian for his beliefs, he will refer you to the Catechism, where all the truths of faith which have been expressed most explicitly and in an existentially clear manner in the history of the Faith up to date, have kept their unchanged place. The orthodox Christian seldom stops to realize that the unprinted catechism of his heart and religious life has quite a different distribution of materials from his printed Catechism, and that in the former many pages of the latter are missing completely or have become quite faded and illegible. He gets on quite well in this way with his printed Catechism. He takes from it what he needs. He finds in it everything necessary for a right way of living and for a happy death. The rest he quietly leaves there: it must be right enough. When a part of it is so good and holy, the rest will be true enough, he would think to himself, if he were to reflect at all on the selective instinct of his practical religious life. And so, on the whole, these other truths too do not cause him much brain racking or many 'difficulties of faith'. It would be interesting to investigate some time the 'interior catechism' of the average Catholic (ten years after his last religion lesson at school) in our day and in our particular region—it will not be the same everywhere in the world. The official catechesis could learn a great deal from this.

The 'unorthodox', the one who has leanings towards heresy, and the 'heretics', open their internal catechism as it were reflectively: whatever they do not find clear in it, they would then like to see removed also from the printed Catechism. They say: whatever *we* today cannot grasp quickly and clearly, vitally and comfortingly in our heart and life, likewise should not weigh down the memory and mind of the Christian of today. The fact that they are so 'difficult' to understand, that they can only be so laboriously reconciled with our present-day religious needs and 'scientific convictions' and generally speaking with everything which we possess in the way of possibilities of belief—this is said to be a sign that these other matters are pious but outmoded notions, fables, outdated expressions of a thought, right in itself, perhaps, but which must be extracted like a kernel out of its shell, myths which must be 'demythologized' to produce the real meaning of Christian thought. This shows, by the way, that the orthodox believer and the Christian heretic differ less from each other in a certain respect than it might seem at first sight. But this also reveals a difference of vital importance (prescinding from everything even more important): once something has been erased from the printed Catechism, how, if what has been erased was true and important for life and shortsightedness and presumptuous modernism (which can be very stupid) have erased it, is it to be reincorporated into it and into the catechism of the heart? Here the *seemingly* so inaccurate and somewhat superficial orthodox person does after all act with a surer instinct; he tells himself: what I do not understand today, what does not mean much to me as yet (in spite of all my good will), can nevertheless be true; tomorrow I will perhaps see it as a most important truth; the day after tomorrow it may be *the* truth of the coming generation.

Does not the 'resurrection of the body' belong to these truths, which are given a wide berth by the orthodox and the heretics alike, but by each in their own way? It is to be found in every Catechism, it is treated of in every course of dogmatic theology and is prayed in every Credo. There are, of course, books—and especially again in most recent times—which try to express this truth more clearly and intelligibly to the present generation. But this has not meant any very great change as yet. Things are really as they were in the early days: 'Now when they heard of a resurrection of the dead, some began to sneer, but others said, "we will hear thee again on this matter"' (Ac 17.32). Since one's 'sneering' can also arise out of profound thought and deep affliction, the present-day sneerers are those who are 'demythologizing'. But the orthodox Christians should not be too quick to become indignant with them. For they themselves are probably those who in their lives today want to hear about it 'again', in other words—never. Nor can it be said that the dogmatic definition of the Assumption of the Blessed Virgin, *body* and soul, into heavenly glory, is a proof of how alive the eleventh article of the Creed is in the hearts of Christians. For it is significant how little, how hesitatingly and really lifelessly the whole literature on the Assumption entered into the *content* of the new Dogma. Hardly any portion of this literature seized the opportunity to re-state more precisely and vitally, and to study more profoundly, *what* precisely is meant by 'the resurrection of the body'. One acted as if nothing new was to be said about *this*, as if everything about this were already clear, in so far as this is at all possible, and as if the question were merely as to whether Mary has already found this consummation *now*.

This article of faith has, if we may say so, always had a troubled existence, ever since it stepped out of the world of late Judaism (since Dan 12.2 *sq.*; 2 Mac 7) and of the New Testament (where it belongs to the first elements of Christ's teaching; Heb 6.1), to begin its journey through the history of the Church and of the Spirit. It was given the assent of faith. This goes without saying. For it is attested by the Scriptures, the word of our Lord and his apostles. Indeed, theology too always pondered on it. In the Middle Ages it was perhaps reflected on even with precision and loving interest (as far as was possible at that time), since the Middle Ages were a period which was still capable of humbly and obediently resisting its own overloud taste and its own tendencies of thinking and living—no matter how much we nevertheless notice, of course, in what direction it actually tended in its theology. They defended the article of faith. Against the pagans and their 'Idealism': Tertullian did so even passionately—*Caro salutis est cardo;* against spiritualistic tendencies among Christians, such as those of the Gnostics and of Origen (interpreted this way); against the Albigenses and Cathari in the Middle Ages; against Rationalism and Enlightenment thought. The populace, the naive man who likes to think pictorially, has always liked to picture the Last Day to himself (more terrified, it is true, than comforted) with the bodies rising from the graves and the Judgement: *tuba mirum spargens sonum.* And even today, this sociological milieu is still favourable for massive images of the resurrection, as is shown by the spread of sects of a chiliastic kind.

Thus far everything in the garden seems to be lovely and in order. And yet the road along which this article has travelled, has been a hard one. Whenever the Fathers became 'philosophers', i.e. platonists, it is noticeable that they find it difficult to include the body in the victory of the 'spirit'. In the history of this Dogma during the Middle Ages, the view of the end veers more and more away from the resurrection of the body to the soul's direct vision of God. And it becomes clearer all the time (even *against* St Bernard) that this *visio* can already be granted to the individual soul before the cosmic resurrection and consummation, until this doctrine is finally enforced in the Dogma of Benedict XII (in 1336). Almost all that the average Christian of today has written in his internal catechism is merely that the good go 'to heaven' after death. He writes on the little in-memoriam-cards: 'What we bury in the coffin is earth's vesture. What we love has remained, and remains to all eternity'. For St Paul the resurrection was the prerequired condition for the participation by the deceased in the full blessing of Christ and in his Second Coming. The average Christian of today, if he were to reflect basing himself on his unwritten catechism, would ask in astonishment why the happily deceased should be so interested in the Second Coming of Christ, since he is after all already with Christ and God in beatitude and so does not need to concern himself very much any more about the fate of this world here below. Even for the theologian, the 'resurrection' is usually an 'accidental' increase in the essentially already fully realized beatitude of the soul, in so far as the body is then reawakened as well and is reunited with the soul. For him too, therefore, the resurrection is very much a supplementary matter. We would suppose that if he had to make a new draft of the Creed, it would be more likely to contain an expression of the 'immortality of the soul'—which after all is stressed in many catechisms as a 'basic truth'—without mentioning in this connection the 'basic truth' of the Epistle to the Hebrews, viz. the resurrection of the dead.

What those who wish to 'demythologize' have to say against this Dogma (and against it especially) because it, practically more than any other, gives rise naturally to objection, does not require to be specified here. All this seems too 'miraculous' for them to dare to expect the contemporary man of physics to accept it. They will then maintain furthermore (falsely indeed, but with a certain semblance of truth) that the Bible itself does already begin to demythologize here and there, in so far as the bodily resurrection does not seem to be nearest to its heart everywhere in the same way, and sometimes no longer appears to be anything more than some sort of covering image for the timeless validity of the victory of the faith over the powers of death and the futility of life. They will point to the fact that medieval theology far into modern times, imagined the resurrection and transfiguration of the body within a world which no longer exists: the *caelum empyreum* as the highest and most sublime world-sphere, which as a 'spatial division' of *this* world exists before the *time*-of-salvation and its events as the fixed framework of saving history. Into this highest sphere, therefore, the bodily substance of man, to which this region has become connatural through the resurrection and transfiguration of the body, can emigrate as to its 'heavenly' place—to Christ who by his 'Ascension into Heaven' has 'ascended' into this sphere. Those who wish to 'demythologize' will ask *where* this heaven is. It must after all be a place, if the doctrine of the glorified bodily nature is to retain any inner content. How are we to 'conceive' this bodily substance? Will we still eat there, and how are we to conceive this, if it happened in the case of the risen Lord, without the wheel of changeableness and perishableness being set in motion again? Can any such bodily substance be thought of in any other way than as a prison, if we remain eternally restrained by it, or does it still make sense and is it honest to speak of a body when we make a spirit or something else unimaginable out of it, in order to render the 'glorified nature' of the body intelligible?

Before we ask ourselves in the concrete what we Christians really believe when we profess the Resurrection of the Body (and whether this is believable and moreover significant for us), we can hardly avoid saying a basic word or two on the subject of 'demythologizing'. It will by no means be a thorough treatise on this question, and even less a historical statement of the pros and cons in this matter. It will simply be a question of one or two remarks to render what follows *à propos* the subject of this chapter more intelligible. All human knowledge is always bipolar: conceptual and intuitional at the same time. Even the most abstract and most precise metaphysical notions still include their particular intuitional element. Under certain circumstances an intuitional *happening* may belong and be suited to this necessary intuitional element just as much as the static image. The boundary between the image and what is meant by it is not to be found at exactly the same point in all 'meant' realities, if only for the simple reason that even something directly representable can be 'meant' (e.g. the cessation of new births, etc.). The 'proto-historical' (Gen 1–3) and the 'eschatological' must of their very nature show the greatest distance for us between their representation or image on the one hand and the intended or meant object on the other hand. Although something can be meant only together with and under cover of a representation (an image, a representable happening), it is possible to mean realities and happenings which cannot be represented (e.g. the 'depth' of the soul, the '*sub*'-conscious, the 'pure' spirit). Man can recognize the inadequacy of such notions, in which the representing element is taken 'as a makeshift' from some *other* reality than the one meant by the notion itself, and hence he can criticize and change this element. He does this, not by doing away with this element and obtaining a 'pure' concept of the object itself and in itself alone—which is beyond what can be represented—but by modifying his representation and looking at the reality anew. This can be done since the reality though not representable in itself can still be conceived from different points of 'view', and thus man gains a clear understanding of the various points where the individual image and representation is merely an image and representation without applying simply as such to the referred-to object in itself.

When someone undertakes in this sense a critique of the representation-schemata of the religious concepts which are used for a Dogma, and does so cautiously and slowly, in the constant endeavour (under the control of the *magisterium* of the Church) of not losing anything of the content of faith in the process, then he does not 'demythologize', but does something which theology has always done and must always do. And conversely, if he does *this*, he can easily see that *he* has no cause to demythologize and that such a 'demythologizing' is ultimately nothing else but his own, in itself perfectly justified method (if properly applied), which has been badly applied in this particular case, because one has—rightly—emptied out the bath-water and—unjustifiably—the child with it. This critique of the schemata of representation always remains unfinished; for we can always conceive something only with the help of *other* 'representations'. The 'critique' is, therefore, of necessity, just as inadequate in relation to the object in itself as the 'criticized' proposition. In many cases in theology it will not be possible at all to say where *precisely* the meant object stops and the '*mere*' image begins. In such cases the believing Christian and theologian will abide by the usage of the Scriptures and Tradition in theology and even more so in the proclamation of the Faith, because he knows after all that he has there an image which has been sanctioned and which allows the matter itself to be seen correctly, even though it is impossible in this case to achieve an adequate reflective separation of the two elements. There are of course notions whose representative element is of such a basically human and at the same time objectively unavoidable kind, that these notions, once they have been found, cannot really be replaced by any better ones. But in every concept there takes place a *conversio ad phantasmata*, as St Thomas says. All knowledge about any reality, no matter how supramundane the object and strict and abstract the notion, is knowledge in 'likenesses and parables'

Now, it is important to observe that the different parts of Scripture, when depicting the events of the consummation of the world and of the resurrection of the dead included therein, give descriptions which simply cannot be combined together into one unified *picture*, however much they mean the same thing objectively and without contradiction. Sometimes our regard is directed to the resurrection of the just alone who, conscious of their salvation, go out happily to meet their returning Lord and come up to join him as his retinue, so that there is no longer any room—in this *image*, it must be added—for a *universal* resurrection and a yet to be accomplished separation of the good and the bad. Or, at other times, the saints are the retinue of the Lord who come with him from above. At one time the end takes place on earth, which only then becomes the place of beatitude; at another time the place of beatitude is the already existing abode above into which man enters on leaving the earth. The figurative nature and the easy freedom and practical variability of the cosmic images (the conflagration of the world, the falling of the stars onto the earth, etc.) is too clear to allow us any possibility of thinking that they were not recognized as being imaginative by the original speakers. Who can seriously doubt that even the writer of Holy Scripture knew that in the case of many the phrase 'the tombs open up' cannot correspond exactly to the actual manner of their resurrection? We do not need to be afraid that we will depart from the teaching of St Paul, if we do not rack our brains too much about how the dead will hear the sound of the archangel's trumpet and how this harmonizes with the sending out of the many angels or with the resuscitating voice of the Lord himself, which we are told about in his own eschatological discourses. We can regard this text as an image and yet be terrified by what it truly means to convey both to the people of those days and to us today: the all-powerfulness of God over the dead, who even when dead cannot escape him; indeed, we may conjecture that God in his omnipotence, just because he is all-powerful and never in danger of being rivalled, will give even the created forces of the world a share in the work of the consummation of the dead into the life beyond all death. It follows from this that we are not 'demythologizing', but that it is an unavoidable and justified task, when we ask quite simply what reality—according to the intention of the Scriptures themselves—these eschatological, popular and poetic illustrations are actually meant to convey. For the reason given, a harmonization of the pictorial elements on their *own* level is quite superfluous and not at all in keeping with the intention of the Scriptures. In this case, too, it will not always be possible to separate the form and the content without ambiguity.

And so when we Christians profess our belief in the 'resurrection of the body', what then do we really mean by it? What is the least we mean by it?

'Body' (*Fleisch*) means the whole man in his proper embodied reality. 'Resurrection' means, therefore, the termination and perfection of the *whole* man before God, which gives him 'eternal life'. Man is a many-sided being which in (and despite) its unity stretches, as it were, through several very different dimensions—through matter and spirit, nature and person, action and passion, etc. And so it is not surprising that the process of man's perfecting and the entrance into this perfection is not in itself a simple and identical quantity in every respect. And it is not surprising that the 'moment' of completion of such a stratified being is not simply the same for every one of these dimensions. Hence, as the Church's consciousness in faith has come to comprehend ever more clearly—instructed as it has been by the beginnings of such a comprehension in the Scriptures—the continuing reality of the personal spirit can already reach the direct communion with God by the event and moment which, looked at from its intramundane side, we experience as death. In so far as this union with God constitutes the innermost being of blessed completion, 'heaven' and 'eternal happiness' can already be given with death (Denz 530). Nevertheless, the deceased remains 'united' with the reality, fate and hence the temporal events of the world, however little we are able to 'picture' to ourselves such a continuing belonging-to-the-world and however few immediately comprehensible statements on this matter are contained in the Scriptures. We must simply try to realize clearly and soberly that a spiritual union with God cannot be regarded as something which grows in inverse proportion to the belonging to the *material* world, but that these are two quite disparate matters in themselves. Thus basically, for instance, there can be vision of God before death, and 'separation from the body' for the soul in death does not by a long way need to mean *ipso facto* a greater nearness to God. Remoteness-from-the-world and nearness-to-God are not interchangeable notions, however much we are accustomed to think in such a framework.

The deceased remain therefore (despite the *visio beatifica*) united with the fate of the world.

This world in its totality has a beginning and a history; it goes on towards a point which is not the end of its existence but the end of its unfinished and continually self-propagating history. It is true, we may not succeed in representing to ourselves concretely *how* it will be possible at some time to separate its continued existence in itself, on the one hand, and its transition into the unknown (to our prevision), on the other hand; it may be impossible to imagine how the former continues while the latter ceases. We may not be able to say what the then remaining world will be like (all attempts to picture this to oneself never get beyond the image). And yet, for all that, this final state of the world as a whole, which will come at a certain point but has not come as yet, is more *conceivable* for us today than it was perhaps for earlier generations and especially for the ancients. For to them this world of their experience gave the impression of being something eternal; change and transitoriness was only a happening in the lowest stratum of all in this 'eternal' world of 'eternal' laws, which was enveloped by the quietly reposing serenity of celestial spheres; for them (even for the Christians[1]), beatitude could, therefore, only mean leaving the sphere of the transitory for the blessed heavenly spheres intended for this 'migration' in the framework of saving history; the history of salvation took place in the 'heaven'-enveloped world, but was not the development itself of heaven. We today are becoming more clearly aware of the developmental character of our world as a whole, in spite of the ultimate uncertainty of the natural sciences and the extremely profound problems of a 'harmonization' of theological data and our natural knowledge of the world. We have come to realize the senselessness of trying to retrace the existence of the world into the infinite; the world itself, practically down to the last detail—and not merely the revolutions of its stars—is temporal.

If we allow the 'becoming', time and history to be really temporal and do not in the end turn them again into a false eternity, then we may say (very carefully): it does not contradict the nature of the world that this open, self-propagating history has a beginning and an end. Who can say how far this end is the very 'running-itself-to-death' of the course of the world itself (which is happening in accordance with its eternal laws), how far a halt is called by the creative and restraining Word of God, how far both of these things ultimately come to the same thing! We know at any rate from the testimony of God that this history of the world will come to an end, and that this end will not be a sheer cessation, a 'being-no-longer' of the world itself, but the participation in the perfection of the spirit. For this spirit is assigned a beginning, but in relation to God. And hence its beginning is not

[1] In their view the world as a whole was created and *temporal*. But this is far from implying that medieval theology could clearly see the radical temporal and historical character, as we experience it, of even the superlunary spheres of the world.

the beginning of the end, but the beginning of a development in freedom towards freely achieved completion, which does not let the becoming end up in nothingness, but transforms it into the state of finality. Furthermore, the deepest conviction of Christianity and of idealism is true: the personal spirit is the meaning of the whole reality of the world and, in spite of all its biologico-physical insignificance, it is *not merely* a strange guest in a world which, standing ultimately untouched and indifferent opposite this spirit, carries on its own history; the personal spirit, precisely as human spirit, is a material, mundane, incarnate—indeed *intra*-mundane spirit. And so the end of the world is participation in the perfection of the spirit: the world remains, beyond its previous history, as the connatural surrounding of the achieved spirit which has found its finality in the fellowship with God and achieves its own history and that of the world at the same point. If this is so, however, it is necessary to consider what exact form this history of spiritual persons has taken and is taking: it is a history which, as the history of mankind, has taken place (consciously or veiled to itself) with, for and against the Person of the One who—right through death and resurrection—possessed the life of God and the history of a human reality at one and the same time—Jesus Christ, our Lord. The end of the world is, therefore, the perfection and total achievement of saving history which had already come into full operation and gained its decisive victory in Jesus Christ and in his resurrection. In this sense his coming takes place at this consummation in power and glory: his victory made manifest, the breaking through into experience, and the becoming manifest for experience too, of the fact that the world as a whole flows into his Resurrection and into the transfiguration of his body. His Second Coming is not an event which is enacted in a localized manner on the stage of an *un*changed world which occupies a determined point in space in this world of our experience (how could everyone see it otherwise, for instance?); his Second Coming takes place at the moment of the perfecting of the world into the reality which he already possesses now, in such a way that he, the Godman, will be revealed to all reality and, within it, to every one of its parts in its own way, as the innermost secret and centre of all the world and of all history.

This is the context into which we must fit what we call the resurrection of the body in the strict sense. The history—which has remained within the framework of the world—of those who by their lives have already effected their personal finality, reaches its real completion and explicit expression together with the consummation of the world. These human beings now become achieved as totalities with soul and body, and their perfection, already begun in death, becomes itself perfected, tangible in the world, embodied. We cannot really imagine the 'how' of this bodily consummation. But we can say in our faith together with God's revelation: I believe, that we will one day be the living, the complete and achieved ones, in the whole expanse and in all the dimensions of our existence; I believe that what we call the material in us and in the world surrounding us (without really being able to say what it is basically, what belongs to its essence and what only to its temporary form and appearance) is not simply identical with what is unreal and mere appearance, with what has been cast off once and for all and which passes away before the final state of man. If, however, the material world is not simply an objective illusion, and is not merely some sort of material which must be taken off and on which the history of souls gets practice in freedom until it has achieved its end, but is a part of the true reality itself, then the material world does for that very reason enter into the consummation in accordance with the divine promise, and it too can participate in the state of finality and completion. When we look at the risen Christ, taking into consideration the experience the Apostles had with him, we may also get some idea of what the perfected condition of the body is like in which the created spirit achieves itself. Only, in doing this, we must not forget that what the Apostles, being themselves as yet unachieved, were able to experience of this consummation, is a somewhat broken, translated experience, and that even then it still remains obscure how the perfected appears to the perfected. In the last analysis, therefore, we can merely say in St Paul's language of paradox: it will be a spiritual body (1 Cor 15.44), i.e. a true bodily nature which, however, is pure expression of the spirit become one with the *pneuma* of God and its bodily existence, and is no longer its restricting and abasing element and its emptiness. It will be a bodily nature which does not cancel again the freedom from the earthly here-and-now gained with death, but will, on the contrary, bring it out in its pure form.

If (and in so far as) we cannot think of the physical nature and concreteness of the risen and real person (even in accordance with what was experienced with regard to the risen Christ) in any other way than together with a definite spatial and local determination, then we must think of heaven as a place and not merely as a 'state'. In so far as there are already human beings (the risen Lord, our Lady and no doubt others: cf. Mt 27.52) who possess a glorified bodily nature, *this* place does already exist as a result, even if not as the presupposition (as the ancients thought), of this transformation of the incarnate human spirit. When we remember the intrinsic finiteness of our own physical spatiality, which is not a presupposition but an inner moment of non-glorified matter and the result of its history, we will not find it impossible to conceive (not: 'to imagine') that this spatiality and the heavenly 'kind of space' are in themselves essentially different and incommensurable quantities. This, however, means then that, on the one hand, it is *a-priori* senseless to ask where heaven is (if by this 'where' we are to understand a location in *our* physical spatial world), and that, on the other hand, it remains nevertheless possible to hold fast most 'realistically' to the conception of the bodily existence of the glorified, including their spatial determination and location. We do not need to accommodate those in heaven in the physical world system of our experience. Since we are, however, learning in physics nowadays more than ever to think abstractly, there will be less of an obstacle in this than before to our taking the existence of those in heaven very seriously in a non-pictorial way. Once the history of the Cosmos and of the spiritual world has come to its complete end, everything will be transformed. It will then be equally correct to call the one new reality a new heaven or a new earth.

The complete, all-embracing solution is always the most difficult, because it must reconcile everything. It is most difficult for such a solution to penetrate the narrow limits of our mind which demand concise and synoptical solutions. And so it is also with regard to the question about the end. Anyone who disposes of the earthly world and dismisses the perfected man from this earth for good, spiritualistically or existentially or in whatever other way, directing him into a beatitude of (supposedly) pure spirits, stultifies and betrays the true reality of man, the child of this earth. Whoever lets man perish, ground to pieces in the cruel mill of Nature, does not know what spirit and person are, and does not know how much more real, in spite of all their apparent weakness, the spirit and the person are than all the matter and energy of physics. Whoever does not believe that both of them, once reconciled, can come to the one completion, denies in the last analysis that the one God has created spirit and matter in one act for one end. The Christian, however, is the man with the complete solution. This solution is the most difficult, the least synoptical. The belief for this solution and the courage for such a solution he draws from the Word of God alone. But God's Word testifies to the resurrection of the body. For the Word himself became flesh. He did not assume something unreal but something created. But whatever is created by God is never something merely negative, is never the veil of maya. Whatever has been created by God, assumed by Christ and transfigured by his Death and Resurrection, is also destined to finality and consummation in us.

7

ON THE QUESTION OF A FORMAL EXISTENTIAL ETHICS

THE subject on which we are going to reflect in this chapter reads: On the question of a formal existential ethics. It is not for the sake of making a gesture of humility that we speak of a *question*: for practically everything we can say here is and remains in fact problematical. What exactly is meant and implied by 'existential ethics' and 'formal' existential ethics should become clear in the course of our considerations.

Our subject must first of all be distinguished from what is nowadays usually called situation ethics. It would be interesting to know who first introduced the term 'situation ethics' into the present-day discussions of moral theology and philosophy. What is meant by this term can be presupposed as known; it is also well known that situation ethics has frequently been discussed during the last few years within the realm of the German language. We may remind the reader (apart from the great names of existentialist philosophy) of the essays and books by W. Dirks, R. Egenter, J. Fuchs, M. Galli, H. E. Hengstenberg, H. Hirschmann, Ernst Michel, M. Müller, M. Reding, G. Siewerth, Th. Steinbüchel and by the author of these *Investigations*.[1] The

[1] W. Dirks, 'Wie erkenne ich, was Gott von mir will?', *Frankfurter Hefte* VI (1951), pp. 229–244; R. Egenter, *Von der Freiheit der Kinder Gottes* (Freiburg[2] 1949); *id.*, 'Kasuistik als christliche Situationsethik', *Münchener Theologische Zeitschrift* I (1950), pp. 54–65; J. Fuchs, *Situation und Entscheidung* (Frankfurt 1952) (cf. pp. 163–168 in this work for further bibliographical references); M. Galli, in *Orientierung* XIV (1950), pp. 13–16, 27–30, 37–39, 52–54; H. E. Hengstenberg, *Die göttliche Vorsehung* (Münster[3] 1947); *id.*, *Die Frage der Individuation als aktuelles Problem: Die Kirche in der Welt*[4] (1951), pp. 349–352; H. Hirschmann, '"Herr, was willst Du, dass ich tun soll?" Situationsethik und Erfüllung des Willens Gottes', *Geist und Leben* XXIV (1951), pp. 300–304; E. Michel, *Renovatio. Zur Zwiesprache zwischen Kirche und Welt* (Aulendorf 1947); *id.*, *Der Partner Gottes. Weisungen zum christlichen Selbstverständnis* (Heidelberg 1946); *id.*, *Rettung und Erneuerung*

general human bases for the rise of an extreme situation ethics are known to us: the intricacy of man's life at the present time and the uncertainty and manifoldness of the ethical norms advocated. The following are the theoretical foundations of situation ethics: on the one hand, an extreme existentialist philosophy, and on the other hand, a protestant repugnance to the validity of a 'law' within a Christian way of human existence. What situation ethics implies in consequence of this is easily understandable: it denies the universal obligation (and one which remains valid in every case) of material universal norms in the concrete individual case, it being quite immaterial whether these norms be conceived as a natural law or as a positive divine law. Norms are universal, but man as an existent is the individual and unique in each case, and hence he cannot be regulated in his actions by material norms of a universal kind. Man is the believer; and faith sets free from the Law. There remains then as 'norm' of action only the call of each particular unique situation through which man must pass successfully, be it before the inappellable judgement of his free decision as a person, or be it before God, whose immediateness to the situation, conscience and faith must not be thought of as mediated by a universal law. A law can therefore only have the function of making man always face up again to each situation peculiar to him, or forcing him to believe, but it cannot be that which has to be fulfilled. How such

---

des personalen Lebens (Frankfurt 1951); M. Müller, *Exkurs über das Verhältnis der 'existenziellen Entscheidung' zur Idee einer Wesens-, Ordnungs- u. Ziel-Ethik: Existenz-philosophie im geistigen Leben der Gegenwart* (Heidelberg 1949), pp. 100–106; Pius XII, *Allocutio* to the Congress of the 'Fédération mondiale des Jeunesses Féminines Catholiques', on 18th April 1952, AAS XLIV (1952), pp. 413–419; K. Rahner, 'Situationsethik und Sündenmystik', *Stimmen der Zeit* CXLV (1949–50), pp. 333–342; cf. also in the *present* volume: 'The Dignity and Freedom of Man' (pp. 235–263) and 'Freedom in the Church' (pp. 89–107), and the works of the author referred to in the notes to the present essay; M. Reding, 'Situationsethik, Kasuistik und Ethos der Nachfolge', *Gloria Dei* V (1951), pp. 290–292; *id.*, *Die philosophische Grundlegung der katholischen Moraltheologie* (Munich 1953); G. Siewerth, 'Von der Bildung des Gewissens', *Mitteilungsblatt des Aachener Bundes und der pädagischen Akademie* (June 1951), pp. 3–36; Th. Steinbüchel, *Die philosophische Grundlegung der katholischen Sittenlehre* I (Düsseldorf[4] 1951); *id.*, *Christliche Lebenshaltungen in der Krisis der Zeit und des Menschen* (Frankfurt 1949); A. van Rijen, 'Situatie Moraal', *Nederlandse Katholicke Stemmen* XLIX (1953), pp. 265–276.

a situation ethics is then established more in detail, whether it is in fact always advocated in the extreme form we have just outlined and whether every theory which calls itself 'situation ethics' adopts this extreme position—all these are questions which need not occupy us here. When we speak here of an (extreme) situation ethics, we mean the explicit or implicit denial of the absolute validity of material norms for the human person as such or the believer as such—the denial of norms which can state something which is also binding in the concrete situation.

That such a situation ethics is unacceptable to a Catholic hardly needs any lengthy proof, however much the practice of many Catholics in the present age is in danger of favouring such a situation ethics unconsciously. This kind of situation ethics comes in the last analysis to the same thing as a massive nominalism; it basically denies the possibility of any universal knowledge which has objective significance and truly applies to concrete reality. It turns the human person into an individual who is absolutely and in every respect unique (which the human person, considered as created and material, is not), and (what is far more important still) it also comes into conflict with divine revelations as given in the Scriptures and *magisterium* of the Church. It is not our intention to expound and establish all this more closely here. All this has, after all, been impressed once more on Catholic theologians in most recent times by 'Humani generis'.[2] Yet we must nevertheless add one thing even to this: one may get the impression that we sometimes make the proof for this rejection too easy for ourselves. For the question is—among other things—the following: *How* do we determine, for instance, the eternal, universal and unchanging nature of man? Is it by a transcendental deduction (and in that case, how and with what results)? Or can this notion of the nature be found in a purely *a-posteriori* empirical fashion? Or partly in the former, partly in the latter way? However, is the *a-posteriori* determined condition of man really unchangeable? How do I recognize in it what really belongs to the nature? Is what we have (until now) been able to find always and everywhere a sure and sufficient criterion for this condition? Can this existence (investigated *a posteriori*), *may* it (morally), be changed by man himself who achieves himself freely? What would follow in this case as to what

[2] Cf. also the Allocution by Pius XII referred to in note 1 above, p. 217.

concerns the moral norms? What would then be the peculiar structure of the knowledge concerning this sort of essential make-up of man (which is first of all effected and delivered in and through freedom) and the moral norms drawn from it? Of what kind would then be the 'necessity' indicated in such norms? What sort of relationship is there basically between law, faith, grace and freedom according to St Paul? There will no doubt be few theologians who can remember from their school years in theology ever having heard anything really exact about these questions. Yet, as has been said, none of these questions are up for discussion here. We have referred to situation ethics at the beginning of our reflections merely because, on the one hand, what we are going to call 'formal existential ethics' must not be confused with the (outlined) situation ethics, and because, on the other hand, this existential ethics is in our opinion the core of truth which is also found in the false situation ethics.

In order to come now to a positive understanding of what is meant by existential ethics, we are going to start from a critical view of the reigning conception in our present-day Catholic Moral Theology and Philosophy about the content and process of a definite moral imperative with material content in a concrete situation of the individual man. It does not really matter to us here whether in the course of this discussion of the common conception, absolutely everything is really brought out which has ever been thought and said about this question in scholastic theology and philosophy by profound and illustrious minds. What is above all important for our purposes is rather what is normally thought about this in the schools and in the *turba magna* of minor theologians. For this is precisely in question for us: whether this common conception really does justice to the way things are in reality.

Let us take a determined material imperative for a particular person in a concrete situation: here and now, this particular thing with this particular material content is to be done by you. Now how, according to the common conception of our present-day moral teaching, does such a concrete and materially determined imperative come about for the individual man in his particular determined situation? Surely it does so by the fact that the application of universal moral norms to the concrete situation results *ipso facto* in the concrete imperative. Naturally this conception knows also that in the concrete individual case there may possibly be several things which can be lawfully done (I may, for instance, in certain circumstances choose to go for a walk *hic et nunc* or say my breviary). Yet this does not alter anything in this way of understanding things as far as the basic conviction is concerned that the concrete imperative arises out of a universal norm and the concrete situation simply given as a matter of fact. Simply, this imperative is in the case just mentioned merely a concrete permissiveness of several possibilities. This permissiveness itself is in this case the norm which arises out of the general norms plus the given situation.

It is not essential for us to know here how these universal norms are founded and how they are recognized. We can presuppose as given that they exist and that they are recognized by the acting subject as being obligatory for him. The question in this common conception is merely as to what is the given situation here, and what application of determined universal norms is demanded by this situation. The situation, as it were, gives the cue for the choice of the universal norms to be considered here and now. What is carried out and applied, are the universal norms and they alone. The situation is conceived tacitly and as a matter of course as *simply pre-existent* to the finding of the norm and the making of one's decision. The coincidence of this simply objective situation and the general norm results, according to the common opinion, in the concrete imperative in this situation, and this quite unambiguously, in such a way that apart from these two factors nothing more is required for the finding of the concrete imperative. Or put in another way: according to the common teaching, ethics is a syllogistic, deductive ethics. I.e., the major premise contains a universal principle: in this situation, under these presuppositions this or that is to be done. It must be noted in this connection that in such a major even the situation is something abstract—something of which it is tacitly presupposed that it can in principle happen often and that it can, therefore, be (adequately) expressed in a universal notion and in a universal proposition. The minor premise of this syllogism then asserts the fact that the presuppositions, the situation is given *hic et nunc*. The conclusion finally converts the major into a concrete and clear imperative. Conscience, accordingly, is conceived exclusively as that mental-moral function of the person which applies the universal norm to the concrete '*casus*'. The difficulty in discovering the moral imperative in the concrete is accordingly seen to lie only in the exactness and adequacy of the analysis of the given situation *in concreto* and, under certain circumstances, in the unambiguous expression of the universal norms. However, if both these things are absolutely clear—this is the tacit view—then there can no longer be any doubt about the concrete imperative. Whoever knows the universal laws exactly and comprehends the given situation to the last detail, knows also clearly what he must or may do here. An ethics whose norms are theocentric, will naturally admit in this theory that the living God can, in the nature of things and basically, manifest his will in the concrete situation—a will which need not be derivable either from a universal norm or from the situation distinct from that manifestation, and which must then nevertheless be obeyed. Yet either such a case will always be regarded as an exception, or such a particular commandment of God will, in spite of everything, be subsumed under the general divine norms or be counted as a factor in the given situation. And so, nothing in the fundamentals of the general theory of a syllogistic, deductive ethics is altered by this case.

Is there any justification for this current view? This question is naturally not meant in the sense of wishing to question the fact that universal norms can and must be applied to the individual case, or that the individual case must obey these norms. Otherwise we would after all fall back into the very situation ethics which we dismissed as unacceptable at the beginning of this chapter. We also do not mean to dispute the fact that in practice, in thousands of cases in everyday life, the method just described suffices for obtaining a concrete moral imperative. This is obvious. And we do not have the least intention of dramatizing the speculative problem towards which we are steering and of acting as if there had been no theory of morals up until now sufficiently acceptable in practice. Yet there remains the following question to be put to the theory described above: is what we are in fact morally obliged to do in the concrete case, also basically identical with what can be deduced from the universal norms in view of a concrete situation? The morally obligatory cannot and must not contradict these norms—this is clear. There can be nothing which actually ought to be done or is allowed in a concrete or individual situation, which could lie outside these universal norms, and to that extent everything which morally ought to be done in the concrete is also the realization of the universal norms. But is it not *more* than that? Is what is morally done *only* the realization of universal norms—is what ought morally to be done in the concrete case *merely*, as it were, the intersection of the law and the given situation? And conversely:

if in a certain situation the universal laws leave room for a free choice, i.e. if according to the universal norms several things are still 'allowed' and ethically possible in a determined situation, can we then do what we want, just because *ex supposito* we do not in such a case offend against any universal laws whose content could be materially formulated? Is the concretion of the individual moral good (i.e. of the concrete morally good action) merely the negative circumscription of the ethical universal by a definite here and now, which carves out a portion for the here and now out of the sum-total of what is ethically possible and allowed, without this becoming and being more than a case or *casus* of the universal?

We should like to answer: 'No'. The reasons for this 'no' and the explanation of the counterthesis lead us into the set of difficult problems regarding the basic relationship between the universal and the individual, applied to the ethical universal and the ethical individual. We cannot, of course, hope to treat this wider question here in the manner demanded by the nature of the matter. The only possible alternative, therefore, is to give a few indications regarding this question. For this question cannot be passed over if we wish to pose the problem at all from which we have taken our departure.

We would really have to ask already at this point as to what exactly is the position of the situation whose existence and perceptibility we have up until now presupposed, following the current conception of the formation of a concrete moral imperative. How does one, as a matter of fact, perceive such a situation and how far can one perceive it reflectively? Can a concrete situation—at least in principle—be adequately analysed into a finite series of general propositions? For there are no other kinds of propositions apart from general ones. For besides such propositions there is only the no longer propositional turning towards the concrete by pointing to it: 'That there belongs to this kind'—a 'sentence' whose subject is not a notion. And now, if there is not (in a complete way), nor cannot at all be, such an adequate analysis of the concrete situation as such into formulable propositions, what follows then from this as far as the theory described above is concerned? I.e. what follows for it, in so far as it alleges that it not merely states something definite and essential about a concrete case (especially by negative judgements and maxims), but also claims furthermore to be able to provide us fundamentally with the clear imperative for a situation which as such cannot, after all, be captured unequivocally and adequately by the syllogism and be built into it? As is well known, the medieval metaphysics of knowledge greatly racked its brain—even as far as the field of the knowledge of the ethical was concerned—about these and similar questions. We do not get the impression that the average textbook ethics of today is very much perturbed by questions of this kind. However, we intend to leave all these questions to one side, although we could—even from this angle—work up to the real question we have proposed to ourselves.

We want to approach our problem from a different angle. Let us presuppose (in an almost impossible oversimplification of the problem) that we have clarified and mentally penetrated a certain situation through and through, and that we have comprehended it by some sort of faculty of human knowledge in the moral field—let us say, by the virtue of prudence, etc. Let us suppose further, that all the universal material norms of ethical action, which can in any way apply to this case, are displayed before our eyes in all their clarity. Suppose that by reason of both these presuppositions, we have formulated a concrete moral demand of which we can say with certitude: by fulfilling this demand, we certainly do not offend against any of the universal norms applicable to this case—and also do not offend against any demand made on us by this situation, in so far as this situation has become a reflex datum for us through its analysis into propositions. The question then is this: is the fulfilment of the imperative identical in the concrete with what we are morally obliged to do here and now? Once more: the question is not whether even what we ought to do here and now might perhaps be permitted to offend against the imperative produced in the manner described. Any question of this being possible must be put out of our mind from the very start. Rather, the question is merely whether this imperative is simply identical with what we are obliged to do here and now. And this question has not yet been answered simply by what we have just described as unquestionable. It has not yet been answered for at least two reasons. Firstly: it is at least conceivable that—even in a concrete situation—all the universal norms that can be found still leave different ways of acting open to us as being allowed and possible in their respective spheres. Indeed, this will happen very often. In such a case, is all of what is allowed before the tribunal of the universal norms actually possible morally, or can it also happen that, from some other source altogether, only one of these 'permitted' possibilities of action is designated as the only morally right one in the concrete? Anyone who opts for the first alternative, presupposes what has first to be proved, viz. the proposition that what ought morally to be done in the concrete is nothing more than merely a case and specifying application of the universal norms. This, however, has to be proved and this is precisely what we are questioning. And secondly: even if in the dimension of what is reflectively assignable, the dimension of the describable difference of possible actions and behaviours, only one action is morally permitted in a determined situation according to the universal norms—when, therefore, the syllogistic deduction has seemingly succeeded unequivocally—even then there still remains the question as to whether just this apparently one and unambiguously determined action could not take quite a different form in a dimension which can no longer be adequately regulated by the universal norms, and yet be here and now the only right one and the one carrying the moral obligation. Taking both reasons together, it is possible to ask: is what corresponds to the universal norms simply identical with what ought to be done here and now, and is what obeys these norms also simply without further qualification what is morally permitted? More concisely still: Is the concrete moral action merely a case of the universal moral good?

This however, seems completely open to question. The concrete moral act is more than just the realization of a universal idea happening here and now in the form of a case. The act is a reality which has a positive and substantial property which is basically and absolutely unique. To prove this in a precise and sufficient manner goes beyond the possibilities offered here. We can only give a few indications of what we mean. We can, to start with, say from a more Christian and *theological* standpoint: Man is destined to eternal life as an individual and someone in the concrete. His acts are, therefore, not merely of a spatio-temporal kind as is the case with material things; his acts have a meaning for eternity, not only morally but also *ontologically*. Now we must, however (even for ontological reasons), hold fast absolutely to the fact—even if this is not obvious to everyone at first sight—that something which is merely a case and a circumscription of something universal, something which *as* an individual and concrete something is just sheer negation, also cannot have—*as* something individual—any real, eternally valid significance. Man with his mental and moral acts, therefore, cannot be merely the appearance of the universal and of what is—in this universality alone—'eternal' and ever-valid in the negative expansion of space and time. In him, the individual, there must rather be a given a positive reality; expressed differently: his spiritual individuality cannot be (at least not in his acts) merely the circumscription of an in itself universal nature through the negativity of the *materia prima*, understood as the mere repetition of the same thing at different points in space-time. We must realize that a contrary view would be profoundly unchristian, and that anyone who does not see this, really has no right to protest against a medieval Averroism or against a modern Idealism. The assertion of something positively individual, at least in man's spiritual personal acts, does not moreover need to appear unscholastic, indeed not even really unthomistic. Of course, anyone who cannot rise to the metaphysical thought that (in good scholastic language) God cannot even *de potentia absoluta* create a second Gabriel—in other words, anyone who cannot rise *at all* to the notion of something individual which is not the instance of some universal idea, of something repeatable—cannot follow our thought here from the very start. Anyone, however, who can grasp this thomistic thought of something real which cannot be subsumed unequivocally under a universal idea or under a law, cannot reject the idea from the very start that something like this is conceivable—indeed, must be postulated—also in man as a spiritual person, as that existent who does not resolve himself completely into *forma-materiae-esse*. We may also say: if (and in so far as) man as a spiritual person participates by his acts in the permanency-in-itself of the pure form, which does not resolve itself in its ordination to matter as the principle of repeatability, then he must also participate in that spiritual individuality of the spiritual which has a positive individuality, an individuality which is not merely the sameness of the repeated universal and not merely a case of the law. Seen in this way, we therefore have to say: in so far as man belongs to the material world by his concrete activity, his activity is an instance and fulfilment of something universal which determines his actions as something different from the individual and opposed to it, i.e. as a *law* expressed in universal propositions. In so far as the same man subsists in his own spirituality, his actions are also always more than mere applications of the universal law to the *casus* in space and time; they have a substantial positive property and uniqueness which can no longer be translated into a universal idea and norm expressible in propositions constructed of universal notions. At least in his actions, man is really also (not only) *individuum ineffabile*, whom God has called by his name, a name which is and can only be unique, so that it really is worthwhile for this unique being as such to exist for all eternity.

It also cannot be said that such an individuality of a spiritual act has no place in the real world, or that one cannot conceive anything by it. For, first of all, there is the whole almost unascertainable field of different possibilities which remain open to the morally acting man within the scope of what is morally commanded and allowed. In every case in which a man decides, *within* the ethical sphere of the universal norms, on one of several possibilities—in which he 'chooses' *within* the sphere of the universally and positively moral good—this (non-derivable) concretion of his moral 'being-thus', brought about by a decision, is undoubtedly conceivable as the 'coming-to-light' of his ineffable moral individuality and not just as the merely arbitrary selection from among certain possibilities, as if these are equally-valid in the last resort and as if, in relation to them, the 'just-this' and 'not-that' has no further positive and ethical meaning. And furthermore: even in a case where the deductive, syllogistic formation of conscience from the universal norms and the concretely given situation seemingly leads to the unequivocal result of a concretely one imperative, the latter can still in actual fact be realized in the most diverse ways and with the most diverse inner attitudes. Even a case where these differences are no longer traceable, where one could conceive of exactly the same case as repeatedly realizable, *only* proves (this and nothing more) that something uniquely and positively individual cannot be expressed reflectively and after the manner of a proposition—that it cannot be the object of a reflective objective knowledge which can be articulated in propositions. It does not, however, prove that there cannot be a case of the positively ethico-individual element of a personal action.

The following must be added to what has been said: this positively individual element in the moral action (an action which is more than the fulfilment of the universal norm or of an abstract being: 'man') is even as such to be conceived absolutely as the object of a binding will of God. It would be absurd for a God-regulated, theological morality to think that God's binding will could only be directed to the human action in so far as the latter is simply a realization of the universal norm and of a universal nature. If the creative will of God is directly and unambiguously directed to the concrete and the individual, then surely this is not true merely in so far as this individual reality is the realization of a case of the universal—rather it is directed to the concrete as such, as it really is—to the concrete in its positive, and particularly its substantial, material uniqueness. God is interested in history not only in so far as it is the carrying out of norms, but in so far as it is a history which consists in the harmony of unique events and which precisely in this way has a meaning for eternity. The fact that this divine binding force, which regards the individual reality as such, cannot be expressed in a general proposition, is no proof of its non-existence, but arises out of the nature of things. The perception of this 'individual norm' (if we are going to use this term for the binding will of God in so far as it regards the uniquely individual which, precisely in its particular positivity, cannot be specified in the universal which can be contracted in 'cases') cannot come about in the same way as the perception of the universal law, viz. by an abstraction which forms notions of essences. Yet this fact is also no proof for the non-existence of such a perception and for the consequent impossibility of such an 'individual norm' or 'existential norm' as something actually binding.[3]

[3] The more familiar notion of 'individual' (individual-norm, -ethics), which would seem the obvious one to use in the context and the nature of things, has been deliberately clarified here (and in what follows) by using the notion of 'existential' (existential-norm, -ethics). We have done this in order to make use even of the terminology to guard against possible misunderstanding, such as that 'individual-' might be understood as being used here in contrast to 'social-', and 'individual-ethics' as against 'social-ethics'. The notion of an 'existential' ethics excludes this misunderstanding; it shows itself unequivocally as the counter- and complementary notion of an abstractly universal 'essentialist ethics'. Yet this 'existential ethics' does not signify an unreal 'ethics of existence' (in the sense of the familiar distinction of existence and essence). On the contrary, it relates—in accordance with the original content of meaning of the modern word 'existential'—to the *substantial nature* of man, in so far as this (at least as φύσις, as principle of the origin and actualizing of the historico-personal activity) must achieve itself constitutively in the positivity of each single, uniquely-one con-cretion of the individual decision. And so this nature in particular cannot have the *all* sufficient condition of its free moral self-realization in an abstractly essential ethics of norms and order, arrived at purely deductively. It remains installed, on the contrary, in just as unnegotiable a manner (i.e. in the line of the *constitution* of the substantial ethico-personal nature) in the non-derivable qualitative property of the unique, individual act—an act which cannot be treated adequately in the manner of a 'case'. An analysis of this 'existential' structure of human nature could provide us with a more exact *philosophical* basis for what we have developed here from a more theological point of view.

No matter how inadequate the reasons offered in the present context, it can surely be said that there is an individual ethical reality of a positive kind which is untranslatable into a material universal ethics; there is a binding ethical uniqueness—by which we do not mean to say that *every* ethical individual reality must also necessarily and always be a binding moral reality, and that therefore there also cannot be anything individually or existentially ethical which remains free. In so far as there is a moral reality in an existential-ethic sense and of a binding kind which nevertheless cannot (in the very nature of things) be translated into universal propositions of material content—there must be an existential ethics of a formal kind, i.e. an ethics which treats of the basic elements, the formal structures and the basic manner of perceiving such an existential-ethic reality. Just as, on the one hand, there cannot be any science of the individual considered as a really individual singular as such and yet, on the other hand, there is a universal formal ontology of individual reality, so (and in this sense) there can and must be a formal doctrine of existential concretion, a formal existential-ethics.

In practice, the most urgent and difficult problem regarding such a formal existential-ethics would, of course, be the question about the *perceptibility* of the individual moral reality and its obligation (when and where such an obligation is present). We may say: there must be some function of conscience which does not merely apply the universal norms to each of my particular situations but which moreover grasps also what has not yet been made absolutely clear by the situation and the universal norms, and which is precisely and as such what has to be done by me individually. And in saying this, we have indeed named an essential, basic function of conscience, which is for the most part overlooked by the usual scholastic ethics, but we have not yet explained how this individual—or existential-function of conscience comes about. We should go on to ask in this regard: how does the individual person know about himself at all as the uniquely individual? How is such a perception conceivable, when basically it cannot adequately be a perception of an objective propositional reflection? How are we to pose and answer the question, when (and in so far as) this individual reality is not the individuality of my being and of my already freely effected state, but the individual uniqueness of something which has still to be done by me? How can this individual future reality be perceived also as something which ought to be done? What does this (moral) necessity look like, which emerges in the approaching history and affects it? It is clear that we cannot really answer all these questions here. We would have to enter into a study of the peculiarities of a non-objective perception which is not merely a subsequent, reflected subsumption and articulation of an (adequately) given condition, but also a constitutive expression of the known thing itself; we would have to go into the question of the peculiar identity of perceiving and acting in the perception of the personal. We would have to treat of the fundamental option of the total (although also in a certain sense empty) basic decision about himself, in which the person, when he begins to reflect about himself, always finds himself already there. We would have to speak of the perception of the future and free individual reality by means of an, as it were, 'playing' and 'attempting' anticipation of what (as something absolutely decided) is still outstanding and in the future, because the quality of the free future can be known only in such an anticipation by testing attempts (up to the point of being 'tempted'). It would have to be asked how all this is modified in a supernatural order where there are the gifts of the Holy Ghost, a supernatural instinct and an individual immediacy to the personal, living God far beyond anything merely in the nature of a norm or law, where there is an inexpressible groaning of the Spirit and an unction which teaches us everything, a secret understanding between the spiritual man and the Spirit of God, so that this spiritual man judges everything but cannot himself be judged by anyone. For the clarification of this non-reflective, non-propositional self-presence of the person to itself in its positive uniqueness we might refer to the dialectic between the uncertainty of salvation, which is an essential property of the condition of a Christian, and the (equally given) testimony of the Spirit that we are children of God (which surely does not refer merely to God's salvific will in general and which cannot be adequately interpreted by a theory of a 'moral' certitude of the individual state of grace); we might adduce certain phenomena of current depth-psychology which manifest something like a co-existence of knowledge about oneself on the one hand, and nescience and displacement of knowledge about oneself, on the other hand, which is nevertheless given. These and many other things would have to be reflected on if we wished to come to a detailed knowledge about our singularity, about the existential quality of our actions as something possible and existentially binding. Yet an exact exposition of all this is more than what can be undertaken in this context.

Since this is therefore not possible, we must content ourselves with pointing out, to finish up, a few things which—as it were as applications of the theory of the truth of an existential ethics and the existentially ethical—can show that the question we have posed ourselves here is not of merely speculative interest. We can merely refer to these things, and even in this we must renounce any systematic method.

It may, for instance, be said that—in addition to its other uses—the suggested theory has its meaning also for the exercise of ethico-theological casuistry. This is not meant to imply that we approve here of the horror against which the traditional casuistry so widespread and frequently engaged in in Germany. This horror rests to a large extent on mental laziness and smugness and on the dread of a clear, discerning and penetrating decision. Yet are there not cases in casuistry where one labours in vain, from the very start, to reach an unequivocal decision of the case by means of a syllogistic deduction in the manner described above, since so unequivocal a clarity cannot be reached in this way, for the simple reason that it cannot be attained by starting with the universal? Are there not cases in casuistry where we make unnecessary work for ourselves in the wrong direction, because we do not reckon with an existential ethics? Is it not conceivable that we also reach for the formal means of probabilism at the wrong time—when there is no possibility of our coming to a decision of an unambiguous kind by means of a universal essentialist-ethics and we then come too quickly to the conclusion that the concrete case must remain open to a decision *in utramque partem* after the manner of probabilism, because the only method known is that of the universal essentialist-ethics? In general, would not an existential-ethics determine the significance and the limits of the different systems in moral theology (i.e. nowadays above all probabilism) from the very start by a more exact ontology and theology of the ethical individual?

A further question would be whether we could not understand the whole teaching on Choice in the Spiritual Exercises of St Ignatius much more profoundly and exactly if we were clearly conscious of such an existential-ethics and the way of finding an ethical existential-imperative. According to the usual theory about the finding of the correct imperative in the concrete (which we have outlined at the beginning of the chapter), the third time for making a choice named in the Exercises would have to be the real and decisive way of coming to a decision. But according to St Ignatius this time is only something secondary compared with the first and second times for choice. We may perhaps hazard the assertion that—as regards this point (as also many others)—our average theology and ethics has not yet caught up with the unconscious theology underlying the Exercises.

In the usual theory of sin we treat sin too exclusively as the mere offence against a universal divine norm. Could not an existential-ethics help us to see more clearly that sin, over and above its property of being an offence against the law of God, is also and just as much an offence against an utterly individual imperative of the individual will of God, which is the basis of uniqueness? Would we not perceive sin more clearly in this way as the failure of the personal-individual love of God? Even though all this has been developed in a formal ontology which in itself is of a philosophical kind, would it not offer a set of categories applicable and useful in a theology of the supernatural as an immediate personal encounter with the personal God as he is in himself?

In an essay about the 'Individual in the Church', the author of the present study has drawn attention to the significance of the question developed here for the position of the individual in the Church.[4] We can merely make reference to this here. If there is an existential-ethics, then there is also a sphere of decision for the individual in and for the Church, which cannot be taken away from the individual by a material command of the ecclesiastical authority.

Has not our theory consequences also for a more profound theology of obedience in general, in the Church, and in the life of the religious? Is obedience to a person giving commands merely the respect for the objective rightness (to be presumed in the individual case) of the individual command, which is right as measured by the objective universal norms of a material kind on which it is based, or must obedience in some cases—and where and when—also be exercised as an act of homage to the individual will of the person commanding which can no longer be thought of as an interpretation and application of the universal and, in themselves, intelligible norms? When and towards whom is this second sort of obedience conceivable?

[4] Cf. *Stimmen der Zeit* CXXXIX (1946–47), pp. 260–276; the same in 'Gefahren im heutigen Katholizismus', in the series *Christ heute* I, 10 (Einsiedeln 1950).

Would it be possible to find reasons, in the proposed theory, for a difference between the teaching and pastoral offices as two spheres which are not adequately reducible to each other? That such a question also has very practical consequences for the life of the Church in the concrete surely does not need a great deal of explanation here.

What are the consequences of our theory for the theory of the choice of calling in the strict sense? Even though we should not dispute the practical usefulness of Lahitton's theory—the usual theory in the Church for the past forty years—about the choosing of a calling and the requirements for being called, especially where ecclesiastical functionaries are concerned (and not the person making the choice), we may nevertheless ask ourselves whether this theory is really quite correct theoretically and in particular where it is a question of the one who asks himself about his being called.

We might also ask ourselves whether the suggested theory could not provide a contribution to the question about the duty of striving for perfection. For if our theory is right, then the question about the duty of a higher moral good is not yet decided in the negative whenever it is impossible to derive this duty from universal norms.

Does our theory not permit us to contribute something also to the question about the relation between the hierarchical and charismatic elements in the Church and in her history? Is not the Hierarchy as such the bearer and guarantor of the correct application of the perma-ment norms instituted together with the Church? However, if the Church acts in her history and if every action is always also more than just the application of the universal norms to the concrete case and given situation, then must there not be a function in the Church which takes in precisely this divinely inspired individual impulse given to the action of the Church and gives it its validity in the Church—a function which cannot be replaced by the administration and right application of the universal norms? Must this function always be originally found and united in the person of the bearers of the hierarchical powers? And if not (as is undoubtedly the case, after all, according to the evidence of Church history), does the Hierarchy not have the duty then to accept such impulses from those quarters in which they originally strike the Church in the providence of God: even from the charismatics, the prophets or whatever one may wish to call these antennae of the individual divine imperatives given to the Church? Can this provide us with a rational basis for 'public opinion' in the

Church?[5] (Seen from this point of view, are—for example—the reasons given for the Sacred Heart devotion completely dependent on the fact that the general and ever valid dogma gives it a Nihil Obstat?)

Such and similar questions could no doubt be still further multiplied. However, these questions may show that the suggested theory is not merely of an academic nature. Certainly, this theory must not be overestimated in its significance. Just as there was logical thought before there was a reflectively grasped formal logic, so there was and is existential-ethical action of a natural and supernatural kind individually and in the Church, even before there is an explicitly developed existential-ethics. And just as, even after the discovery of formal logic, applied logic was not essentially improved, so it will also be in the present case. And yet, just as no one will on account of this hold formal logic to be a superfluous matter of idle curiosity, so, we would think, it will be necessary also to think about an existential-ethics of a formal kind. Such an ethics might have its uses from many points of view. For this it must, of course, be presupposed that it is right and is first of all developed explicitly. We did not mean to do more here than to raise a few questions in this direction.

[5] Cf. by the author: 'Die öffentliche Meinung in der Kirche', *Orientierung* XXIII–XXIV (1951), pp. 255–258; the same under the title of *Free Speech in the Church* (London and New York 1960).

8

THE DIGNITY AND FREEDOM OF MAN[1]

THE general theme of the Austrian Catholic Congress (*Katholikentag*) is 'The Dignity and Freedom of Man'. The significance and aptness of this theme for the present state of the world is obvious. Yet so also is its obscurity. We need only remember that the word 'freedom' in particular has been the motto and war-cry of the most diverse intellectual and religious movements in the West. It was Paul's cry against Jewish legalism. It was the cry of the French Revolution and of Liberalism in their fight against the political and social system of the Christian Middle Ages in the West and against the Church. . . . And strange to say, one hundred years ago under Pius IX, 'freedom' was the object of criticism and reservations on the part of the Church, whereas today under Pius XII it is the motto of a '*Katholikentag*'.

There can be no question here of formulating stirring slogans with regard to this theme. Our intention is rather to put forward—quite soberly and almost in thesis form—a few basic reflections on this subject which might to some extent supply the basis for the various specialized group-discussions. These reflections, therefore, must not remain too much on the level of mere generalities and yet they must not be so 'concrete' as to anticipate and make superfluous the work on individual problems.

I. THE DIGNITY OF MAN

1. 'Dignity' in general signifies the fact that a being has of its very nature a determined objective position within the manifoldness and

[1] This Essay was originally given as a Paper at the opening meeting of the Study Session of the Austrian 'Katholikentag' (Catholic Congress) in Mariazell on 1st May 1952. This fact determined its subject. We have not tried here to disguise its thematic thought and form as pre-determined by the leading ideas of the Vienna 'Katholikentag'.

heterogeneity of being which demands respect and protection as well as realization both in its relations to others and in itself. Thus 'dignity' is, in the last analysis, objectively identical with the being of an entity—understood as that which is given necessarily in its 'essential structure' (*Wesensstruktur*) *and* as that which is given as a task (*Aufgegebenes*) to be accomplished. And in the present context 'essential structure' means everything man necessarily is and must be, whether this—regarded in itself—be a natural essence (*Natur*) or whether it be—with reference to the basic structure—a free gift of God, a grace and hence supernatural.

2. For the exact nature of the dignity of man we must consult Reason and Revelation. We cannot give a detailed explanation here either of the methods of natural knowledge by reason and the science of revelation or of their respective possibilities, validity, differences and mutual relationships. We must simply mention two things:

a. With regard to objective rank, subjective claim to lead and comprehensiveness in content, the knowledge and science of revelation as found in the believer is superior to rational metaphysical knowledge. This is true even though, conversely, a certain 'natural' knowledge is also required as an irreplaceable prerequisite for the knowledge of faith. For this 'natural' knowledge itself is effectively exercised through God's saving grace, as well as being co-revealed as a guarantee for its true contents by the God of revelation. Hence our method in attempting to express the nature and dignity of man will be to start from revelation and to try to determine, as far as possible, the 'natural' remainder of that dignity from this starting-point, i.e. from the whole of this (historical) 'nature' of man.

b. In view of the biological, cultural and cultural-historical mutability of man, it is no easy task to attain an exact metaphysical understanding of the permanent, necessary nature of man underlying his historical mutability. Such a knowledge is not to be gained by a mere collection of factual evidence of what can be observed at a moment of time in the individual man—by using, as it were, the methods of the natural sciences. For this would imply that what can be thus observed is 'everything', or that everything observed is necessary for the nature or in accordance with it. A knowledge of essences (*Wesenserkenntnis*) which includes the concrete knowledge about the possibilities of nature (which in part are to be freely realized), must rely rather on a twofold method:

(i) On a transcendental method. Everything which already reaffirms itself with implicit necessity in the very *question about* the nature of man and in the very way man puts this question (i.e. more strictly speaking, in the metaphysical aspect of the knowledge man has of himself), belongs to the metaphysically necessary nature of man and to the moral perfection of that nature. Anything in this knowledge which is not transcendentally 'lasting' in this sense, need not on that account be accidental; but the question of its belonging to the necessary nature of man does in this case require to be proved separately and cannot be presupposed as self-evident.

(ii) The reflection on the historical experience man has of himself, without which the notion of man remains 'empty' and without which this notion has no clearness and consequently no power in history. Such reflection is indispensable because only in this way can we recognize the metaphysical possibilities of man as a free being which, because he is free, cannot be adequately deduced from something else clearly given. Since this reflection, being itself a 'historically becoming' process, is essentially unfinished, the understanding of the essence is permanently *in via* in spite of its *a-priori* and transcendental metaphysical element. To give an *adequate* design of man (what he is and ought to become) by an *a-priori*-rationalistic reason is impossible. Man must always refer *also* to his history and thus even to his future in order to know what he is. And conversely, the critique of the experience of self, which is necessary because not everything which is, is right and 'rational', refers the historical experience back to the transcendental, metaphysical method of self-knowledge and to God's judgement on man in revelation. Because man really knows 'concretely' about himself in this historical experience only—an experience which is still in a state of becoming—there is no manifest knowledge of essence without *Tradition* (of a natural kind and of the kind of saving history) and without a *venturing*, planning, devising anticipation of the future (which is itself grasped in an intramundane, 'utopian' manner and in a revealed 'eschatology'). All that follows, about the dignity (i.e. the nature) of man, must be understood with the reservation that the second element of this knowledge of essence is brought out merely formally and not in its reflex content. Finally, it must be noted that nothing can be explained here regarding these questions by something which is itself no more than an independent and lucid hypothesis, but that every notion refers to everyone for its explanation, and that such explanation must always merely elucidate the explaining and the explained and at the same time remove them into the obscurity of mystery.

3. The essential dignity of man consists in the fact that, within a sexually differentiated community in spatio-temporal history, man, by spiritually recognizing himself and freely identifying himself, can and ought to open himself (in the direction of immediate personal communion with the infinite God) to the love in Jesus Christ which communicates God himself. His dignity may be regarded as something pre-established (*vorgegebene*), i.e. as a capacity and a task, or as something fulfilled. Fulfilment, the gaining and preservation of the pre-established dignity constitutes itself the final and definite dignity of man (which, therefore, can be lost). The pre-established dignity cannot simply cease or become non-existent, but can exist as something denied, as foundation for damnation and judgement. In so far as this nature is from God and directed to God, receiving from him and opening itself in his direction, it is a nature in which the given dignity is always both the innermost being of man and what lies above man and hence partakes in the remoteness, the mysteriousness and namelessness of God. It only unveils itself completely in the knowing-believing-loving dialogue of man with God, and hence can never be given simply in the manner of object-like objectivity. We perceive God in a mirror and in images only; the same is equally true of man and of his destiny, for he is from God and directed towards God.

4. The dignity of nature is *pre*-appointed (vor-*gegeben*) to man for his free self-understanding—as the goal of his freedom, as its salvation or judgement.

5. The dignity of man's nature may be regarded formally, i.e. in advance of the question whether, by exercising his free choice, which is dependent of course on redemptive grace and the judgement of God, his dignity brings about his salvation or God's judgement upon him.

Regarded in this way, the dignity of man's nature embraces the following moments which mutually determine each other:

a. Man's personal nature (in its specifically created and human characteristic), i.e. the 'natural' being of man. This means:

(i) *Man is Spirit*: in the perception of the spatio-temporal, he is always dependent on the total unity of reality, i.e. on God, who existed before the multiplicity of his immediately-given objects. This is true even in his own case, understood as a subject set off from the object and (implicitly) perceiving.

(ii) *He is freedom*: about this we will have to say more later.

(iii) *He is an individual*: he is not merely an instance of the universal; each man is someone unique and ultimately never someone who can be totally deduced; his individuality in being-thus and in action is not merely the negatively spatio-temporal application of a universal or of a universal idea, which circumscribes him in the here and now. Because he is an individual, he has a valid existence which, as a real existence, does not coincide with his spatio-temporal existence; he is 'immortal' and the subject of an eternal destination and destiny. This is why the individual man, who is now, may never be forcibly sacrificed, in a manner which destroys him, for the future of 'humanity', of the others who come after him. The present is never just the material for a utopian intramundane future.

(iv) *He is a community-building person*: Person is not the opposite to community; rather, both are correlative realities, i.e. *qua* person, man is intended for community with other persons (God and men), and there is community only where there are *persons* and where persons are protected; he is a perfect person in the measure in which he opens himself in love and service for other persons. A genuine problem of opposing tensions exists only where (and in so far as) there is a question of striking a balance, in the plurality of human existence, between personality (or community) on *one* particular human level (as, for instance, on the level of economics, of the State, of the Church) and the same sort of community (or personality) on *another* level.

(v) *He is* (qua *human* person) *an incarnate*, *mundane person* who realizes himself in his ultimate core only in a spatio-temporal, pluralistic expansion, in concern for his bodily existence (economy) and within a community communicated in a tangible manner (marriage, parent-and-child relationship, the State, Incarnation, Church, sacraments, symbol, etc.). The personality of man, therefore, cannot be relegated to an absolutely internal realm. It requires of necessity a certain space for realizing itself. Such a space, although it is to a certain extent 'external' to it (body, earth, economy, sign, symbol, State), is nevertheless essentially necessary and hence must be so constructed that it permits personal self-realization. Seen even from this point of view, a retreat into the merely 'private', the inner 'conscience', the 'sacristy', etc., is contrary to nature.

b. The supernatural existential. This means: the person, as we have just outlined him, is called to direct personal communion with God in Christ, perennially and inescapably, whether he accepts the call in redemption and grace or whether he closes himself to it in guilt (by the guilt of original sin and of personal sin). The person is addressed by the personal revelation of the Word of God in saving history which finds its climax in Jesus Christ, the Word of the Father become flesh; the person is unquestionably situated within the offer of his interior, saving and divinizing grace; he is called to the community-forming visible manifestation of this personal state of 'being directly called before God' which is the Church.

c. The supernatural existential is related to what we have called the personal nature of man, as a gratuitous gift of God, as grace. In this way man exists in nature and 'supernature'. This does not, however, mean that it is left to his free choice whether he intends to understand himself as a purely natural person or as a person called to direct communion with God by grace.

6. With this essence and this dignity of man there is given a plurality of human existential dimensions (Existentialien):

a. He is a *corporeal-material* living being, in a biological community of life with its material surroundings, and with a care for its will to live.

b. He is a *spiritual-personal*, cultural being with a diversity of personal communities (marriage union, family, kinsfolk, a people, the State, the community of nations), and with a history.

c. He is a *religious*, *God-centred* being (by nature and grace), with a 'Church', in a history which either damns or saves.

d. He is a *Christ-centred* being, i.e. his being possesses an ontic and spiritual-personal capacity for communicating with Jesus Christ in whom God has forever made the countenance of a man his own and has opened the reality of man, with an unsurpassable finality, in the direction of God; only thus was the real possibility of a direct communion of all men with God established with finality. Hence we can only speak ultimately of God by engaging even in the midst of all this (in the midst of theology) in anthropology; and ultimately any information about anthropology, about the nature and dignity of man, can be given only when we engage in theology about God and from God.

7. a. While the many existential dimensions must be distinguished, they and their achievement cannot be divorced from each other 'spatially' in the concrete. Each one of these existential dimensions is really dependent on the other. The lowest dimension is determined by the highest and vice versa; the whole being of man must work itself out in each one of them in particular. Every attempt by a dimension to make itself independent and self-sufficient, even merely in its own realm, contradicts the fact that man, without prejudice to any true and genuine plurality of his ontological moments, is first and last, originally and by destination, *one person*. Hence, for instance, economics or even economic legislation do not enjoy a 'pure' autonomy from the laws of the spiritual person, i.e. from ethics.

b. On the other hand, man in his self-knowledge, which must always proceed from a *multiplicity* of perceived objects and remains dependent on this multiplicity as such, can never perceive himself adequately from *one* principle, in such a way that he could adequately deduce from this his existential dimensions and their structural laws. There is, therefore, a permanent plurality of sciences of man and a relative individual structure of laws for each existential dimension and of the powers administering and forming it, which must be respected by every other.

c. Because this plurality possesses in its turn a structure and a superior and lower order, the claim of the higher dimension takes precedence over that of the lower one in any (apparent or, for the meantime, rightful) case of conflict.

8. The nature and dignity of man are threatened. And that in a twofold way:

a. From without: Man as a bodily being, before he has made his personal decision, is open to being seized by a creaturely influence which is independent of him: the influence of material forces and other created persons (men and angelic powers). Although an ultimate and final damning situation for man can arise only through the free decision of man from within, nevertheless such interventions from without, which touch the person and his personal and indeed supernatural dignity, are possible and hence menacing. There is no 'zone' of the person which is absolutely inaccessible to such influences from without. Every 'external' event can be significant and menacing for the ultimate salvation of the person, and is, therefore, subject to the law of the dignity of the person who as such can be degraded by some intervention from without (cf. 7a and 7c above).

b. From within: Since the dignity of man is imposed as a task on man who disposes of himself in freedom, man can fail to find himself and his dignity by a free offence against himself in any one of the existential dimensions, in so far as this offence touches the whole of man essentially. Man cannot, indeed, cancel out or change his pre-established essential dignity as he pleases; but in practice he can understand it in such a way that this dignity contradicts its own pre-established nature ontologically and hence ethically, even by the way it is activated; in this sense, he can degrade it by becoming culpable before God. The use of his freedom necessarily poses man with the choice of degrading his dignity or preserving it by the grace of God and converting it into achieved dignity.

c. External and internal threats mutually determine each other, seen from a total view-point. Speaking theologically, the fact of being threatened from without is, in its post-paradisian characteristic, a consequence of man's perversion from within. And at the same time, this external threat is the situation in which the inner defection of man from his own nature achieves itself in a characteristically post-paradisian, impelled and concupiscent manner, so that ultimately for us—*before* the revelation of the judgment of God—guilt and fate become unceasingly intertwined.

9. One of the results of this situation of being threatened is that man inevitably finds himself either in a state of guilt or in a state of redemption, in so far as he has had any free control at all over himself

(we prescind here from the manner of original sin's sinfulness). As a spiritual person, control over himself is for him inescapable. If, however, he has control over himself, then he has control (implicitly or explicitly) over himself in accordance with all the existential dimensions of his being. He accepts, therefore, his concrete being (including the supernatural existential of this being), or he possesses it in the manner of rejection and then he is guilty. There cannot be any existential neutrality in the face of the historical being of man. The question can only be how far man—precisely by *objective reflection*—must be explicitly conscious, in his understanding of himself (which of itself need not be adequately reflex), of the depth of his being and of his dignity. Men acting historically among each other are, therefore, in actual fact either men with a dignity which they have culpably degraded or men with a dignity redeemed by grace. The precise position of the border-line between the two within the saving history of humanity only God knows. It does not, at any rate, coincide unequivocally with the boundaries of Christianity or of the visible Church. There is also a battle of light and darkness within the Church.

10. Where the pre-established nature and dignity of man is preserved, and where the individual realizes it in the particular manner which was assigned to him alone, there is redemption by the grace of Christ. This means:

a. There is preservation and realization of a nature to which belongs the *super*natural existential of being called to immediate participation in the life of God, i.e. participation in the grace of the Son of the Father become man.

b. This act of preservation and unfolding of nature has a reality which presupposes the entitative, gratuitous communication of the divine nature to man.

c. The accomplishment of this act is itself, without prejudice to its freedom, a gratuitous grace of God, considered even as an accomplishment in actual fact.

d. In so far as this act aims, in its reflex-objective explicitness, at the preservation and unfolding of the natural essence by observing the 'law of nature' (i.e. in so far as this act is considered as nothing more than this), it is in itself basically possible without any *super*natural help of grace and external revelation of God. However, in so far as even such a taking possession of oneself as regards one's natural essence requires quite a long temporal duration for its accomplishment, it needs the help of God's grace:

(i) In the concrete, post-Adamite situation of man, an actually undimmed and sufficiently unfolded perception of the natural essence of man, taken as the norm of his natural moral acts, can be obtained only with the help of the revelation of God's Word.

(ii) The actual accomplishment of such acts (in their longer temporal duration), even in their natural aspect, can take place only by the help of God's grace. This grace is not owed to the individual *qua* individual with regard to his actions (over and above his mere potency), it is given to him with a view to the total salvation (and hence also that which embraces the supernatural dimension of man) of the whole concrete human being in Christ and as destined for the eternal life of God.

Hence the *actual* preservation of the dignity of man, even in its natural dimensions, depends on God's supernatural will of grace in Christ Jesus. Any actually preserved dignity of man, wherever it is to be found, is a part of Christian salvation—it is redemption in Christ Jesus. This does not necessarily mean, however, that man must thus be always and everywhere conscious of this source of his actual preservation, that he must explicitly accept it *as* redemption, or that the preserved dignity in its natural and supernatural dimension can on this account be found only within the visible framework of Christianity. Where and to whom God gives the grace of Christ, this he alone decides. It is his secret. What we know about the conditions of such a distribution in the actual order (necessity of faith and, in certain circumstances, of baptism), does not permit us to make any unequivocal judgement in the concrete, individual case about whether grace has been given and thus the vocation and dignity of man has been preserved.

11. Accordingly, it is absolutely possible in the nature of things, it can and should be our aim, to reach a mutual understanding with unbelievers even *qua* unbelievers (i.e. with non-Christians) about the natural part of the actual constitution of the nature of man, about his dignity as a person and the 'natural moral law' resulting from it. However, the following points must be observed:

a. Wherever and in so far as such an understanding is wholly or to a large extent successful, it is also in actual fact itself the result of the indirect influence of revelation (through the believer in revelation) on the unbeliever who otherwise would not actually see without error what in principle he is capable of seeing.

b. The practical consequences arising from the formal principles regarding the natural being of man and his dignity, thus accepted in common, will again differ essentially in the case of the Christian and of the unbeliever, since they do not yet give the former a grasp of the totality of the actual man. The significance of this agreement, possible in principle, must therefore not be overrated. This agreement does not in practice lead to any real concrete settlement, not even in a partial sphere of human existence, but at the most to a provisional agreement in tolerance which, even in the particular sector which really cannot be adequately separated from the rest, signifies a certain *modus vivendi* and nothing more. (Think, for instance, of the questions of education and schools, cultural-political problems, etc.)

12. If we have in this way to some extent circumscribed the dignity of man in its objective content, we can now define it in its formal quality and draw the most fundamental conclusions from the definition.

a. In so far as man is a person, who possesses himself knowingly and in freedom—in other words, is always objectively referred to *himself* and hence does not ontologically have the character of a means but of an end, an end by a reference away from himself, indeed, to *persons* but not to things (which themselves are rather referred to persons), he has an absolute value and hence an absolute dignity. What we call the absolute, unqualified validity of moral values is essentially based on the absolute value and the absolute dignity of the spiritual and free person. 'Absolute' means here the same as 'unconditional' (but not 'infinite'). This means that all subhuman things and values of an objective kind are conditional, i.e. they are dependent on a free (even ethically) determination and choice of values: *if* (you are not obliged to) you want this or that, then you must do, prefer, respect, etc., this or that. The human person by its nature and dignity demands an unconditional respect which is independent of any freely exercised determination of an end and value—i.e. is absolute.

b. This dignity of man as a person is given an even greater quality essentially and in the actual order, in respect of its absoluteness, by the fact that man is called to be the direct partner of God, who is the simply Absolute and Infinite.

II. THE FREEDOM OF THE PERSON IN GENERAL

Because one of the existentials of man, viz. freedom, is particularly threatened today in its right understanding and its exercise, we must turn to it in particular at this point.

1. Freedom of choice (or of decision), being a basic condition of the person, can be defined only with difficulty. It is the possibility for the person to dispose himself in such a way that this disposal in its concreteness cannot be entirely resolved or analysed into something different from itself from which it could be deduced, so that in such a case it would be, and be thus, because its prerequisites happened to be such and not otherwise. By prerequisites we mean here both internal and external presuppositions, the inner disposition of the person, the external circumstances and conditions, present before the decision. The causality of free action must, therefore, be understood as a free openness to more than what is realized by the decision. This causality can, therefore, be possible only when faced with the finite, or the infinite conceived as merely finite, and hence can have meaning only in the face of the finite. Of course, in so far as the source of the existence of an affirmative or negative attitude towards the absolute God lies precisely in the adoption of a right or wrong attitude towards finite goods (or those conceived as finite) in their divinely caused order, in virtue of the necessary relation of the spirit to the absolute which supports freedom, freedom is in the last analysis the possibility, through and beyond the finite, of taking up a position towards God himself. This position is taken up by the person himself and he himself is responsible for it. Freedom is possible, therefore, only as the transition from the open choice of infinite possibilities to the definiteness of the finite realization, in which and passing through which the infinite destiny of man is gained or lost in a personal manner. And so freedom is possible only where there is a transcendental openness to the infinite God, that is to say in the spiritual person. Freedom is self-achievement

of the person, using a finite material, before the infinite God. It is, therefore, a datum of theology, of theological anthropology. For without freedom man could not stand before God as a responsible agent, in dialogue and partnership with God; without it he could not be the subject of guilt before God nor of profferred and accepted redemption and pardon.

2. However, *finite* freedom is preceded, without prejudice to genuine spontaneity, by interior and external conditions different from its act, and hence it presupposes also a law of the ontological and ethical order. It is the freedom to say yes or no to a call; it is not an absolutely creative freedom. Of course, this call must not be understood here *merely* as a universal law, nor the 'yes' *merely* as the realization of universal norms of being, as if it were merely a 'case'. These preliminary conditions, which are constitutive conditions for the exercise of finite freedom, are themselves finite and thus limit the possibilities of freedom. They are not equally great in every case and they are changeable. It follows that we cannot demand a determined and fixed magnitude of such prerequisite conditions and of the possibilities of freedom pre-established in them, as arising out of the nature of creaturely freedom. Herein consists the ontological and ethical basis for a legitimate limitation of freedom. This must be noted if we wish to distinguish the legitimate and the false meaning of an equality of rights for everyone and of the equality of all before the law. Basically, such an equality of rights can merely mean that everyone shall have *his* rights protected, rights which only coincide with the rights of everyone else in certain basic points, but not in every point of an objective kind. The tendency towards the attainment of an adequate material equality of rights for everyone would only mean the oppression of everyone, because it would be based on an interference with the different scope for freedom objectively ordained for every individual in particular.

3. Freedom, on the one hand, is the *manner* of the appropriation and realization of the person and of his absolute dignity before God and in the community of other persons, using finite, decided materials. And yet, on the other hand, freedom must not on that account be

conceived as a merely formal capacity which receives its significance *only* from the result realized by it but different from it. The person and, consequently, freedom are themselves existing realities of the highest order and are, therefore, even in themselves absolute values. Thus freedom is *also* meant to be for its own sake, so that, even if all its results *were* attainable without it (which is not so in reality), it would still have to exist, and the frustration of its exercise would still mean an attempt on the absolute dignity of the person. And so it is *not* in the least a matter of indifference whether a result is brought about with or without freedom.

4. If, on the one hand, freedom considered simply in itself, i.e. freedom of exercise and not merely freedom in what is done, belongs to the absolute dignity of the person and if, on the other hand, it is dependent for its exercise in the concrete on conditions of an external and internal kind, then the *concession* of these possibilities of the exercise of freedom to a sufficiently large extent is demanded by the dignity of the person. To deprive the person totally of this scope for freedom would, therefore, still be a degradation of the person even when the thing to be done would still be attainable without this concession of scope for freedom. *Simply* to deprive a person of the scope even for morally wrong decisions of freedom (even if or in so far as such a thing is or were possible) cannot, therefore, be the business of any man or of any human society in its dealings with other men. Even this would be an attempt on the dignity of the person and of his freedom which is not merely a means to an end (i.e. of the good realized without freedom) but is also itself a part of the goal (viz. of the person). The *unconditional* refusal of the possibility of an objectively and morally wrong decision would amount to a suppression of the very scope for freedom itself. It is no counter-argument to this to point out the fact that it is impossible for the Blessed to sin. For they have already achieved their freedom totally. Freedom, however, does not consist in always being able to do the opposite of what has been done up to now, but it consists in being able to effect oneself once and for all into finality. This does not postulate any real 'right' to what is morally evil which would relate to the morally evil as such. We merely mean to say by this that the attempt to make what is morally evil more or less completely impossible by coercion is not only in actual fact

quite utopian in this world, but must in the concrete degenerate into a morally wrong attempt to eradicate the scope for freedom itself.

5. The scope for freedom thus demanded as the possibility of the exercise of freedom must—without prejudice to the plurality of moments of human existence—extend through all the dimensions of this existence on account of the mutual interconnection of the dimensions of human existence. To try to exclude some particular material of finite goods for freedom from this scope for freedom right from the start and absolutely, and to try to limit freedom *a priori* to certain other fields of personal freedom, would violate against the principle formulated above (I, 7a) and would represent a grave injury to the dignity of the person. Hence there must be a zone of personal freedom in the sphere of economy, of the formation of communities, of the creation of objective cultural values, in the religious field, in the sphere of Christian values, whether or not these realms in particular and taken simply by themselves could 'function' sufficiently even without such a concession of freedom.

6. The moral law as such (in contrast to the forced compliance with it) is not a limitation of freedom, since it does after all presuppose freedom of its very nature and turns to it (since it is fulfilled only when it is obeyed freely), and since it orientates freedom to its own essential goal, viz. the true achievement of the person. The law (*qua* liberating law of freedom) can do this, to be sure, only if it is more than a merely destructive demand which provokes guilt, i.e. in so far as it is not a demand made on the powerless from without but the imperative expression of a power from within which is granted to the person in the concrete order of salvation only by the pneuma of God (cf. above I, 10).

7. The freedom of the personal decision for which we are responsible ourselves and the consequences of which we must bear ourselves is a higher value (because more personal) than material security of physical existence as such. The flight from freedom into the enclosure of a merely secure life is, therefore, immoral. Wherever (and in so far

as) a certain freedom and security of the material conditions of life belong to the necessary practical prerequisites of personal freedom, they are sanctioned by the dignity of human freedom and must be demanded in the name of this freedom—they must, therefore, be fashioned in such a way that the freedom of man itself is not sacrificed to the desire of possessing these material goods.

8. There can nevertheless be a justified limitation, not indeed of freedom as such, but of the scope for freedom. For the latter is (a) changeable and finite from the very start and independently of any human intervention and (b) is unavoidably changed in one person (even to the extent of a restriction) by the claim to freedom made by another person. Restriction of the scope for freedom of one person even when voluntarily posited by another cannot therefore be immoral, but flows precisely from the nature of the freedom of finite persons who exercise their freedom in a common space of human existence.

9. Such a limitation of the scope for freedom is thinkable as legitimate on various counts and in different ways:

a. As making it impossible to have a total or partial, but unlawful, restriction of some people's scope for freedom by others. For instance, the principle of the lawfulness of compulsion in a formal democracy: the freedom of political groupings is conceded only to those who also recognize this freedom in others; against enemies of democratic freedom we may proceed with compulsion. Or: anyone who steals is put in prison; society's reply to the unlawful limitation of freedom in the material realm of the free shaping of one's life is the enforced limitation of the freedom of movement. This principle of the enforced protection of the freedom of the many against someone who threatens freedom is not, however, the sole principle of the lawful restriction of freedom. There are others which are equally essential.

b. As an *educative* restriction of the scope for freedom with a view to the liberation of freedom. Man, on account of the uninvited influences exerted on him from without, is not simply and from the very start in lordly possession of complete control over his personal power of decision. He can be swept away involuntarily (before any action of his freedom takes place) to do actions which either lack freedom and responsibility completely or possess them only to a diminished degree, and which then become an obstacle to and restriction of the possibilities of his freedom for good. He can be corrupted in advance of his decision. The enforced restriction or elimination of such influences imposed by others (viz. 'those charged with upbringing', such as the State, the Church, etc.) is not an attempt on freedom, even when it is done in the face of objections from the one who is not really limited by this in any proper sense. In this respect it would be a false, utopian outlook of an optimistic or pessimistic kind if we were to think that man can, from a certain age onwards, do without any such, to-a-certain-extent enforced education by others (i.e. an education which does not merely appeal to the free good sense of the other by exhortation and instruction, etc.) or if, on the other hand, we tried to keep *every* possibility for evil always and everywhere away from him.

c. Whenever the legitimate demand for an objective action (be it legitimate by reason of the things itself or by reason of obligations freely contracted towards it) is of its nature independent in its objective being of whether its performance is constituted by freedom or without it—and to the extent in which this applies—then the enforcing of some action is not contrary to the nature of freedom.

d. Difficulties arise in the case of someone, on the grounds of conscience, refusing to do something which is objectively justified and hence legitimately enforceable, by maintaining that conscience forbids him to perform this task (refusal to do military service, etc.). In such a case the following has to be said:

(i) The one who makes the demand must re-examine the justification for his demand very closely, out of respect for the freedom and conscience of the person who refuses.

(ii) He must ask himself whether he has merely the right or is furthermore morally bound to make this demand.

(iii) If the former, then he can desist from enforcing his demand. In many cases such a course will even be advisable or demanded by general considerations.

(iv) If the latter, then he has the right and duty to enforce his demand (in so far as this is possible) by using coercive measures proportioned to the importance of his demand. For it is then not really a case of a conflict between freedom-conscience, on the one hand, and coercion, on the other hand, but between freedom and conscience *on both sides*. The tragic conflict between the objectively justified and obligatory demand, on the one hand, and the subjective conscience in good faith, on the other, is insoluble in practice. Its tragedy must be accepted with patience and mutual respect as a sign of the imperfection of the order here below.

e. The performance of actions and adoption of attitudes which essentially include the free 'yes' as one of their internal constitutive moments (and to the extent in which they do this), must not be coerced. The only law that remains valid in this case is the law of what ought to be done, and no longer the law of what must be done. The actual demarcation of the one case from the other is indeed difficult, because the concrete execution can include both moments. On account of the higher dignity of freedom as compared with the doing of something, we must decide against the use of coercion in a doubtful case.

10. Since there is, therefore, a legitimate (and of its nature, higher) principle of freedom and a legitimate (although of its nature lower) principle of justified coercion—and since both these principles are *not* capable of simply being divided between separate dimensions of human existence and action in such a way that they do not come into conflict from the very start—there arises the problem of drawing the right line between coercion and freedom in the same realm of freedom. The following has to be said on this subject:

a. Every demarcation in the concrete is morally justified and feasible in the long run only when it respects both principles. Anarchic freedom and absolute totalitarian coercion both equally misunderstand the nature and dignity of the human person and of freedom.

b. It is impossible to find a demarcation which can be deduced *a priori*, which is valid once and for all and in every case and which is at the same time exact, because the finite realm of freedom possesses an objective variability the exact magnitude of which itself depends again both on the concreteness of the situation and on the free decision of man.

c. It is also not possible to discover such an unequivocal demarcation from revelation and the teaching of the Church. Even these sources do not provide us with any possibility of a theological rationalism in the construction of a fixed system of the right proportion between freedom and coercion in society, the State, the Church, etc., which would be valid always and everywhere.

d. Hence it is a duty of man for the preservation of his dignity and freedom continually to renew and re-establish a correct proportion between both these factors—a moral duty which he has as a man and as a Christian.

e. The demarcation of boundaries is variable. It must be undertaken, within the framework of the general principles:

(i) In accordance with the objective and changing circumstances of mental disposition, economic situation, the real possibilities of the use of freedom, etc., which objectively can prescribe certain obligatory changes of demarcation. To these 'objective' circumstances of the situation can also belong those which in themselves have arisen from the wrongly employed freedom of men but which in actual fact have already taken root in an objectified manner in certain attitudes and needs, etc. In this case it would actually cause even more serious damage to freedom and the objective order not to take cognizance of such real facts. This is the right place for showing a legitimate 'tolerance' in the proper sense of the word, which puts up with what objectively is not justified but nevertheless is given in actual fact, because its removal would in fact cause more evil than good. (Where freedom of conscience is respected as *such*, even when it—i.e. obeying the dictum of conscience—realizes itself in the wrong object and yet exists as freedom of conscience itself, it would be more correct not to speak of tolerance or 'toleration' but of active esteem and respectful deference before the conscience of another. Objectively false situations must in certain circumstances be tolerated; positions adopted by conscience which are subjectively right or must be imputed as subjectively right, even if they have a false object, must always be respected and never be injured.)

(ii) As a historical decision. This means that even bearing in mind the general principles and taking into consideration as objectively as possible the concrete situation, there still are (at least in principle) several possibilities open which form the object of the free historical decision of the powers appointed for this (both individuals and groups). This means that here the result is not merely a deduced application of formal principles to purely static, objectively established circumstances, but that it has the characteristic of historical uniqueness and of creative originality in which the dignity of freedom reaches its highest achievement.

f. Hence the historical way of acting of Christians in society, the State and the Church, has inevitably the character of a bold venture, of uncertainty, of walking into the dark, of 'not knowing what we should pray for', of praying for gracious guidance from above to lead us beyond that which can be calculated in advance, of 'art' (in contrast to theory). Anyone who believes himself to be dispensed, at least *as a Christian*, from making such a decision, on account of the fact that the shaping of the future is in the nature of a venture, offends against the historicity of his existence and becomes all the more guilty. The Christian has not *merely* the duty of proclaiming and commending the ever valid principles; he must place his trust in God and venture a concrete future. Even *as* a Christian he must not only suffer but also act without the rightness and the intramundane powerfulness for the future of his concrete actions being *materially* and concretely guaranteed for him simply by the rightness of his principles. This is true in general and especially is it true of the courage needed for freedom and coercion and their concrete balancing. That we always have to deal with a fluid, unstable and provisional balance arises ultimately not from any cheap cowardly willingness to compromise on the part of the Christian, or from an uncreative decadence of man at a certain period, but from the essential creaturely nature of man; man in his knowledge and freedom as a creature does not stand at the absolutely *one* point of origin of all reality, but must master what is for him an indissoluble plural reality in the one realm of his free actions by human truth and creaturely freedom. Compromise, the middle way, the 'on the one hand—on the other hand', a seemingly uncreative lack of originality, incompleteness, provisionality, making an attempt with right of recall and with reservations, the abandoning of a position, being willing to learn from new experiences, slow evolution, the lack of any clear sustained construction, etc.—all these are, in their right place, signs of genuineness and of genuine humanity. We do not have any reason for letting ourselves be impressed by the unbending monoideism of other '*Weltanschauungen*' (outlooks on life). Anyone who believes that he can open all locks with one key, arrogates God's position to himself, is lying and has no genuine future. All this does not in the least signify a confused, vague both-yes-and-no-programme for the Christian. Precisely because, on the one hand, the concrete imperative programme of action is not unequivocally deducible from metaphysical and theological principles and yet, on the other hand, because it is something necessary, it does not need to be a popular repetition of eternal principles in uniformly balanced vagueness but ought rather to command courageously and with justified one-sidedness (i.e. subjection to the situation) what ought to be done at this particular moment. For however true both 'sides' of a question (the question of coercion and freedom, for instance) usually are in theory, both of them are not equally urgent for action at every moment. Watchword and theory rightly have different structures. The Christian must not only have the courage to uphold a balanced eternal theory but must also have the courage and decisiveness to pass a clear, even though time-bound, watchword which *he*, in certain circumstances, can utter in the name of Christianity although it has not been and also cannot be proclaimed by the Church as such.

g. The execution of such a shifting of the boundary between freedom and coercion must generally take place by evolution, making full use of the legal possibilities already given. Whenever the present state of affairs encloses an essential and general annulment of the rights of freedom granted by natural law, the changing of this state is permitted (from the Christian point of view) even by the employment of revolutionary acts; and indeed, if there is any real hope of success, such a method of removal is demanded of those who have the necessary means at their disposal.

h. The boundary between freedom and coercion lies *within each* particular dimension of human existence, each of which regarded by itself differs from the others in the nature of things. The more material such a dimension, the more confined may be the field of freedom in principle; the more personal the dimension, the greater the actual freedom must be. The Christian is, therefore, quite rightly, more touchy about the interference of the State in matters of cultural import, for instance, than about its interference in economic matters. Although the Church is not a free association of men but rather (like the State) has a right to exist prior to such associations, she cannot force anyone to enter her against his will.

III. THE STATE AND FREEDOM

1. The State exists for man and not vice versa. It must serve the personal dignity and freedom of man. It is true that the communities of

interest and the orientation of man to a 'thou' in love and mutual service already belong to the nature of man from the very start. And yet the State is not the first and decisive organization of these communities but merely a subsidiary social organization which must serve these more primitive and essential communities (such as the marriage community, the family, the clan, local and vocational communities, the community of friends, a people, communities arising from common possession and creation of cultural goods, etc.). The State presupposes these; it does not first invest them through itself with their rights.

2. And yet the State is a natural institution, founded on the natural law wherever a greater number of people are living together. Its final structures and rights are not arbitrarily assigned to it by its citizens.

3. The State does not grant the original rights and the scope for freedom of the individual and the smaller but more primitive communities (which are more primitive because arising more closely from the core of the person). Rather, it must protect them and, where necessary, regulate and harmonize them with each other. It must, therefore, always authenticate its right to make a particular limitation of freedom in a concrete case—it cannot simply presuppose such a right. And it must in the case of such limitations of freedom and use of coercive measures keep to the already mentioned principles. It must in certain circumstances refuse to further its citizens' flight from freedom. There are also instances of a 'voluntary' transference of rights which the State ought not to accept so long as the individual or the smaller communities can look after these rights.

4. Even those laws of a formal democracy which have come into being in a formally incontestable manner, are only then justified when they do not annul the freedom of the individual in some sector of his sphere of existence or curtail it beyond right measure. Otherwise democracy becomes the dictatorship of the numerical majority, which is just as immoral (because ultimately the same) as a totalitarian State in which every right of the individual is merely a concession granted by the apparatus of the State.

5. The (written and unwritten) constitution of a State will be all the more the way it ought to be, the more that State is so constituted as to allow the citizen the effective use of his native rights and freedoms, even against the State itself, be it by a division of powers and an independent administration of justice orientated by the natural law, or be it over and above this (which is ultimately something absolutely necessary and cannot be replaced by formal State laws) by an effective appeal to the conscience of the supreme rulers of the State who bow before and know themselves responsible to God and his law. Wherever man no longer has such a possibility of exercising his rights against the State, there we have the Moloch of the totalitarian State, no matter what its written constitution may be.

6. The universal and equal suffrage in a formal democracy is neither a necessary right flowing everywhere and always from the nature of the human person nor is it a sufficient safeguard in itself of the right order of a State or of the just laws and the right demarcation between freedom and coercion. It may even stand in the way of a reform of conditions and outlook and cover up the fact that not only must everyone be given an equal right but *his* right. Of course, this universal and equal suffrage may in a certain historical situation be in actual fact an indispensable, even though by itself insufficient prerequisite for the maintenance of the citizen's freedom against the State. Yet we must not then grow forgetful on this account of the other necessities for the State: the education and formation in principles and practical acquaintance with affairs of the rising generation of political leaders, legal measures against the dictatorship of political parties, care and maintenance of the communities which have a midway position between the individual and the State, delegation of specialist problems away from the political parliament to appropriate specialized organs (which have to be set up if need be).

7. There are unchangeable principles akin to the natural law and of a Christian kind which are valid for every State and for the constitution of every State and economy. To see that they are observed in the State and in the economy as well as in their constitutions, is the duty of every Christian. Their observation would be a blessing for every-

one which cannot be exaggerated. However, there is no constitution of State or economy which could simply be deduced from these unchangeable principles in its concrete form. Over and above these principles, Christians (not the Church) in a certain period, culture and historical situation need a correspondingly determined *concrete* conception of how this State ought to look in the concrete here and now, especially with regard to the division of freedom and planning (coercion). The fact that they cannot simply obtain this concrete conception, the imperative of the present hour, from the Church, does not dispense them from this duty; and nothing much is achieved by a common consent to the principles when people are not clear and agreed about how these principles ought to be realized in this particular place and at this particular time. The fact that this concrete and communal, courageously forward-looking picture of order is not sufficiently present, has a paralysing effect on Catholics and turns them into an object rather than the very subject of history—in contrast to much smaller groups who have a different way of thinking.

IV. THE CHURCH AND FREEDOM

1. The Church is an indispensable shelter of freedom in the world; she teaches, lives and defends the dignity and hence the inviolability of the individual man: that he is a person, has an eternal destiny and has freedom. She places man before the living God and hence before the Guarantor of the right of the weak as against the physical power of the stronger. She proclaims the Judgement of God, before which there is no respect of persons. By her independent existence from the State she is the living protest against every caesaropapism, every idolization of the State and absorption of the whole life of the individual, considered under the spiritual and material aspect, by the State bureaucracy and by a total planning which necessarily means the death of all spiritual creative life. By professing eternal life based on the grace of God beyond history, she relieves man of the pride and the anguish of life, both of which lead to a violent attempt—and one which enslaves the present in favour of an utopian future—to achieve the kingdom of God already here on earth. She educates man to be moderate and humble, which in the long run serves the real and ever-new improvement of earthly conditions better than any utopian radicalism. In so far as she places all men before the one Lord and

Father and before the one goal, she creates the only really objectively tenable basis for a permanent and really sacrificing love of neighbour.

2. Today more than ever the Church must be on her guard not to appear in the eyes of men as a clerical, religiously camouflaged kind of totalitarian system. Her objective nature is not that of a totalitarian system, since the dignity of man, the directness of man's relationship to God and freedom are part and parcel of the basic principles proclaimed by her herself and established by constitution in her very being. Moreover, she has been given God's promise that she will be preserved by his grace until the end of time from every essential defection from this her true nature. However, since the Church is always a Church made up of sinful men, even as far as the holders of her authority are concerned, she can in her individual actions also offend against her own principles and against the freedom of the individual both within and without. This has happened often enough in the course of history. It can happen even today. And this is what the Church must guard against, for today more than ever she must be the champion of true freedom. But even by such individual offences she does not become a totalitarian system. For she acts in these cases against her own proclaimed and practised principles, whereas a really totalitarian system does not recognize such principles of the freedom or dignity of the individual either expressly or tacitly, but on the contrary idolizes the collectivity and degrades the individual. But the Church must reckon with the real danger of giving the scandal of an apparent totalitarianism. This is particularly the case because, no matter how clear her ultimate basic principles may be, there can be, and in fact there has been, a subjective development of the Church's consciousness in articulating and applying more particular and proximate principles with exactitude and sureness. And this also explains how it is possible for the Church to violate the legitimate claims of freedom both from within and from without, even in cases where she has not become clearly conscious of this.

3. Even in the Church there is to be found an application of the principle of subsidiary function in respect of the functioning of her hierarchically constructed authorities, without prejudice to her basic

God-given constitution and the direct origin of her fundamental authorities and powers in her divine founder. This means that even in the Church every individual, community and authority must, indeed, be fitted into the whole structure of the Church and subordinated to the highest authority of the Church; but this does not mean that the members of the Church (both individuals and communities), which are thus incorporated and subordinated, cannot and ought not to have their own relatively independent functions; it does not mean that the life of the Church is directed by an omnipotent central body of bureaucrats, and that all others have merely the duty to receive orders passively, without any responsibility or initiative of their own. Even in positive Canon Law (which is not unchangeable) changes can take place in the boundary between freedom and compulsion and in the distribution of duties and rights. The Canon Law obtaining at any particular moment in time does not need to be regarded as something immutable. Because someone does not have a divine right in a certain respect and in a particular case, does not mean that the Church herself may not invest him with such a right in the form of a *ius humanum* which can be a true right and not merely a privilege. Thus it is conceivable that in this respect the rights of lay people might be further extended and re-extended, since in the long run this is the only way in which the layman can be brought to a consciousness of his duties in and on behalf of the Church.

4. Even within her life of religion, the Church must combat the tendency among her own members of taking refuge in the mass and taking flight into a merely collective religious life, as manifested by too great a dependence on others, by shying away from personal responsibility or waiting for ecclesiastical directions from above in the wrong circumstances, or by the opinion that everything is morally as it should be merely by the fact that the Church has not issued an explicit and detailed verdict, and by the dwindling of a *personal* private life of piety both of the individual and in families, in spite of their participation in the official liturgy, etc.

5. If we are to give some indication of certain concrete instances where room should be left for freedom *inside* the Church particularly at the present time, then the following must be said:

a. Even within the Church there should be room and toleration for the expression of opinion, i.e. Public Opinion. Pius XII himself pointed this out and stated that the absence of such public opinion in the Church would be a fault for which both the pastors and the flock would have to take the blame. The following are the Holy Father's actual words (*Osservatore Romano*, 18th February 1950):

> Public opinion is the natural portion of every normal society composed of human beings. . . . Whenever there is no manifest expression of public opinion at all, and above all whenever one must admit that public opinion does not at all exist, this lack must be regarded as a fault, a weakness and a disease in the life of that society. . . . In conclusion, We wish to add a few words about public opinion within the pale of the Church (in respect of those matters, of course, which are left to free discussion). Only those will be surprised at this who do not know the Catholic Church, or at least know her only badly. For, after all, she too is a living corporate body, and there would be something lacking in her life if there were no public opinion in the Church—a lack for which the pastors as well as the faithful would be to blame. . . . (German translation: *Orbis Catholicus* III (1950), pp. 313–316).[2]

b. There must be room in theology for research, for different schools and directions of thought, for experiments and progress, within the framework of actual dogmas and any other really obligatory doctrines.

c. There is, if we may express our meaning in so profane a manner, a lawful 'freedom of association' for Christians.[3] Even in this sphere is it a valid rule that higher forms of organization must not be allowed to suppress the spontaneous individual life of fellowships which grow up within the Church from below, in favour of a kind of 'State Socialism' which organizes things in a bureaucratic manner from above? Such methods would be more convenient and would make it easier to survey everything, but they would not be more successful in the long run and

[2] Regarding the object, limits etc. of public opinion in the Church, cf. K. Rahner, 'Öffentliche Meinung in der Kirche', *Orientierung* XV (Zurich 1951), pp. 255–258. The same in: K. Rahner, *Free Speech in the Church* (London and New York 1960).

[3] Cf. on this: K. Rahner, 'Peaceful reflections on the parochial principle', pp. 283–318 in the present volume.

would, in fact, mean the death of any true Church life. An exaggerated principle of parochial and natural social groupings offends against the rightful freedom of the Christian in his religious life.

d. Side by side with the official function which is transmitted in a juridical manner, there is and must also be the charismatic and the prophetic in the Church which cannot be officially organized right from the start but must, in all patience and humility, be given sufficient room for growth, even though its bearers are sometimes rather 'inconvenient'. It is written: 'Do not extinguish the Spirit'.

6. If the non-Catholic fears the Church as a potentially totalitarian system which would oppress him in his freedom once it became sufficiently powerful for this, then the following must be pointed out:

a. In those cases where coercion would be directly or indirectly aimed at what can of its nature take place only by free consent (i.e entry into the Church, etc.), the Church of its very nature cannot and will not want to use coercion. In these matters she desires freedom for herself and for others and nothing less.

b. Since the line of demarcation between coercion and freedom has in the nature of things a variability determined historically and by circumstances, and since this change in situation can bring with it not only the right but in certain circumstances also the absolute moral duty of shifting the boundary between freedom and coercion—and this even in favour of a greater freedom—the Church is not simply and absolutely bound by old ideals of protection for the Catholic religion by the State; she is not bound by ideals which restricted non-Christians in their freedom. Such ideals can be absolutely justified in a certain situation, so that the Church does not need to be ashamed of her ideals even in this respect (at least not of everything appertaining to them). Yet these ideals do not have any ever-valid binding force on the Church herself. It is not as if the Church had still to regard these ideals in every respect even today as being valid everywhere and as having to be realized 'of their very nature'. Neither the Holy Empire nor the sectarian, territorial State with special privileges for the Church as the State-religion need nowadays be the Christian ideal in our country. Although there can be no right to a false cult *as such*, there can certainly be a right to scope for freedom within which a false cult is possible, and within which it would not be permitted to suppress this false cult by external force merely because it is false, when (and because) this would be possible only by a restriction of what is a legitimate scope for freedom in a determined historical situation. Suppose the State permits all its citizens, and hence also the Christians, the freedom which is their due by natural law and uses only that coercion to which it can be proved to have a right by natural law, materially and not merely formally.... Suppose further that it does not engage in culture-politics, which goes beyond the kind of politics really incumbent on the State (which is of an essentially negative and subsidiary character[4]).... Suppose finally that the State above all does not engage in an anti-religious culture-politics (directly or indirectly) and does not conceive the 'separation of Church and State' in this anti-religious sense, as did the liberalistic State of the nineteenth century.... Then, under such conditions, we Christians need not nowadays nor in the foreseeable future demand any patronage for the Church by way of political coercive measures from the State, a patronage which would restrict the freedom of the non-Christians. Nor ought we to demand this, but should rather believe in the power of the Gospel. There would be no harm if we who historically speaking still come from a sectarian State with a State-Church, were to re-examine out situation and practices to see whether we do not here and there still hold fast to things from that bygone age which are or were historically justified, thus giving grounds for continued anticlerical feelings to the detriment of Christianity's real power for winning souls.

[4] And hence the State must, for example, respect the wishes of the parents even in its State schools, since the parents have the primary right and duty to be the educators of their children.

9

GUILT AND ITS REMISSION: THE BORDERLAND BETWEEN THEOLOGY AND PSYCHOTHERAPY[1]

PERHAPS the most important question theology can address to psychotherapy today is whether the latter claims to be or hopes to become the secularized form of what takes place in the realm of the Christian Faith, of the sacrament and the proclamation of the faith, viz. the remission of guilt. If psychotherapy does not make this claim, since it would be senseless to believe that it could perform such a function, then we must ask ourselves where we should draw the real, basic line of demarcation between the activities of the Church and those of profane psychotherapy concerning guilt and its remission. For obviously it cannot be said that psychotherapy is in no way concerned with guilt and remission of guilt, just because it is an activity in the field of medical psychology which, unlike the activity of the Church, does not require any divine mandate. Consequently, we must determine the line of demarcation.

In the following pages we will attempt to define this boundary. We will do this in as concise a manner as possible, almost in bare thesis-form. The metaphysical anthropology underlying our reflections would, of course, require to be worked out and proved more exactly. Nevertheless we may hope that what will be said can be fairly well understood even in the form given.

[1] The following was first published (in an abbreviated version of a lecture) in: *Angst und Schuld in theologischer und psychotherapeutischer Sicht*, A collection of lectures, edited by Wilhelm Bitter, M.D., D.Ph. (Stuttgart 1953). Unabridged reprint in: *Anima* VIII (1953), pp. 258–272.

Throughout this particular treatise, the author uses the term '*Schuld*' almost exclusively—a term used equally by the theologian and the psychotherapist (although in different senses). Hence we have translated it throughout by the term 'guilt'. It should, however, be noted that, whereas the German term (in its theological sense) refers directly to the free and responsible offence against God, the English term refers rather to the result of such an offence—*Tr.*

1. 'Guilt' is one of the most fundamental notions in theology, for theology has to do with God and his word to man. This word, addressed to man in the totality of his being, declares him to be a sinner in the sight of God and one who is redeemed by God and his action. This at once implies a threefold truth for theology:

a. Sin or guilt, as understood in theology, is indeed an occurrence capable of description, even definition if you wish, but is not at all events a *derived* phenomenon reducible to other, more original phenomena. The theological meaning of guilt has, for instance, nothing to do with a problematical interpretation of states of depression, disturbances of the psychical mechanism, etc.; it is in no way an ideological superstructure imposed on the facts of immediate experience. Guilt is not the same as illness, 'evil' is different from 'neurotic', 'ill', etc. Theocentric ethics is neither an unwarranted *interpretation* of psychical events nor merely some sort of ideal standard *to which* the physics of the spirit ought to 'conform'. Rather, it expresses the true reality of the spiritual, God-related person and *is*, together with Logic, the 'physics' of the spirit, so that any 'setting-in-order' or 'disposing-to-the-good' of spiritual-personal reality cannot escape the question of truth. This means that since really existing guilt is an intentional happening with an *intrinsic* constitutive moment of truth or falsehood, moral right or wrong, even 'existing' or, if you like, 'physical' guilt can be repaired only by attaining the objective truth or good. In the personal dimension, to which guilt belongs, there can be no question of 'repairs' or 'setting-in-motion' of the 'physical apparatus' (which does not really exist in this dimension), except as a result of its assimilation to the objective norms of truth and goodness which express not only an objective duty but the true essential structure of this 'apparatus'.

b. Guilt in the theological sense is not an offence against some universal custom, civic morality, public penal laws or conventions, the laws and conventions arising from normal upbringing, etc. Nor is it merely a wrong action with harmful, destructive, pathogenic, physically and socially perturbing effects. Sin and guilt in the theological sense are to be found only where man, addressed by God, acts in God's sight and together with Him (as is his will), even though the overriding refusal to admit this fact and the suppression of this truth (viz. of the dialogical structure of guilt) is one of the essential moments of guilt and one which is not confessed until there is a conversion by grace: *Tibi soli peccavi.*

c. Only when someone sins knowingly against God can there be guilt. It is quite a different matter (and one into which we do not wish to enter more closely here) to determine the extent to which there must be objective and reflex 'awareness' of saying 'no' to God and his will and of thus (and only thus) establishing guilt. The fact, however, that real guilt before God is possible only as a knowingly perpetrated act, does belong to the theological notion of guilt. Unconscious and involuntary personal guilt before God does not and cannot exist. There can be extremely reflectionless, forgotten, dissimulating or suppressed guilt, but not guilt brought about unknowingly and involuntarily. The different degrees of guilt, therefore, depend absolutely on the degree of knowledge and freedom. Yet, although there cannot be any unknowing and involuntary guilt before God in the theological sense, there can of course be wrong decisions or actions which are guiltless and yet offend in their material reality against the objective structures and rules of man and his world. Such decisions and actions can, without detracting from their guiltless character, have such injurious and pathogenic effects on man as to encourage and eventually induce him to incur real, conscious and voluntary guilt. In so far as there can be guilt only before the One God and his undivided will (which ultimately is the only binding one), man can also never find himself, objectively speaking, in the tragic situation of being able to choose only between different ways of becoming guilty, so that no matter what alternative he chooses, he necessarily incurs guilt. In certain situations the only choice open to us may lie between two actions, both of which must be regarded as harmful and wrong in a certain respect; yet, objectively speaking, no situation can ever force us into guilt. For this would imply the contradiction that God at the same time imposes and condemns the self-same behaviour. It is, therefore, also quite contradictory and immoral to say that we must learn to have the courage to incur guilt and to recommend such courage. It is true, however, that under certain circumstances man may have to learn to act courageously even though his action may, in certain more restricted aspects, harm him or others in some specific realm of human existence.

2. For theology and according to revelation itself, guilt and sin are principally and originally acts or events and not states, even though the very frame of mind produced by the sinful act helps to cause further

sinful acts and constitutes the atmosphere in which sin thrives. Sinfulness arises ultimately from sin—the first theology of sin, the account of the Fall given in Genesis, already shows this. By depicting man as becoming guilty through a deed in the state of paradisean goodness, it tells him that his sinful state does not simply come into being without reference to his own active freedom but arises out of his responsible act. It tells him that he cannot shift responsibility for his guilty acts to a dark, impersonal, anonymous fate or to an 'Ego' from which he, the one who acts and suffers, can separate himself and which he can accuse as the tragic and incomprehensible power disposing of him, the active subject. On the contrary, it tells him that he must hold himself and no one and nothing else responsible for his guilty state, in so far as he acts and suffers. Man has entered fully into the biblical truth only when he no longer makes any distinctions in this, and when (since the account in Genesis is the aetiology of man's disastrous state of suffering) he confesses the state from which he suffers to be his doing, which should not have happened and indeed did only happen because he who suffers, and he alone, willed it. He must not accuse his tempting surroundings or the woman or nature (real temptations all) of being the cause of his state; he must see that cause in himself and in his own inalienable act of freedom—he himself in his free act is the one whom he must accuse as the cause of the state making him now suddenly ask the question which really ought not to have been asked at all: how did all this happen? It is certainly true that, in spite (and because) of his consciousness and freedom which are the *a-priori* conditions making a guilty act possible, the reflecting man always encounters himself in his reflection as someone who has already decided, i.e. as someone in a determined moral disposition, and never as someone who makes a decision arising out of pure moral indifference—in short, as a sinner or as someone redeemed by God's grace. And to that extent his reflection is never capable of retracing his own particular sinfulness sufficiently clearly in the unique direction of his sinful act *or* of simply attributing his sinful act to his sinfulness (brought about by previous decisions). Guilt, in spite of its basically active character and its nature as an event, has a diffused existence for us in the whole course of human history, even simply on account of the fact that ultimately our subsequent and always unfinished reflection and 'analysis' can never adequately resolve the conjunction of act and state, habitual disposition and new original decision, sin and sinfulness. We can, no doubt, say with some probability or practical moral certitude that there and in this way, at this spatio-temporal point in this particular history, guilt began. And yet we must also say: it 'could' not help coming this way, in view of the 'sinfulness' which reigns throughout the whole of existence and out of which this culpable act arose. Our meaning here is not only that the culpable act was preceded by a dangerous or tragic but actually still innocent state, but also that it was preceded at least by an always possible, truly sinful state which was expressed in a consistent manner by this particular culpable act. It is of course true, as already stated, that the sinful state referred to must ultimately have sprung from an act of decision, but this does not mean that the latter must necessarily have been stored up in the person's historical memory and thus be always available for renewed reflection. Consequently, the fact of our getting the impression that this or that could really have happened no differently—'I *acted* thus because I *am* that way'—does not necessarily argue against guilt considered as an act and thus for the tragedy of a development opposed to the responsible freedom of one's personal state; it is merely an indication of the fact that the person had always understood and accepted himself in a certain manner even before the action in question occurred, and that he had performed the act out of and in accordance with his freely acquired attitude and frame of mind.

3. Man is that strange being who attains self-consciousness only by being conscious of something other than himself, who deals with himself by occupying himself with something else (even if this be merely the perception or thought of himself), who catches sight of himself only by perceiving an object. Man always requires some material distinct from himself which will act as the Archimedean point, so to speak, from which alone he can attain himself. He must be in-the-world in order to be capable of being personal; he must diffuse himself in order to concentrate himself on himself; he must 'go out' (as the German mystics used to say) in order to be able to enter into himself and into the very core of his person. Thus we may quite rightly say that in the case of man, who is a creature and essentially in-the-world and who is at home with himself only by being-with-others, the act of freedom springing from the core of his person, where man is ultimately concerned with himself and his relationship to God (both insolubly

bound up with one another), is necessarily achieved in a material which, although different from the real spiritual core of the person, is nevertheless the prerequired object on which the act of freedom is exercised. Man's relationship to himself, and his action on himself and before God, is inevitably mediate, i.e. by means of ob-jects. Man's culpable desire-to-be-God and his emancipation from the all-embracing will of God, who wants him to be always open to his infinity, operate within man's attitude to the fruits of the world and in the face of commandments relating to this or that finite object in the world. This is why there is, according to the Scriptures, more than one divine commandment and more than one human sin, each distinct from the other although (and because) the same reality of 'becoming-guilty' before God is realized in all of them. There is, therefore, a peculiar dialectic relationship between guilt considered in itself and as arising originally, and the material of guilt in which guilt, actualizing itself, is posited—a relationship similar to that existing between spirit and body: one cannot exist without the other and yet they are not the same; each refers, for its understanding, to the other which it is not itself. The objectively tangible offence against man's nature, against his due relationship to God which can be formulated as a law, and against the intramundane, ordered structure of persons and things in his surroundings, is the constitutive *sign* of the real revolt against God taking place in the depth of man's soul and utterly determining it. We call this objective falseness of man's concrete act a 'sign'. For firstly, it is not strictly identical with what is properly speaking meant in theology by the guilt of the person as such and before God as he is in himself; this is clearly shown even by the mere fact that the same objective perversity of the action, considered as an offence against a restricted material law, can also come about, indeed can even be induced from outside, without there being any personal guilt. And yet, secondly, this objective falseness also indicates the presence of such a guilt (in the normal case), and man looks at himself in it and recognizes himself reflectively as a sinner. For example, drunkenness is normally *physically* wrong because it normally offends against man's bodily health which, as the health of a spiritual person, is also subject to the binding sovereign dignity of the spiritual person assured to him by God. Now, in certain cases a person may make himself drunk quite innocently, either because he does not know that it is contrary to nature or because he lacks the necessary moral freedom in doing it; in other cases, drunkenness may be brought about by external force and still other cases, it may be the concrete material or the sign-like manifestation of personal guilt, by and within which the personal turning-away from God realizes itself *in concreto*. In this last case the concrete action is called a *constitutive* sign, because personal guilt can realize itself only in this (or a similar) sort of concrete form. This dialectic unity, this difference between personal guilt and its constitutive, concrete manifestation still exists even when we are dealing with 'internal' sins in the superficial sense given to this term in everyday experience (or, in the language of Holy Writ: when it is 'merely' a case of 'lusting after'), or when it is a question of an apparently explicit and direct refusal to submit to God himself and his will. For even the merely 'internal' act of sin is an 'em-bodied' act (in the original sense of the word), which changes man's bodily, physiological, etc., constitution and, in consequence, in-dicates its presence, like the external sinful action, in the 'otherness' of external reality. In other words, it indicates its presence by expressing it in the 'other' of its own bodily reality (to be understood as an animated reality which consequently includes the psychical as one of its inner constitutive moments), i.e. it shows itself as 'now-existing' by positing itself. And similarly, even when sin seems to be directed explicitly and reflectively against God himself (in a judgement and objectively), it nevertheless takes place in the material of the world and hence with a constitutive sign-likeness. For propositional thought about God is even in this case constructed with the use of the 'materials' of the world. Also, there is a difference between '*thought* about' God and God meant 'intentionally' and aimed at by the transcendental nature of *original* thinking and willing. And thought about God, like any other 'inner' thought and act of the will, does include a physical manifestation in the form of a sign. Thus it is conceivable, for instance, that in certain circumstances such an opposition to God, although objectively wrong, may nevertheless not be existentially culpable (i.e. in the very core of the person), because in such a case God is denied in the objective concept but not with that real, fundamental grasp (*Zugriff*) which occurs in the basic act of freedom.

4. We started above with the simple fact that according to Scripture and Tradition sin against and before God is always the same and yet

there are *sins* (in the plural), which must be given specifically different names and must be appraised in a specifically different manner. Proceeding with logical necessity, we have now arrived at an ontological conception of man's nature, which we now intend to outline again in greater detail so that it may then be easier to understand our subsequent propositions about guilt, recognition of guilt, guilt and suffering, divine remission of guilt and earthly triumph over suffering.

Man is a being constructed, as it were, from the interior towards the outside. He has, on the one hand, a spiritual-personal nucleus giving him an 'intentional' transcendental relation to 'Being as such and in its totality', and hence to God, and rendering him capable of hearing the word of God as such. Man's transcendent orientation and consequent freedom and openness towards all being, allow him to maintain a selective, de-ciding, consenting or denying attitude towards individual things (and the merely *represented* totality of being and hence God in this sense), since he always transcends everything limited and desires the whole, Being as such, God. On the other hand, man always has to achieve himself *qua* transcending person in a relationship to something which is neither himself nor the transcendent counter-pole to his spiritual openness for the whole as such. In short, he must constantly achieve himself as a person in an 'intermediary reality' (*in einem Mittleren*), formed by the union of his animated corporeality and embodied spirituality together with their concrete, material and propositional objectifications, and by the external world of equally real persons and things as well as by the objectifications produced there by 'external' actions. This 'intermediary reality'—which alone provides man with the means of cognitive access to himself, free control over himself and a conscious, free attitude towards God—is at the same time different and unseparated from the 'seminal' (*ursprünglich*)[2] human person. There is no permanently fixed boundary-line between these two spheres of man which are continually undergoing osmosis into one another; man constantly transforms himself into the objectifications of his body, thoughts and actions-in-the-world; he deposits himself into them without being absorbed by them (like brute-animals) and without having to deliver himself to them

[2] We have translated '*ursprünglich*' by 'seminal' rather than 'original', since the 'seminal person' is a *continuing* dimension of the one person, fulfilled in the 'achieved person' via the 'intermediary reality of the person' —*Tr.*

completely; and when he objectifies himself in this way in the world, he is constantly referred back again to himself and to God. These objectifications are 'he himself' and yet not he himself; he is in the Other and becomes the Other, but never in such a way that he can be in the Other as he is in his own self. For he is never contained totally in the Other which expresses him and shows him to himself and to others. And the Other is also never completely only his expression, since the intermediary material itself includes structures alien to the person to which the person cannot refuse to submit himself up to a certain point and in varying degrees, if he is to be at all able to express himself in the Other by forming himself into it and so fulfil himself in this intermediary reality. Only by passing out of the depth of his being into the world, can man enter into the depth of the person where he stands before God; this is roughly what the medieval mystic would already have said. Thus we may say that we must distinguish between the '*seminal*' person (*ursprünglicher* Person), understood as transcendent spirit and as freedom before God; the world-like and piecemeal 'intermediary reality' (*Mittleren*) in which the person, searching for himself, must achieve himself; and the 'achieved' person (*endgültigen* Person) who has freely fulfilled himself *via* his intermediary reality. By the fact that the seminal person achieves himself in the intermediary 'world' of his animated body and external surroundings, this constitutive sign (i.e. the intermediary reality of the person) becomes relatively independent; it may even remain when the act of the seminal person no longer persists. The connection between the act of the seminal person as such and its constitutive sign in the intermediary 'world' of the person is fluid, both as regards their interdependence and as regards the expressive capacity of the constitutive sign. The intermediary 'world' of the person is at the same time the medium of the constitutive sign and the medium of influences exerted on the person by the 'Other'. Realities different from the person, the surrounding world, Nature, heredity, other persons, etc., reflect themselves into this intermediary reality and create in this way an *a-priori* basis for the possibilities of personal self-achievement in the sphere of the constitutive expression of the person; for personal self-achievement requires such an expression in the same medium as the 'Other'. In this way (and only in this way) the 'outer world' influences the person himself; it naturally does so in the many different ways in which the intermediary sphere of personal exercise of freedom can be determined: by physical influences, psycho-somatic influences of speech, etc. In so far as the seminal person *and* the Other find fulfilment in identically the same realm of the intermediary 'world' of the person, there is 'interpenetration' in this medium between Action and Passion, between what is done and what is imposed, one's own and the Other; one's own is covered up by the Other and the Other becomes the property of the person; thus, the person posits the constitutive sign as the 'other part' of himself, becomes a stranger to himself and divests himself of himself—while, conversely, the surrounding world, originally strange to the person, finds fulfilment by forming itself into the very medium belonging to the person as sphere of his self-fulfilment.

5. The person finds certain pre-determined structures in its nucleus, psycho-somatic medium and surrounding world which precede freedom and its formative control over the person. What in particular these structures are and how they are recognizable cannot of course be explained here; the analysis of the nature and necessity of these structures is the task of theology, metaphysical anthropology, ethics and all the other anthropological sciences (in so far as they do not regard themselves as purely positivistic descriptions of merely *temporary* conditions). Now, if an act freely performed by the seminal person (who is spiritually and freely referred to God) contradicts the right structure of the person and his proper relationship to God, i.e. if the person turns an intermediate reality and his own expression contained in it into an absolute (in other words, mistakes it for God and idolizes it), then there is sin *qua* act. The constitutive sign of sin, i.e. the embodied reality of the seminal, personal act and of the seminal person in his intermediary being, is called 'suffering' in theological language. Such a sign of the sinful act has necessarily a painful effect on the person. For the medium is not absolutely indifferent, or *pure* possibility of personal 'expression', but has its own *a-priori* structures, independently of the freedom of the person. And so when the seminal, personal act is formed into this medium in a manner contradicting its *a-priori* structures, it experiences the resistance offered by these structures as a conflict and hence as suffering (for the medium is inevitably also the medium of the '*passio*' of the person). However, in so far as the surrounding world can also enter into this

same medium by its painful influences, not every suffering is a constitutive sign of personal guilt. Yet, because the state of suffering induced from without (independently of guilt), or continuing even after its originating guilt, constitutes in its turn a question posed to the person (about how he is to understand it), it can and must be answered either in a guilty or in a true manner. When answered in a guilty manner, the state of suffering becomes the 'tinder' of sin and hence the source of its own or new guilt. When it is accepted by faith as a sharing in the Passion of Christ (i.e. answered truly), the state of suffering becomes the means of making Christ's Passion one's own. The sinful act of the seminal person, achieved *via* the intermediary reality of the person but able to remain thus achieved even after its constitutive sign has ceased, is the state of sin, i.e. sinfulness.

6. The essential freedom of the seminal person, i.e. freedom as distinct from its exercise in the intermediary outer world of the person, is of its very nature a conscious occurrence. This does not mean, however, that basic freedom strictly as such is an objective datum of consciousness and can, therefore, be the direct object of reflection. Man can look at himself and his freedom only in their constitutive sign (by considering himself as an object) and in the objectifications of his freedom which are different from freedom itself even though they are its *constitutive* signs. This leaves him in an essentially ambiguous situation as far as his knowledge of guilt is concerned. To understand this we need only consider the sober facts of theology, even before making any deductions from what has been said so far. According to the Scriptures, man ought to confess his sins; he ought to say (hence *can* also say) that he has sinned in this way or that, and not merely make a general, vague statement about his sinful state. Now, in so far as he makes an explicit confession or admission, he must have an objective knowledge of his sinful acts which is expressible in concepts and propositions. He must, therefore, be able to gather sufficiently certain information from the objective, material data of his internal and external life to be able to say that he has sinned. The material of his consciousness, tangible to reflection and open to analysis, must really be the *sign* of the personal guilt of the seminal person about which he wishes ultimately to make a statement. And yet, according to the same Scriptures, man is not only commanded not to 'judge' others, i.e.

not to make *absolute* assertions about the real state of a person deep down and in the sight of God, but he also cannot and is not allowed to pass such an absolute judgement on himself and declare himself to be either absolutely justified or an absolute sinner, in the sense of declaring that a justifying or sinful act has *certainly* taken place here and now. Thus, the constitutive sign on which such a judgement would have to be based, cannot be *so* absolutely unequivocal that it allows him to pronounce such a judgement *before* the *divine* tribunal. In spite of the real informative function of the constitutive sign, the *real* information given by it is of an essentially equivocal character. In the light of what has been said previously, it is easy to see the reason for this ambiguity; since the constitutive sign is 'embedded' in the very same intermediary reality as that which acts as the medium for passive determinations from outside (i.e. outside in the widest sense, including the antecedents of the person as regards free, personal self-determination and the inner conditions making it possible), there is at least in principle absolutely nothing in this medium which could not be an impression received from outside as well as an expression of the original, personal act. When reflection interprets the realities in the intermediary medium of the person as expressions or impressions or both, this cannot basically be anything more than an approximate, provisional interpretation. Such an interpretation may be sufficient for practical conduct and the duties imposed by it—and indeed will be sufficient for it in the normal, everyday case—but it will not be an absolute interpretation and will always remain subject to reservations; it will always remain exclusively reserved to God, the only Judge. Only in this way can the interpretation correspond to the indistinct situation with which the creature must bear patiently to the end. By its character of 'not being absolutely clear about oneself', of 'not being able to deal definitively with oneself', this interpretation not only realizes a regrettable fact but also a basic and essential situation of the creature, since it is precisely at this point that the creature surrenders himself unconditionally to God. Any would-be final analysis of guilt and justice implies usurpation of God's Judgement. Reflection can never 'catch up' with man, for the simple reason that every reflection, whatever its pretensions to objectivity, is itself a morally good or evil act demanding a new reflection on its own quality and so on *ad infinitum*. A reflective self-knowledge and analysis of guilt (by oneself or with the help of others) means primarily an analysis of the constitutive sign of guilt and only indirectly (and with reservations) a knowledge of the guilty act committed by the seminal person. *Qua* analysis of the constitutive sign and of the 'deposit' of the seminal person in his psycho-physical external nature (i.e. of everything which is at all analysable in itself), our analysis can of itself and *in principle* reach real certitude, even though it will not usually do so in actual fact. But even if we were to attain certitude in this, it would not be an absolutely safe foundation for an unequivocal decision about the seminal or achieved person who remains in himself necessarily unattainable by analysis. *Homo videt faciem, Deus autem cor.* The 'science of the heart' is even today reserved to God alone. Any progress made in any of the ways and techniques of psychology is amazing and important; but it is always concerned only with the outer zones and not with the real centre of the person or the 'heart' in the biblical sense, which never objectifies itself adequately. We can draw conditional conclusions from these zones, applicable to the 'heart', and these will be important, indeed may even involve practical consequences. Yet this is all we can do. The 'heart' remains the secret of the King, a secret known to itself and God but not to the Ego as it faces itself by reflection and self-expression, and not to others either. In parenthesis, it should also be remembered in this connection that every analysis even of the intermediary dimension of the person changes the data to be observed, rather like (but even more than) the effect produced by observation in physics. And so, what is observed is not the pure constitutive sign of the personal act but rather a synthesis (no longer adequately dissoluble) of the sign and the change resulting from its being observed by the self or some other person. Consequently, this observation itself is again no purely theoretical matter untouched by ethics, but a moment in that chain of moral decisions which no man can escape during his life; and so man can never, not even for a single moment, become a purely objective observer. In short, every reflection is always faced with an ultimate ambiguity: what seems to be guilt, when read off the supposedly or really constitutive sign, may ultimately be guiltless suffering alien to the person due purely to the 'passio' caused from outside; and conversely, what seems to be suffering tragically inflicted from without, may in reality be a proper constitutive sign of one's own guilt, at least by the fact that it would not have assumed its present form if man had not been guilty of misunderstanding this originally non-personal suffering by his inevitably-activated personal decision. An adequate analysis of this synthesis of possibly culpable Action and possibly merely endured Passion would be feasible only if we could stop this continually flowing process of synthesis and turn ourselves for a single moment into a purely active or purely passive subject. Man never is, however, either of these while living here below. And when the ontological difference between the inner and outer person is removed in death, man is no longer the judge but God alone judges, looking into the heart and from there to the works (not vice versa); he can judge them from this viewpoint—they are the works in which the heart has fulfilled itself.

7. The foregoing considerations allow us also to see the already-mentioned connection and ontological difference between guilt and suffering (illness in the widest sense of the word). Suffering is the constitutive sign of guilt. Accordingly, it is not the same as guilt. It is *not* always and unequivocally a constitutive sign of *personal* new guilt, actively caused from within, or the simple expression of the suffering person's guilt. It is certainly, according to Scripture, always a sign of guilt, but this may be the guilt of the race, original sin. Yet it is not a neutral suffering for all that. Since (and in so far as) man had already understood himself, and taken up a position towards himself, even before making any *reflective* stand by his original free choice, suffering (in man already grown up to personal freedom) is never a merely neutral, personally indifferent happening simply to be deplored. Rather, it is suffering understood and responded to in this way or that and thereby actually becoming the expression of our own guilt *or* the material for justifying faith and the expression of our appropriation of redemption by sharing in the Passion of Christ. In consequence of this double possibility, always decided but veiled, suffering itself is also ambiguous.

8. Only through God can man be delivered from guilt in the strict sense. In the first place, the original, personal act of guilt of the seminal person and the sinfulness of the achieved person, of the person who has fulfilled himself, cannot be removed by evading the freedom of the person. Such removal demands at least a free personal act of conversion. We do not wish to enter here into the question of the conditions

under which such a conversion is even thinkable, in view of the fact that the person has *completely* activated, 'understood', and (apparently) exhausted himself in the choice demanded by the previous, presupposedly guilty 'option fondamentale'; it is—let us note—not very easy to explain how this person, who has not only done a guilty act but also *has* become guilty as a result of this act, can still be capable of such a fundamental transformation of the whole nucleus of the person. In any case, this transformation alone does not yet wipe out guilt. For the wiping out of guilt is essentially a kind of dialogue, the adoption of a position concerning God and in the sight of God. God, in spite or rather because of his absolute nature, is not an impersonal 'It', or the stationary, unattainable vanishing-point of the spiritual person's transcendence. He is the 'living God'; relative to him, every human act is essentially a response to his call, so that after the creature's 'no' to this call, the dialogic process of human existence can really continue only by a new Word of God. HE must forgive the guilty act committed against him. Guilt can, therefore, be remitted only by his act, and this act can be known only through *his* Word and can be decided upon only by him. This word, if it is to take place in the tangible manner of this world, can be spoken only by a man if and in so far as he can truly say that he has been appointed and sent to accomplish this word and be its servant. To the '*Tibi soli peccavi*' corresponds God's '*Ego te absolvo*', and this alone delivers from guilt. This deliverance remains in the nature of things just as transcendent to empirical reflection as guilt itself; it must, therefore, be heard and accepted by faith—only in faith does it become real and known.

9. This-worldly victory (at least partial) over suffering and cure of sickness in the widest sense of the word are quite a different matter. Sickness and suffering differ from guilt as such (even though they spring from guilt in certain circumstances), just as the constitutive expression (sign) is different from the reality expressed or signified; they extend over the intermediary, world-like reality of the person, where they receive their objective character. And so, suffering and sickness can be reached also from without by somatic and psychical intervention, for the dimension in which they exist is exactly the same as that in which these determinations from without are received. Combative outside interventions against suffering are possible even

independently of the question whether suffering in a particular case is due to personal, past or present guilt, in so far as the relationship between guilt and its constitutive sign is a fluid one (i.e. in so far as there is no unequivocal and absolutely fixed connection between them, in the sense that guilt can exist without any adequate expression), and the expression of guilt, i.e. suffering, can still continue to exist even after guilt has been remitted by the word of God. Since suffering is never an absolutely unequivocal constitutive sign of guilt, it is also morally justifiable to fight against it by direct means intended to destroy it, even when it can be supposed with sufficient practical certitude that the suffering comes from still unremitted guilt. Whether this attempt to remove suffering under these presuppositions will be successful in a particular case, is quite a different question which cannot be answered *a priori*. It must, however, be stressed also that there is a Christian way of overcoming suffering which does not consist in removing suffering (sickness, etc.) from the intermediary realm of the person, but in faith's acceptance of suffering—of the suffering which continues to exist in this world of transitory things and of probation, as a means of sharing in the redemptive Passion of Christ. Consequently, the phenomenon of suffering will always remain ambiguous, and this ambiguity will always put man in doubt whether he is not after all merely a sinner and will always incite him to renewed efforts in his fight for perfect happiness in this world, offending thereby against faith and hope; accepted in faith, on the other hand, suffering is the very way in which redemption, the eschatological good coming from God alone, appears. On this basis, it must be asked whether every kind of combat against suffering in this world (which in itself is permitted and a duty for the Christian) is not itself culpably based on the secret opinion that there 'really' should be no suffering and that, with a little bit of energy and cunning, suffering can really be banished through the progress of technical science, medicine and psychotherapy, even while the economy of this world is still in existence. To say 'no' to the sufferings of this world is at once a sacred duty for the Christian in the sight of God and, at the same time, the greatest danger of allowing himself to steal past the Cross of Christ. This 'no' can ultimately consist only in helping man, by means of teaching and God's merciful benevolence, to shoulder the Cross in spite of its continued weight, so that he may carry it without bitterness and despair and go on believing in the promise of eternal life.

10. As a result of the dialectic unity and ontological difference between guilt and its constitutive sign, between sin and suffering, regarding their actual dimensions, natures and conquest, the respective tasks of priest and physician are also mutually related and different from each other. Each has a different object and procedure. The priest in himself can only be the mediator of the word of God which remits sin but which as such does not simply and necessarily remove the constitutive sign of sin, viz. suffering, even when the latter has arisen from personal guilt. For once the suffering springing from sin has arisen, it attains its own manner of existence, like any other objectification of the personal spirit and freedom, since it is supported by the intermediary reality of the person and not by the personal nucleus and the seminal person himself. The physician (both of the body and psyche) aims directly at the pathogenic suffering and not at the sinful act or state of the seminal or achieved person. He must not, indeed, simply bypass the question of real guilt in the theological sense, for his own proper object may be a constitutive sign of real guilt, and this question inevitably poses itself for the sufferer. Moreover, suffering often (though not by any means always) cannot be removed from the person, i.e. from his intermediary reality, without a conversion—*μετάνοια*—having taken place in the seminal person; and such a conversion can take place, at least in actual fact, only when man, believing, accepts remission of his real guilt from God. Yet the object and activity of the physician as such remains strictly different ontologically and theologically from that of the priest. The physician should not indeed be merely a healer of the body; but even in so far as his 'patient' suffers or may suffer spiritually, his task still differs from that of the priest. His task remains, directly, confined to the objective materializations of the proper guilt of the seminal person in this world; it confines itself, if you wish to put it this way, to the psyche and does not directly reach the immaterial, personal ground of spiritual freedom as such, where man is called directly by God and answers him with a 'yes' or a 'no'. In so far as guilt and suffering are nevertheless connected, though not identical, i.e. are connected in the unity of the dialectically 'veiling' and 'revealing' relationship between origin and the originated, between sign and the signified, expression and the expressed, the priest and the physician are referred to each other and dependent on each other, in spite of all the differences of their task and commission.

10

PEACEFUL REFLECTIONS ON THE PARAROCHIAL PRINCIPLE[1]

I

PRINCIPLES are good in themselves. Anyone who has no principles is like a 'jelly-fish'. Yet principles can also become 'fads'—and be 'flogged to death'. And that does not do any good even to the most sacred of them.

It might be advisable to distinguish first of all between two classes of principles concerning human conduct. One class consists of those which are always the only correct and valid ones, no matter how much

[1] Cf. J. Höffner, 'Um das Pfarrprinzip', *Trierer Theologische Zeitschrift* LVI (1947), pp. 60–62; O. von Nell-Breuning, 'Pfarrgemeinde, Pfarrfamilie, Pfarrprinzip', *Trierer Theol. Zeitschrift* LVI (1947), pp. 257–262; J. Höffner, 'Nochmals das Pfarrprinzip', *Trierer Theol. Zeitschrift* LVII (1948), pp. 236–239; A. Schrott, *Seelsorge im Wandel der Zeiten, Formen und Organisation seit der Begründung des Pfarrinstituts* (Graz 1949); M. Marchi, *Esperienze parrocchiali* (Rome 1949); A. Kirchgässner, *Pfarrgemeinde und Pfarrgottesdienst* (Freiburg 1949); C. Noppel, *Aedificatio corporis Christi*[2] (Freiburg 1949); K. Lechner, *Laie und Pfarre* (Vienna 1949); R. Perenna, *Innovazioni o rinnovamento della parrocchia?* (Como 1950); B. Socche, *La communità parrocchiale* (Rome 1950); A. Ryckmans, *La paroisse vivante* (Tournai 1950); G. Viviani, *La parroquia* (Rome 1950); H. Légaré, *Introduction à la sociologie paroissiale* (Lille 1950); J. Miller, 'Beiträge zum Pfarrprinzip', *Orientierung* XV (1951), p. 163; F. Benz, 'Die neuen französischen Seelsorgsmethoden und ihre Bedeutung für Deutschland', *Tübinger Theol. Quartalschrift* CXXXI (1951), pp. 208–247, 320–339, 464–486; L. Borlée, 'Structures sociales et ministère paroissial', *Rev. Dioc. Tournai* VI (1951), pp. 427–446; J. Peitzmeier, 'Jugendgruppenarbeit und Jugendpsychologie', *Theologie und Glaube* XLII (1952), pp. 454–461 (important for an evaluation of the 'parochial youth movement'); R. Spiazzi, 'Spunti per una teologia della parrocchia', *Scuola Catt.* LXXX (1952), pp. 26–42; A. Schrott, 'Pfarrseelsorge und überpfarrliche Seelsorge', *Der Seelsorger* XXIII (1953), pp. 202–208; P. Virton, *Enquêtes de sociologie paroissiale* (Paris 1953); *Die Pfarre, Gestalt und Sendung* (Vienna 1953); *La Maison-Dieu* XXXVI (no. 4 1953): 'Problèmes de la Paroisse'.

they may be violated. This is the sort of principle which is meant to govern its particular objective domain exclusively (e.g. 'Thou shalt not commit adultery'). The reason for this is that such principles alone express the whole objective structure of the reality over which their validity is meant to extend. The other class is composed of those principles which are meant 'also' to have validity in a sphere of human conduct, but together with others; they must divide their authority in this sphere with other principles and must be applied in proper doses, as it were, if they are not to become harmful (e.g. 'The economy must allow for the development of private enterprise'). Such principles not only permit but, in the very nature of things necessitate, 'compromise', (if we may use such a suspect term to express what we mean here); they demand that other principles be allowed their rights, and they themselves must be applied 'more or less'. For such principles do not of themselves alone express the whole intrinsic law of the reality to which they are applicable. Hence, if they are to be applied justly, they must leave room for the application of those other principles which flow equally well from the same multiform structure of the reality concerned. With these principles we have to be very careful not to defeat their purpose by becoming obsessed with them. In their case there are inevitably different 'manners' in which the opposing principles may be 'apportioned' and applied in the concrete (there can, for example, be freer or more restricted forms of economic organization). One of these principles may take the place of the other, and there will be no great sense or hope of success in combatting the desired new 'apportionment' of practical application by defaming the newly adopted 'manner' as being a denial of the one and only principle. There simply are no clear-cut boundaries in these cases. It will always remain a debatable point whether one of two principles opposing each other in this way has enough scope in practice for being realized (whether, e.g. in a particular system of education the right of authority is sufficiently preserved as against freedom). In such cases, even legal demarcations and stipulations concerning the principles can never replace the honest and decent attitude of *men*. The proof of the presence of such an honest attitude is given when the champion of one principle really and honestly recognizes the right of the principle professed by his antagonist, successfully keeps the extremists in his own 'party' within bounds and is capable of granting greater force to the opposite principle (when he sees that the concrete state of affairs demands it), without fearing the reproach of being unprincipled and of betraying the party doctrine.

Let it be understood from the very beginning that the 'parochial principle' belongs to the second category. The first thing to do now, though, is to discover what we mean by the parochial principle.

Before we attempt to do so, we would like at once to suggest a distinction which is usually overlooked but which would seem to be important both in theory and in practice. We have to distinguish two principles contained in the parochial principle. We will call them the 'parish-priest principle' and the 'parish principle'. As an abstract 'principle' (i.e. one formulated on its own, before entering into an objectively-justified—not 'lazy'—compromise with other 'principles' in practice), the 'parish-priest principle' demands that all pastoral work in a determined community be exercised and directed by the parish priest of that community and his assistants, curates etc. It is quite indifferent whether these assistants are permanently at his disposal or are called upon by him (N.B.) as the need arises. It follows immediately (in principle, or at least in practice) that according to this principle the care of souls refers here only to those who belong to a particular parish. The 'parish principle' demands that all pastoral work be done within the parochial territory, in other words that pastoral care devote itself in its various activities to people belonging to the same parish. Hence this principle, looked at purely theoretically, does *not* require every particular pastoral activity to come (permanently or only for the occasion) under the authority of the parish priest or of the assistants under *his* authoritative direction. It requires merely that the group of people given pastoral care belong to the same parish. An example of what is meant here would be a parochial youth group directed by an independent diocesan youth chaplain, answerable to the bishop alone, or a parochial branch of a men's society directed by a member of a religious Order who is responsible for the work in this particular field. We do not mean to dispute that the transition between the 'parish-priest principle' and the 'parish principle' is fairly fluid in practice. Nevertheless, as we will see later, the distinction between the two is important both theoretically and practically, if we are to get a really clear idea as to what is demanded when the parochial principle is advanced. Our distinction would, for instance, make it easier at least to determine the point at issue in the debate about the line of demarcation between 'ordinary' and 'extraordinary' care of souls.

Following on the distinction of concepts just made, let us at once add a further distinction concerning the concept of 'extraordinary' and 'ordinary' care of souls. For we must somehow balance the 'parish principle' with the right of the representatives of 'extraordinary pastoral work'. Looked at purely in the abstract, pastoral work could be called 'extraordinary' for several reasons: either because and when it happens only occasionally (e.g. a parish Mission held only every ten years); or because it is performed by someone who does not belong to the ordinary parochial clergy even though it is done *in* the parish and by the authority of the parish priest (as for instance a course of Lenten sermons preached by a Regular in a parish at the invitation of and as the representative of the parish priest); or because it is carried out independently of the parish priest's directing authority and, therefore, (at least in most cases) outside the framework of a parish (such as work with a Third Order group formed in conjunction with a non-parochial Friary Church). It will be useful, for the sake of clarity, to apply the term 'extraordinary' (at least here) only to this third kind of pastoral work. The other two kinds are really only more exceptional cases of 'ordinary' pastoral work, since they are after all directly or indirectly borne by the parochial clergy and take place within the framework of a parish.

After this preliminary, formalistic distinction of concepts, we must now go more closely into the matter in hand. What in the concrete is meant by the parish- and parish-priest principle? Is there, and why should there be, such a principle? Although we ought to distinguish these two principles in theory and, as will appear later, also for practical reasons, they do nevertheless stem from the same (or related) objective conditions and may consequently be described and appreciated together for the moment. The 'parish-priest principle' (taken in the abstract) indicates the exclusive competence of the parish priest and *his* assistants regarding the pastoral care of the people under his jurisdiction. The 'parish principle' is ultimately concerned with the same object, but more from the point of view of the people given pastoral care. Thus it demands that that care must be exercised primarily and exclusively in a territorially-defined congregation, in the sense that wherever men come together for the care of their souls, they must do so as members of the same parish.

Whenever such principles have been given a new emphasis and it has been demanded that they be carried out to the full, two factors have always been associated with such a tendency: a changed general situation in the spiritual field and theoretical reasons recalled to mind as a result of this new situation. We have seen the gradual development of a new situation in our day. There have been times in the Church when the ordinary parish clergy felt, rightly or wrongly, less qualified for dealing with the greater pastoral tasks. At such times they were, therefore, quite pleased to leave certain pastoral activities, demanding greater accomplishments, to the 'extraordinary' pastoral work especially of the regular clergy—thus, e.g. Missions, pastoral care for special groups of men making greater demands on the intelligence and spirituality of the chaplain, etc. So the parish clergy confined themselves at such times more or less to their administrative functions, regular Church services (with a sermon or Sundays), catechism lessons in the schools, instructions and the administration of the sacraments. Today the secular clergy, especially in our great cities, feel themselves fully qualified even for further and greater tasks. And since the secular clergy of today are rightly of the opinion that the responsibility for sufficient pastoral care as a whole falls ultimately on them, they also are no longer willing to confine themselves to that sector of the care of souls which might easily give the impression (at least when looked at superficially and in comparison with the tasks previously left for the most part to the 'extraordinary' pastoral care) of consisting of bureaucratic and administrative functions. The seculars are no longer willing to limit themselves to those duties which make great demands on time and man-power, but for which the representatives of 'extraordinary pastoral works' easily tend to consider themselves 'too good'. Wherever the 'ordinary' care of souls is at a high level, the work will tend to be as self-sufficient as possible. If it did not show this tendency, this would merely be a sign that things are not all that they should be. In addition to this, there is a second determining factor in the matter under discussion, viz. the newly-reawakened will to community among lay people, who are the object of pastoral care. We live, from a cultural-historical and social point of view, in the period of the 'collective man', of the mass, and also in the age of the dissolution of those social forms and structures ('classes', etc.) which, by their diversity and peculiar characteristics, facilitated the formation and growth of more independent, more strongly-marked individual personalities. Although this development has been attended by its own extremely grave dangers for man and for the Christian in man, it has also created a renewed understanding and will to community within the sphere of Christian life, a will to form 'communities' and, concretely, a desire for the parish. Indeed, in so far as modern communization threatens and diminishes the sense of security and inviolability of the individual, who is left to the tender mercies of anonymous, vast, soul-less and brutal collective powers, the parochial community in particular, with its religious foundations and spirit, will appear in an ever-increasing measure as a haven of refuge to the threatened individual. Living in this parish-community and finding support in it (which can in certain circumstances go far beyond the purely religious sphere through such factors as '*Caritas*', Christian neighbourhood, and the creation even of a high intellectual and moral 'milieu'), man is no longer a helpless, solitary individual and yet is not merely a 'cog' or 'number' in a soul-less collectivity. It may well be that the meaning of the parish community can still increase a great deal in this direction and that parish-life may be developed much further still, especially since the Christian of today—even in so-called Catholic countries—lives in pagan surroundings.

Perhaps something of the social, economic and cultural organization found in the Jewish community in the great pagan cities of hellenistic antiquity is necessary also for the Christian parish of today, situated as it is in the midst of the unchristian and humanly formless mass-society of our day. The parish would have to develop to a far greater extent into the complete home of the Christian man. (Yet this must not give rise to a ghetto-mentality, and Christianity must remain active in its missionary task, continuing to feel responsible for the life and salvation of all people. And so the Christian congregation must not only be self-sufficient as far as possible, but must also be mentally and spiritually alive and must regard itself as the germ-cell for the re-christianization of all the people.) '*Junge Mannschaft*' and similar phenomena are in fact the first steps towards a re-formation of the Christian parish and the Christian 'home-land'. We cannot enter further into these questions here. The little we have said, however, may suffice to indicate that even the present-day situation of the layman has urged a more *vigorous* emphasis on the parochial principle.

When we debate nowadays about the parochial principle and try to discover how it is logically and legally reconcilable with other 'principles' and to what extent it is actually limited by them, it must not be forgotten that the present state of the world certainly demands a more intense life in the parish, and in that sense also a more vigorous application of the parochial principle, than was the case in former times. The fact that present-day parishes (and especially parishioners) to a large extent do not as yet, and indeed will not very quickly, correspond to the demands of the situation, is no argument against these demands.

In such a situation one naturally recalls the fundamental, and in a certain sense 'always valid', arguments for the parochial principle. These arguments can perhaps best be divided into two groups, viz. those based on dogmatic reasons and those based on pastoral considerations. The dogmatic argument is founded on the fact that the Church has an episcopal structure by divine, and hence always valid, law. We quietly leave to one side the question of whether everything attributed directly to the concrete (territorial) structure of a diocese is really as immutable by divine right as is the dogmatic notion of the Church's episcopate. (Actually, there would be quite a few debatable points in this matter.) The Church as a whole is divided into different territorial parts. And each of these parts, defined by *spatial* boundaries (and not by difference in social station or other conceivable principles of organization), is subject to a bishop. The bishop is in his own person the pastor of his diocese, with full responsibility and rights. Any pastoral care in his diocese is his responsibility, is exercised in his name and by his authority, and is concerned with those who are subject to his authority because they, as Christians, live within the boundaries of his diocesan territory. (We prescind here from the case of the exempt Orders where the spiritual care of their members within the Order lies outside the competence of the local Ordinary.) The reason for this spatial structure of the Church is a very profound one precisely because of its primitive nature, and is easily comprehensible: the Church's pastoral care is concerned with the *whole* man and with men in so far as they form a 'people' which as such is to enter into the Kingdom of God. Both of these purposes are accomplished by addressing man as a being with a home. For 'at home', where he is rooted with his past and his relations, where he has his house and home and where his life is lived, there man is wholly present because that is where he has his habitat both bodily and mentally which determines his characteristics, and that is where he is directly the member of a people to which the Church has been sent by the commission given to her by our Lord.

Now, the parish (which in the early Church coincided practically with the diocese) is in a sense the diocese in miniature. The parish in itself exists indeed only in virtue of human law and hence has not basically the same irrevocable necessity as the diocese. Thus the bishop can to a great extent (and within the framework of canon law) make use also of other instruments besides the parish (and parish priest) in the fulfilment of his pastoral duty.[2] Nevertheless, the parochial structure is a consistent development and practical application of the principle of the territorial diocese ruled by the bishop as pastor of the whole flock. The parish, too, can in this sense claim to be a realization of the divinely-wise and ever-valid principle which the Founder of the Church has established within her for all time, viz. that she should convert men into Christians, men who have a home and are a people. When principles of pastoral organization begin to vie with one another, it remains an indisputable fact that the parochial principle can claim to be the oldest and most venerable principle applied by the Church on the authority of Christ; one man is in charge of the whole pastoral work done among a group of people who are collected together under him because they have their home on the same soil. If this principle has eternal validity for the over-all structure of the Church (and hencealso permanent meaning and utility), it cannot be absolutely false for the smaller structures of the Church.

Let us pass on now to the pastoral argument for the parochial principle. The pastoral effort requires a living centre on account of the unavoidable and immense variety of its activities, means and forms and of individuals with whom it is concerned. From this centre everything derives its proper place, right measure and correspondingly greater or lesser importance, and this centre is a safeguard both against a kind of planless hypertrophy and against an atrophy of particular pastoral activities. This living centre can only be the Altar, even though genuine Christian life and ecclesiastico-sacramental life do not by any means coincide, i.e. even though Christian Priesthood and Liturgy are not the same thing[3] and genuine Christianity itself must come to grips with the whole of reality (and hence also with 'profane' reality),

[2] The reserved rights of which the bishop cannot deprive parish priests according to Canon Law, form only a small sector in the business of present-day care of souls.

[3] Cf. my essay 'Priesterliche Existenz', *Zeitschrift für Aszese und Mystik* XVII (1942), pp. 155–171.

making it subject to its law. Yet it remains true that wherever pastoral care exercised in federations, associations, organizations, etc., more or less cuts itself loose from the central concern of all Christianity which man, as a member of the holy people of God, adores through the Sacrifice of our Lord and—truly and historically—encounters in the Sacrament of the God of grace and eternal life, this 'care of souls' becomes a mere empty busyness, an exclusive interest in local club life, a rationalistic urge to reform the world and an officious organization-fever, by which the members seek their own advantage and not God. The Altar, however, stands first and foremost in the parish church. For the parish church is the representative of the diocese and the primary place for the care of souls according to canon law (if only for the reason that the parish priest has the right and duty of the care of souls of *all* Christians living in his territory). Hence, if every pastoral work finds its central point in the Altar of Christ, then the life of the parish, issuing from the altar of the parish church, is and remains *the* basic form of the care of souls. In this way we also have a guarantee that individual pastoral endeavours preserve their mutual relations and proper proportion, by the very fact that in the parish they reach man under the very respect which even by nature is one of the most many-sided and yet most uniform, viz. man as member of a natural, spatial community. Such an organization has also fundamentally the greatest stability in times of crisis. The most primitive structure is also the most indestructible. The bond uniting kith and kin, as realized in the natural community, belongs to the most primitive forms of human society. And the parish builds on the foundations of the natural community. Consequently, taking things as a whole, the parish, and hence also its pastoral function, has (after the family) the greatest social, spiritual and thus also pastoral resistance of all human associations, both against internal tendencies to dissolution and against external influences.

We have tried in the above to give at least an indication of the *inner* justification of the 'parochial principle', an indication of its 'essence' as it were. Since this principle is, however, of human law in the Church (though in practice an almost self-evident conclusion from the territorial principle of the episcopate, going back to a divine ordinance), it follows that the parochial principle, taken as something actual, can be given 'existence' (i.e. its real validity) only by Canon Law, and not merely by basic considerations about its meaning and actual fitness for the matter in question. Now, the parochial principle has in fact been instituted by Canon Law. There are three canonical prescriptions which together bring what we call the 'parochial principle' into existence: firstly, the Tridentine provision that a diocese must be wholly divided into parishes (CIC can. 216); secondly, CIC can. 464 § 1,[4] which lays down the parish priest's pastoral duty with regard to all his parishioners; and thirdly, can. 94 §§ 1–3, which determines that every Catholic Christian acquires the parish priest of his place of residence or, if he has no domicile, of the place in which he is actually staying, as *his proper* parish priest. It follows from this that where the law itself does not make an exception, every Catholic Christian is inevitably made subject to a parish priest who has the right and duty of pastoral care in his regard and who carries the responsibility before God and the Church for the salvation of those Christians whose parish priest he is. There can, therefore, be no doubt about the existence of a 'parochial principle'. Nor can there be any doubt about the fact that every Catholic Christian is basically placed under a parish priest (apart from certain exceptions which are of no practical interest here, since in most cases they concern only exempt Religious). Two observations should be made here on this canonically formulated parochial principle. *Firstly*, although there can be only one parish priest in each parish (can. 460 § 2), his right and duty to exercise his pastoral function among his parishioners does not imply that he is necessarily the only one who has a pastoral duty towards the parishioners. The pastoral right of the parish priest can basically be a cumulative right and is not necessarily an exclusive one. Thus the parish priest has, for instance, a duty to instruct the children in the Catechism,[5] and yet this is (obviously) also the duty of the parents;[6] similarly in the case of those charged with seeing to it that children make their Easter duties.[7] Thus it is obviously in no way a violation of the parish priest's pastoral right when the bishop grants a certain limited right and duty of exercising pastoral care among the parishioners of a parish to someone other than the parish priest (e.g. to a teacher of religion in the school; to Religious at their own church: can. 1334), without thereby releasing the parish priest from his obligation to exercise the same function (in such a

[4] '*Parochus ex officio tenetur curam animarum exercere in* omnes *suos paroecianos, qui non sint legitime exempti.*'

[5] CIC can. 1329, 1330, 1333 § 1.

[6] CIC can. 1335.

[7] CIC can. 860.

case, those appointed to the same task may, of course, 'share' the actual carrying out of this task). *Secondly*, it is important to make a further observation with regard to the more precise nature of the canonical 'parochial principle'. There is no duty on the part of the parishioner, corresponding to the parish priest's pastoral rights, to make use of the parish priest's 'services'. The parish priest must preach, proclaim the doctrines of Faith, hear Confessions, distribute the Eucharist, officiate at divine service on Sundays.[8] These are indeed most important, if not *the* most important, functions of his pastoral right and duty. The Christian obviously has the duty of knowing the teachings of the Faith, of receiving the sacraments and of attending Mass on Sundays and Holydays; and the parish priest can exhort the Christian to fulfil this duty.[9] Yet in the very matter of these most important and frequent duties of their religious life, the faithful are *not* bound to fulfil their duty specifically in the *parochial* sphere of the care of souls. According to can. 467 § 2, the faithful should indeed be admonished to attend frequently, where this causes no inconvenience, the services and sermons in their parish church, but, according to the meaning of the word 'admonition',[10] this urgent recommendation is not intended to impose an obligation in the strict sense and is in itself already limited by the '*frequenter*' and '*ubi commode fieri potest*' expressly added by the canon. Hence, in so far as Canon Law itself authorizes the admonition of the faithful to take part in the *parochial* life, this admonition can concern only a 'frequent' participation (a notion which is still realized even if someone does not attend the parochial services absolutely every Sunday) and may be given only if the parishioner does not thereby experience any additional inconvenience. Thus current Canon Law (contrary to the law of previous ages) quite logically does not speak of any duty of attending the *parochial* Mass on Sundays, since the duty of Sunday Mass can be fulfilled also by attending Mass somewhere else (except in Private Oratories).[11] The same is true of the reception of Holy Communion,[12] even of Easter Communion (which we are merely advised to receive

[8] CIC can. 467 § 1, 1344 § 1, 1329–1332, 863, 892 § 1, 873 § 1.

[9] CIC can. 863; 854 § 5; 1348.

[10] Cf. Benedict XIV, *De synodo dioecesana* lib. XI, cap. 5, no. 5; Wernz-Vidal, *Jus canonicum* II 'De personis' no. 736, IV (Rome 1943), p. 937.

[11] Can. 1294.

[12] Can. 869.

in our own parish church)[13] and of the annual Confession.[14] So it is clear, even from these considerations that, in so far as it has been established as an actually valid principle by Canon Law, which alone is capable of so establishing it, the parochial principle is of itself not an absolute and exclusive principle. Otherwise the parishioners would necessarily have a duty strictly corresponding to the parish priest's pastoral right. The fact that this is not the case, that, in other words, the parochial principle determined by Canon Law presupposes that the faithful may fulfil their religious duties outside the parish, shows that Canon Law recognizes a pastoral activity of the Church which is not based on her parochial-territorial structure. Nevertheless, there is a parochial principle since Canon Law has established it, and it is also possible that future legislation will once more extend its validity further than is the case today.

II

That, then, is one side of the picture. But, as already stated at the beginning, the parochial principle is not the only valid one and must not be the only one which governs our pastoral activity. Side by side with it there are other principles which must also be given their due place in the concrete structure of the care of souls. We must not complicate matters, nor must we oversimplify them. 'Clear, simple lines' can be just as dangerous as the confusion created by discordant tendencies. No matter how justified the parochial principle is, it must never become the weapon of an (unacknowledged) 'State Socialism', which would equate, level and centralize everything from above, even if this 'above' and the 'central point' be merely the parish.

In the first place, the parish (and hence also the parochial principle) is merely of *human* right in the Church. Parishes and parish priests are not divine, unchangeable realities in the Church, like the Primacy of the Pope, or the Episcopate. The territorial parish exists because and in so far as Canon Law and the bishop desire its existence and the measure of its functions. The same holds good for the parish priest. Now, it follows from this that the standard for judging the legitimacy of this humanly-given right is not the parish and its greatest possible self-sufficiency (for the parish is the measured and not the measure) but man, the object of the care of souls. And the concrete application of

[13] Can. 859 § 3. [14] Can. 905 *sq*.

this yard-stick, i.e. the actual organization of pastoral care as divided among the work of the parochial and non-parochial clergy, is a matter for the bishop. Besides basic clarity, this application will always require a 'prudent estimate' which can never be replaced by 'unequivocal principles'. Since the parish and the office of parish priest are merely a canonical development of the diocese and the episcopal office, which can differentiate their functions not only in this particular manner but also directly in extra- and supra-parochial organizations, it would be wrong to say that e.g. ecclesiastical associations and their chaplains can and must properly and lawfully present themselves *only* as structures arising out of the *parish* as such, although it would be very regrettable if the parish were to deteriorate into a kind of 'blanket-organization' for such associations and groups within its territory.

When it is a question of how the pastoral office should be exercised—whether parochially or supra-parochially, according to the parish- and parish-priest principle or (partly) without it—then the only objective yard-stick is furnished by the answer to the question as to how the pastoral office attains its goal, which is the transformation of man (both as an individual and as a member of a community) into a Christian so as to enable him to lead a Christian life (in knowledge and adoration of God and by imitation of Christ). For pastoral care exists for the sake of the Christian, and not the Christian for the sake of pastoral care, and certainly not for the sake of the one who exercises it. No pastor (whether 'ordinary' or 'extra-ordinary') has the right to judge and shape the technical structure of pastoral work according to whether and how far it will offer him as unhampered and undisturbed a sphere of activity as possible. Professional or 'bread-and-butter' jealousy (of a material and spiritual kind), bureaucratic 'tidiness', a schematic 'planned economy', a need for self-assertion, fear of losing the justification for one's existence—such and other 'motives' which often play their part on both 'sides', are not a fit basis for discussion whether in favour of or against the parochial principle.

The only question to be considered is how the object of the care of souls (viz. the Christian man) can best be attained. Now, the parochial principle in its intrinsic reasoning is itself ultimately based on a natural view of man, the 'object' of pastoral care, for it makes use of a basic fact of human life for its particular view on the care of souls, viz. of the fact that man has a home somewhere. In this view, pastoral care must approach man from this particular side of his existence. And this is quite right as far as it goes. Man, however, is in fact a many-sided being; 'having a home' (having roots in a place) is not the only existential of his life. For he has a certain individuality endowing him with individual talents, experience of life, temperament, etc. He is differentiated according to age and sex. He has a particular occupation. As a rational being, he is free to form associations which may cut across his territorial community. He can change his place of residence. He has individual needs not catered for where he lives. And man is this many-sided being even *qua* the object of pastoral care. By the very fact that the parochial principle is based on a natural existential of man, it is obvious from the very beginning that other natural existentials of man may equally serve as a basis for the possibility, right and duty of pastoral care. In other words, the care of souls can also deal with man in so far as he is conditioned by these other existentials, i.e. it can make him its object in so far as he has a certain occupation, enters into certain free associations, etc. If this right and duty are denied to it, or these opportunities are not utilized as far as lies within its capability, then the pastoral ministry does not address itself to the whole man in the manifold plenitude of his being and life, and man cannot become fully Christian nor Christianity fully human. In other words, since man's being embraces different natural dimensions, the pastoral ministry may basically be exercised from the viewpoint of all of these dimensions, and indeed must be so exercised if it is seen that complete christianization of man is in fact impossible merely from the point of view of his living in a certain place (i.e. merely by applying the parochial principle).

This is, however, in fact the case. It is in fact impossible, as can be seen from the point of view of both the object and the minister of the care of souls. To these we must add a third consideration which points in the same direction.

Considering man who is the object of pastoral care, it is obvious that wherever we have to deal with simple human conditions—in other words, with agricultural communities where practically all the happenings of human life (such as work, cultural life, etc.) occur within the confines of a parish which can humanly speaking be surveyed by an individual—the pastoral ministry can deal with man in accordance with the parochial principle, i.e. basing itself on the fact that his home, interests, etc. are centred in this one place. Thus it will still be able to reach man in all his relationships, for the simple reason that his whole life unfolds itself in practice within the parish. Something similar (although sociologically quite different) happens where the number of Catholics scattered over a large area in a non-Christian district is comparatively so small that Church life can of necessity unfold itself only in the form of parish life; for in such circumstances there can be no other way of exercising the pastoral ministry since the number of people who could, for instance, be interested in any particular 'society' is so small. So in this case, too, the parish is in fact the only possible soil for the care of souls. Prescinding, however, from such cases, the narrow confines of their immediate home can no longer embrace all the activities of townspeoples' lives in present-day circumstances brought about by urbanization, greater freedom of movement and the extensive departmentalization of modern man. The location of man's material and spiritual home (if we may be allowed such a distinction) differs widely. Modern man living in towns (in contrast to the farmer or perhaps even to the small-town artisan) pursues his occupation outside of the parish. He visits schools which are very often in no way connected with his parochial district. Like a nomad, he changes his residence so frequently that he cannot possibly have the farmer's sense of 'belonging'. He often knows his next-door neighbours least of all. Differences in intellectual and cultural needs deeply separate people living in the same place and lead to the formation of communities which are not in the least recruited from the immediate neighbourhood of their domicile. Man's life, lived in his society (clubs, communities of interest, etc.), side by side with his professional and family life in the narrowest sense, takes him just as far away from his immediate local surroundings. His travels, hikes, recreations and amusements, looked at territorially, all take place, in the majority of cases, outside of the narrow confines of his place of residence and hence outside of the parish. The ties binding him to his relations (if such ties still mean anything at all to him) also transfer his life out of the parish, since a man's kindred too are scattered in these days of shifting populations. We may regard these conditions as unavoidable, regrettable, requiring to be reformed or in any other way you like; the fact remains that the pastoral ministry cannot directly change this state of affairs (based on social transformations) to any considerable degree by its own proper means. It must, therefore, reckon with this general state of affairs as an established fact (for an unforeseeable length of time), just as life in the parish in bygone days did not create (though it did strengthen) the territorial community and its solidarity, but presupposed and accepted it as the obvious norm for pastoral organization. This means, consequently, that the possibility of getting a hold of the *whole* man by pastoral means, basing one's efforts merely on the parochial principle, i.e. on the principle proceeding from the place where man lives, has diminished considerably as compared with what was the case in times past. If the pastoral ministry is to meet man on all levels of his actual life, and if to a large extent man does not actually live any longer in the community corresponding to the parish, then pastoral care must not limit itself obstinately to meeting him on the level of the parish alone. If school-children, for example, live more in the school and in youth groups created by these surroundings than in the district of the town where they happen to live at any particular moment (until their parents 'move' once more), and if our pastoral work must in its own interests meet them on their *own* ground, where they actually feel 'at home', how can the parochial youth group, i.e. the youth of their 'district', be the only and decisive meeting point between Church and school-child? If the teacher's nearest neighbour is not actually the milkman or dressmaker living next door, but his or her professional colleague with whom he shares his economic endeavours, his level of education, general interests, etc., how can the pastoral ministry refuse to create a 'personal parish' in a certain (*non*-canonical) sense for such people and refuse to christianize the spiritual sphere in which these people actually live? If young craftsmen, apprentices, form economically and intellectually a specific type of man, who inevitably also expresses and asserts himself in associations (if not in a religious then at least in a profane sense), can pastoral care renounce the formation of apprentice-associations, merely because these are contrary to the 'parochial principle' or because it must then answer the question as to how the Christian 'congregations' thus springing up may be coordinated in a vital union with the parochial congregation (which is most desirable) —simply because it is easier 'without all this'? If an intellectual, even one who is very much a man of the people and who does not wish to cut himself off in a separate caste, nevertheless has his own intellectual and social needs which only come into their own if he and his colleagues are allowed to be 'among themselves' sometimes (not because they cut themselves off and exclude others, but because the 'others' exclude 'themselves' for want of corresponding interests), and if these associations are 'supra-parochial' (if only for numerical reasons), are we to say that even religiously-guided circles for such men (in any form whatsoever) are forbidden simply because this would offend against the parochial principle? There may be still other needs of association according to profession, social position, age, sex, etc. (Other examples, apart from the ones already given, might be associations for priests, soldiers, students, young workers, etc.) Since these cannot be condemned together with their non-conformist, exclusive, singular and small-minded abuses, but must be judged by their natural and rightful purpose, viz. to create human and spiritual homes for the men of today who can no longer find such a home merely among their local neighbours and relations, any truly up-to-date form of pastoral activity which is trying to reach and christianize the whole man under as many aspects as possible, cannot base itself simply and solely on the parochial principle. By thus contesting the exclusive validity of the parochial principle, we do not mean to deny that it is imperative for such an 'association-minded ministry' (in the widest sense of the word) not to forget that the right structure of its activities must come from what is essential to Christianity—from the 'altar' (and that there is a real danger of forgetting this which certainly has not always been avoided in past decades). For, on the one hand, we do not deny the justification of the parochial principle nor, on the other hand, is it impossible for an 'association-minded ministry' to observe this imperative even within its own form of activity.

The conditions of social structure in which modern man lives forbid any exclusive application of the parochial principle. The latter is not the only valid principle for the organization of pastoral activities. This does not—for the reasons indicated—apply only where there is an almost compelling movement today towards some form of *organized* extra-parochial associations as an indispensable basis for the care of souls, but even where otherwise strongly differentiated groups of people (though not strictly organized) may be given sufficient pastoral care only on a supra-parochial level. We are thinking, for example, of the specific public catered for by our works of religious formation, or of converts in large towns.

Finally, there is a further factor which must be taken into consideration in this connection. Our city-parishes are very often so large that there cannot possibly be any sense of neighbourly 'togetherness' among *all* the members of a parish to the required and desirable extent; yet this is the natural basis for any parochial ministry. Among ten-thousand people there is no neighbourliness in the way in which a parish of the old type could presuppose it. In such large parishes there may, of course, be a certain circle of people (the 'faithful' parishioners) whose whole Christian life is centred in the life of their parish with the kind of Christian 'togetherness' which is the ideal sought by the parochial principle. In this way even a large modern parish may give the impression of having a 'flourishing' parish life. Yet this impression is secured at the cost of the many others who remain strangers. Should not our pastoral ministry 'get hold' of them too?

The care of souls as practised in the nineteenth and twentieth centuries (in Germany) has, of course, recognized this added need for an extra-parochial ministry and has taken pains, with greater or lesser success, to fulfil it. Yet for the last fifteen years the more vigorous emphasis laid on the parochial principle has given cause for pointing out expressly the continued existence, as far as the object of pastoral activity is concerned, of the sociological presuppositions which have led during the last hundred years to an ever more wide-spread ministry conducted *also* extra- and supra-parochially; indeed, these presuppositions have if anything become even stronger today. So it would be high-flown romanticism (even when it can apparently appeal to 'dogmatic' reasons) and typically German pedantry, or a leaning towards false ecclesiastical State Socialism, if we were to throw the experience and methods acquired by the extra-parochial ministry during the last hundred years completely overboard, in the name of the parochial principle, and regard them as something utterly out of date for modern pastoral work. We do not in any way mean to deny by this the fruitfulness and necessity of the renewed pastoral-theological appreciation of the significance of the strictly parochial pastoral ministry, extending from the '*Grossstadtseelsorge*' (1911) of the Viennese Heinrich Swoboda to the '*Aedificatio corporis Christi*' (1937) of Konstantin Noppel, S.J. Nor must it be asserted that every 'organizational development' which has ever existed has a right to existence today. Nevertheless, the fact that during the last years of National Socialism pastoral care was to a very large extent reduced to a purely parochial ministry, does not prove that we may still make a present-day virtue out of the necessity of that period of persecution, in times which now permit once more of a freer and more comprehensive development of the Christian missionary mandate.

The conclusion that the parochial principle (or more exactly: the 'parish-priest principle') cannot be the only legitimate one for present-day pastoral activity follows also from a second point of view, viz. that of the pastor himself. The more departmentalized man is nowadays as the object of pastoral care, the more difficult and multiform the pastoral ministry must be, if we do not intend to subscribe to the pious and merely comfortable illusion that the care of souls is required to concern itself only with the 'universal human element' in all these differentiated people and yet can christianize them sufficiently and in all the different spheres of their lives. If, however, there ought to be special ministries concerned with priests, artists, students, converts, etc., and if such a pastoral ministry exercised on highly-differentiated groups of people presupposes a great deal of specialized experience and knowledge about the occupations, living conditions, spiritual origins, etc. of these people, then there surely cannot be anything sinister in supposing that not every priest is called to and capable of such a ministry merely by the fact of his belonging to the parochial clergy of a particular parish. In short, there is surely nothing sinister about suspecting that in such cases the parish-priest principle is insufficient (quite apart from the fact that in practice these different ministries cannot be carried out within the confines of a single *parish* and hence the parish principle cannot be applied even for merely technical reasons). It is no disgrace, and no reflection on their own human, scientific and moral-ascetic qualities, if the parochial clergy draw the logical conclusion from the fact that it is impossible for the parish priest and his curate (in every parish) to be qualified (humanly, scientifically and pastorally) for all these necessary specialized forms of the care of souls. *Non omnia possumus omnes*. A capable doctor—to draw a parallel—does not feel ashamed, but feels it to be his duty as a doctor in certain cases, to send a patient to a specialist or to a hospital. A sober and objective estimate of the capacities of the parish clergy, on the one hand, and of the demands of youth on the other, will make us realize that we cannot even expect to find *the* youth-chaplain in *every* single parish who will —humanly and pastorally—be equal to the demands of present-day youth-work and will have the time for it. If in this case a better pastoral care of youth can be achieved extra-parochially (e.g. by supra-parochial youth-groups organized in conjunction with the schools, or in 'federations'), then the parochial principle must not be allowed to stand in the way, nor must such a settlement of the matter be regarded as a 'sign of the poverty' of parochial care of souls. Such a scheme would be nothing more than the recognition of the limitations of any man, even of the pastor, in the matter of the salvation of souls, a limitation which, after all, applies equally, in other spheres, to those to whom the clergy of a parish surrender the pastoral ministry of certain groups of men. Moreover, such an arrangement does not deprive the parish priest of his right and duty to see to it that the task of educating the youth of his parish, imposed on him as the representative of the Church, (which has the autonomous right to educate), is actually carried out to the full in these circumstances (even though partially by others).

Although we must for the reasons given dispute the exclusive validity of the parochial principle, even considered from the viewpoint of the pastor, we do not deny by the same token that *often* (though certainly not always) the parish principle may still be observed even when we have to diverge from the parish-priest principle. For instance, a men's society directed by a Regular may have its 'parochial groups', or a group of a youth federation equally directed from 'outside' may be recruited from young people of the same parish. In many cases, certainly, even the parish principle will not be applicable, if only because the number of extra-parochial pastoral 'specialists' is so small; in other words, the special groups under the care of these 'specialists' will in such cases require to be organized also supra-parochially, even when the number of members belonging to the same parish would otherwise be sufficient for the formation of a parish group. In these instances the impracticability of the parish-priest principle also requires us to abandon the parish principle.

There is yet a third point of view from which the exclusive validity of the parochial principle may be contested. As we have explained in a previous essay,[15] the individual has his own independent rights in the Church, i.e. (applying the matter to our present question) the individual must in principle be left enough scope in the Church to be able to express his individuality. This applies also to his freedom to form associations even when these arise, as in this case, 'from below', by the free initiative of the Christian individual himself.[16] The authoritative

[15] 'Der Einzelne in der Kirche', *Stimmen der Zeit* CXXXIX (1947), pp. 260–276.

[16] We do not need to make a detailed examination here of the many possible motives for the actual formation of such associations. In cases applicable to our question, these motives will usually arise in some form or

ecclesiastical government (i.e. the bishop and the Pope) has the right and the duty to decide whether in the actual individual case such a 'free group' (as we are going to call it) corresponds in its *concrete* characteristics to the basic norms of Christian Faith and Morals. This authority has the right and duty of deciding whether a 'free-group' is in this particular instance a necessary or desirable realization of the Christian individual's right, or at least one which may be tolerated, and whether in the concrete case the Church wishes to use such a 'free-group' as an instrument of her care of souls (e.g. by giving the group a 'spiritual leader', 'spiritual director', 'president', etc. who then owes his right and duty not only to the group but also to the Church). Thus, 'permission' or 'refusal of permission' for such a free-group does indeed lie with the Church authorities in individual cases, but it is not an act left simply to the good pleasure of this authority. For it too finds its objective norm in the basic right of the individual Christian to form such groups; it is rather an act binding on the conscience of ecclesiastical authority by objective norms, even though the actual observance of these norms is not in its turn subject to the judgement of the individual believer. Before the conscience of ecclesiastical authority, the right of the individual to free association is first of all *in possessione*; moral justification for '*non*-permission' of such an association in a concrete individual instance must, therefore, be proved and not presupposed. As Pius XII himself emphasized in an address to the College of Cardinals (20th February 1946),[17] the principle of subsidiary functions is valid even in the Church, without prejudice to her hierarchical structure; but this means that fundamentally the free formation of associations from below may be prevented and replaced by organization from above only when there are compelling reasons. Hence, Christians have fundamentally the right to form such associations arising from their own initiative, because there is an inalienable right of the individual in the Church; such a basic right of free formation of groups must actually be capable of being realized, and its realization cannot always be limited of its nature by the framework of one

---

other from the already suggested need of a '*spiritual*' home characteristic of the differentiated man of today. This need is nowadays no longer satisfied simply by the person's residential neighbourhood.

[17] AAS XXXVIII (1946), pp. 144 *sq*.

and the same parish. A group of young Catholic Christians, formed by its members on their own initiative, a Catholic students' Union, a 'Christian Section', a 'local academic group' not established by ecclesiastical authority, a Catholic Sisterhood which is not necessarily an ecclesiastical association, even the first seed-bud of an ecclesiastical Religious Order (when religious enthusiasm brought like-minded Catholics together)—all of these are free-groups which, even though they may not be (or are not yet or not necessarily) *fidelium associationes* in the canonical sense of CIC lib. II, tit. 18–19, have basically nothing 'unecclesiastical' about them and do not require to owe their origin to any official initiative on the part of the Church. This is all the less necessary since even Canon Law (CIC can. 684) recognizes *associationes* of the faithful which are not 'erected' by the Church. The Church, therefore, recognizes the right of the faithful themselves to form such societies; of course, even in these cases the Church reserves the right to approve or disapprove of them and of keeping a *legitima vigilantia* over them.[18] Moreover, it is self-evident that such a formation of groups cannot claim to be an 'ecclesiastical association' in the *proper* sense without approbation by the Church,[19] which again does not mean in the least that a free-group which is not an 'ecclesiastical association' must by this fact alone be 'unecclesiastical'. Such 'free-groups' of Catholic Christians will not in practice pursue exclusively or primarily religious ends in the strictest sense (we are thinking here, e.g. of a Students' Union, a youth group, etc.). Nevertheless, if they pursue a relatively comprehensive goal and have of their very nature a greater formative and educative influence on their members, they can provide a very suitable basis for the pastoral work of the Church. Thus since, on the one hand, the formation of such 'free-groups' independent of the parochial territory is fundamentally an inalienable right of the individual believer (which cannot be choked off merely by an appeal to the parochial principle), and if, on the other hand, since sufficient scope must basically be allowed to them, such groups do actually come into being and as a result offer an important opportunity to the Church for influencing their members by her pastoral activity, then the parochial principle is not justified in preventing the Church from making the best use of these pastoral opportunities. In other words, the Church

[18] CIC can. 684; cf. also can. 336 § 2; can. 469.
[19] CIC can. 686 § 1: *in Ecclesia . . . associatio.*

must be allowed to fulfil her pastoral office in the soil of such 'free-groups', by providing them with spiritual guides, particularly since the bishop, precisely speaking, has no power whatsoever by current Canon Law to impose a duty binding in conscience on the believer of participating in an association established authoritatively by the Church herself (and, let us say, erected in a parish). Even the suppression of 'free-groups' would not guarantee the growth of the official Church societies. If, for instance, youth groups or 'federations' of Catholic youth have a basic right to originate in a 'movement' coming from their own free initiative—a right which the Church is *a-priori* and fundamentally in no position to annul (she has after all until now not even absolutely forbidden her young members to take part in inter-denominational youth organizations)—and if such groups actually offer an excellent opportunity for the Church's pastoral work (desired by themselves), should or may the Church, by refusing to give them the requested spiritual guides, leave this pastoral possibility unexploited merely because such a 'free-group', or such groups of a federation, 'offend' against the parochial principle?

Such an attitude could only with difficulty avoid the suspicion of being an ecclesiastical 'State Socialism', which recognizes only an ecclesiastical 'State youth movement'. It would not in the long run prevent such free-groups from springing up, but merely cause them to become indifferent religiously or cause their members to leave in order to join inter-denominational federations. The Church has certainly the right, as the divinely authorized educator of youth, to create those institutions by which she believes herself to be best able to fulfil her own task of education. She certainly has the fundamental right to make these institutions (whatever they may be) obligatory for her young faithful. But, if the right of individuals to unite freely in groups is not annulled by this right of the Church, and yet must also not be placed in the dilemma of having either to renounce its own actualization altogether in the face of institutions created from above (such as parochial youth groups) or to actualize itself merely in the formation of a religiously or even denominationally indifferent group (such as in a club without any connection with the Church whatsoever), then the only practical conclusion to be drawn from this will be that the Church ought to use the free-group itself as an instrument of her formative activity by appointing her spiritual assistants to guide it. The Church can, of course, make it a condition for such a spiritually-guided free-group that it become suitably incorporated, without losing its own characteristics as a 'movement', into wider ecclesiastical institutions (e.g. into 'Catholic Action') and that the free-group for its part see to it that its members associate themselves with the pastoral youth work taking place directly within the framework of their parish (corporate Mass and Communion for the youth of the parish, etc.). It follows from what has been said that the parochial principle is neither in a position today nor basically entitled to set itself up as the *sole* organizational principle of the care of souls.

Looking back over the reasons against the exclusive validity of the parochial principle, the *conclusions* so far reached may be easily formulated. The parochial principle, in its fundamental reasoning, is the 'territorial principle', since the objectively decisive reason for it lies in the fact that man becomes the object of the care of souls in a suitable, and indeed unavoidable, manner precisely in so far as he has a 'home' (*Heimat*), a '*place-where-he-is-quartered*' (*Stand-ort*). The reasons which militate against the exclusive validity of the parochial principle, both on the part of the object and on the part of the minister of the care of souls, are all based on the fact that man has his 'station' (*Stand*) in life (taking the word here in its widest sense as referring to the differences in occupation, intellectual differences, differences in sex, age, culture), which owing to present-day sociological conditions no longer corresponds completely in practice with the narrow confines of the immediate locality where he lives. Now, in so far as man's social differences in this widest sense furnish a basis for the possibility and duty of an extra-parochial care of souls exercised in view of these differences, we may speak of the application of a 'social-differential principle' (*Standesprinzip*) to the care of souls. Our third reason against the exclusive validity of the parochial principle for the pastoral ministry was based on the fundamental right of the individual in the Church to form 'free-groups'. In so far as such extra-parochial 'free-groups' give grounds for the possibility and (in certain circumstances) duty of an extra-parochial pastoral care, we may speak of a 'free-group principle'. And so we may formulate the results of our inquiry so far by stating that the parochial principle is not the only legitimate principle for present-day pastoral practice. Side by side with it, and possessing their own validity, there are the '*social-differential principle*' and the '*free-group principle*'—even if social differences (in the meaning used here) and free-groups do not take the form of mere expressions of the individual parish. The 'federation principle' implied several times during our discussion of the parochial principle is, in the terminology adopted here, a combination of the social-differential and free-group principles. For a 'federation' (*Bund*) (prescinding from its *supra*-diocesan organization) is a 'free-group' whose organizational principle is to be found in the 'social-differential' (i.e. occupational and similar differences). To this extent the 'federation principle' is also justified by our reflections.

In actual fact, the parochial principle has never governed alone in the *history* of the Church's pastoral ministry. The Apostles themselves had no territory as the limit of their commission and work. Already in the Didache[20] we find mention of 'wandering apostles' engaged in pastoral work, side by side with the local clergy. We have accounts of such migrant ascetic teachers as late as the third century.[21] The ever-growing importance acquired by the monk in the Eastern Church right up to the tenth century as confessor and moral adviser as compared with the secular cleric points to another chapter in such extra-parochial care of souls. The 'guest-master' who, in accordance with the rule of St Basil, gave spiritual direction and counsel to those coming from outside the monastery,[22] was also engaged in extra-parochial pastoral work. The ancient institution of 'visitors' (περιοδευταί)[23] points in the direction of an 'extraordinary' care of souls in country districts, practised by 'wandering physicians of the soul' in the name of the bishop of the town. Wherever we find the influence of monks on their surroundings in the early Church (and their influence was indescribably great), there we see also an 'extra-ordinary' pastoral care at work. The missionary migration of Irish-Scottish monks in the seventh and eighth centuries all over the Continent was equally an 'extraordinary' form of the care of souls, since it took place mostly in established Christian lands. Already towards the end of the eleventh century, we hear of a slight controversy concerning the right of extra-parochial pastoral care, an *altercatio monachi et clerici, quod liceat monacho praedicare* according to

[20] Chpts. 11 and 13.

[21] Ps.-Clemens, *Epist.* I, 10 *sq.*; *Ep.* II, 1–6 (Funk II, Tübingen 1901, 8 *sqq.*, 15 *sq.*).

[22] *Reg. brev. tract.* C-CI; *reg. fus. tract.* XXXIII, 2 (PG XXXII, 1152 B *sq.*; PG XXXI, 997 *sqq.*).

[23] First Synod of Laodicea, can 57 (Mansi II, 574).

the title of one of the writings of Rupert of Deutz.[24] Similar treatises were written by Idung of St Emeran[25] and Honorius Augustodunensis.[26] We might also just mention in this connection the controversy in the twelfth century between monks and Canons Regular, since it also touches on the justification of the monks' apostolate.[27] As early as 1096, a Synod at Nîmes[28] had defended the right of the monastic apostolate, in the presence of Urban II. From the thirteenth century onwards, the pastoral ministry in medieval towns is no longer even conceivable without the extra-parochial apostolate exercised by the Mendicant Orders. In the middle of the thirteenth century, the Church experiences the first really important controversy about the 'parochial principle', in the fight between the Mendicant Orders (on the one hand) and William of Saint-Amour and his followers (on the other). This controversy ended theologically and canonically in favour of a less absolute parochial principle.[29] Of course, this does not mean that the defenders of the parochial principle did not also have very good reasons on their side; and, above all, there has undeniably been a reverse movement since the thirteenth century with regard to the subordination of the pastoral ministry of the Orders to the *bishops* as against the privileges of the Mendicant Orders. Arguments like those put forward by Thomas of York,[30] Bonaventure,[31] or Thomas Aquinas[32] in favour of the extra-parochial care of souls exercised by the Mendicants are still worth reading, and not a few of the arguments with which they had to deal in favour of the parochial principle sound surprisingly modern (as e.g. when they speak of the nuptial relationship of the parish priest to his church in which no one else may inter-

[24] PL CLXX, 537–542; cf. also PL CLXX, 541–544; 609–664; 663–668.

[25] Pez, *Thesaurus anecdotorum novissimus* II, 2, pp. 507 *sq.*

[26] Text in: I. A. Endres, *Honorius Aug.* (Kempten 1906), pp. 147 *sqq.*

[27] Cf. e.g. Anselm of Havelberg (PL CLXXXVIII, 119–140); Arno of Reichersberg (PL CXCIV, 1493–1528).

[28] Mansi XX, 934 *sq.*

[29] The official Church documents on this controversy can be found e.g. in Cavallera, *Thesaurus doctrinae catholicae*, no. 414 *sq.* (Denz 458 *sq.*).

[30] '*Manus, quae contra Omnipotentem tenditur*' cap. 13–18: Bierbaum, *Bettelorden und Weltgeistlichkeit an der Universität Paris* (Münster 1920), pp. 134–167.

[31] '*Quare Fratres Minores praedicent et confessiones audiant*', *Opusc.* XIV, Quar. tom. VIII, pp. 375 *sqq.*

[32] '*Contra impugnantes Dei cultum et religionem*' cap. 4, cap. 10, 12 (*Opusc.* I, edit. Parm. XV, pp. 13–23; 52 *sq.*; 54–56).

fere, or when the parochial right is said to be analogous to the exclusive right of the bishop with regard to the care of souls). This mid-thirteenth-century controversy about the right of existence of the extraordinary pastoral ministry had its sequel in the doctrine of John of Pouilly, condemned by John XXII in 1321.[33] The significance, extent and influence of the extra-parochial pastoral ministry exercised mainly by the regular clergy (though not exclusively so; cf. e.g. the Oratories of St Philip Neri), has fluctuated slightly even in subsequent history. But basically and in practice the right and possibility of the extra-parochial care of souls has remained essentially uncontroverted since the thirteenth century. Even the Council of Trent does not represent an essential deviation in this matter, although it ordered the absolute division of dioceses into parishes.[34] If anything, it is the pastoral theology of Jansenism and the struggle against it which show signs of a revival of the former controversy about the parochial principle. The 'parochialism' of Jansenism[35] and its doctrine of the incompatibility of the Religious life with pastoral activity[36] signify objectively a dogmatic and pastoral absolutist view of the parochial principle, which has its echoes also in the polemic of the Enlightenment against the Religious life. We cannot, of course, go into details here regarding the whole history, which to a large extent is still unwritten, of the fluctuations in the relationship between the parochial principle and the principle of the 'extraordinary' care of souls. It would be a history which would reflect a great part of the history of the spirit, economics and Canon Law of the Western world. We would have to speak about many matters in the course of it: about the history of conventual exemptions, about the slow transformation and abandonment of the law imposing a duty of attending the *parochial* Mass on Sundays or the duty of confessing to one's own parish priest (at least at Eastertide). We would have to speak of the history of the right to preach possessed by non-parochial pastoral ministers, of the Third Order sodalities of the Mendicant Orders, of the 'Compagnies de Prédication' in the France of Philip II Augustus (†1223), of the controversy between secular and regular clergy in the Middle Ages regarding burial rights. We would have to deal with the history of private Oratories and non-parochial churches, and to speak of the

[33] Cf. Denz 491–493.
[34] 24th Session (11th November 1563), *de reformatione* XIII.
[35] Denz 1510 *sq.* [36] Denz 1580 *sqq.*

efforts to incorporate churches into monasteries, of the history of the pastoral ministry of pilgrimages, of the development of confraternities and Marian congregations, of the history of parish Missions, of the medieval guilds as spheres of extra-parochial pastoral activity among people of different social stations, of the development of Catholic life in associations during the nineteenth century, and of many other matters. At any rate, such a survey of the pastoral ministry would show that the parochial principle was never exclusively in force in the Church and that the Church, on the contrary, protects the many facets of life even in the pastoral sphere, by her healthy instinct for life which defends itself against every form of pedantry.

It has already been shown in part, in connection with our treatment of the parochial principle, that other pastoral principles too are known and recognized as valid by current Canon Law, which alone, in the final analysis, can create really valid principles for the care of souls beyond mere considerations of their suitability (viz. laws which are more than, and more exact than, the merely natural law and the general norms of the Church's mission determined by divine institution). The same follows also, on the other hand, from what still remains to be said about the pastoral apostolate carried out by members of Religious Orders in accordance with Canon Law.

Since a large part of the extra-parochial pastoral ministry is carried out by Religious, it will be well to say a few words about the *Orders-apostolate* to conclude this Section. It is an undoubted fact that the final purpose of the life of an Order is absolutely compatible with the care of souls in general. St John Chrysostom and Pope Siricius already tried to attract monks to the priestly apostolate. Men like Eusebius of Vercelli, Paulinus of Nola, Martin of Tours and Augustine already tried to shape the life of the clergy after a monastic pattern. The ancient institution of episcopal monasteries, the establishment of the Clerks Regular, the almost untold number of Orders and Congregations founded since the twelfth century which count the pastoral apostolate as part of the express and ecclesiastically approved purpose of their Order, the clarification of this question by the great medieval theologians, and the already mentioned decisions by the Church's magisterium,[37] make the compatibility of life in an Order with pastoral activity a theologically indisputable truth. Nevertheless, it

[37] Denz 458 *sq.*; 1580 *sqq.*; 491 *sqq.*

may not be utterly useless today to call this truth expressly to mind. The pastoral ministry as exercised by Religious even in hierarchically organized countries does not of itself necessarily mean (either conceptually or objectively) an extra-parochial ministry. For such a care of souls can basically be exercised within the framework of a parish. In other words, the pastoral ministry exercised by Religious can basically be in keeping with the 'parish principle', either because the Orders take over parishes of their own (as happens frequently and is also provided for in current Canon Law)[38] or because they perform other pastoral duties *in* parishes at the invitation of the parish priest[39] (as is in fact true of the greater part of their pastoral ministry), so that even these activities of 'extraordinary' care of souls in a wider sense do not overstep the parish principle. Yet actually the pastoral activity of the Orders does very often pass beyond the boundaries of the parochial principle. And if anything, it is this alone which can be regarded as a serious question. What is to be said about this? First of all, we must emphasize that the extra-parochial pastoral ministry exercised by Religious is in no way a violation of the hierarchic principle of all care of souls, i.e. of the principle that every pastoral ministry must be carried out as a result of a mission and mandate given by the Pope and the bishops, and as their instrument. The great medieval theologians already referred to the fact that the Pope and the bishops have an original and inalienable right and corresponding duty to minister to the faithful, and that they do not lose the right of ministering *directly* to all the faithful (i.e. to the whole Church or the whole diocese respectively) by charging parish priests with the maintenance of their rights and the fulfilment of their duties, in a measure and to an extent left to their own discretion (determined by the purpose of the measure and not by any 'parochial rights' existing before their ruling). These theologians already concluded quite rightly from this that when the Pope or a bishop entrusts Religious with the exercise of this ministry (originally devolving on the Church's Hierarchy) even without parochial-territorial limitations, this care of souls is a function of the Hierarchy, and hence of the organism of the Mystical Body founded by our Lord himself, in exactly the same way as is the territorial parochial office. Since the Roman Pontiff has

[38] Cf. especially CIC can. 456; 630 *sq.*
[39] Cf. e.g. CIC can. 608 § 2 together with 1334; 1341 § 1.

universal and *immediate* jurisdiction over all the faithful (even the individual),[40] he can or could also transfer such pastoral functions to Religious without using the bishop as an 'intermediary'. Even in this case it could not be said that the hierarchical principle of the care of souls has in any way been violated (although, of course, such a measure which is in keeping with the existing Canon Law, is in fact only rarely taken, apart from marginal cases which in the main concern the internal life of the exempt Orders of Clerics). Now if, secondly, the full accomplishment of the pastoral task did and does in fact also demand *extra*-parochial care of souls, then the Pope and the bishops are absolutely justified in calling also on Religious to help in this task. The reason for this is not that members of Orders desire to be pastorally 'employed' in accordance with the Rule of their Order and cannot in practice find such employment in the parochial ministry alone. Just the reverse is true; because the care of souls must, for reasons arising out of its objective needs, be carried out partially in an extra-parochial manner, this extra-parochial ministry may also in such a case—and in the measure of its needs—be carried out by Religious, if they are called to this by the Hierarchy. It also follows from this, however, that Religious should not include those works within the sphere of their supra-parochial, 'extraordinary' pastoral ministry which can be performed within the parish ministry, i.e. anything which does not of its very nature require to be done supra-parochially or can be done in the parish without loss of any really special benefit. If and when they are not in a position to engage in objectively supra-parochial pastoral work (either because of a lack of such work or because of a shortage of suitable men who could do it), then they should, to the extent to which they dispose of men free to do pastoral work, either do real 'supplies' in secular parishes by arrangement with the parish priest, or (in the spirit of their Order) take over humble and 'stony' parishes or found new ones. If, for example, a non-parochial Orders-church is simply an exact copy of the parochial church in whose territory it is situated, i.e. if it does not exercise a really specialized pastoral function which cannot be performed by a parochial church, then let it quietly 'shut up shop' or become a parish church in its own right in cities where parishes are too large.

It is to be expected that much could still be done in this direction to

[40] Denz 1827.

make better use of those among the Religious who are able to do pastoral work, and to remove in this way much unnecessary friction between the pastoral ministry exercised by Orders and that exercised in the parish. Since there must, however, be a supra-parochial ministry in the nature of things and since it can be exercised by Religious, the existing Canon Law (thirdly) also envisages, sanctions and protects an extra-parochial ministry carried out by Religious. Thus Canon Law commands bishops not to refuse Religious the faculty to preach or confessional jurisdiction without grave reasons.[41] The bishop is not allowed to interfere in the internal discipline and spiritual direction of an ecclesiastical association of lay people erected by apostolic privilege in conjunction with the church of an Order.[42] The ecclesiastical law governing associations[43] recognizes and sanctions ecclesiastical lay-associations (Third Orders, Confraternities, etc.) which very often have a supra-parochial organization and are often (in keeping with their characteristics) directed by Religious. The bishop may for a grave reason withdraw Religious Houses and Pious Institutes from the care of the parish priest, even though they be situated within the boundaries of his parish and are not exempt *de iure* from his authority.[44] The bishop can thus create as it were a 'personal parish', a congregation without any proper territory, whose pastoral care is therefore also extra-parochial. Canon Law[45] envisages that the bishop may also require the help of Religious, when necessary, for giving Catechetical instructions, especially in their own churches. It positively desires that there should be sermons at Sunday Masses even in non-parochial churches (even those of Religious).[46] If a bishop permits the erection of a Clerical Religious House in his diocese, he must also inevitably grant to it the right to a church or public oratory in which religious services (including Sunday Mass) may be held for the laity, according to the rules governing 'churches' and 'public oratories'.[47] Thus, wherever there exists a properly-erected house of a Clerical Religious Order, even the bishop cannot forbid a certain measure of extra-parochial ministry by these Religious, especially[48] since the permission for the erection of a Religious House includes also (unless something else was explicitly agreed upon at the time) the faculty for the Religious

[41] CIC can. 1339 § 1; can. 874 § 2.
[42] CIC can. 690 § 2.
[43] CIC can. 684–725.
[44] CIC can. 464 § 2.
[45] CIC can. 1334.
[46] CIC can. 1345; cf. also can. 483, 1°.
[47] CIC can. 497 § 2.
[48] CIC *loc. cit.*

to exercise the activities proper to their Order, and thus in certain cases also to exercise pastoral care beyond the boundaries of their own church. Although the foregoing provides us with only general, skeleton-directions which by themselves do not give a full guarantee of the *objective* justification of extra-parochial pastoral work by Religious in any individual case (even of such pastoral work as remains within these limits), these canonical regulations do nevertheless show clearly that current Canon Law does regard even extra-parochial pastoral care as something basically justified and desirable. Since these regulations were not after all drawn up expressly 'in favour' of Religious, in order to give them 'work' or 'rights' and privileges, but for the sake of pastoral work in general, these canons show that evidently the same considerations lie behind these norms of present-day Canon Law as we have adduced above on the limits of the parochial principle from the point of view of the object of the care of souls. The 'existence' of principles even of extra-parochial care of souls is therefore as much warranted by Canon Law as the 'existence' of the parochial principle which is also merely established by the fixed law of the Church.

III

In conclusion, we would like to make a few reflections, based on our theoretical considerations, which may perhaps be of some little use in pastoral practice. There can, of course, be no question here of defining concrete boundaries and lines of demarcation of competence between parochial and extra-parochial ministries. Such an undertaking would require a more exact examination of pastoral work according to task, available man-power, and specific situations, which is a matter for the appropriate diocesan authorities. Yet a few matters pertaining to the intermediate sphere between extremely general theories and extremely particular practice may perhaps still be added to the practical insights we have already discovered here and there.

If, besides the parochial principle (both *qua* parish- and parish-priest principle), other organizational principles of pastoral care also have validity *de iure* and *de facto* (i.e. at least the 'social-differential' and the 'free-group' principle), and if there are to be settled and comprehensive (which does not mean, primitive and narrow-minded) conditions, then this requires on all sides a good and selfless will to live in harmony and to work together. Although we may not simply turn the parochial principle into an absolute norm in order to create a clear situation even without good will on all sides, the advocates of the parochial principle must be able to find among the representatives of supra-parochial associations and alliances (based on different social stations) understanding of their insistence on the importance of a living parochial pastoral care and on the importance of parish life, since the parish cannot be merely a subsequent blanket-organization of groups and associations or federations in which these other organizations are not really interested. Conversely, the advocates of the 'social-differential' and 'free-group' principle must be able to feel that parish priests do not have a clerical craving for power but are possessed of that attitude which enabled St Paul for his part to solve a similar quarrel about relative competencies : *dum omni modo . . . Christus annuntietur.*[49] Whenever *several* principles are entitled to demand their rights, a ready attitude of understanding and of love will always be the deciding factor. Without it, even the reduction of the theory to *one, unique* principle will fail to succeed in practice; with it, even the difficult task of allowing several principles their rightful place within the same sphere is really quite simple when all is said and done. Selfless, unassuming love is most practical; it teaches us to recognize the justification of several principles and reduces them in practice to *its* own common denominator. Norms, no matter how clearly and subtly reasoned out in a legal sense, can never replace a right moral attitude on the part of those who must put them into practice. Frictions arising from the lack of such an attitude can never be avoided by guiding principles and fixed spheres of action, no matter how exactly thought out they may be. Whenever such frictions arise, we must first of all call for an examination of consciences and not for an examination by the jurists.

If we have given support in the preceding pages to the necessity and right of extra-parochial care of souls, this does not mean that we are in favour of a wild, excessive creation of extra- and supra-parochial groups, federations and associations. It does not mean that in this respect the situation as it was before 1933 has canonical validity for all time, that everything should remain as it was in 1933. There will be no harm done if many phenomena which existed at that time remain buried, for they were manifestations of singular German tastes and

[49] Phil 1. 12–20.

exclusive interest in local club life rather than of genuine pastoral needs and genuine 'freedom of the spirit'. Whenever something old or necessary which has proved itself, or something new which is useful, revives again, it must have the will to real cooperation with the parochial ministry. Let those appeal to the 'social-differential' and 'free-group' principles who have the greatest love for the altar of their own parish and who prove their Christian liberty by being prepared to serve and love *the whole* which does, after all, find its first and clearest expression in the parish, in the 'Church'. Whenever the right attitude is present on all sides, this cooperation with the parochial pastoral care can be achieved, even though it will often not be easy to formulate it in legal arrangements and norms in a manner which will satisfy everyone. Anyone who has grasped the fact that such arrangements remain lifeless without the proper living spirit, will not be terribly unhappy if he feels that these agreements do not offer to all sides the desired 'guarantee' of such cooperation and settlement.

Whenever several valid 'principles' strive for and demand realization in one and the same set of circumstances, *cooperation* is impossible without some 'compromise'. In such cases, to come to the sort of understanding we have indicated is not a 'lazy' compromise. Whenever it is ultimately a question of everyone's seeking not the triumph of his own principle but rather the salvation of souls, such a compromise will *not* create the impression in those concerned that they have made a 'painful sacrifice' in the cause of mutual understanding. Since there can, in the very nature of things, be different solutions to the question of how in practice the many principles are to be reconciled, the final solution is a matter of decision; in other words, it is a task to be left to the authority of the Church. Once this decision has been made, after mature deliberation, in favour of a really workable agreement, then we should not go on debating endlessly but should set to work. For pastoral care does not consist in a debate about principles. It is better to work without '*the* ideal solution' (which in this matter can never be found), than to wait idly for principles regarding the care of souls which are still more ideal, just and wiser than those which have in fact been arrived at by an authoritative decision. Seeing the spiritual distress in which man finds himself today, it is high time we stopped fighting about the principles according to which these human beings are to be saved. When someone saves another, he does not require anyone beside him to ensure that he is doing it in accordance with principles. Although there cannot really be a 'best' synthesis of the different pastoral principles deducible *a-priori*, and one which is valid once and for all, there is nevertheless a very clear criterion in practical life as to whether a possible synthesis has actually succeeded, not only on paper and as a legal arrangement, but in the hearts of the advocates of particular principles. Such a synthesis has been successful only when the parish priest of the parochial principle shows a positive, active interest in the various forms of 'extraordinary' pastoral care, when he tries to bring his parishioners into contact with these forms (federations, Orders, associations, literature, etc.) according to their (not his) needs. It has been successful only when the clerical representatives of extra-parochial care of souls have an active consciousness of their responsibility as regards the life of the parish and when they, on their own initiative and as far as in them lies, stimulate the people under their pastoral care into real service to the life of the parish.

Cooperation and right order does not exclude 'competition'. It is not at all a bad thing if a preacher knows that his listeners can go away to someone else if he preaches badly. If we were to attempt, even on the pastoral plane, to make 'competition' impossible from the very start by legal measures (e.g. by a parochial principle made absolute), this would merely be a sign of weakness and a proof that we seek ourselves and not the salvation of souls. To suspect every variety, every form of competition in the pastoral realm at once as 'chaos', 'disorder' and a 'frittering away' of our forces, would be a sign of the same evil or of very shortsighted pastoral politics. Even if things (i.e. in truth: for the man of the 'competitionless' institution) went more smoothly and with less hindrance for a time without competition, such advantages would have to be paid for in the long run by the slow but sure degeneration of such an institution into self-complacency. Thus the desired cooperation between the parochial and extra-parochial care of souls must not be thought to have succeeded only when the different institutions no longer 'compete' with each other in any way whatsoever. The will for right order and a living will to honest and objective competition are absolutely compatible. Even in the pastoral realm we do not need any 'controlled economy' bureaucratically imposed from above right down to every detail.

Finally, it should be expressly emphasized that we have nowhere in the course of our deliberations defined our attitude to the question of *supra*-diocesan societies and of the possibility as well as the limits of a central direction of such societies. This is a special question which would have to be considered separately.

The work of St Bonaventure, one of the Doctors of the Church, which we have cited previously, was also really concerned with the *ius positivum* of the parochial principle. Thus it was concerned with the question of how we must act if charity, in the face of men's needs of salvation in the concrete situation of the times, demand that we do not make the parochial principle the only organizational principle of our pastoral ministry. The final words of his whole investigation contain the kernel of all our reflections and should, therefore, also conclude these considerations: . . . *rigor iuris positivi, ubi expedit, servandus est, ubi autem salutem impedit remittendus est . . . Quod enim pro caritate institutum est, non debet contra caritatem militare. Amen. Et sic est finis illius quaestionis.*[50]

[50] Quar. VIII, p. 381.

II

NOTES ON THE LAY APOSTOLATE

If we are to attempt to say anything precise about the lay apostolate, we cannot avoid saying something about 1. What is meant by a 'layman', 2. the 'apostolate' in general, 3. the nature of the 'lay apostolate' and 4. the significance of the lay apostolate today.

I. THE LAYMAN

1. The concept of 'layman', in the ecclesiastical sphere, has nothing to do with that of the 'profane' or 'ignorant', of someone who on account of his inexperience is helplessly dependent on the expert, or of the 'unecclesiastical', religiously indifferent, the mere object of hierarchic powers. In this sense there are, or should be, no laymen in the Church. For a layman in the theological sense is one of the λαός of God; in other words, someone eminently sanctified, consecrated, called from a world lost in sin and death into the ἐκκλησία of God and of his Christ, into the host of those who have been visibly and tangibly called to salvation by baptism. The notion of 'layman', therefore, does not mark the boundary between the sphere of the profane and the sphere of the sacred and sacral; rather, it refers to someone who has a *definite* position *within* the one consecrated realm of the Church.

2. This determined position which constitutes the layman *within* the sacral sphere of Holy Church, can first of all be described negatively (by contrast with the non-lay in the same Church) and then positively (by description of the inner characteristics of the lay state).

3. *Negative description*:

a. The layman must first of all be distinguished from those who have proper hierarchical powers in the Church (CIC can. 948). These powers comprise the *potestas ordinis* and the *potestas iurisdictionis*. The 'power of orders' consists of those full powers, which of their very essence are primarily of a sacramental nature; they either *can* only be conferred by the sacrament of Holy Orders (thus the power to absolve, confirm, ordain, consecrate) or at least are in fact only given in a *permanent* fashion by Ordination (thus the powers of the Diaconate and the lower Orders). The 'power of jurisdiction' is made up of those powers which belong to ruling and concern the authoritative instruction and direction of the rest of the Church's members. Lay status in the Church means, in the strict sense, that one does not have these powers. It must, however, be clearly underlined, in this connection, that there are powers in the Church which do not require to be transmitted exclusively by the sacrament of Holy Orders or cannot even be conferred by it strictly as such. Complete sovereign power (jurisdiction) is not transmitted by the sacrament of Orders but by a non-sacramental, sovereign act of the (highest) Church authority. The full powers of an acolyte, subdeacon, etc. are in fact (often) conferred by Ordination, but they can also be given without such an act (of a sacrament or perhaps merely of a sacramental). We cannot then differentiate a lay person from a cleric, with reference to these powers, by the *manner* of their transmission but only by the *content* of what is transmitted (viz. the power). And so a clear and exact theological terminology must state that anyone who is, in any way, rightfully in *habitual* possession of any part of liturgical or legal power (over and above the basic rights of every baptized member of the Church), is no longer a *layman* in the proper sense, i.e. no longer belongs to the simple 'people of God'. It is most important for our further reflections to understand this and grasp the reasons for it. An officially commissioned 'lay-catechist', a woman officially employed as 'parochial helper', an official sacristan, etc. are not indeed ordained; yet if these are their principal functions, they are no longer, properly speaking, lay persons. This is apparent even in the sentiment of the early Church. She conferred all these offices by Ordinations; thus the old 'Minor Orders' were *not* in fact merely transitory 'steps to the priesthood' but conferred a permanent 'minor' office in the Church through which its possessor belonged to the clergy. The same conclusion follows from the very nature of things; the precise powers by which the clergy is distinguished from the laity are of their nature *divisible*, according as the Church may think fit (as far as jurisdiction and the sacramental powers are concerned). Hence, whenever the Church gives someone—whether with Ordination or without—some part of the power distinguishing clergy from laity, and does so, not merely for an individual occasion, but habitually, and as constituting a calling and office, she makes him a cleric, whether we would apply this term or not. In this strict theological sense, it is absolutely possible for a woman to belong to the 'clergy' even though, according to the will of Christ and already in the practice of the Apostles, the extent of such hierarchic powers conferrable upon her is much more limited than that accorded to men. The fact that in *current* Canon Law a woman cannot have ordinary jurisdiction in the narrower sense, because in current Canon Law such jurisdiction is an ordinary 'office' reserved to men, does not alter anything about the basic principle which concerns us here. Regarded from the viewpoint of purely divine law alone, it is absolutely conceivable that a woman, e.g. an abbess, should have the permanent right of patronage of a parish, as was the case at the time of the right to 'private churches'. If in fact the 'clergy' is normally composed of men only, it is because (at least in the case of *higher* offices) the power of ruling *and* the power conferred by Ordination are meant to exist normally in one and the same person according to Christ's will; now the powers conferred only by Ordination are reserved to men and that already *de iure divino*. And so we must be extremely careful in the use of theological terminology. Even a simple question, such as the following, will make this clear: Can a layman, who is elected Pope, accepts the election and thus already possesses the absolute plenitude of all jurisdictional power in the Church before he has been ordained and consecrated, still seriously be called a 'layman' in theological terminology, until he has been ordained? A negative answer to this question logically involves saying with us that the lay status ceases whenever there begins, in any measure whatsoever, a total or partial participation in the *potestas iurisdictionis* or *potestas ordinis* or both. It is, of course, debatable whether this or that actual, small ecclesiastical office can still be considered as participation in the proper powers of the hierarchy, or whether it merely implies obligations which can no longer be looked upon as such a participation (as e.g. the duty merely of lighting the candles); it remains therefore a debatable point whether the bearer of such an office still belongs to the clergy in the theological sense or not.

b. Secondly, the notion of 'layman' must be distinguished from that of the 'Religious' (and members of 'secular institutes' properly so called, since they also, take the vows of the Evangelical Counsels). We cannot explain here the nature of the Evangelical Counsels and of vows, especially under their truly ecclesiological aspect. We wish simply to state it as a fact here, in pure thesis form and without proofs, that the vows taken in respect of the Evangelical Counsels have of their nature an ecclesiological aspect. This does not indeed mean that these vows give the one who takes them a hierarchical power and a *status* in the Church based on *this* power and distinguishing this status from that of the people of the Church as such; but it does mean that the Evangelical Counsels are an expression, visible manifestation and representation *in* the world of a very definite essential characteristic of the Church, viz. of her world-transcending origin and destination. They must, therefore, be found in the Church, considered as the historical, visible form of the world-transcending and eschatological grace of Christ; they consequently provide the basis *in* the Church as *such*, for a proper status, so that the one who has this status is theologically, and not merely canonically (CIC can. 491 § 1: *religiosi praecedent laicis*), distinguished from the people of the Church in general and hence from lay people.

4. *Positive description*:

a. From the point of view of the *world*. Up until now we have merely given a negative description of the layman, i.e. he is not one of those who have hierarchical powers and he does not belong to the Religious. Both of the 'estates' from which he is thus distinguished are 'states', i.e. (relatively) stable, permanent forms of life (even though they are not always irrevocable), which—each in their own way—take their subjects out of the 'world' in virtue of the content of their tasks. Correspondingly, the layman is a Christian who remains in the world, not in the sense of the profane which we have already excluded above, but in the sense that the layman must have a specific task towards the world and in the world which determines his 'status' in the *Church* and not merely in civil life. Being a layman, seen from this point of view, does *not* mean being a Christian who does not really have much say in the Church and who is merely a passive object of the pastoral endeavours made by the Church (= the clergy) for his salvation; a layman is not one who *for such reasons* occupies himself with those worldly-profane matters lacking any religious relevance which would occupy him just the same even if he were not a Christian. Being a layman in the Church (and also to have the qualification of a Church member in this sense) means rather, having one's place in the Church as her member and exercising her functions wherever there is the *world* (all this referring, of course, to the lay-*Christian only in so far as* he is *distinguished* from the clergy and from Religious). For the 'world' is not merely constituted by sinful and rebellious opposition to God, Christ, grace and the Church; the world is also God's creation, a reality which can be redeemed and must be sanctified (i.e. the Kingdom of God); and even in this respect the world is not simply identical with the Church, but rather the Church is the historically tangible and socially constituted instrument used by Christ for the coming of the Kingdom of God through the redemption and sanctification of the world. In this world the layman has his determined place according to his historical situation, his people, family and calling, the individual possibilities furnished by his gifts and capabilities, etc. And he has this, his place-in-the-world, basically *in*dependently of and prior to his Christianity; after all, he is born before he is re-born. This original independence of the layman's place-in-the-world is the element of truth in the notion of the 'lay' considered as the 'profane' which we rejected above as false. The layman is originally in the world in virtue of the *pre*-Christian (but not 'godless') position of his existence; in *this* place, and not in any other, is he to be a Christian. This he must be, not just 'in addition', but by christianizing his original pre-Christian situation, which is the very essence of lay-existence, in such a way that precisely where there is the world and not the Church, the Kingdom of God may begin to exist through him as a member of the Church. We will, however, have more to say about this later on. For the moment it is important to realize the fundamental point that the Christian *qua* layman is distinguished from the non-lay (i.e. the clergy and the Religious) not merely by the fact that he has an original place-in-the-world even *for* his Christian existence (which is true of every Christian), but that he also *retains* this place *as* a Christian and for his Christian existence as such, and does not leave it even in the fulfilment of his existence (at least not by living a new kind of life which takes on the permanent form of a new 'state'). In other words, when we rightly say that 'the Christian layman remains in the world', this does not mean that the layman is a Christian and in addition also a man, a member of a family, the father of a family, a tailor, politician, art enthusiast, etc. Rather it means that his being-in-the-world which preceded his Christian being, remains and is not changed as a 'state' by the fact of his being a Christian; but it is now both the material for his very being as a Christian and the *limit* of this being, as far as his *exterior* life and the structure of his state are concerned. As far as his state is concerned, if he goes beyond the limit set by his original situation-in-the-world, he ceases to be a layman. What has just been said provides us also with the right meaning of the expression, frequently used nowadays, the layman's 'mission in the world'. Such expressions must always be understood to refer to a twofold fact: the layman is placed in the world as a member of the Church at a determined point, given prior to his Christian being, *and* this is positively and negatively the place of his being as a *Christian* (i.e. it is a calling and the limit of his commission).

b. From the point of view of the *Church*. The positive determination of the concept of 'layman' (i.e. one which does not distinguish him merely negatively from the clergy and Religious) must not only consider his specific situation-in-the-world when trying to define his Christian being. It must also say what the layman is in the Church, as such, and what he brings with him to his place-in-the-world and what he can realize there as a member of the Church. We can obviously give here only a very brief indication of this, since it involves, or should involve, almost everything affecting Christian existence.

(i) The layman is someone called by God, in Jesus Christ and through grace, to eternal life. He is the justified and sanctified, the gratuitously adopted son of God. He shares in the one grace which in Jesus Christ was promised and communicated to redeemed humanity, to *holy* Church.

(ii) Within the Church, he cooperates in rendering this grace historically tangible (a visible manifestation which in its totality is nothing other than the Church). For the layman has received the sacrament of baptism; he offers the sacrifice of holy Church together with the priest; he is given his Christian mission in the world by the sacrament of confirmation which commissions him personally, expressly, and in a sacramentally tangible manner. He takes part in the Church's life in many other ways too, so that as a result, this, his life in holiness with, in and through the Church (its direction, divine service, power of grace, proclamation of the Word, charity, etc.) becomes part of the manifestation of the Church. Thus he shares in making the Church what she always is and must always become more and more, viz. the historically tangible, spatio-temporal presence of the redemptive grace of God in Jesus Christ.

(iii) The life of the Church is more than just the exercise of their functions by the holders of hierarchical offices (instituted once and for all by Christ as her permanent organs) in the authoritative proclamation of the Word, administration of the sacraments, direction and celebration of divine services and government of the ecclesiastical community in all the other forms of its Christian life, on the one hand, and the acceptance of these exercised functions by the people of the Church, on the other. In spite of her permanent proper structure and hierarchical organization, given to her by Christ, the Church must always remain open to that unpredictable initiative taken by her Master through his Spirit and the charisms of this Spirit which cannot be institutionalized. Over and above the static element of official functions there must be, and is, the dynamic element of charisms. We cannot give here a closer definition of their nature and importance for the Church. It must suffice to state that even laymen can be the subject of such charisms; these charisms are not only gratuitous graces and aids granted by God for the private life of their recipients, but are also given to them for the salvation of the Church. A message received from heaven and passed on to the Church, a life giving outstanding example and which has a type-forming power in a determined situation, the discovery of a new aspect of the Christian Faith and life, a historical decision of universal significance inspired from above, a God-given impulse to perform a certain work in the public life of the Church, etc.—all these are to be understood as charisms inspired by the Holy Spirit. And even lay people can receive such charisms, for the Spirit has not limited himself in the distribution of his gifts by any rule known to man and applicable by man. The poor, children, women, married people can equally well be the recipients of such heavenly impulses and the point of entry of the divine Spirit's permanent influence on God's Church. God has in no way guaranteed that the movement of his Spirit should always and necessarily begin at the summit of the hierarchy. The hierarchy has, on the contrary, a strict duty to discern and further the Spirit wherever he may act; it must not extinguish the Spirit simply because he has not inquired beforehand whether he is everywhere seen to be in conformity with the plans and the opinions 'in high places' on pastoral matters and the affairs of ecclesiastical politics. Ecclesiastical authority has certainly the duty, right and power of discernment of spirits (even though it is not necessarily capable of an infallible decision in every case), but it is not the original and sole owner of this Spirit. Laymen too can be the recipients of charisms which exercise an irreplaceable function in the Church, side by side with her official functions, laws, rules and everything which can be deduced *a-priori* both dogmatically and rationally. In so far as such charisms (in this narrower sense applicable here) are of their nature free, non-organisable, unpredictable and hence also uncontrollable gifts of God, they also do not give rise to a 'state', unlike the hierarchical offices or the Evangelical Counsels which for all their gratuitous realization are intended to constitute a permanent form of life. Hence even when these charisms are bestowed on a layman, they do not remove him from his situation in the world. He does not cease to be a layman by being the recipient of such charisms. It should just be mentioned in passing that we must not confuse these charisms in themselves with a possible enthusiastic manifestation of such charisms. Even absolutely normal fulfilments of Christian life can be counted as charisms, if by their strength, purity and depth (i.e. as 'moral miracles') they bear the stamp of their divine origin even in their outward appearances. This is true even when their recipient is not a clearly determinable individual but when the Spirit takes hold of many; thus the liturgical movement, for instance, can perhaps be looked upon as a charismatic happening in the theological sense just as much as, let us say, Fatima. In both cases, there will always ultimately be certain side-effects which do not have a particularly spiritual origin.

(iv) In so far as the layman is a member of the Church both in the dimension of inward grace *and* her outward (quasi-sacramental) visibleness, he also shares necessarily in the Church's mission and responsibility. He not merely enjoys the use and advantages of her activity and is not merely subject to her direction or a passive object of her missionary mandate; but by the very nature of being a member of the Mystical Body of Christ he is also an active cooperator in the fulfilment of her mission and mandate, in so far as these can, and must be, predicated of the Church as a whole and in so far as the fact of a determined mission and a definite mandate does not itself constitute the essential difference between certain members of the Church and others who are called lay people. We cannot say exactly what this cooperation means in a positive and negative sense, until we deal with the lay apostolate itself. The important factor at this point is merely the most general conclusion which follows immediately from the positive content of the fact of being-a-layman-in-the-Church : the layman participates in the mission and task of the Church (which does not by any means signify that he participates in the mission of the hierarchy or the clergy, etc.).

(v) Up till now we have spoken of the layman in so far as the meaning of this concept results from the permanently established nature of the Church and of Christianity. It remains now to be seen that being-a-layman-in-the-Church can also be given content by positive ordinance and legal disposition on the part of the Church (i.e. *iure humano*). A layman can be a godparent, can fulfil certain functions in ecclesiastical associations, can have the right of patronage, can, by right, assist in the administration of Church property, etc. All these are functions which belong to him *de iure humano*, and they signify services in the Church which do not destroy his nature as a layman, since they do not deprive him of his proper station in the world.

Human law could, of course, assign certain ecclesiastical tasks, rights, duties and powers to laymen by which the latter would cease to belong to the lay state, in accordance with what has been said above, as for instance by ordination to the priesthood. It will, however, always be possible to state in such cases—and it must already be stated at this point—that the Church can give an assignment of such dimensions, which results in a change of the layman's specific situation, only with the free consent of the individual concerned. It is true that by virtue of her pastoral office the Church can impose certain tasks and duties (together with any rights which may be involved) on the layman, even by a *uni*lateral decision, but this possibility is not unlimited. It may not be absolutely determined in its extent, and may vary to a certain degree, according to the conditions of culture, the circumstances of the times, etc.; but it has undoubtedly an intrinsic limit beyond which the Church authorities may not go by a unilateral act. This already follows clearly, for example, from CIC can. 971 and can. 214 § 1, which declare a forced ordination to be immoral and without any of its purely canonical effects on the ordained. It is certainly not a question here merely of an ordinance by positive law, but it is ultimately a matter of natural law which applies not only to third parties but also to the Church herself. Thus, *if* the Church on her part were to confide such tasks and duties to a layman in the service of her mission by a unilateral decision and as a permanent measure, so that it would have to be said that such a person had essentially been deprived of his intramundane state without his voluntary act (whether with or without ordination), then such a commitment of a layman by the Church would be immoral and without effect. It at once follows from this that the Church cannot charge a layman, of her own initiative, with collaboration in the tasks of the hierarchy to any extent she cares to choose. It is also impossible to determine the limits of this possibility simply and solely by reference to the needs of the Church's apostolate. For there are needs and obligations which must be borne collectively, without it being possible to come to a binding conclusion from this as to the obligation of any particular individual; it must surely be supposed that God, in his providence, will also provide for these needs in the measure really willed by him, without imposing an express moral obligation on the individual *qua* individual. The human race, for example, 'must' be propagated. But in the nature of things, nothing at all really follows from this as to the individual's duty to marry. Similarly, the Church 'must' have priests. But this premise, as such, and on its own, in no way implies the consequence for the individual that he must become a priest. The Church also, cannot impose this obligation on him of her own initiative, however urgent her needs and great her lack of priests may be. The same would consequently apply also to similar duties which might be imposed on a layman because allegedly the Church would otherwise be unable to fulfil her responsibilities. If such obligations (e.g. of always handing over half of his income) were to imply an essential change in his lay station in the world, the Church cannot *iure humano* impose them on him by a unilateral decision. The 'imposition on the layman' of the tasks of the Church by positive Canon Law has its intrinsic limits. Nothing, of course, is as yet decided thereby about any possibly existing *moral obligation* on the part of the layman to do more than he has done hitherto, whether by reason of the general principles of love of neighbour or as a result of a special divine vocation. We have merely contested the *Church's* moral right to impose and enforce such an obligation. The Church obviously, always has the right and indeed the duty to give general indications, to exhort, to describe a critical state of affairs and thus to canvass among, and appeal to, the ranks of the laity to provide those who will assist her hierarchy in the fulfilment of its obligations; she may appeal to them to do this by entering into the clerical or religious state or by taking upon themselves some other measure of Church work which, because it essentially modifies their very state in the world, cannot be imposed on them as a duty by the Church as such and by her unilateral ordinance; nor, therefore, can the Church deduce from general principles and in the form of a definitive and authoritative ecclesiastical decision that this measure of work is a duty *hic et nunc* and in this particular case. For the latter would objectively, and in practice, amount to the same as the former, which has already been proved to be beyond the competence of the ecclesiastical hierarchy.

A further point, connected with the present question, to which attention must also be drawn right away, is that current Canon Law does not give a great deal of legal determination to the tasks, rights, and duties of laymen which according to the divine law of the Church can basically be theirs without their ceasing to be laymen, and to the tasks and duties which they can morally be expected to fulfil and which can actually be imposed on them by human Canon Law. I venture to suggest that as long as this state of affairs persists, we will never have the kind of lay Catholic Action desired by us. Real responsibility and duty will only be accepted and borne where the *law* grants a certain realm of freedom (even though merely *iure humano*) for autonomous fulfilment of such duties and responsibilities. The laymen engaged in Catholic Action should not in every individual case be merely the executor of someone else's will (even though this be the will of a priest or a bishop), without any autonomy of his own which, even though always granted by the hierarchy alone, is also respected by the hierarchy in the individual case. In other words, there should be a more exactly established *right* of lay people in Catholic Action which protects the layman even vis-à-vis the hierarchy. As long as this is not the case, we will wait in vain for a Catholic Action, a direct cooperation with the clergy and the hierarchy, in which others take part besides young idealists and 'pious old busybodies' or those in whose case the suggested difficulty has been overcome by the fact that there happens to exist a relationship of personal friendship and trust between them and the Church authorities concerned. It cannot be expected that such a right of the layman will in the first instance be promulgated by Rome as applicable everywhere in the world. Conditions throughout the world are too varied for this. Could it not, however, originate carefully, but also courageously, in individual dioceses and countries? Only once he knows what he is actually permitted to do in the Church *iure humano*, will the layman assume duties seriously.

5. Everything mentioned so far has been intended merely as a positive and negative clarification of what is meant by 'layman', in preparation for the treatment of the lay apostolate. The following are the salient points to be kept in mind. The lay state in the proper sense ceases whenever there is real and habitual participation in the powers of the hierarchy in such a way that the exercise of these powers characterizes the life of such a person, i.e. determines his station (in life). It is theologically indifferent in this connection whether in the actual practice of the Church these powers are given by ordination or are (or can be) bestowed without it. This is merely the reverse side of the fact that the layman has his place-and-station-in-the-world which is his permanent 'domicile' as a Christian, and one which is characteristic of him as a Christian, as well as providing the material, and setting the limit for his Christian existence, in so far as the latter is distinguished from that of the cleric.

II. THE APOSTOLATE IN GENERAL

1. By virtue of divine right and institution by Christ, there are hierarchical and non-hierarchical functions in the Church, those who have hierarchical functions and the people. The hierarchical ministry is exercised *in* the Church and for the Church; as far as its purpose and meaning are concerned, it has been designed entirely with a view to the Church and as a function of service to the Church which is the communion of all believers. Yet, as regards its existence and the extent of its powers, it does not come from the Church, but from Christ; it represents, in the Church, Christ's position as Lord in relation to the people of the Church. The same holds good both for the hierarchical ministry in itself and for those empowered to exercise hierarchical functions. No matter how much the whole Church (including the laity) has cooperated in finding suitable candidates for the hierarchical ministry, it is through those who possess hierarchical powers, and through them alone, that the hierarchical ministry and its powers are

transmitted, in the name of Christ and not in the name of the Church in so far as she is distinguishable from the members of the hierarchy.

2. The hierarchical ministry has, therefore, powers in which the layman cannot participate in any way, unless he becomes himself (in the manner just described) a holder of hierarchical functions and thus ceases to be a layman. The teaching and discipline of the Church show that she is conscious of her absolute power of being able to *divide* the fullness of her hierarchical ministry according to its individual functions and to make divisions even within a single function, and thus to make others share in this ministry in different degrees. But this in no way alters the fact that everyone who shares in her official ministry ceases to be a layman in the theological sense. Now the hierarchical office, considered in its aspect of full power, gives a most specific commission and a most definite mission. For *this* mission, with its own purposes, is the highest characteristic of that office. Particular persons have this office with these powers, because a definite purpose is to be achieved by possessing this office with these powers. This mission is the apostolate peculiar to the hierarchical ministry in the Church. It follows then that there is an apostolate in the Church which can be exercised only by hierarchical functions and their powers. It is impossible, and would be absolutely self-contradictory, for the laity to participate in this apostolate; to insist nevertheless on speaking of it, would be unenlightened and airy-fairy talk, merely appearing to be pious. To put it in another way: participation in the hierarchical apostolate, in the strict and precise sense of 'participation', can only mean the reception of part of the hierarchical *office* and hence also of the apostolate and mission included in this office—in other words, ceasing to be a layman. If the term 'participation' is *not* to be used in this sense, but rather in a vague sense, then it can mean two things: (a) the 'participator' is a 'subsidiary worker' of some sort in the actual carrying out of the hierarchical apostolate (in modern terms, the bishop's chauffeur, for instance, the girl employed in the office dealing with Church funds, the housekeeper in a parish house). It is obvious that such a meaning does not realize the content and dignity of the proper lay apostolate. Or (b) it means that the apostolate of the hierarchy and the lay apostolate meet in the same object, i.e. the

particular people served by both (even though they have quite different starting-points and are achieved in essentially different ways), and that both of them have the same ultimate *goal* in view with regard to the same people, viz. their salvation. This is of course true and does happen. This fact alone does not, however, make the lay apostolate a proper 'participation' in the hierarchical apostolate. For it is logically incorrect to regard something as a participation in something else merely because both of them agree in certain of their characteristics. And the fact that the lay apostolate falls in a certain sense and to a certain extent under the supervision and direction of the hierarchy and its apostolate does not alter the case. After all, this fact does not 'constitute' the lay apostolate in the first instance. For the real lay apostolate is already constituted—as will be explained more in detail—by baptism (and confirmation), by membership in the Church and by the motive force communicated to the member by the infused habit of supernatural love. If in a particular case an apostolate must first be constituted by an individual mandate given by the ecclesiastical hierarchy, it can only be because the hierarchy is drawing upon an auxiliary force for the actual accomplishment of her own permanent task, or because it gives proper participation in her mission and powers. There is no conceivable reason or necessity for giving an individual mandate apart from these two cases. In both it is no longer a question of any real lay apostolate, since the first represents less and the second more than it. In short, there is an untransferable apostolate of the hierarchy which must not be confused with the lay apostolate. We call the former apostolate—in an attempt at clear terminology—the 'official apostolic mission'. Hence we may say that the official apostolic mission is not a lay apostolate. Where the layman arrogates such a mission to himself, or really receives it, he ceases to be a lay person, if it is given to him even though without ordination as constituting a permanent state. This statement, of course, merely provides us with a first formal distinction which in content and objectively does not yet tell us anything very enlightening about the reality signified. For the question arises as to what element of transmitted power is contained in the concrete in this official apostolic mission. For if there, nevertheless, is an apostolate of the laity (which no one seriously denies), then it is reasonable to suppose right away that both apostolates have certain generic traits and constituent elements in common. The important thing, therefore, is to ascertain which constituent elements are reserved and proper to the official apostolic mission as against the apostolate of the laity, and how we may in contrast to this characterize the apostolate of the layman as such.

3. Now, the official apostolic mission (or better, the 'office' of apostolic mission, since it is not merely a question of a mission given by an official order but of a mission constituting an office and one which is to be exercised as an office) might be characterized by simply enumerating those apostolic actions and powers which undoubtedly identify someone who does and can do these things, as a non-lay person, i.e. as someone belonging in some (perhaps humble) degree to the hierarchy of God's people of the Church; thus, sacramental absolution, transubstantiation, power to confirm, to anoint the sick and to ordain, the power to teach independently and authoritatively as invested in bishops and the Pope, the right to make Church laws in the real sense etc. Yet this method is insufficient. For it does not give the basic notion and structure of the non-lay apostolate common to all these functions. Nor is it capable of shedding any light on the question where it is most needed, viz. on the border-line cases in which the hierarchical apostolate seems to become very lay and the lay apostolate very clerical, and where we are not quite certain, therefore, whether these are unavoidable 'transitions' or dangerous 'encroachments'. To get a clear view of that basic structure,[1] we must remind the reader once more of what we said above. There is in the Church, considered as the holy union of the redeemed in a visible society juridically ordered by Christ himself, a power of directing, a pastoral office, which extends in its functions into the various dimensions belonging to the nature of the Church which is the visible presence of the truth, of sanctification and of the will of Christ. This office has been transmitted by Christ to certain men, to the exclusion of the many others who are also members of the Church, and these men pass it on in the same exclusiveness by apostolic succession. It is an office constituted by the mission and power to christianize individuals and peoples, and then to maintain their Christianity permanently, and to direct the community of Christian existence, as such, as a community of truth,

[1] Cf. for what follows: K. Rahner, 'Priesterliche Existenz', *Zeitschrift für Aszetik und Mystik* XVII (1942), pp. 155–171.

of the new and eternal worship, and of sanctity. As is already clear from Scripture, the bearers of this office are already clearly stamped by Christ in two respects: they are those, from the viewpoint of their *origin*, who have been taken out of their original place-in-the-world; they must give up their jobs; they leave their nets, their kinsfolk and family, they live by the altar; they take their mission as their calling, even regarded from an empirical, intramundane point of view. Their mission, having become vocational and proper to their state, may, and indeed must, realize itself as the characteristic form of their earthly life: in their dress, their poverty, their non-stability etc. It is quite irrelevant to this how far all these factors can assert themselves in detail, in the life of the individual bearer of the office. They may take the most varied forms and have (as they have had) different degrees of intensity and clearness. Nor does it mean that the clergy will always be *de facto* a sociological 'state' and 'calling' in a profane, civil sense, as it actually is and has been for the last fifteen hundred years in the West. It is sufficient if we see that there is a fundamental 'form' which is given, together with the office and mission, and which takes hold of the office-bearer; this 'form' removes him basically from his original place-and-state-in-the-world, and is intended to integrate his whole life into his mission, so that he carries it out, not only *in* his life, but *through* his life, through the distinct characteristic of his life and the way he uses it. This official apostolic mission claims the whole existence of man, in such a way that it shifts him from his original station in life. From the viewpoint of its *destination*, this official apostolic mission sends a man away; it sends the messenger into spaces and dimensions of human existence which are not his proper place, before 'kings' and the 'Gentiles'; his message must be delivered even 'out of season'. Although such an apostolate demands committal of the messenger's whole existence, it at the same time surpasses fundamentally the person of the messenger: he does not bear witness to 'his' Christianness (although using it as an instrument), but bears witness to Christ alone; he is not the religious genius who overflows, but the messenger who delivers a message. He bears witness to Christ, not where he would stand by virtue of his own worldly existence, or where in the world *this* existence takes place of its very nature—but always and everywhere; in other words, particularly where of himself he 'has no business', where he has been sent 'from above' and not where he has been placed by his own human existence. He must always, therefore, put up with the unavoidable fact of being mistaken for an indelicate fanatic who interferes in other people's 'private business' and of thus arousing anti-clerical feelings. His new station can be justified only by faith. It is generally understood, of course, that everybody has the inclination and the right to make known and to communicate his opinions. The *content* of a profession of Christian belief, made and conceived in this way and limited to such a situation, would perhaps surprise and seem offensive to an unbeliever, but not the actual happening of such a profession. The apostolate of one officially sent, however, does more; it does not merely communicate, and is not merely an apostolate, as it were, arising from the already given human fact of 'rubbing shoulders' with the people concerned, an apostolate 'on the spot'; it is aggressive, the apostolate of the 'itinerant preacher', of the 'traveller' going from door to door, concerned with the 'places where we still have to go' (in a spatial and especially *spiritual* sense). No wonder that such an apostolate at its summit, i.e. in the priesthood, demands the grace of a sacrament of its own.

Let us recapitulate. An official apostolic mission exists wherever there is any degree of habitual exercise of hierarchical powers (of the *potestas ordinis* or *iurisdictionis*); this is the case when that exercise provides the basis for a new existence; in other words, when it suppresses the apostle's original station in the world—his human, pre-Christian existential situation (at least in part)—and founds a new state and calling, with a new place in the world for the apostle and his own life, allocated to him by his very mission.

4. Hence we may say conversely, and at first negatively: wherever *such* an official apostolic sending-out is *not* given and there is nevertheless a genuine apostolate, i.e. a justified influence on others for their salvation, we are dealing with the apostolate of the *layman*, an apostolate which is still to be determined in its positive nature.

5. This definition of the hierarchical apostolate and the negative distinction of the lay apostolate included in it, can be applied only with care in *practice* and leaves still much to be desired as regards its clarity in border-line cases. Yet it is not without significance even in the practical sphere. As we have already pointed out, no one without free

consent on his own part can be obliged by the Church to accept a share in an hierarchical apostolate. We are now in a position to add, that if one were to bring pressure to bear on a lay person to make him accept an apostolate characterized, as we have seen, by a being-sent-out and a being-removed-from his original place-in-the-world, and to accept it as a duty imposed on him on account of the 'requirements' of the Church, one would do something which one has no right to do. This fact is already no longer mere theory. It might be asked from this point of view whether, for instance, the apostolate of the Legion of Mary with its (in itself wonderful) aggressiveness and intensity (which already turns it almost into a vocation), can still be called *that* kind of lay apostolate which belongs to the duties of every Christian flowing from baptism and charity. Or does such an apostolate already verge very closely on the hierarchical apostolate? Is it the on-the-spot apostolate of neighbourhood (like the lay apostolate) or is it an apostolate constituted by a sending-out, away from one's own original place-in-the-world (like the apostolate of the hierarchy)? And conversely, our reflections show that many forms of apostolate which we are inclined to regard as lay apostolate, turn out to be an apostolate of hierarchical mission. It is, for instance, impossible to regard the life and work of Maria Theresa Ledochowska (1863–1922), the foundress and directress of the Sodality of St Peter Claver and one of the chief supporters of our modern missionary movement, as still a lay apostolate. Is a 'layman', whose profession it is to administer Church finances and who does so with a sense of his responsibility in the religious sphere, a 'lay apostle'? What is the position of a 'lay' teacher whose main employment is teaching in a junior clerical seminary? Such and similar questions are not merely questions of an idle categorization which does not change anything in reality. These are questions which may be basic for deciding about the obligatory nature of an apostolate, as well as basic for the ideal and spiritual foundation of such an apostolate, the formation required for it and the aptitudes for such a calling. It must first of all become clear that 'someone properly entrusted with an hierarchical apostolate by official mission' and 'someone ordained with a vow of celibacy' are not identical notions. It will then be possible to dispel the instinctive feeling which often has very bad effects in practice in the way the clergy treat 'laymen' employed in the service of the Church, viz. the opinion that such non-ordained laymen, by the mere fact of their not being ordained, cannot also be charged with a hierarchical apostolate in a legally well-defined sphere of activity within which and for which they are truly responsible, but must inevitably be merely subordinate employees and handy men who by law itself must always take second place to any 'ecclesiastic'. Furthermore, there could then take place a gradual reawakening of the sense of the 'sanctity' of *all* official functions which in fact belong to this hierarchical apostolate; it might then become a living question once more whether this sanctity might not also be made visible again in every case, as in the early Church, by ordination transmitting such an official function. When the question of married deacons came up recently at a sacerdotal congress in Berlin, it was not a proposal to slacken clerical celibacy. Basically it is rather a question of reconstituting the diaconate itself as an hierarchical ministry with its own sphere of responsibilities and apostolic labours (which it no longer has in fact), and of handing over these apostolic responsibilities by ordination. Once we come to look upon this office as a permanent state in its own right and not merely as a 'step towards the priesthood', there would be no reason for thinking that it must necessarily be fulfilled by celibates, and yet it would be a grade in the hierarchical apostolate and not of the 'lay apostolate'. If there were such grades of hierarchical apostolate—transmitted with or without ordination but clearly, officially constituted as ministries and without celibacy, with their own dignity and rank, and with their own sphere of activity—it would perhaps be much easier to avoid demanding too much of the layman proper and *his* apostolate. A tree grows and thrives only when it has been planted in its natural habitat. There are many tasks in the realm of the Church's apostolate as a whole which cannot be fulfilled on the plane of the lay apostolate; it would be necessary rather to create a new theological, psychological and legal sphere for them, on the level of the hierarchical apostolate.

From what has been said, it can also be seen that the transition from one of these apostolates to the other is quite fluid in practical life. This is not surprising when we remember that it is not easy to distinguish, even merely in general, between the calling, the goal towards which the calling tends and the beneficial side-effects produced by it, or between the main occupation and that pursued 'on the side', between the temporary and the permanent, between a specific and an accidental change of situation. Thus it can also happen that in a particular situation the lay apostolate may be much more intensive and comprehensive in its *final effect* than an hierarchical apostolate. It may be that the hierarchical apostolate gives very much the impression in the concrete of being occupied merely with the administration of what is already established, and of being preoccupied with keeping the established machinery running, whereas the lay apostolate (especially in the case of charismatic impulses) gives the impression of aggressive conquest, discovery and original missionary spirit. Yet none of this can alter the essential fact that the hierarchical apostolate is the apostolic mission constituting the office in virtue of which the apostle is sent *out*; the lay apostolate—when it remains true to what distinguishes it from the hierarchical apostolate—is, as will be shown more clearly still in what follows, the apostolate of man *in* his original place-in-the-world.

6. One of the consequences of what we have seen must be emphasized once more, both in general and in particular. The organizational staff of Catholic Action, composed of men who more or less give their whole time to this work, is not part of the lay apostolate, but a concrete form of organization of the hierarchical apostolate for the purpose of stimulating the apostolate of laymen. This is not the same thing. The hierarchical apostolate does not become a lay apostolate merely because non-ordained and married leaders form part of this organ of the hierarchy. This fact alters nothing regarding the hierarchical character of this administrative authority. It is merely a consequence of the realization that there is a shortage of priests and that people who come from the lay state in their more mature years and married, are fitted for certain tasks of the hierarchical apostolate; this situation will continue, particularly as long as the ordained clergy remain, sociologically speaking, a sort of caste in this country (i.e. the author's) and hence find it still rather difficult to establish contact with certain circles and strata of society. And since it is in the nature of 'Catholic Action' to be an organization for setting the action of Catholic laymen in motion, it follows also that the exact proportion of priests and laymen directing this organization is purely a question of using the most suitable means to the end and not a question of principle. Neither the priests nor the non-priests engaged in this work are 'laymen'. In consequence, it is also difficult to see why the non-priests in 'Catholic Action' must necessarily be inferior in rank to the priests (*de iure* or *de facto*). It would be quite a good thing if there were men today who

could play the same role in the Church as, in days gone by, did Tertullian, Clement of Alexandria, Origen, Didymus the Blind, Catherine of Sienna, Karl Löwenstein and M. Th. Ledochowska, etc.

III. THE LAY APOSTOLATE

1. It should be clear already from the foregoing that the real lay apostolate is what we nowadays like to call 'action of Catholics' in contrast to 'Catholic Action'. Bearing in mind what has been said above about the notion of 'layman', and just now about the hierarchical apostolate of the official apostolic mission, the nature of the lay apostolate might be circumscribed as follows: it is the kind of concern for the salvation of others incumbent on every baptized Christian by the duty of love of neighbour and through the force of this love in the place in the world which belongs to him, without participating in the hierarchical ministry and its apostolate. It is not the apostolate constituted by the official and vocational sending-out, but the apostolate of love in the situation-in-the-world in which the layman finds himself and which belongs to the nature of a layman. Every Christian has been given the right and duty by baptism and confirmation, without any further commission, to bear witness to his Faith and even to concern himself with the salvation of his neighbour. It is quite possible, that by doing this, he may *in actual fact* do more for the spread of the Faith, and instruction in the Faith and moral formation, than the hierarchical apostolate of the Church (as happened, for instance, in the early Church or during less formalistic ages than ours). Yet when he acts as an apostle, he bears witness to *his* faith and *by it* naturally to Christ himself). This is true when he defends himself against attacks on his Christian existence. It is also true when, and in so far as, his existence *in the world* (i.e. his family life, friendships, life with neighbours and in civil society, and his occupation) makes such active witness to his own faith necessary, obligatory and unavoidable, since the Christian layman must obviously 'declare' himself in all these situations for what he really is, viz. a Christian. The apostolate of the layman is, therefore, directly founded on his *own* Christian being, and is not determined in its extent and manner by a proper mission from above, but from below, i.e. by his situation in the world. His Christian influence is conducted through his worldly 'connections', and is not specially constituted by an additional mission and

mandate. He does not go out (in a spatial or spiritual sense), but works 'on the spot'. He is a missionary by the living example of his Christianity. Naturally, this life considered as a productive example includes also the Word, testimony and exhortation given by one man to another, encouragement and warning. Yet all this is legitimized and supported by the fact that the Christian lives from the start in the same spatial and spiritual sphere of human existence as does the one towards whom he is an apostle.

2. Such a lay apostolate is obligatory for the Christian. It flows from his Christian being and from the duty and strength of that supernatural love of neighbour which commands and enables the Christian not merely to regard others as his neighbours in the wordly sphere but also in the realm of salvation. Although such love of neighbour embraces all men, in the sense that it does not exclude anyone *a priori* and in principle from its proximity, it has a certain gradation by its very nature as a realistically-Christian and not abstractly-idealistic virtue: it begins nearest home, with the family, etc.; it favours those belonging to the household of the faith; in brief, its radiating power is permitted to remain rooted in its 'domicile', it is not sent-forth. This is not only its limitation but also its strength: it is an apostolate in the concreteness of the familiar milieu, heart to heart, in the reality of earthly life, in the concreteness of everyday happenings and not in abstract theory, by real living example and not in doctrinal, general norms, in demonstration of the power of grace within the prosaic context of everyday life.

3. Such an apostolate is therefore exercised essentially by the example given by the layman fulfilling his Christian role (proper to the layman as such) as a member of the Church, which consists in using the world *qua* world as the material for Christian existence, and redeeming and sanctifying it. In other words, science, art, medicine, politics, economics, work, marriage, etc.—in short, all the dimensions of human existence—although they all have a relative legality of their own, are an open challenge in the concrete order of salvation and damnation which can be answered in the concrete only by the Christian in the grace of God. If the Christian living in the world answers this challenge

by a life of patience, interior freedom, sincerity, perseverance, earnestness, etc. in these different spheres, *then* and in this way does he effectively exercise his lay apostolate.

4. If the lay apostolate as such is thus primarily the fulfilment of Christian existence in a place in the world with responsibility for one's neighbour and his salvation, and in so far as that fulfilment has a salvific significance for the other, then it follows that the lay apostolate must be exercised in all the situations which constitute the layman's place-in-the-world. First of all in *marriage*, as a father or mother, and in *public life*; these two dimensions of Christian existence are sanctified by the sacraments of matrimony and confirmation respectively. In addition there are the tasks and opportunities provided by the layman's neighbourhood, community of work and of country, citizenship, participation in the community of minds in science and art. In all these dimensions and tasks of human, and at the same time Christian, existence, the lay apostolate—it should be underlined once more—does not essentially consist in direct recruitment and propaganda, or in persuading, converting, warning and exhorting, etc., as is characteristic of an apostolic mission, but in the dynamic and effective example given to others by the layman's Christian living in these dimensions. This naturally does not mean that the Christian must be silent, is not allowed to speak of his Christ-life and must carry discretion to scrupulous extremes. No, a *Christian* may and ought to speak a *Christian* word wherever *man* normally does, may or ought to give expression to the inner motivations of his heart and life, i.e. wherever he gives a fraternal word of advice or instruction and, if necessary, a word pertaining to his responsibilities as a father or mother, teacher, master, or as one more mature. But the Christian has no apostolic duty beyond this. We need not be afraid that this represents too great a restriction of the realm of the lay apostolate. This realm, even understood in this way, is still infinitely wide. The lay apostle is not restrained by this as far as the goal and object of his apostolate are concerned, but only as regards a certain *way* of achieving them for which he is not suited. Any priest who has experienced the suffering caused by the 'inopportuneness' of his aggressive apostolate, will understand what we mean. If lay people would cultivate this apparently 'limited' field of their apostolate to the full, then the world would be Christian within half a

century. This theory naturally does not mean either that the Christian layman may be apostolic only in the 'private' sphere of his life. Since every Christian is a *human* being, and thus has his original place-in-the-world and hence is unavoidably involved in public life (even though with varying intensity), he has an apostolic task to fulfil even in his public life. But he must fulfil it in such a way that he occupies the very place in public life which he has as *man* (as citizen, scientist, artist, etc.) and also as what he really is, viz. a Christian. He is not, however, required to seek and gain a new place for himself in public life *for the express purpose* of carrying out the missionary task imposed on him. Not that he may not do this also, should he so desire. But if he does, then it is his own free and praiseworthy decision and not his apostolic duty necessarily imposed on him as a baptized Christian; also, whatever he does in this way, is not really a lay apostolate in the strict theological sense, but part of the hierarchical apostolate accepted with express or tacit approval of the hierarchy. This can happen '*per modum actus*' (something like 'managing a business without a mandate') or '*per modum habitus*', i.e. as a vocation and principal function, and then the person concerned is not indeed 'ordained' but no longer a layman either.

5. It is of the highest importance to understand the above clearly, for only then do we have a clear idea of the goal towards which any apostolic formation of the layman must be directed. Once this is clear, it immediately becomes clear also that any education for the lay apostolate is senseless from the very start without education for a holy, interior Christian life. Drilling, with a view of training an aggressive militant of the 'Salvation Army' type, is not a Catholic schooling for the *lay* apostolate, but could at best be training of subordinate functionaries for the hierarchical apostolate. A functionary of the hierarchical apostolate (ordained or not) can more easily forgo personal fullness of Christian life than a lay apostle. For the former has something which is effective without personal sanctity, viz. sacramental or juridical powers. A layman, on the other hand, must be apostolic precisely *by* his Christian life; his *Christian life* itself must be the testimony which wins souls for Christianity; actions and words enter into this merely in so far as they themselves form part of man's own action in his human existence. In other words, formation of lay

apostles is formation of the action of Catholics, not formation for Catholic Action; and education for the action of Catholics is formation for that true and full Christianity which is necessarily dynamic. Religious associations of lay people under the direction of the Church ought to reflect well on this. There naturally is also 'education for Catholic Action'; but objectively this is a recruitment of lay people for participation in the hierarchical apostolate of the clergy by which, if this participation becomes a vocation and alters his station in the world, the layman ceases to be a layman. We naturally do not mean to dispute that a layman may also participate in the hierarchical apostolate of the Church to a small extent only or *per modum actus* without ceasing thereby to be a layman. But then it will be in a way analogous to the case of the layman who on a particular occasion replaces the subdeacon at High Mass: what he does in this case is not the business of the layman in principle and habitually, although he does perform this function here and now and may even, in case of necessity, be invited and summoned to perform it. Catholic Action is, therefore, in no way forbidden by what has been said to recruit lay people to help the parish priest, notify him about the sick and the dying, etc. Such activities are not only good and useful; they are not merely an apostolate which deserves great credit and is often exercised in an admirable manner; but it may even from a human point of view be a recommendable complement in the life of a Christian layman who in effect is not 'fulfilled' by his worldly profession (and the opportunities for the lay apostolate offered by it), which is very often the case especially nowadays.

6. The layman's tasks and hence also, if you wish, his apostolate naturally include also all those factors which result from his relation towards the Church and 'within' the Church. He pays his Church dues and thus supports also the hierarchical apostolate. He takes part in divine service and thus shares in the 'edification'[2] which all members give to each other in spirit by divine service, for even these lay people are not merely passive recipients of a grace of truth, love and strength communicated by the clergy alone. He is a godparent, member of Church Committees, etc.

[2] Cf. H. Schlier, *Die Verkündigung im Gottesdienst der Kirche* (Cologne 1953).

7. The layman can possess charisms in the narrower sense, which are continually bestowed on his Church by the Holy Ghost. But we have already spoken about the most essential aspects of this, so that we do not need to say any more here about this possibility of the lay apostolate.

8. A further consequence of what has been said is to be found in a clear distinction of two kinds of 'ecclesiastical' (in the widest sense) organizations of the laity, their formation, the sources of their authority and of the influence exerted on them by the hierarchy of the Church.

a. Firstly, there are *Church* organizations in the proper and strict sense of the word. These are organizations created by the ecclesiastical hierarchy itself for the accomplishment of its own apostolic tasks. The Church's hierarchy creates such organizations by recruiting laymen on a voluntary basis who put themselves at her disposal for the accomplishment of these tasks; this they do either by opening themselves to the sanctifying action of the Church in a more than generally obligatory measure, or by being prepared to cooperate themselves in the apostolic mission of the hierarchy, or in both of these ways.

In the case of strictly ecclesiastical organizations existing for the purpose of cooperation by laymen in the task proper to the hierarchy, it can be a question either of cooperation by such non-ordained persons as their principal function (so that, as has already been underlined several times, they then cease to be laymen in the theological sense), or it may be a question of their putting their time and energy at the disposal of the hierarchy, but only to a limited extent (so that they then do not cease to be laymen). It depends on this distinction whether it makes sense to speak of a lay organization or not. Cooperation which constitutes one's principal function, a vocation and a state, may involve an express or actual participation in the very powers of the hierarchy or not. If the former, then it would objectively be a case of a body of Church-officers who are lay merely in appearance; if the latter, then it would be a case of a body of subaltern Church employees. All properly speaking *ecclesiastical* organizations, being organizations concerned with the object (personal sanctification) or the subjects (those engaged in the apostolate) of the truly hierarchical activity of the Church, take their origin *de iure* and by nature from a direct initiative of the hierarchy. They are founded *by* the Church. They also essentially depend in their activity on the hierarchy and its direct and positive, directing and commanding influence. In consequence, they necessarily are *de iure* under spiritual direction with authoritative powers. They do what the hierarchical Church tells them to do; and conversely, whatever they do is a manifestation of the Church as such, part of the life of the Church as *such*, i.e. not merely Christian Church life in the world, but the Church herself. Such ecclesiastical organizations in the strict sense are, for instance, the Third Orders, the Marian congregations, fraternities (in the strict, specifically religious sense), associations for the support of the Missions, etc. No matter how much they *direct* their members *to* the lay apostolate, they themselves do not constitute a lay aspostolate as such but are particular forms of organizations of the hierarchical apostolate enabling the latter to exercise its functions towards the laity (by forming a personal and apostolic Christianity in these lay people) or to be supported by laymen in the fulfilment of some particular task of the hierarchical apostolate as such.

b. Secondly, there are organizations of the laity as such by means of which the laity seek to further their Christian life as laymen. We are thinking here of student associations, federations of youth groups, unions of university men, etc. Such organizations are characterized, on the one hand, by the fact that their primary and immediate objective aim is not the religious[3] as such, but has a profane, civic, mundane, cultural, human content (or whatever name we wish to give to the difference from what is formally and strictly religious as such). On the other hand, such Catholic, 'temporal' lay organizations are characterized by the fact that they recognize the 'temporal' as a sphere for Christian action, a task which is of basic relevance for eternal salvation, is subject to God's commandments and is a commission given them by God in such a way that it cannot be determined in its ultimate concreteness and precise details simply by the hierarchy *alone*, and merely with the help of the general principles confided to

[3] For it will have to be said that a religious fellowship, whose *immediate and main purpose* is a religious one (such as prayer, divine service, religious formation, practice of the Evangelical Counsels, etc.), can be nothing other among Catholics than an *ecclesiastical* organization in the sense of a). For such a fellowship can be justified only as a function of the whole Church, and that also in her visible, hierarchic dimension.

the teaching and safekeeping of the hierarchy.[4] Hence the layman has in this sector of the 'temporal' been given a Christian task in which he possesses real independence, and leads *these* organizations himself. The priest can only be an 'assistant', 'adviser' and, if necessary, a pastor in this field. In other words, the priest can only use these groups as the sociological basis for the fulfilment of his own task.

It is understandable that in *practice* the transition between properly ecclesiastical organizations and Catholic-Christian temporal organizations can be rather fluid. It may even happen that one and the same organization, regarded sociologically and theologically, realizes both the first *and* the second type of organization, because it objectively seeks two completely different ends simultaneously. And yet it is basically necessary to recognize this distinction with all its consequences.

9. Let us try to clarify the preceding statements by indicating their consequences for 'Catholic Action'. Thus:

a. Catholic Action is the organization intended to *form* and *school* Christians *for* their apostolic task in the world, in marriage, at their work, in the public life of community and of the State, in the realm of culture. The object of this schooling is the laity, the subject is the clergy and those laymen who assist them in this *their* task (cf. (c)).

b. Catholic Action is an organization for the purpose of safeguarding the rights of the Church in public life, a task which is practically indispensable in the age of mass-democracy.

c. Catholic Action is an organization of lay people (not simply: of the *whole* laity), constituted for the purpose of assisting the clergy in *its* apostolic task, in the measure possible to the layman without his ceasing to be a layman. It can be part of this task of the layman to see to it that the first two aims of Catholic Action just mentioned are really fulfilled, by forming an 'elite of militants' or a 'pool of leaders'.

In so far as the first two purposes are concerned, Catholic Action seeks by the very nature of these aims to form and school as many Catholics as possible. With regard to its third purpose, Catholic Action is neither simply an obligation incumbent on every good Christian, nor a task for which we can hope in practice to win every Christian,

[4] Cf. above, the essays on a formal existential ethics and on the parochial principle.

much less be obliged to do so. The first task mentioned above is undoubtedly also the task of every particular Christian organization (congregations, Christian vocational associations, etc.). It follows, therefore, that Catholic Action can *in part* play only a subsidiary role with regard to this task (i.e. try to reach and school those for their Christian ministry in the world who for some reason or other would otherwise not belong to any other Christian organization), and *for the rest* be merely a 'blanket-organization' coordinating these other organizations for this same (first) purpose shared by them all. In practice, Catholic Action will also have to be such a coordinating blanket-organization, joining the many other organizations together, it order to achieve its second purpose, even if only to avoid any unnecessary bureaucracy and so to attain as many Catholics for its second purpose as possible. Only in this way will it be possible for it, for example, to effect a 'plebiscite', a mass petition, a school-strike, etc. From the point of view of the first two purposes, therefore, Catholic Action cannot in any sense renounce being a blanket-organization. This naturally does not in any way prejudge the question as to the possible and desirable constitution of this blanket-organization in relation to particular associations, congregations, etc. By 'blanket-organization' we mean here merely that Catholic Action embraces groups which are autonomous in themselves and which are not merely dependent functions of an organization (called 'Catholic Action') instituted from above, nor merely its subaltern ramifications. Such a conception would mean a violation of the historical rights of these groups (which existed before Catholic Action understood as an organization), a violation of the principle of subsidiary functions (which is valid even in the Church), and a violation of the right to free association. Such an ecclesiastical 'State Socialism' would inevitably choke the life of the Church eventually, no matter how clear and ordered its forms might seem at first.

And so we must come to the conclusion that Catholic Action as such cannot be the organization of the apostolate of the laity as such, and that Catholic Action and action of Catholics do *not* coincide. They do not coincide because it is absolutely impossible that what is called Catholic Action[5] in the concrete should penetrate to the place

[5] In so far as it is not a 'blanket-organization' and in so far as we can apply to it what must be attributed to the groups organized by it. If such a group

where the apostolate of the laity is exercised, viz. in the family, by one's occupation and in one's work in the concrete. Catholic Action can form and educate *for* this Christian life in temporal situations (which imposes an apostolic and missionary task and responsibility), but, because certain aspects of this life cannot be organized at all, e.g. the task of the father in his family, it cannot itself take charge of this life. Other sectors can be organized, e.g. the Christian organization of an actual industrial concern, where several laymen can coordinate the carrying out of their proper lay and yet Christian task by common deliberations, mutual aid, etc. But *such* organizations arise then in the nature of things from below, from the temporal situation; they are organizations dependent on the inalienable decision of the lay people themselves, for which as such the Church therefore cannot take over responsibility, as she does with regard to what is called Catholic Action. It follows that such organizations of the proper lay apostolate cannot really form part of Catholic Action in the proper sense, in so far as the latter is more than a blanket-organization which as such does not interfere in the 'private business' of its member organizations and which therefore is also not responsible for it.

IV. THE IMPORTANCE OF THE LAY APOSTOLATE AND FINAL SUMMARIZING REMARKS

1. We do not need to add much to what has already been said here about the importance of the lay apostolate, as understood by us. We will therefore content ourselves with making two remarks, one positive and the other negative.

a. The mission of the Church has encountered a special difficulty in the post-medieval period and particularly today when, the modern age having passed away, a new age is dawning. This difficulty consists in the fact that the non-religious spheres of man's existence have today become much more closely knit, full, complicated and capable of

---

is really an apostolate of laymen (as, for instance, a students' union, a vocational organization, a Catholic workers' union), i.e. action of Catholics, then it is of course possible from this point of view to ascribe the proper apostolate of the laity to Catholic Action—if these groups belong to Catholic Action.

absorbing man's interest than in past ages. We need only ask ourselves quite simply about the situation in general: what could interest and absorb man spiritually in the past, over and above the satisfaction of the most immediate requirements of life? The answer must be: on the whole, only religious questions of human existence. For besides this there was nothing. Anything else was (like art and science) itself a moment of the religious question. When we pose the same question for the man of today, we must answer: apart from the religious, there are innumerable other factors calling for his interest and attention. These new realizations of human existence (such as the profane sciences, art, technology, politics, a highly complicated economy, etc.) must themselves be mastered by man in new ways; they demand an original response from Christian experience, a response of such a kind as to prevent the religious and Christian element in these new realizations being covered over and being crushed by the weight of the non-religious. Only the layman can do this, in the last analysis, not the priest. A priest, in virtue of his very vocation, cannot have the same full and original relationship to these dimensions of human existence as the layman; such a relationship is an indispensable condition for making the best possible use of these opportunities given to man. The layman, and he alone, as we have tried to bring out, is given the mandate and is enabled to do this precisely by the lay apostolate. Thus the new (contemporary) situation has brought out a completely new significance of the lay apostolate which it did not possess before in this respect. For in a completely new historical sense, the 'world' has, really only now, begun to exist, i.e. the world which man himself has brought forth out of Nature; ultimately, this world can be christianized only by the one who has fashioned it, viz. the layman. The task of the priest does not become any less urgent, irreplaceable and holy on this account. The priesthood holds the sacred reality and administers the sources of all that the layman has to introduce into his world. It has the ever recurring task of forming men into Christians who must in turn fulfil their Christian mission in the world. The priest and the Religious are meant at all times to be a tangible sign in the world, by their celibacy and the other Evangelical Counsels, of the fact that the Christian is in the world but not of the world, that all fidelity to earth and man signifies eternal life only once it becomes suffused and transformed by the grace which comes from beyond the world. Layman and priest are not in competition as regards their apostolic, missionary task. Each has his own place which no one else can fill. Yet in as far as every man lives in his own world and no longer merely in the world created by God alone, the lay apostolate has taken on a new and irreplaceable significance.

b. Everything which is not lay apostolate in this sense (hence all Catholic Action), can and will nevertheless have a great importance of its own. But we must realise that everything else is important only in so far as it serves to stimulate, educate, coordinate, etc. the action of Catholic laymen. Catholic Action, taken as a whole, will in practice only be effective on and through the action of Catholics. It follows from this that every organization, and all organizational machinery, which is superfluous viewed in this light, is really superfluous, indeed harmful, because it ties up the energies of priests and laymen in the wrong place. In brief, the nature and extent of the significance of Catholic Action depends on the significance of the action of Catholics.

2. If we may be permitted finally to refer once more to a few important points which have been discussed in the course of these reflections and which may not always have been self-evident for everyone in the past, we would recall the following:

a. Serious thought should be given—slowly but courageously—to the question of whether and how the law regarding laymen could be further developed (at least in the form of diocesan, particular laws). First of all, with regard to laymen who are engaged full-time in the governing bodies of Catholic Action. I have not been inspired in this by anyone else and am perhaps just constructing theories in my study. But it seems to me that in the long run we will have people of real greatness and initiative, men with ideas on these bodies, only when they are given a sector of activities, with its corresponding rights, for which they are themselves responsible and within which they enjoy real autonomy. If this be undesirable, then we should revert to the old methods which admitted only priests, together with housekeepers and sacristans (and possibly also auxiliaries taken from the ranks of the Religious), in the hierarchical apostolate. When we speak in this respect of a development of the law regarding lay people, we do not refer *in the meantime* (and perhaps not for a long time yet) to the drafting of laws with a multitude of paragraphs but, to begin with, only to the following: if someone is entrusted with a task, *he* should also be allowed to fulfil it.

It should be clear who is really competent for what. Higher authority should not intervene as soon as it disagrees in some vague way. In the normal case the responsibility and role of higher authority consists in putting the right man in the right place and then leaving him free to act. Any other attitude would be symptomatic of the Church being influenced by the totalitarian spirit of the age. Once relations between priests, bishops and laymen within the hierarchical apostolate are governed by the right outlook and attitude, and once this attitude takes ever deeper roots, it will perhaps be possible gradually to give a more precise *legal* formulation to everything involved in this; in this way we might then clarify the situation even where human limitations would otherwise prevent us from hitting on the right solution by mere improvisations. This applies also, *mutatis mutandis*, to the law concerning those laymen whose participation in the hierarchical apostolate by Catholic Action is not their principal function or their calling, but who are merely laymen. Their proper and essential apostolate in the world, in the place where they find themselves, does not permit of juridical formulation. Nevertheless, they have, or may have, certain tasks in and towards the Church which are not impossible even for a layman as such, since the tasks referred to are not their official function and calling, and do not change their situation in the world. We all want the layman to take a greater interest in many of the Church's concerns. He will do so once he sees that he is not merely expected to take an interest and share responsibility when it happens to suit the clergy, and that he does not need to become paralysed in mute and respectful passivity whenever the clergy happens to find this more convenient. What we have just said about the basis of such a law, regarding those who direct Catholic Action, naturally applies with even greater force in this case. Consider one example alone: responsible and conscientious laymen who are editors of magazines, should not have to ask themselves, as apprehensively as is sometimes the case, whether the opinions expressed in their periodicals are agreeable to those in high places or not. It would be good if one or other of the leading articles in *Wort und Wahrheit* in the last few years had been taken seriously, calmly and soberly instead of being merely treated as that kind of journalism which is used for the sheer sake of assuming an air of importance and of attracting attention.

b. Let us not impose an apostolate on the layman to which he is not suited existentially and to which in general he is not called. To assume such responsibilities may appear heroic and fruitful—for a time; after that such undertakings are swallowed up. Better to take the longer but more effective road: let us form laymen so that they may be Christians in the place where they are or should be—in the world. It is there that they must bear witness to Christ by their life. If they do this, then they are lay apostles.

INDEX OF PERSONS

SUBJECT INDEX